Britain in the Wider W

M000313605

Britain in the Wider World traces the remarkable transformation of Britain between 1603 and 1800 as it developed into a world power.

At the accession of James VI and I to the throne of England in 1603, the kingdoms of England/Wales, Scotland and Ireland were united only by having a monarch in common. They had little presence in the world and were fraught with violence. Two centuries later, the consolidated state of the United Kingdom, established in 1801, was an economic powerhouse and increasingly geopolitically important, with an empire that stretched from the Americas to Asia and to the Pacific. This book offers a fresh approach to assessing Britain's evolution, situating Britain within both imperial and Atlantic history and examining how Britain came together politically and socially throughout the eighteenth century. In particular, it offers a detailed exploration of Britain as a fiscal–military state, able to fight major wars without bankrupting itself. Through studying patterns of political authority and gender relationships, it also stresses the constancy of fundamental features of British society, economy, and politics despite considerable internal changes.

Detailed, accessibly written, and enhanced by illustrations, *Britain in the Wider World* is ideal for students of early modern Britain.

Trevor Burnard is Wilberforce Professor of Slavery and Emancipation at the University of Hull. He is editor in chief of the Oxford Bibliographies Online in Atlantic History and the author of *Jamaica in the Age of Revolution* (2020) and *The Atlantic in World History, 1492–1830* (2020).

Countries in the Early Modern World

Available titles:

Early Modern Ireland
New Sources, Methods, and Perspectives
Edited by Sarah Covington, Vincent P. Carey, and Valerie McGowan-Doyle

Britain in the Wider World
1603–1800
Trevor Burnard

For more information about this series, please visit: www.routledge.com/
Countries-in-the-Early-Modern-World/book-series/CEMW

Britain in the Wider World

1603–1800

Trevor Burnard

Routledge
Taylor & Francis Group

LONDON AND NEW YORK

First published 2020
by Routledge
2 Park Square, Milton Park, Abingdon, Oxon OX14 4RN

and by Routledge
52 Vanderbilt Avenue, New York, NY 10017

Routledge is an imprint of the Taylor & Francis Group, an informa business

© 2020 Trevor Burnard

British Library Cataloguing-in-Publication Data
A catalogue record for this book is available from the British Library

Library of Congress Cataloging-in-Publication Data
A catalog record for this book has been requested

ISBN: 978-1-138-31359-0 (hbk)
ISBN: 978-1-138-31360-6 (pbk)
ISBN: 978-0-429-45752-4 (ebk)

Typeset in Bembo
by Apex CoVantage, LLC

Contents

Figures

Acknowledgements

I am a late convert to the writing of British history, having spent my career as a student of early American history, notably of the Chesapeake and the Caribbean. The usual move in scholarship is for scholars of England in the seventeenth century or Britain in the eighteenth century to extend themselves from the study of the small islands that made up the British archipelago to a study of what Britain wrought overseas. I can think of works by my friends Steven Pincus, Kathleen Wilson and Sarah Barber as examples of outstanding British historians applying their insights from British history into the history of the British Empire. It is less common to move the other way, from studying British America to look at Britain itself, although it was always impossible to study early America without knowing a good deal about British history. And as an Atlantic historian with an increasing orientation to studying the relationship between the Atlantic and the rest of the world and in understanding themes in Atlantic history that have a transatlantic dimension between Britain and its overseas possessions, such as imperialism, gender relations, migration and slavery, I argue that seeing Britain and its involvement in the wider world has become an increasingly interesting imperative.

My first exposure to early modern British history came at undergraduate level in a subject on Stuart Britain taught at the University of Otago by Michael Cullen (now Sir Michael Cullen, after leaving historical scholarship to take up a distinguished political career). An equally distinguished New Zealander, John Pocock, introduced me further to British history at graduate level. But I never really got to grips with the rich historiography and excitement that is involved with understanding how Britain began its involvement in the wider world alongside the making of a British nation within the seventeenth- and eighteenth-century British archipelago until I taught a course at the University of Canterbury in New Zealand with three brilliant historians of Britain – Glenn Burgess, Marie Peters and John Cookson. This course, from 1992, was a pioneering subject in what John Pocock had asked scholars to do in 1973 in a famous memorial address to John Beaglehole, the great scholar of James Cook in the Pacific. That address was as much an expression of rage against Britain for abandoning New Zealand when it joined the European Economic Community as it was a call for a new historical approach to Britain. John was concerned then and now at expanding what he saw as parochial visions of what constituted being 'British' then and in the past. Pocock asked British, and by implication British American, scholars to try a new subject, which was to expand their vision beyond the shores of Britain (which for most meant just the land of England) to examine all kinds of Britains, from North America to the West Indies to South Africa and to Australia and New Zealand. The course that Glenn, Marie, John and I taught was probably the first course in Atlantic history and in the British world to be delivered in the Southern Hemisphere. And the rage that Pocock expressed against the historical amnesia that sometimes affects the British in Britain about its role in the past in the world is just as significant in 2019, two months before a possible exit from the European Union, as it was when Britain left New Zealand to its own devices in 1973.

Moving from Jamaica, to New Zealand, to Britain, to Australia, and then back again to Britain, where I am the Professor of Slavery and Emancipation and Director of the Wilberforce Institute for the Study of Slavery and Emancipation at the University of Hull, has made me aware of the multiple links that Britain forged in the seventeenth and eighteenth century throughout the world. In Britain, a key moment was at the University of Sussex in 2007, where Huw Bowen persuaded me to put on a conference on a project he was running with Elizabeth Mancke and John Reid comparing the eighteenth-century Atlantic and Indian Ocean worlds. I think Huw took advantage of my susceptibility to flattery while out drinking at the Merchants pub in Rugby, where we were then both living. He persuaded me to do some of his conference preparation for him by providing him with a venue for discussions. It was a good thing that he did so. The result of this conference, held in the beautiful weather of early-summer Sussex, produced a wonderful book that includes among many better offerings an essay from me when I began my first exercise in comparative oceanic history, asking what studying the Indian Oceanic world would do to inform studies of the Atlantic world. I soon realised when I presented an embryonic version of this paper to colleagues at my new university, the University of Warwick, that my knowledge of the Indian oceanic world was very limited. David Arnold pointed this out with his customary tact and helped set me straight on how to think of British overseas expansion into Asia. Huw also helped me develop greater knowledge and interest in British history when he invited me to a fabulous conference at Aberystwyth, two months after our conference in Sussex. This conference, which Huw organised entirely this time, was on Wales and the British overseas empire. It allowed me not only to benefit from the wisdom of some great historians of Wales and Scotland but to write my first essay that was on a British history topic. While I was at Sussex, I discussed many of the themes of a British world and what was distinctive about British European expansion with Saul Dubow, a great scholar of South Africa and nineteenth- and twentieth-century African themes that have had a bearing on this work. My thinking was also strongly influenced by what I learned at Sussex from Richard Follett, Clive Webb, Richard Whatmore, Naomi Tadmor and Paul Betts.

The month of the conference on Wales and Empire saw me move from the University of Sussex to the University of Warwick, as professor of American history. Warwick is a major centre for global history, and my colleagues there in global history, notably Maxine Berg, Giorgio Riello and Anne Gerritsen, along with colleagues in Caribbean and American history – Gad Heuman, Tim Lockley, Rebecca Earle, Cecily Jones, John Gilmour, David Dabydeen and Tony Macfarland – and colleagues in early modern British history – Steve Hindle, Bernard Capp, Peter Marshall, Margot Finn and Beat Kumin – instructed me in how to think about British, American and Caribbean history more globally.

My thanks are due to all of them, but my most important thanks are to Mark Knights. We arrived at Warwick together in September 2007 and became fast friends and intellectual companions, although his historical and exposition skills are far superior to mine. A highlight of our intellectual life together was a series of workshops and seminars for advanced graduate students that we held at Warwick and most memorably in a hot Chicago summer in 2011 where we compared scholarship on Britain and British America in two weeks of incredibly intensive and massively rewarding teaching. These two weeks were the most intensive teaching either of us had ever done, with constant guests, loads of readings and brilliant graduate students, many of whom have gone on to very promising careers. If you want to know something, however, you must teach it and after those two weeks I was convinced that I had something to say about Britain and the wider world between the seventeenth and the early nineteenth century that others might be interested in. This book is thus the long-term result of the Mellon funded set of workshops on Britain and the wider world held in 2010 and 2011. I thank the Mellon Foundation for their support of this project. It is also a by-product of an Australian Research Council Discovery Grant and the product of fellowships in Paris between 2015 and 2018, courtesy of Cécile Vidal, Bertrand Van Ruymbeke, Marie-Jeanne Rossignol and Allan Potofsky.

Many other people in Britain, France, the Netherlands, Germany, and the United States have contributed to the work that is presented here, but I hope these friends and colleagues will not mind me making a special acknowledgement of my long-time friend and collaborator, Andrew O'Shaughnessy. Once again, this work is indebted to both Andrew's scholarship and to his encompassing historical vision. Andrew is the perfect embodiment personally of some of the themes in this book – the quintessential English gentleman who has lived in America for much of his life (albeit in that English outpost of Charlottesville, Virginia) and who has written penetrating work on the British West Indies, British North America and the ruling elite of Britain during the American revolutionary war. Every page of this work bears some indebtedness to my deep immersion in Andrew's work.

I believe that this book shows that I have the sort of lasting appreciation of Britain that only those of us not born in Britain can have. My ancestors left for New Zealand between 1858 and 1905, some from Scotland and more from southern England, especially from Buckinghamshire and London. My wife, Deborah Morgan, had ancestors from Britain who arrived in New Zealand from 1840 to 1880, including a long-lived ancestor called Henry Burling who died aged 104 in 1910, leaving well over 600 descendants. Given her devoted Anglo-philia, Deborah may find this volume the rare work of mine that is of interest to her and to the general reader. As always, she did not involve herself with the writing of this book and neither did my wonderful children, Nicholas and Eleanor Burnard. But without their support, especially in this year, which has seen several challenges I have not experienced before, I do not think I could have written this book. My former colleagues Joy Damousi, Jennifer Milam, Peter Otto, Clara Tuite, Andy May, Tim Parkin, Mark Edele, Gillian Wigglesworth and, as always, Deirdre Coleman have been equally supportive in difficult times.

I would like to dedicate this book to a brilliant academic couple whom I have known since my first arrival at the University of Canterbury and whose emotional and practical support for me and my work has been always more important even than their intellectual example. Glenn Burgess and Mandy Capern are now, once again, my colleagues at the University of Hull. It makes going to this lovely region of Britain and to a great job in a premier research institute even more enjoyable. I hope that Glenn and Mandy will ignore the errors and misstatements in this book and think of it as but a small token of a lifelong friendship.

1 Britain in 1603

Introduction: Old Tom Parr

Old Thomas Parr, a poor man of modest habits but an active libido, died in 1635, allegedly (although improbably) 169 years old. If he had, in fact, lived between 1483 and 1635, he would have lived in one of the rare periods in its history where England was relatively little involved in the world. It was, like all long time spans, a period of momentous social, economic and political change, including the English, Welsh and Scottish, although not the Irish, shifting from Catholic to Protestant allegiance. But it was not a period in which the wider world intruded much on British life, except perhaps at the very end of Parr's supposed long life. If we imagined another Thomas Parr living 169 years before him (in other words, from 1314–1483), that Parr would have lived during a period of intense involvement of the four nations of the British archipelago with each other, where Wales and Ireland became aligned with England and when Scotland engaged in frequent conflict and a time when England was heavily involved in western Europe as a result of the First Hundred Years' War. If we imagine, moreover, a Thomas Parr born in the year of Parr's death in 1635 who lived as long as Parr was meant to have done (i.e. between 1635 and 1804), this Parr would have lived in a world of many transformative events, including a calamitous civil war, the overthrow of monarchy and a successful foreign invasion and a revolution in the economy of Britain away from agri-culture to industry.

What might have been most remarkable to this new Old Thomas Parr would have been how by 1804 the people of his small village in Shropshire would have been participants in the titanic struggle between France and Britain for mastery of Europe and the world. Britain was once again involved in world events in a way it was not in 1635 but which it had been around 1400. Indeed, Britain – an entity that did not exist in 1635 but which in 1804 comprised all four nations of Britain and an enormous worldwide empire – had never been so involved in the world as it was in this year, one year before the battle of Trafalgar ensured it had mastery of the seas. This book covers the changes that this imaginary long-lived Englishman would have experienced in a period of dramatic internal and external change for Britain in the seventeenth and eighteenth centuries, with special emphasis on how society changed in this period and even more on how Britain became a global player. It will note also that while the greatest change that the Thomas Parr dying in 1635 would have experienced would have been the transformation of England from a Catholic to a Protestant country, one of the changes that the imaginary Thomas Parr dying in 1804 would have experienced would have been a diminishing in the patriarchal principles that governed marital and family relationships in early modern Britain. He would also have died just as Britain's population was exploding and as fewer people lived the sorts of rural life that a poor man such as Parr would have lived in the sixteenth and seventeenth centuries. He also would have died just as Britain, through the Industrial Revolution, was becoming 'the workshop of the world,' a country that had developed a brand-new and radically successful form of economic organisation with worldwide historical impact. Exploring change through the lens of family and gender helps to balance political and economic change with major currents in social history.

Plan of book

Between 1603 and 1815, a small island in the North Atlantic came to dominate international affairs. By 1815, the United Kingdom of Britain and Ireland (formed in 1801 with Britain created when Ireland became part of the union of England/Wales with Scotland in 1707) was poised to become the leading global power in the nineteenth century. This book shows how this unusual chain of events came to pass. It looks both at the formation of Britain and then the United Kingdom and at the development of Britain's empire in the Americas, Asia, Africa and the Pacific in the seventeenth and eighteenth centuries.

How Britain became a global power by the early nineteenth century was remarkable. By 1815, Britain controlled a quarter of the globe with influence far beyond it, especially if we link Britain with the fledgling but rapidly growing ex-colony of the United States. This increase in global power and influence would have astonished historians and empire builders in the past. Britain had a bad reputation for much of its history. Procopius, a great historian of late antiquity, thought Britain such a dreadful place that he declared it inhospitable, a place where the air was so poisonous in some places that it could kill if the wind changed direction. It was a place, moreover, inhabited by Britons, whom, another medieval chronicler declared, had a name that showed the people's true character – *Briton* was a word, he claimed, that derived from the Latin *brutus*, that is 'irrational' or 'stupid.'

The countries that in 1603, when this book begins, made up the British archipelago – England, Wales, Scotland and Ireland – had become separated from patterns developing in Europe in ways that may seem familiar in Brexit Britain today. That was especially true for the largest and most important of these four countries, England. By the second quarter of the sixteenth century, when Henry VIII broke with Rome to achieve a fleeting marital harmony, England had become close to a pariah state in Europe. It was, from the mid-sixteenth century, Protestant in a mostly Catholic continent, and it was provincial and philistine in its culture and standard of living compared to life in the great cities of France, Italy and northern Europe. England appeared to be a country that was irredeemably culturally and politically barbaric without much redemption either in a faltering economy. One sign of this cultural barbarism was Henry VIII's appalling treatment of his legal wife, Catherine of Aragorn. Catherine was the aunt of Europe's richest and most powerful man, Charles V, Holy Roman Emperor, ruler of Spain and master of a fabulously rich American empire. This was the man the rash and impecunious Henry VIII had decided to pick a fight with. Elizabeth, his daughter and queen of England between 1558 and 1603, was a much wiser ruler than her father, but even she continued the English practice which horrified Europe, which was of killing a rightfully crowned monarch, in this case, Mary, Queen of Scots, the mother of her successor.

The opinion makers of sixteenth-century England tried to suggest that as a Protestant kingdom, it was a virtuous alternative to the growing empire of Spain under Charles V and Philip II. Writers argued that Spain, as could be seen in its conquest of the Americas, was a cruel and vicious nation. They argued that its empire was one characterised by violence, intolerance and persecution. The problem with this argument was that the English in the second half of the seventeenth century stood on very weak ground. It did not have yet an American empire to exploit but its initial forays abroad suggested that it followed the example of Spain as seeing the world as a place to exploit for personal gain. The English might criticise the Spanish for their moral delinquencies, but the fact was that England was a scavenger nation, grateful for whatever crumbs came their way in explorations of the Americas and Asia. And its actions towards Scotland and especially Ireland, where a ferocious quasi-genocidal war was fought in the 1590s, showed it to be as barbaric towards other people as Britons imagined was the case for the cruel Spanish.

The start of the seventeenth century promised little better. Elizabeth was replaced as monarch of England/Wales by James VI of Scotland, the son of the Scottish monarch whom Elizabeth had ordered to be executed. James's accession meant that Scotland and England were theoretically connected. The peculiarities of the monarchical settlement of 1603, with the smaller nation providing the ruler for the larger, provoked considerable anxiety in England, as well as resentment against Scottish pretensions. Conflict of all kinds marked the reign of James VI and I (where this book starts) and even more so that of his incompetent son, Charles I. Religious strife, tumultuous civil wars in all three British kingdoms, monarchs who were incapable of ruling successfully and rebellions of all kinds (political, social and familial) made the seventeenth century an especially difficult one for Britons, both those in Britain and the numbers of migrants and adventurers who ventured into North America, the West Indies and, to a lesser extent, Africa and Asia. It is not surprising that the seminal work of political philosophy in the mid-seventeenth century, Thomas Hobbes's *Leviathan*, was written in England in the immediate aftermath of a calamitous civil war and the execution of yet another British monarch. Hobbes's theme was conflict and how it could be managed. His realisation was that competition between men and between states was brutal and relentless. Only an Englishman living in the mid-seventeenth century could have concluded that the natural state of man was to be in a constant state of violence, and only an Englishman could have been right in thinking such thoughts.

After the Glorious Revolution of 1688, however, England and Wales (and after the formal union with Scotland in 1707, Britain) experienced a marked change of fortunes. In the eighteenth century, especially during the Second Hundred Years' War with France (1689–1815), Britain swept everything before it and became a global power. The former pariah state became the envy and concern of other states in Europe. By the end of the Seven Years' War in 1763, its world and European position had been transformed from a century earlier. It was not only powerful geopolitically; it was also an economic marvel, developing the first industrial economy in history because of the Industrial Revolution which started in the early eighteenth century and which picked up momentum after 1760. This new system of economic organisation allowed Britain to provide ever-increasing standards of living for its growing and demanding population, even if the birth of an industrial working class and a growing population of the rural poor made observers worry whether resources could increase quickly enough to keep up with rampaging population growth. By 1815 and the defeat of Napoleon Bonaparte, however, Britain could lay claim to be the dominant world political *and* economic power.

The shift in power in the eighteenth century from first Italy and the Mediterranean, then from the Ottoman world and eventually from the great agrarian empires of Asia towards northern Europe and increasingly Britain is an event of global historical importance. So, too, is Britain's development of settler societies in the Americas, showing how Europe could extend its reach in multiple and different ways to other parts of the world, adding European settlement to normal patterns of colonial exploitation. This book traces first how the composite monarchy of England/Wales, Scotland and Ireland became the polity of Britain in the eighteenth century and what this meant for social and economic patterns in the British archipelago. It examines how this developing world power became increasingly important in Europe, eclipsing Spain and the Netherlands and competing, successfully, with France for European and then global dominance. It then connects this development to the creation of a vibrant British Empire in the Americas and increasingly in Asia which by 1760, as the American Benjamin Franklin claimed, promised to eclipse just in British North America alone the mother country in population, wealth and influence. Franklin warned, however, that this happy situation would continue only if Britain continued its salutary practice of not interfering in how colonial settlers organised their lives, including how they treated non-white subjects, both Native Americans and African Americans. Sadly, Franklin's advice was not heeded, leading to the first big rupture in settler colonialism, the American Revolution of 1776–1783.

In short, this book traces a remarkable transformation. When the book starts, in 1603, Britain was separated from the rest of Europe by the English Channel. Its connections eastward were patchy to non-existent. And it had hardly ventured westward, except, mostly disastrously, to Ireland. It was distant, isolated, and peripheral to world and European history. These weaknesses, however, became strengths in the seventeenth and especially the eighteenth century, underpinning the rise of one of the greatest Empires in modern history. Yet, as this book makes clear, these movements towards Britain having a global presence and an ability to influence events in Europe that it had never had before (except perhaps briefly and less decisively in the early fifteenth century) had problematic elements. One reason why Britain was able to do as well as it did in the eighteenth century was that it developed, first in the world, effective ways in which to harness the ability to make war to a fiscal system that was not destroyed by the enormous costs of state-sponsored violence. Britain was not a pacific state. Its fiscal-military success enabled it to use coercion remarkably effectively in multiple parts of the world to acquire the land and resources of other peoples for its own use. Its commercial success was also not unproblematic. Britain enjoyed remarkable economic growth in the eighteenth century, developing an embryonic industrial economy within an innovative population in which invention and the pursuit of scientific knowledge were encouraged as in no other place of the world. But that commercial inventiveness had dark aspects, not only in the treatment of poorer people in Britain but also in the development of highly exploitative and morally dubious traders such as the commerce between Africa and Britain in weapons and, most of all, people.

How did Britain do it? One reason was social and economic. Britain's social and especially familial structure was distinctive and well suited for imperial expansion. Inequality was lower than elsewhere in Europe and much lower than in Asia, and the bottom tier of the population had noticeably higher levels of calorie consumption than in much of the rest of Eurasia. Its economy was both growing and efficient. And Englishmen, although not Englishwomen, were more prepared than other Europeans to move away from Britain – to Europe in the case of the Scots and Irish and to the Americas in the case of the English. Britain's success also owed much to the fact that it was home to many innovators from the late seventeenth century onwards, as well as being the centre of major innovations in science and especially in finance and fiscal policy. Britain not only benefitted from the Scientific and Industrial Revolutions but also pioneered what historians call the fiscal-military revolution. By working out how to pay for military expansion and for expensive wars, Britain was able to defeat its wealthier and larger neighbour, France and expand throughout the world without bankrupting itself. In addition, fertility levels, which were relatively low in the seventeenth century, although high as this book ends, also had an important correlation with per capita incomes, as resources and assets poured into the hands of both the aristocracy and middling sorts, making the rich and well-off of the archipelago truly formidable and an important counterweight to a relatively poor monarchy.

Geography, however, was important. Britain's distance from Europe and the natural barrier of the sea helped Britain withstand military threats, at least after the Glorious Revolution of 1688, when one aristocratic faction welcomed in a foreign invader to counter what was considered religious and political tyranny. It also meant that Britain did not have to devote large resources to maintaining a standing army, as France had to do. Britain could thus stay out of many European problems. As a result, the British learned to intervene judiciously, taking advantage of circumstances that were in their favour but staying out of it when the dice were loaded against them.

Of course, the rise of Britannia was neither a one-way process nor uncontested. Plenty of Britons, women prominent amongst them, found what Britain did overseas anathema to their idea of Britain as a civilised and civilising nation. If Britain's increased involvement in the world changed the world, so, too, the world changed Britain, especially from the middle of the eighteenth century onwards. Until the middle of the eighteenth century, imperial matters intruded relatively seldom into more important local matters, such as the forming of a British world in the British archipelago and renegotiating power relationships both between ruled and ruler and between men and women. The triumph of the Seven Years' War, 1756–1763, and the recognition that Britain was now a great global power led to worries about what all this wealth and power were doing to the British character.

The first concerns came from an understanding of what the East India Company was doing – avaricious and immoral Englishmen filling their boots while enjoying Asian corruption and allowing millions of Bengalis to starve in the great famine of 1770. Such concerns spread to the Americas, especially in the revolt of colonists in North America in 1776. This revolt provoked much soul-searching in Britain as to how it should treat both British subjects abroad and the millions of non-British subjects under British control in Asia, the Americas, Africa and the Pacific. Contestations over Britain's role in the world became normal from the American Revolution through the French Revolutionary and the Napoleonic Wars. Yet the loss of part of the American Empire did little to dampen British enthusiasm both for the empire and for increased involvement in the world. The French Revolution and the Napoleonic Wars, 1793–1815, made all previous wars, even the Seven Years' War, seem relatively small-scale and limited in aims and objectives. These latter wars were both the biggest global crisis Britain had ever faced, leading to an unprecedented mobilisation of men and a huge inflation in the country's debt, and the greatest opportunity Britain had ever had of putting distance between itself and its most formidable global competitor, France. Britain's great victories at Trafalgar in 1805 and Waterloo in 1815 placed this small island state at the edge of Europe in a perfect position to establish itself as the world's leading power in the nineteenth century.

What made this possible, however, was not just military victory in 1815 but also the profound transformations of the British economy resulting from the Industrial Revolution of the eighteenth century. The Industrial Revolution was a transformation in economic activity in which Britain became the first industrial nation that had long roots reaching back to the financial revolution and development of long-distance commerce in the 1690s, but which accelerated remarkably from the 1760s. The Industrial Revolution led to changes as profound for the British people and for people in neo-Britons in the Americas and Pacific as was for the case for any period in Britain's history. The Industrial Revolution allowed Britain's rapidly rising population to be fed and maintained in ways that theorists such as Robert Thomas Malthus, writing about the relationship between population and resources in the 1790s, thought unlikely. Britons were the wealthiest people in the world by 1815, with the best standard of living of any people save for its ex-colonists in the newly formed United States of America and its colonial subjects in Canada and Australia. Such an expansion of wealth through trade and industry had its price, however. The burden of British imperialism was considerable, especially for subject peoples in a deindustrialising India and for non-white peoples in Africa and the West Indies.

The book concludes with an appreciation of the new worlds that Britain was involved in in the late eighteenth and early nineteenth centuries, connecting them to a two-hundred-year transformation of the three kingdoms of Ireland, England and Scotland from places relatively uninvolved in the world to a single nation intensely involved in global commerce, colonisation and Christianisation. It does so in two ways, congruent with themes running through the book. It examines the ways in which the British state had developed in ways that made it able to run a growing domestic population and have as well a large empire while ensuring its ability to keep Europe stable, balanced and divided. It also looks at how Britain had changed domestically, with emphasis on the changing positions of women and men, especially challenges to the overwhelming assumption of patriarchal principles that pertained as a basis for social order in 1603. The just-over-two-hundred-year period studied in this book was pivotal for the making of Britain and for Britain's involvement in a much wider world than was the case in 1603. It also was central to the making of the modern world and an integrated global economy in the nineteenth century. By the time that Victoria, Queen of Britain and its empire between 1837 and 1901, was born in 1819, just four years after the Battle of Waterloo, Britain was immeasurably stronger, wealthier and more outward-looking than the narrow and insular England/Wales and Scotland that James VI and I faced when becoming monarch in 1603.

Throughout the book, I concentrate on gender as a counterpoint to traditional interpretations based on politics and economics. There are a number of ways in which the considerable social changes that transformed Britain and its empire can be addressed, such as through changes in standards of living, an analysis of differing class relationships over time, the many ways in which religion sustained and gave meaning to peoples life while religious difference polarised people as no other set of beliefs did or through explaining the extreme litigiousness and devotion to the law of Britons. The history of gender seems to me, however, to be crucial to understanding changes and continuities over time in British life and in their understanding of other peoples. When Britons wanted to understand the basis for political authority, they turned, as did James VI and I in his address to his people when becoming English king in 1603, to familial and gender analogies. When English travellers to America and Africa tried to make sense of the new people and societies they encountered, the first thing they did was to try to make sense of how man and women interacted. Gender will be woven throughout each chapter as a way of measuring change in a vital area of British life.

Wales and empire

One weakness of this book is that it pays less attention to Wales than it does to the other three kingdoms of the British Isles and to British possessions abroad. This absence is not part of the usual condescension to Welsh history common within English historiography, or least I hope not deliberately so. The reason for not spending much attention on Wales is because Wales and the Welsh have always been located at the very outer margins of British imperial historiography and that the British Empire and British overseas expansion has never loomed very large in writing as the domestic history of Wales. Of course, individual Welsh people were important in the seventeenth- and eighteenth-century empire. The most famous Welshman and Briton in the seventeenth century Atlantic empire was Sir Henry Morgan, the famous privateer and governor of Jamaica. Sir William Jones, the notable orientalist scholar and founder of the Royal Asiatic Society in 1784, and Elihu Yale, governor of Madras between 1687 and 1699, were as important in British Asian history as Morgan is in British Caribbean history. But it is hard to discover a Welsh perspective on overseas expansion that was different from that of either England or Scotland. Wales remained tightly harnessed to England politically in the early modern period and increasingly economically integrated with its larger neighbour. Consequently, Wales established few direct links of its own with the British Atlantic world or with the East India Company. There was in effect no clearly defined Welsh nation or self-standing Welsh economy separate to England. But I would not want to suggest that this means that Wales can be collapsed into England, with Wales as an undifferentiated junior partner of England. Wales was the most deeply and extensively colonised part of the English, then the British, Empire, with a colonisation that never, as in the United States or Australia, turned into postcolonialism. Overseas expansion solidified this colonialism, incorporating Wales into a pan-British enterprise without giving that enterprise any distinctive Welsh flavour. For some Welsh commentators, the idea that Wales is a colonised, rather than a colonising, country, unlike Scotland or England, is a comforting thought. The literary critic Ned Thomas argued that he preferred to be part of an oppressed group, like the Welsh, 'precisely because [the Welsh] lack[] the strain of militarism and imperialism which there is in on the British identity.'[1]

Unlike the Scots and the English, the Welsh seemed to have little need of empire to establish a sense of their identity and destiny, one tied to the preservation of their language and dissenting religion rather than to assertions of Welshness overseas. Historians of Wales, at least until recently, have not worried much about empire. Glanmor Williams, for example, the most prominent late twentieth-century historian of modern Wales showed no interest in empire. The defining work on empire produced at the end of the twentieth century, the five-volume *Oxford History of the British Empire*, contains just eleven references to Wales, with the number declining from seven in the seventeenth-century volume to zero in the volume on the twentieth century. By contrast, Ireland has 303 references, 201 for our period, while Scotland has 130 references, of which 111 are in our period. In some ways, this absence of Wales is surprising, because, as Gwyn Alf Williams has stressed, the very idea of Britishness was derived from Welsh sources. Britishness was first enunciated in the Legend of Madoc, a Welsh prince who supposedly sailed to America in 1170, and the London Welshman, John Dee's first use of the term *British Empire* in 1577.[2] Moreover, the Welsh economy – copper and slate in the early modern period – had strong imperial connections, especially with the Caribbean.

Fortunately, historians of Wales are starting to see Wales within an imperialistic framework and are moving away from depicting Wales in purely domestic terms, with Welsh involvement overseas of minor or accidental interest. After all, the name of the British colony where European settlement is one of the concluding parts of this book has a Welsh name – New South Wales in Australia. An example of this new work is by Chris Evans, who compares the three south-western areas of Britain (the English south-west of Devon and Cornwall and Munster in Ireland and Wales) in an Atlantic context. He shows how wool from Wales found a ready market in the Atlantic slave empire, clothing enslaved people in the West Indies. Meanwhile, Welsh copper was essential in the plantation economy and connected the copper capital of Swansea to the Atlantic port of Bristol. These three regions became increasingly integrated into the Atlantic in the eighteenth century, with Devon's worsted incorporating Munster yarn; Welsh copper containing Cornish ore and the south-west Atlantic fishing fleet, sailing for Newfoundland in Canada via the ports of Munster, where salted provisions could be loaded. These regions provided fish, animal flesh, woollen textiles and copper to Britain's eighteenth-century empire. It was a contribution that foundered in the late eighteenth century, causing revolutionary turmoil, agrarian crisis and the intertwined processes of industrialisation and de-industrialisation in the nineteenth century. Only copper, industrial in nature, survived fully into that century.[3]

Chris Evans focuses on the expansion of Wales outward. I have written on the Atlantic's effect on Wales through an exploration of the reintegration of the Pennant family into North Wales after its members had made a fortune in making sugar through the exploitation of thousands of slaves on large plantations in central Jamaica. The Pennants were one of the rare families who used profits from slavery to invest in British industry, building near Bangor the largest slate factory in the world. Richard Pennant, Lord Penryhn, the founder of this North Wales Empire, used his experience in managing (from a distance) enslaved people to integrate production efficiently and to maximise labour organisation in his slate factory in ways that made working in this factory that eventually it led to the lengthiest strike in British history, between 1900 and 1903. His family made their colonialist intentions clear by building between 1820 and 1845 a neo-Norman castle in Bangor as their principal residence. To build a neo-Norman castle in a landscape where real Norman castles were built by the conquerors of an independent Wales in the fourteenth century was a potent symbol of Welsh defeat and dependence that residents could not fail but to recognise. It was an actively aggressive act of cultural defiance that mocked the Welsh through parodying its colonial history.[4]

James VI and I

Let's start our story with the accession of James VI as James I of England and Wales. James VI of Scotland left Edinburgh on 1 April 1603 to take up his new role as king of England following the death of Elizabeth I without direct heirs on 24 March 1603. James VI was the heir through his grandmother, Margaret, sister of Henry VIII, and thus the heir of his great-grandfather, Henry VII. He became the first of six Stuart kings and through his great-grandson, George I, the progenitor of the still-reigning Hanoverian dynasty. He was a man of mostly Scottish and Welsh descent, more British, although not English, than more than most monarchs, including his Stuart descendants, children of foreign princesses. He was the first king of England with living sons since Henry IV in 1399. That he gave up his Scottish home for a new English residence is telling about the greater advantages England had over the perennially poor and divided Scotland.

England was not without its problems, however. Its royal revenues were dreadful, meaning that its monarch was not wealthy or even financially stable. It had just finished a bloody invasion of Ireland, and civil unrest was always likely, as had been seen in the abortive rebellion of Elizabeth's favourite, Robert Devereaux, Earl of Essex in 1601. Because the decade of the 1600s had the peerless playwright, William Shakespeare, at the height of his powers, and because it was very soon after James VI and I took power that the Bible he commissioned, the Authorised Version, or the King James Bible, published in 1611, still the best-selling book in the English language ever published and, with the words of Shakespeare, the language whose cadences resonate in the English-speaking world most of any literary work, we tend to invest that decade with a specialness it perhaps does not deserve.

England was a religiously divided nation, with fierce antagonisms between various Protestant sects, and had experienced one of its worst economic crises in the 1580s and 1590s, with harvest failure, plague, record unemployment, inflation and a huge crime spree, leading to unprecedented levels of public executions, some of which when given to traitors and Catholics were extremely gruesome. It was in the middle of a population boom, with the population increasing by 80 per cent between 1540 and 1640, by which latter year there were 5 million people in England. For the moment, there was no Malthusian crisis, with population increase outstripping the capacity of the nation to feed all its new mouths. Resources continued, just, to increase at a rate enough to prevent starvation among the poor. But social unrest was ever-present. There were thousands of so-called masterless men (young men outside established employment structures, the most important of which were indentured servitude for teenagers) travelling the roads and getting into trouble, a body of people always able to be mobilised by popular leaders willing to air their grievances against the cards they had been dealt to the wider public and to the political nation. England always teetered on the verge of serious revolt, even though such revolts were few and viciously crushed by a state willing to exercise its powers when it felt it needed to. The English population was one that was always in search of wealth or at least better forms of sustenance: it was restless, aggressive and always on edge.

The Tudor and early Stuart period saw a great increase in inequality. Alexandra Shepherd has calculated that while overall per capita wealth increased from £33.61 to £51.62 between James VI and I's reign to that of Charles I, the gains from increased national prosperity were unevenly divided. The major beneficiaries were yeomen in the south-east, whose wealth increased by 80 per cent in a generation. The losers were husbandmen, labourers, some tradespeople and single women. Inequality by class was matched by inequality by region. London, East Anglia and the south-east were much richer than anywhere else, especially the poor north-west and Cornwall. The number of poor people was exploding. There may have been a fourfold increase in poor relief between 1500 and 1700, an increase greater than population increase as a whole.[5]

James VI and I was fortunate too that other nations did not take advantage of an unusual succession. The accession to a throne by someone not a son of an existing monarch usually in early modern Europe caused an eruption of social unrest, as viable candidates for monarchy tested their case. It was true, of course, that it was hard to dispute James VI and I's legitimacy, given the paucity of legitimate heirs to the Tudor throne. But we need to recall that when Anne died in 1714, in the next change of dynasty to the English throne, the succession went to a man with numerous better candidates to the throne ahead of him. It was not a foreordained certainty that James VI and I would be accepted onto the English throne in 1603, especially as a Scotsman arriving in a country with a lasting antipathy to people of that nation. He was not tested by foreign opposition. The nation that was most likely to cause trouble, France, was going through severe problems of its own and its attention was focused on domestic rather than foreign concerns. Philip II of Spain, who might have been king of England himself if his father's wife, Mary Tudor, had survived longer, was unhappy with this second Protestant succession in a row to the English throne, but he was more concerned in 1603 with fighting the Turks and dealing with rebellion in the Spanish Netherlands than with causing trouble in England.

This silence from Europe was a welcome break from continual problems from Europe in a period in which the Continent was in constant turmoil during what Mark Greengrass has nicely termed 'Christendom destroyed.'[6] Reformation and Counter-reformation had unleashed waves of religious warfare throughout western and central Europe, which were only to become more intense from 1618 and the start of the Bohemian Crisis that became the devastating Thirty Years' War. Meanwhile, military technology had advanced rapidly, making wars more expensive, armies larger, casualties more frequent and conflicts longer in duration. James VI and I's principal foreign policy objective was to stay out of European conflict, but that objective proved impossible to sustain. Even Elizabeth I had been drawn into European wars from 1585, despite all her diplomatic skills. The European wars she was forced to enter during the last eighteen years of her reign depleted the English treasury so much that it was virtually empty when James VI and I took over, causing him immense problems domestically as well as in foreign affairs.

James VI and I has had a bad press in history writing, in part, because he followed as monarch one of England's most renowned and glamorous monarchs and, in part, due to his admittedly uncharismatic personality. We have been especially influenced in our poor opinion of him by the penetrating but unfair portrait of him put forward by a disgruntled and deliciously bitchy courtier, Sir Anthony Weldon. Weldon depicted James as a freakish creep – he may have had mild cerebral palsy – with an uncouth Scottish accent and a tendency to drink too much and swear with abandon while being cowardly, lazy and obviously homosexual (then a capital crime). There is not much evidence that James VI and I actively engaged in sodomy, a capital felony which James himself declared 'ye are bound in conscience never to forgive' (although he also said the same about swearing, which he frequently engaged in). Nevertheless, his fawning over attractive young aristocrats, most notably his favourite, the Duke of Buckingham, created scandals at court. Still, perhaps because of homosexual inclination, James VI and I seems never to have taken a mistress, unlike most monarchs (most notoriously his grandsons, Charles II and James VII and II) and was at least formally faithful to his wife, Anne of Denmark, with whom he secured the reign through having an heir and a spare (the latter becoming king in 1625).

Weldon's caricature was malicious, as James VI and I was by any measure a skilled and resourceful king, with thirty-six years' experience under his belt before coming to London. He made a good fist of dealing with England's many problems while sustaining his reputation as a reforming king in Scotland and being a monarch able to keep Ireland under some sort of control. His ability to keep Ireland at least quiescent is in stark contrast to both his predecessor and his successor, both of whom found Irish affairs impossible to manage. But the problems he faced were formidable. He had to improve royal finances, deal with three different forms of ecclesiastical establishments in each of his three kingdoms, keep his subjects from succumbing to religious hatred and bring harmony in both church and parliament. He just about achieved this aim, making him probably the most successful monarch of the century and perhaps the most accomplished English monarch since Henry V.

A king needs luck, and James VI and I's greatest stroke of luck was the failure of the Gunpowder Plot in 1605, a potentially devastating terrorist strike against Protestant rule by discontented Catholic gentry from the English Midlands. The Gunpowder Plot was an audacious attempt to blow up the houses of parliament, thus killing most of the representatives of the political nation, when it was in session. The plot was discovered on 4 November 1605, and England was cast into one of its periodic intense bouts of anti-Catholicism. A national holiday of thanksgiving was declared to mark England's fortunate release from Catholic tyranny, and that day is still celebrated, often, as in the famous celebrations in Lewes, Sussex, containing significant anti-Catholic rhetoric. The defeat of the plotters confirmed once again that England, Scotland and Wales were determined to hold to their Protestant heritage, no matter what. The actions of the plotters gave James VI and I a popularity he was never to achieve again in his reign. Assumptions of Catholic conspiracy were only enhanced by the assassination of the once-Protestant king of France, Henri IV, in 1610 by a Catholic fanatic.

Nevertheless, this show of support for James VI and I early in his reign did not mean that he was given much leeway in implementing policies that the English Parliament and peerage disagreed with. James VI and I failed in his major objective on taking the throne of England, which was to make a permanent political union between England and Scotland. The English were prepared to have a Scottish king but only if he knew his place. They were unpersuaded that the act of succession meant that they needed to combine with a nation whose poverty meant that they felt that they would get nothing in return for Union, except increased debts. The only model for Union that the English understood was that of Wales, which was a union with a conquered country. English parliamentarians and peers were unwilling to entertain a different kind of Union, one based on presupposed equality. James VI and I's resorted to symbolic gestures, such as declaring himself on accession as 'the Emperor of the whole Island of Britain' and entitling his coronation medal as 'Caesar Augustus of Britain.' No union ever eventuated in the seventeenth century. The Commons insisted, contrary to James VI and I's argument, that creating a union was not easy. The laws of England were English laws, Sir Edwin Sandys argued, and if the name England was lost when incorporated into the larger entity of Britain, then England and its laws would fail.

James VI and I was more successful in his foreign policy at the start of his reign, quickly ending in 1603 a long war with Spain begun in 1585 and making peace also with the Dutch. Overall, however, it is hard to see that many of the problems that faced James VI and I at the start of his reign had been solved when Charles I took over in 1625. What was true, of course, was that James VI and I managed these problems better than did his son but that is saying little, given how disastrous a king Charles I was. James VI and I's solutions to problems were controversial. He tamed Ireland but at some cost, with the native

Figure 1.1 The coronation of James I

Source: Chronicle/Alamy Stock Photo.

Irish and the Old English starting for almost the first time to combine against the Crown. His religious policies in Scotland did not bring religious consensus but instead stirred up greater discord, with Scots suspicious of an episcopal and non-Calvinist thrust in his policy. In England, few of the problems he faced went away after his death. He did not solve effectively either the problem of royal finance or the relationship between Parliament and the Crown. He had a bad relationship with that institution, a turbulence that compromised his chances of getting money from it and limiting his foreign policy options.

The Thirty Years' War and the rule of kings

He might have done better if a crisis not of his making had not occurred: The Bohemian crisis of 1618 in which Protestants rebelled against their Roman Catholic Habsburg king, Ferdinand II. The resulting Thirty Years' War devastated Europe and caused major problems for James VI and I. He had wanted to trim between Protestants and Catholics (and, if possible, stay out of the conflict all together) but that neutrality was hard to achieve when it was his son-in-law, Frederick V, Elector of Palatine, who was fighting the Habsburg rule. The Thirty Years' War saw the first crisis of the Stuart monarchy, a multidimensional crisis in which agricultural depression and religious tensions combined with foreign policy problems to make the difficulties inherent in a composite monarchy very real. What was especially worrying were calls by Puritans for military intervention in Bohemia and an outbreak of anti-Catholicism which was often orchestrated by Calvinist clergymen in England whom James VI and I had himself put into office. Supporting Frederick V was problematic, however, as it suggested resistance to monarchical rule was possible, even desirable; James VI and I was furious at a son-in-law he felt obliged to support but whose actions he deplored.

James VI and I had very firm views on the role of the monarchy and the limits on popular resistance to a monarch's rule. He made several pronouncements about what he considered were the lineaments of royal rule, such as his *Trew Law of Free Monarchies* (1598) and *Basilkon Doran* (1598). He believed that the king was 'accountable to none but God,' a statement extreme to modern readers but generally accepted by most political theorists at the time, The king, James VI and I asserted, was above the law and did not have to share his sovereignty with anyone, which was one consequence of the break with Rome in the 1530s – before that time, the papacy had some claim to sovereignty throughout western Christendom. If this seems tyrannical, we need to consider that it remains the position about the power held by most recent presidents of the United States, at least for actions taken while they are in office. James VI and I insisted that God had installed kings to 'minister Justice and Judgement to the people,' 'advance the good, and punish the evil' and act as 'a natural Father . . . bound to care for all his subjects.' He thought there was no practical limits on the power of the Crown, just an expectation that he ruled according to the law and for the benefit of the people.

England, of course, had often objected to kingly rule. Several of its kings had died suspiciously, such as Edward II (1327), Richard III (1399), Henry VI (1471) and Edward V (1483). The Tudors and Stuarts undermined the medieval assumption that the king of England 'was under God and the law, because the law makes the king,' an assumption encapsulated in the famous Magna Carta forced on John in 1215. James VI and I stridently disagreed. It was his view, taken up with severe consequences for his authority by Charles I, that formed the crux of the conflict between Parliament and Crown in the seventeenth century, The king might pronounce all he wanted about his rights and his divinely guaranteed powers, but it was difficult for him to rule if Parliament objected even if, on the surface, Parliament had no existence independent of the king who determined if and when Parliament met. In practice, ignoring Parliament was impossible, given the weight attached by the populace to the so-called ancient constitution, ensuring a sort of partnership between the people and the monarch. Moreover, as often noted in this book, royal rule depended on a host of amateur lawmakers in local government. In any given year, perhaps fifty thousand officeholders served in England and many more were placed in lesser offices and served in the militia or as jurymen. In theory, in a ten-year period, one-half of the adult male population served as officers. As Tim Harris concludes,

> ordinary people played an important role in governing their own commu-
> nities, and the central government could find it very difficult to get those
> at the local level to enforce unpopular policies and initiatives, unless pres-
> sure could be brought to bear to persuade or compel local officeholders to
> do their duty or else some measure could be devised to sidestep the local
> agents of law enforcement.[7]

Independence was especially pronounced in towns and cities, with London notably cantankerous in defence of its traditional privileges, not least those of its ancient guilds through which much of the commerce of the town was funnelled. Monarchical principles lived in uneasy tension with traditional commonwealth inheritances that saw politics as dependent on civic-mindedness, mutuality and an absence of people acting in their own self-interest.

The final question in discussing royal authority is, What happened if a king did not rule by law or ruled unjustly or was a tyrant? If what a king did contradicted what God wanted, you had to obey God first. But you could not actively resist lawful authority and had to accept punishment for non-compliance, even if you were obeying the dictates of God. James VI and I thought that resistance to a lawful monarch was theoretically possible but hedged how this might occur with so many qualifications that, in effect, it was practically impossible – the advice he gave was that if a realm had a bad ruler, that was both God's decision to punish a people for previous misdeeds and something that needed to be accepted until a new and better ruler emerged, arising out of God's will and presumably as a result of a people being forgiven for their sins. Opponents of the Stuarts thought rebellion undesirable but potentially allowable if there was no other option. They argued that it was legitimate to oppose the Crown when the Crown violated the law or even if it did not act in the people's interests. They were able to couch such opposition in ways that connected it to England's ancient past and to firm ideas about commonwealth values of self-government. Thus, their actions could be seen to be in accord with consensual values and norms and based on long traditions – it was the Crown, in this view, not the Parliament or the people, who were trying to change customary relationships and bring doctrines from a Europe tending towards absolutism into a land devoted historically to personal and political liberty.

But relatively few Britons put the conflict between king and parliament, at least until the late 1640s and between 1685 and 1688, in such starkly antagonistic terms. In short, the current consensus is that we should not see the political problems of the seventeenth century as a fundamental constitutional battle between a Stuart monarchy determined on absolutism and a Parliament that was sharply hostile to infringements on its 'rights' and as being the protector of the ancient constitution and the peoples' rights against monarchical tyranny. Glenn Burgess has made it clear that there was considerable political and constitutional consensus in England until the 1640s and that when conflict occurred before that decade, it did so less for grand ideological reasons but because of factional rivalries or even from misunderstandings.[8] Such a view might be thought to drain the seventeenth century of much of its drama and its primeval explanatory power as a century of debates and fights over the meaning of liberty. It does allow, however, for a greater appreciation of both contingency and continuity in British history over the long term. As always, when things ran smoothly, as they did in the 1610s and 1630s, and for most of the eighteenth century, it was possible for people to live with ambiguity about the roles of various parts of the English constitution and for a natural tendency in English politics for consensus to hold sway.

Composite monarchy

James VI and I was the ruler of several realms – multiple kingdoms, in one telling, or composite monarchies, in a more recent formation. A composite monarchy is a polity including more than one country under the sovereignty of one ruler, meaning the existence of a 'profound respect for corporate structures and for traditional rights, privileges, and customs.'[9] James VI and I did not always pay respect to such traditions as he professed, his views also tending towards expressions of absolutism, where he proclaimed himself above the law. But the reality of his situation as a monarch of several realms, in which power was always something to be negotiated between monarch and representatives of the people, meant that reciprocal relations between composite states were crucial and that a composite monarchy had a plurality of jurisdictions and coercive powers. The king had an *absoluta potestas* (direct authority), but he did not have a monopoly on violence and jurisdiction. Other political agents, such as Parliament, the nobility, the church and corporations enjoyed political, juridical and economic privileges, which, in many cases, emanated from their own natures and traditions, not necessarily flowing directly from the monarch, as suggested in absolutist regimes.

The idea of a composite monarchy is of relatively recent invention, introduced by H. G. Koeninsberger in 1975 and enhanced and explained in 1992 by J. H. Elliott. As Elliott describes it, a composite monarchy was not a unified kingdom but many kingdoms that had only one thing in common, a single ruler who ruled these states as a personal, as opposed to a real, union. A 'personal union' was one in which boundaries, laws and interests remained distinct while a 'real union, as occurred when England and Scotland joined together in 1707 was one in which the constitutional states were interlinked. Wales and Ireland never fitted into the pattern of a real union, as they were conquered places, assimilated into the larger unit, without being able to contribute to the structures of the subsequent new state. In the seventeenth century, however, Ireland was different constitutionally from what it was to become, hovering uneasily between being a colony, subject to English laws, and a kingdom, with its own tradition, customs and jurisdictions.

In general surveys of monarchies in the early modern period, the composite monarchy is seen as ill favoured. More than one-half of the seventeenth-century revolts in European states occurred in composite states, comprising a well-integrated territory linked by loose and often-contested bonds to other autonomous regions. At least in Britain, the core and peripheral regions were contiguously linked, unlike those of the Spanish and Austrian Habsburgs. These composite monarchies were politically unstable for two reasons, only one of which really applied to the composite monarchy under James VI and I. The one problem that was not that important was what was a major concern in France, which was repeated endogamy among monarchs which reduced the gene pool of the dynasty and led in Spain to the physically deformed and mentally challenged and sterile Carlos II, whose parents had such a limited number of ancestors that their genetic legacies were heavily compromised.

The second problem was vitally important in the Stuart monarchy. James VI and I and Charles I wanted their kingdoms to be unified in politics and religion, but their kingdoms preserved their own institutions and collective identity with a distinct religion and, to an extent, separate languages. As a 1641 English pamphleteer noted, disintegration of the Stuart personal union was inevitable 'because there was not heretofore a perfect union twixt England and Scotland, incorporating both into one body and mind.'

For early seventeenth theorists, diversity in a kingdom was not a strength but a weakness. Francis Bacon wrote an essay 'Of Seditions and Troubles' where he noted that 'discontents' are 'in the politique body like to humours in the natural, which are apt to gather a preternaturall heat, and to enflame.' An 'enflamed' part of a composite state – such as Scotland in 1638 and Ireland in 1641 – would create instability in all parts of the composite monarchy, which a ruler was powerless to counteract, as he had few coercive powers and had to realise that solving, or attempting to solve, a problem in one part of the composite monarchy (or, later, in the empire, which was not a composite monarchy strictly speaking but which had different parts that expected to be treated differently) caused resentment and strife in other parts. It was in the peripheries that power was especially problematic – England, for example, was the last of Charles I's kingdoms to rebel against him. Diversity frequently led to 'sub-imperialism' and that 'sub-imperialism' bred resentment, mainly because the peripheral parts of the composite state, such as Scotland, possessed extensive privileges, guaranteed by the monarch and would not give these up when a central government tried to enforce conformity in all parts of the state.

In the case of Britain, the composite monarchy was always under stress, in part, because what united the kingdoms was much less than what divided them. England and Scotland had been at loggerheads for many centuries, and the mutual hatred between them could not be easily assuaged just because from 1603 they had a common king. Their economic and social differences were exceeded by their incompatible religious regimes and doctrines, each strictly enforced in law. Even geography caused a problem, as each kingdom, even England, had places that were too poor to have had much contact with London (e.g. Westmoreland and the Cambridgeshire fens) and where religious and political decrees from London were routinely ignored. Wales and Ireland were even less tractable. Just because James VI and I claimed to have made laws that all had to obey, that did not mean that he was correct that this meant that obedience had to happen. In the highlands of Scotland, for example, clan chieftains generally ignored the Crown and pursued their own policies and engaged in local feuds that had nothing to do with government commands.

James VI and I tried hard to overcome this diversity of views, religions, and geographies. He tried to foster a common loyalty, based on himself, among all his subjects. He stated that his fondest 'wish above all things was at his death to leave one worship to God, one kingdom entirely governed [and] one uniformity in laws.' In practice, that uniformity meant Anglicisation, or the adaptation to the mores and power of the south-east of England and, above all, to London. It was not just the Scots, Irish and Welsh who were unprepared to follow such a policy. So, too, were many English people, living in places distant from the metropolitan centre and opposed to Stuart centralisation and the efforts of these Stuart monarchs to try to overturn long-established local customs for their new and very popular idea of 'British' solidarity.

Notes

1 Ned Thomas, *The Welsh Extremist* (Ceredigon, Wales: Y Lolfa, 1973), 33.
2 Gwyn Alf Williams, *Madoc: The Making of a Myth* (London, 1979); idem, *When Was Wales? A History of the Welsh* (London: Eyre Methuen, 1979).
3 Chris Evans, 'Wales, Munster and the English South Wales: Contrasting Articulations with the Atlantic World,' in H.V. Bowen, ed., *Wales and the British Overseas Empire: Interactions and Influences, 1650–1830* (Manchester: Manchester University Press, 2011), 40–61.
4 Trevor Burnard, 'From Periphery to Periphery: The Pennants' Jamaican Plantations and Industrialisation in North Wales,' in Bowen, *Wales and the Overseas Empire*, 114–42.
5 Alexandra Shepherd, *Accounting for Oneself: Worth, Status, and the Social Order in Early Modern England* (Oxford: Oxford University Press, 2015), 69, 80, 95, 115.
6 Mark Greengrass, *Christendom Destroyed: Europe 1517–1648* (London: Penguin, 2015).
7 Tim Harris, *Rebellion: Britain's First Stuart Kings* (Oxford: Oxford University Press, 2014), 27.
8 Glenn Burgess, *Absolute Monarchy and the Stuart Monarchy* (New Haven: Yale University Press, 1996).
9 J.H. Elliott, 'A Europe of Composite Monarchies,' *Past & Present* 137 (1992), 68–9.

Bibliography

Burgess, Glenn, *Absolute Monarchy and the Stuart Monarchy* (New Haven: Yale University Press, 1996).
Croft, Pauline, *King James* (Basingstoke: Palgrave Macmillan, 2003).
Elliott, J.H., *Empires of the Atlantic World: Britain and Spain in America 1492–1830* (New Haven: Yale University Press, 2006).
Harris, Tim, *Rebellion: Britain's First Stuart Kings* (Oxford: Oxford University Press, 2014).
Houlbrooke, Ralph, *Britain and Europe 1500–1780* (London: Bloomsbury, 2010).
Kearney, Hugh, *The British Isles: A History of Four Nations*, 2nd ed. (Cambridge: Cambridge University Press, 2006).
Sharpe, Kevin, *Image Wars: Promoting Kings and Commonwealth in England, 1603–1660* (New Haven: Yale University Press, 2010).

2 England enters the world, 1600–1700

Origins of settlement

The English were late colonisers, especially in the Americas, where they lagged well behind the Spanish and Portuguese. Indeed, England had a presence in India before they had one in the Americas, with the charter given to the East India Company being granted on 31 December 1600, and in Africa, with a trading station in Sierra Leone probably beginning around 1606, when a factor employed by John Davies, a London merchant, engaged in the redwood trade from 1611 onwards. Of course, the English had made tentative forays into the New World in the sixteenth century, with a couple of early contacts from perhaps as early as 1481. But apart from slaving ventures in West Africa, fishing in Newfoundland and pirate raids in the Caribbean by Sir Francis Drake, Sir Humphrey Gilbert and Sir Walter Raleigh, colonisation was limited before 1607 to a failed settlement at Roanoke in North Carolina between 1588 and 1591. English colonisation (there was none to speak of from the other three nations in the British Isles) was mostly in the mind, with works on the desirability of settlement in the Americas written by Richard Hakluyt in 1584 and 1589 and a travel guide to Virginia, written by Thomas Hariot, in 1588, alongside Walter Raleigh's evocative and largely imaginary 1596 boastful account of his travels to the South American lands of Guiana. It was not until April 1607 that the first permanent settlement of Virginia happened, at Jamestown, in the tidewater region of Virginia. By this time, the Iberian nations of Portugal and Spain had established viable colonies in South America and the Caribbean and in parts of southwestern North America and Florida.

Yet England and Britain quickly made up for its late start. By the middle of the eighteenth century, Britain's Atlantic possessions, including Ireland, were second only to Spain's in size and importance. By 1760, the British Atlantic, excluding Ireland, comprised 23 colonies, with a total population of 1,972,608, of whom 1,326,306 were white and 646,305 black. In addition, large numbers of unsubjugated and unincorporated Native Americans lived in the American interior, and a proportion of them were allied to the British and attached, very loosely, to the British Empire.

How do we create a chronology of British colonisation of its Atlantic world? The first distinct period, done by the English, involved the imagining and then the realising of late sixteenth-century colonising projects urged on the English Crown and English merchants by propagandists such as Richard Hakluyt. This initial period of imagined colonisation lasted from the 1580s to the 1620s. By the latter date, the English had viable settlements in Virginia and Bermuda and were starting to settle the West Indies and New England. English colonial enterprise in this early phase of colonisation emerged from a heady combination of national ambition, economic pragmatism and a thirst for individual and collective glory. English entry into the Americas was shaped by competition in Europe with Spain, a desire to supplant the Catholicisation of the Americas with aggressive Protestantism and a utopian urge to end English poverty through the exploitation of Atlantic resources.

In one sense, this early colonisation was a last act of the Renaissance more than an act that looked forward to the Enlightenment. English colonists tended to look back to older precedents when envisioning their empire in the early seventeenth century. The treasurer of Virginia in 1626, George Sandys, for example, published an edition of Ovid's *Metamorphoses*, which he wrote in his spare time. Sandys was interested in how the classical works on civility that Ovid represented could be reproduced in the Virginian wilderness, a wilderness in which the Virginians had only just survived a massacre of them by Native Americans of the Powhatan nation in 1622. In London, William Shakespeare was inspired by colonisation in Bermuda in 1609, to write his last play, *The Tempest* (1611) about how colonisation wrought a 'sea-change' in Europeans so that the Europeans were transformed in the Americas – metamorphosing, in short – 'into something rich and strange.'

Early English settlement failed to meet the expectations of its projectors, almost all of whom lost most of their money in early settlement schemes. The main achievement, as seen in the Virginia massacre of 1622, was negative, a prolonged assault on the vibrant yet vulnerable cultures of indigenes, through the occupation of Native American land and the rapid deterioration of English–Native American relations, as initially positive views of the indigenes were replaced by highly negative views that led to violent conflict and racial denigration within a decade of permanent settlement. For their part, Native Americans came to realise that English settlers were not just a fresh, if unpleasant, set of invaders like other tribes of Native Americans, as was customary within North America, who came and harassed residents of desirable locations but who did not try to fundamentally change social relations. These English were here to stay, were determined to either get rid of or reduce into servitude and dependency the owners of land they desired and were completely unwilling to even try to learn much about the people they wanted to displace.

What made this early settlement distinctive compared to Iberian colonisation, which was conducted very much under the aegis of the Crown acting on its own behalf and which was controlled in all aspects by the state, is that English colonisation was mainly done by private initiative, usually chartered under the Crown. In effect, the state subcontracted out colonisation to the private sector. The leading colonisation companies were all joint-stock companies, in which investors pooled funds in order to spread risk and increase the amount that could be used to attract settlers and pay for settlement. The most famous of these companies was the Virginia Company, which founded Virginia in 1607, but also important was the Massachusetts Bay Company, the Providence Island Company and the Newfoundland Company. Not all companies lasted a long time, and none did especially well. They were mostly intended to foster trade, and trade, as much as settlement, was the aim of most early settlement endeavours. The major enclaves of settlement at Jamestown, Bermuda, Plymouth Plantation and Boston were the models for future ventures. These companies may not have been terribly successful for individuals, but the Crown found doing colonisation this way very easy, as most of the hard work was done by the companies rather than itself.

As joint-stock companies fell from favour in the 1620s, the Crown moved to proprietary charters. The Courteen syndicate established tobacco planting, copying Virginia, in Barbados, and the Catholic Calvert family settled Maryland, adjacent to Virginia, in 1634 as a Catholic-friendly colony. The willingness of the English Crown to privatise the business of colonisation shows its desire to have colonies be oriented towards commercial profit and indicates its indifference to the forms of government that were established overseas. The result was by 1640 a bewildering variety of governmental forms that had a long-lasting legacy, meaning that when the Crown wanted to tighten up imperial legislation after 1660, it faced a hard task reconciling that standardisation of practices with the diversity of governmental forms that arose at the founding of colonies. What tended to happen in most colonies, however, was that settlers quickly founded representative assemblies modelled on the English parliament, where they created their own laws, designed for their own circumstances. Settlers took the localism of seventeenth-century England into life overseas, claiming the right to govern themselves based on their inheritances as English subjects who may have left the shores of Britain but who maintained their English identity abroad. That the Crown was willing to allow colonists to govern themselves and exercised little oversight over such self-government persuaded settlers that their assumptions of the rights of Englishmen abroad was uncontroversial and acceptable. The governments that resulted usually had a governor appointed by the Crown and a scattering of other colonial officials who thought themselves as part of an embryonic imperial system of control.

When they tried to impose themselves on assemblies, however, they often met with indifference or opposition. Usually, instability in colonial governments, which was frequent and often bitter, if usually rooted in local concerns, was seldom based on antipathy to Crown interference, mainly because the Crown was noticeably absent from most areas of colonial governance, but came from conflict among factions in a colony, each attempting to gain an advantage for themselves but with few factions having any legitimacy besides self-promotion of individual interests. In the main colonies of the American

South and the West Indies, it was hard for any ruling elite to emerge as mortality rates were so high that most residents had arrived recently, had few firm roots in the places where they lived and found it difficult to gain the support of fellow residents. English politics had a strong deferential aspect to it, with authority derived from residence, wealth and membership of the landed gentry or aristocracy, groups assumed to have the right and ability to rule. Settlers found it difficult to be deferential towards rulers who often came from the same circumstances as ordinary men but who had been fortunate in their settlement histories.

The second stage of settlement, from the mid-1620s to the mid-1680s, was much more successful than the first stage and marked the period in which an English Empire really started to emerge. Settlement in most areas, however, remained difficult in the face of sustained Native American resistance and given the hardships of clearing land and establishing viable economies. Only the West Indian island of Barbados, significantly without a Native American population and small in size, meaning that forest clearing and the development of plantations proceeded relatively rapidly and which was transformed in the 1640s and 1650s by the first successful introduction of plantation agriculture based on using the labour of Africans shipped to the island in the burgeoning Atlantic slave trade and employed as hereditary chattel slaves in a new institution predicated on unfreedom, had truly performed according to expectations.

Nevertheless, progress was substantial in all colonies, even if none matched Barbados for its ability to give its residents wealth and its ability to make its society seem demonstrably English in character (even if based on slavery, which was an institution unknown in this form in England). Within a generation of settlement, English settlers in most colonies had established viable political and social structures, had developed economies that provided at least a decent subsistence living and which pointed to future wealth and had started to articulate visions of what they wanted their embryonic societies to become. Those visions usually revolved around turning these places into places that were recognisably English, with the colonies of New England, settled by Dissenters who adhered very much to the idea that what they were creating was a godly commonwealth in the wilderness, a city on the hill that would be a shining light for future generations, as the founder of the Massachusetts colony, John Winthrop, put it in his 1630 treatise, *A Model of Christian Charity*, having an idea of Englishness which differed markedly from the more commercial and competitive idea of England advanced by the setters of the Chesapeake and West Indies. These differences between North and South reflected differences in settlement patterns, and economic orientation (New England had few goods to offer for sale in Britain while with sugar and tobacco the plantation colonies in the south and in the islands produced things that the metropolis wanted). It also reflected the divisions in Britain itself over what a proper society should look like.

The foundation of success in the southern and Caribbean colonies was African slavery, which by mid-century was deemed essential to produce luxury tropical goods for European markets. These colonies could by mid-century be sharply delineated from northern colonies by their commitment to enslaved labour, a delineation which persisted for several centuries to come. These societies, north and south, resembled each other in being far from civilised places. Indeed, conflict between classes was endemic, as embryonic elites with few pretensions to civility and little inherited authority, as noted earlier, attempted, with some success, to impose themselves on their poorer compatriots. Poorer men, in the age of the small planter and tradesman, were resentful about these richer men's nouveau riche pretensions and were especially resentful that they were being excluded from political power. Thus, the successes of seventeenth-century English colonisation seemed to observers to be unimpressive, given how low average standards of living were and how combustible, while primitive, was social and political life. One reason why England paid so little attention before the late seventeenth century to the societies it had established in the Atlantic world is that they seemed chaotic and barbarous, as much as they provided relatively little economic benefits to the English population.

The key event in English settlement was also the key event in British life in the seventeenth century, which was the implosion of the metropolitan centre during the British Civil Wars. The colonies were left behind to fend for themselves in this period while Britons quarrelled at home. As Carla Pestana claims, the importance of the Civil War to early American history is that 'no American colony of any other European state experienced a comparable breakdown at the imperial centre until the French Revolution.'[1] This breakdown of authority came at a crucial time, just as the colonies were starting to gain some understanding of their peculiar cultures and developing their own histories. Thus, the breakdown in imperial authority gave emerging settler leaders confidence that they could control their own affairs. They consolidated local power in the 1640s and 1650s at the expense of proprietors and the Crown. British American colonies never lost this capacity for self-government, despite attempts by the later Stuarts to claw back control to the imperial centre.

The Glorious Revolution in America

The Glorious Revolution confirmed, at least to colonial minds, that they were entitled to self-government, The colonial rebels of 1689, who were numerous and in many North American colonies, although not many West Indian colonies, shared objections to James VII and II's Catholicism and absolutist tendencies and used the revolution to eradicate the most authoritarian features of later Stuart colonial rule while bolstering the ultra-Protestant and anti-Catholic character of religious life in English America. Maryland, for example, ceased to be a Catholic refuge from this period. As in England, the 1670s saw tensions grow between colonists and a very narrow elitist government where, as in Virginia and Jamaica, governors ruled like independent potentates. Around 1675, the imperial government embarked on a new policy intended to shatter colonial self-governing tendencies by binding every colony directly to the

Crown. This initiative occurred in a time of troubles in many colonies. In New York, taken from the Dutch in 1660, a temporary recapture of the colony in 1673–74 encouraged the large Dutch population to oppose the Duke of York, later James VII and II, who was in control of the colony, in his attempt to control all officeholding. In Massachusetts, the bloodiest war per capita in American history, King Philip's War, in which Native Americans directly challenged English authority, put great strain on a system in which only a minority of adult males who were members of the Puritan Church could participate in politics. Another war against Native Americans, Bacon's Rebellion of 1676, in which divisions between big planters and poorer men were highlighted, convulsed Virginia. Maryland also had a rebellion in 1676 while, in Jamaica, there were continual battles between one political faction who favoured Jamaica becoming a plantation society and another faction who believed that plundering Spanish America was the way to fortune and prosperity. When James VII and II took over as king, he wanted to tame these unruly places by consolidating all the American colonies into three or viceroyalties on the Spanish model. Only one was established: the Dominion of New England, which incorporated eight previously separate colonies into a single province, extending from the Delaware River to the Canadian border. James VII and II also continued his brother's policy of squeezing, as settlers saw it, the colonies for money through their rapidly expanding plantation economies. He persuaded Parliament to raise duties on sugar and tobacco, which were meant to be a tax passed onto the English consumer but instead were costs mostly borne by the American producer. For tobacco farmers, this was especially bad, as they were facing a prolonged slump in tobacco prices in the 1680s.

While colonists complained about imperial policies, shaping their complaints in terms that were to become familiar a century later during the American Revolution in terms of executive 'tyranny,' there was also a strong desire among many colonists for a closer relationship with the imperial state. Settlers were tired of their isolation from England and often saw, as with large sugar planters in Jamaica in the 1680s, advantages from their close connections with rent-seeking imperial merchants that made closer imperial control welcome. For every alarm against the centralising tendencies of the Crown, there was a corresponding welcoming of what the government was doing, As Richard Dunn notes,

> never before, and probably never since, were such toadying letters and grovelling addresses sent to Whitehall . . . in Jamaica Governor Albemarle toasted the [birth of the] Prince [of Wales in 1688] so immoderately that he plunged into a fit of jaundice and died.[2]

Nevertheless, when news of rebellion in Britain came to America, settlers quickly joined in, with serious revolts in Massachusetts, New York and Maryland. Each of these rebellions was very different, primarily because each rebellion occurred around local issues that varied from colony to colony. Ironically, the people who did best from the Glorious Revolution were the Caribbean colonists, who had not risen on behalf of William III. They used the influence of absentee sugar planters living in England and their connections with London sugar merchants, who had strongly backed William III, to get special favours, including the end of the Royal African Company's monopoly on providing slaves to the West Indies and some dropping of sugar duties. The main effect of the Glorious Revolution for both mainland and island colonists was that it became very clear that henceforth they would have to operate in a transatlantic system, with London as the metropolitan core.

Studying English America in the seventeenth century as opposed to British America in the eighteenth century, a century when the dynamic Atlantic world became increasingly important to Britain economically and geopolitically, is a useful corrective to notions of a smooth colonial progress over time to increasing sophistication, complexity and success. The varieties of colonial experience before 1688 were bewildering. That complexity reduced over time – the colonies each became more internally diverse, but that internal diversity made each colony increasingly resemble each other in its fundamental features. In the seventeenth century, the colonies in the Americas were varied in their histories, their ethnic and religious mixes and their commitment or lack of it to either religion or slavery. If we stopped our analysis in 1692, perhaps the most disastrous year in all of American history, with a disastrous earthquake in Port Royal Jamaica; the first outbreak of yellow fever in the Caribbean, a disease which more than anything else hindered white settlement in that region; the beginnings of serious warfare in the Caribbean; the tumult of a witchcraft trial in Salem, Massachusetts; a foiled slave revolt in Barbados; the Keithian schism between Dissenting groups in the new province of Pennsylvania; and the Leisler revolt in New York, pitting the Dutch against English colonists, we would not see success but an America unravelling. We would also see a remarkably under-institutionalised world full of unassimilated populations, red, white and black, with little to unite them except mutual fear and misunderstanding.

The threat and application of force and the acceptance of extreme levels of violence marked the peripheries of empire as savage and outside the normal experience of Europeans, themselves far from unfamiliar with brutality. Wars could be especially brutal, from the near extermination of English settlers in Native American raids in Virginia in 1622 and 1644 to the near-genocidal destruction of Native Americans in the Pequot War in Massachusetts in 1637 to the savagery of Bacon's Rebellion and King Philip's War in 1675–76 to the unremitting brutality that accompanied the introduction of plantation slavery in Barbados and then the rest of the Caribbean and the American South, that made these years probably among the worst years in African American history. The objective of these Atlantic conflicts with people thought of as 'other' was not just military victory but cultural destruction and genocide. Bernard Bailyn has termed the seventeenth century the 'barbarous years,' reflecting less European notions of Indian behaviour but his modern perspective that these years saw European settlers do things that marked them out, more than

Native Americans, as barbarians.[3] Thus, while the settlement of the colonies was increasingly celebrated by Britons and Americans alike as bringing wealth to the empire and providing opportunities to ordinary Britons to establish new, remarkably egalitarian and politically strongly participatory societies that gave white settlers some of the best standards of living in the world, it was a success gained through the immiseration of others – the taking away of Native American land and assaults on their cultural autonomy and the brutalising of African slaves in harsh conditions in the developing plantation economy.

Britain in India

The Atlantic world was the most important but not the only region of the world into which England expanded during the seventeenth century. It also gained a toehold in India. The East India Company was a joint-stock company established by royal charter in 1600. It was founded, like the Virginia Company of around the same time, by a corporation of merchants and investors who had exclusive rights to trade between South Asia and Britain. It was relatively small in the seventeenth century, lacking the resources to mount a sustained challenge from the Dutch Vereenigde Oosindische Compagnie (VOC), which also trade in Asia. The latter was 40 per cent larger than the East India Company between 1613 and 1617. The East India Company did not get permanent status in Asia until 1639, when it was invited to establish a presence in Fort St George, near Madras, India (now Chennai). It was slower still to establish itself in Bengal, not having a factory there until 1651. Each English factory reported directly to company officials in London. The main trade was in textiles, sent to both Europe and Africa, where they proved almost immediately popular.

The East India Company was founded with very high hopes of great profit, which was one reason why it was founded as a joint-stock company with monopoly powers. It did reasonably well, accounting by the 1690s for 13 per cent of England's imports, mostly from India, Bombay, and Madras. These imports comprised cotton, silks, spices and indigo – tea came later. Its physical presence was small. By 1713, it owned ten sizeable bases or 'factories,' but the total number of Europeans in the East India Company was tiny: only a few hundred at its major base in Calcutta. The Company was the largest business enterprise of seventeenth-century England, drawing on large amounts of capital and being a significant employer of people in London. Its wealth and importance stirred envy and resentment. Critics resented how it took away most of the bullion England had gained from Atlantic trade, as gold was the only European commodity in demand in India. It was suspected, rightly, of being corrupt, a charge that continued to be laid against it until its demise in 1857 and especially as it moved to worldwide prominence after 1760. Other critics believed that its importation of calicoes and cheap silk and cotton undercut English weavers. In 1719, there were riots in London against women wearing foreign silk and calicoes while in 1721 a ban on wearing calico goods was put into place for a brief time. The ban showed how domestic concerns outweighed overseas interests in political calculations.

However much the company's early operations were driven by commercial motives, the Indian trade was always an armed trade. The East Indian Company relied on both maritime force and on diplomatic relations with powerful Asian territorial states where it was often in competition with the more powerful and better connected Dutch, who kept the East Indian Company largely out of south-east Asia. Its relationship with the English Crown was fraught and contested. The government exploited merchant resistance to the company's monopoly by revising and reusing charters as tools to get more money from the East India Company and to receive more loans, to keep the Crown quiet. Despite the intrusion of greater parliamentary inspection from 1688, the East India Company weathered a period of competition in the early 1690s and received a charter for its reincorporated company in 1700.

Its real period of growth came after 1700, with a dramatic increase in the sale of Indian textiles, as such goods became increasingly fashionable in Britain. The rationale for state intervention grew as the company's wealth, prestige and military power steadily expanded. That expansion coincided with the rapid Mughal decline from the 1720s, a development the company welcomed, as it could exploit, and did exploit, fractures within Indian politics. The East India Company was always notorious for its ability to play high-level politics, both in India and in Britain. Its involvement with Indian society, however, was limited. It kept mostly to Indian law during any disputes. The company's presidency towns (where its factories were located) increased their population greatly, were large wealth creators for Britain and their Indian associates and increasingly claimed immunity from Indian law. They became engines of empire by the late eighteenth century.

The East India Company was not just a corporation like other corporations. As Philip Stern argues,

> from its very origins, as a Corporate body politic, the East Indian Company was deeply concerned as an institution with not only government and its employees, shareholder, and corporations but increasingly broad claims to jurisdiction over all English subjects in Asia as well as an expanding network of coastal and island populations, their cosmopolitan Eurasian populations, and the maritime space that connected them.[4]

For Britain, such corporate diversity was confusing and improper. It eventually came to fold the East India Company into a more coherent and centralised imperial network, but this only occurred in the nineteenth century. In the seventeenth century, however, despite the occasional efforts by the English state to exert more coherent authority over Indian affairs was met with the same response that the state faced in the Americas – resentment and passive and sometimes active resistance.

The East India Company needs to be seen in a global context. When the Crown allowed the company to augment its powers in the 1670s and 1680s, including the ability to punish English subjects, the same centralising impulse was also in play in proprietary colonies, such as Pennsylvania and South Carolina, and the chartering of companies which built forts and settlements overseas, such as the Hudson's Bay and Royal African Company. The East India Company was more successful than its counterparts in America in keeping its distance from such regulatory regimes, becoming more independent and thus more powerful by the end of the seventeenth century. Like its jurisdictional authority more generally, the company's right to rule came from a variety of sources, including English charters, Asian grants and what it had gained for itself as an aggressive power broker.

What made the East India Company successful in the late seventeenth century after contraction and difficulty between the 1620s and the 1660s was the textile trade from Gujarat, Coromandel and Bengal. It supplied both Britain but also much of Europe, displacing the Dutch in the process. Its success relied on meeting not just the demand for cloth but in catering for the tastes of discerning female consumers. And its success relied on the latitude it gave to its employees to trade on their own account while limiting the expenses of the East India Company considerably. Its success meant that it got enemies in London but also friends, notably the Crown. Moreover, the wealth of the Indies was narrowly concentrated, with large London merchants the major beneficiaries, with profits reinvested in the growing stock market.

Migration to the Americas

What made British involvement in the world different from other Europeans' involvement in overseas expansion was the willingness of Britons to move outside of Britain. Reflecting the notion of England and Scotland as societies on the move from the mid-sixteenth century onwards, migration to the British Atlantic world was considerable. Few people travelled to either Asia or West Africa and migration to Ireland from England and Scotland is dealt with elsewhere in this book. But migration was substantial to British America, dwarfing all other European migration to the Americas from the seventeenth century to the early nineteenth century.

The peak period of seventeenth-century migration came between 1640 and 1700, with 303,000 Britons leaving for the New World, a figure nearly twice that of all other European migrants combined moving to the Americas. The 1640s were the high-water mark for white migration, with about 70,000 settlers going to British America, especially to the Chesapeake and Barbados. Before 1675, European migration to the Caribbean was substantial, at 145,000 compared to 110,000 people moving to North America. European migration declined after the introduction of chattel slavery, being half of the migration to North America in the last quarter of the seventeenth century.

People migrated for many reasons but economic vicissitudes in Britain and perceived opportunities in the Americas motivated free settlers, and, to an extent, indentured servants. The main cause of mass migrations was the enormous and continuing demand for field labourers in the plantation colonies.

Before 1650, these labourers tended to be young white male indentured servants. These people were replaced from mid-century by enslaved Africans. Debate rages over whether the increased migration of the latter precipitated a decline in the former. The best evidence we have is that if whites had wanted to go to America, planters would have found a place for them, either working alongside or instead of African slaves. White servants came less frequently to British America in the late seventeenth century because they realised that opportunity in British America was not as abundant as pictured and because the English economy picked up after 1660. Thus, for a mixture of demand and supply reasons, servant migration declined just at the point that the number of enslaved people increased within plantation societies.

Most migrants, white or black, came as either coerced or unfree people. Of the white migrants (we deal with enslaved people later), indentured servants were usually young and had, over time, an increased amount of skills that made them instantly employable. Convicts, by contrast, were drawn overwhelmingly from the lower social ranks. Most settlers in the seventeenth century came from London, the south-east, East Anglia, and the West County – the heartland of England, in short. In the eighteenth century, this heartland migration dried up almost totally, with English and Welsh migrants being noticeably fewer on the ground in the eighteenth century than in the seventeenth century. These seventeenth-century settlers lived on the coast; their eighteenth-century followers, who tended to be Irish Catholics, Ulster Protestants or Germans from the Palatine or Swiss, populated the interior. The unfree nature of the population, including slaves, lasted until the American Revolution, after which migration moved from being mostly of unfree people, white and black, to mostly free white people.

These migrant groups tended to want to replicate the societies they came from, but that was seldom possible. Migrants came as a heterogeneous mix, in the main, with considerable diversities in backgrounds, occupations, and places of residence. D. W. Meinig suggests that this diversity eroded the sharp edges of regional and national identities – migrants identified more with the country of origin than with their religion or with the small places they had been born in.[5] Mobility and sustained contact with other people and cultures led to the evolution of new identities that frequently coexisted alongside older identities. Colonial societies were always more pluralistic than their metropolitan counterparts, even than London.

The most significant characteristic of seventeenth-century migration, alongside its mostly non-free nature, was that women were reluctant to move to the New World, Surprisingly, gender hardly features in migration narratives even though the disproportionate number of men among migrants made European society in the Americas highly masculine, ridiculously so in places such as Jamaica and Antigua. European women did not like America and did not see in it the opportunities that encouraged men to migrate there. From the 70 to 80 per cent of migrants who moved to plantation colonies, men outnumbered women by six and eight to one, depending on the time period. It was only in

New England, singular in this respect as in so many others, that women moved in large numbers, usually as part of married couples or in family groupings, and even there the sex ratio in the first decades after settlement was three males to two females. Overall, women made up between 10 and 15 per cent of all European migrants to British America before 1776.

It is hard to know why women stayed home rather than move to the colonies (they were also less likely to move within Britain, although the disparity between men and women in internal British migration was less than to the Americas), but it is probably a combination of 'push' and 'pull' factors. Women had better opportunities than did men in Britain, as domestic servants, who were always needed in local economies. They may have been more family-oriented, with more obligations to elderly parents or siblings, and they were probably put off America by tales of women there having to do unfamiliar work for British women, such as working in the fields. They may have heard also of the propensity for sexual violence to be common among indentured servants, who served without the protections offered to such people in England. Some historians have argued that seventeenth-century English America was a good place for women to go to, as the shortage of men meant that they could marry more easily, and to better kinds of spouses, than at home. But a good marriage hardly compensated for the lack of amenities to run a household, the lack of family support and the likelihood of becoming a young widow with dependent children, given the high mortality rates in places such as early Virginia. The absence of women in colonial society undoubtedly contributed to seventeenth-century America being a highly masculine place, where masculine values such as competition, aggression, carousing and a strong devotion to achieving the main chance and to make money at all costs pertained in most places except for New England.

Native Americans

In a sweeping summary of social patterns in colonial British America, John Murrin has declared that the colonies were the 'beneficiaries of catastrophe.'[6] That catastrophe preceded English colonisation by a century and started with Columbus' arrival in the New World in 1492, accompanied by microbes and pathogens that Native Americans had no immunity from. The result was rapid depopulation through disease and poor treatment of Native Americans by the Spanish. The first and most intense bout of depopulation was in the Caribbean, where up to 95 per cent of the Native American population died in the first half-century of contact with Europeans, leaving many major islands, from Hispaniola to Cuba to Jamaica and Barbados, denuded of indigenous inhabitants during the sixteenth- and seventeenth-century phase of colonisation. The disaster of the Columbian exchange then spread to the rest of the Americas, including North America, where the effects came later, in the seventeenth and eighteenth century and which was less affected than more tropical regions to its south. This book is about Britain and its relation to the wider world and thus not directly concerned with the expropriation of Native American land after 1492 and the displacement of Native Americans from dominance in the Americas, so my treatment of Native American interactions with the English in the seventeenth century is necessarily brief and oriented around the narrow issue of Native American encounters with the English.[7]

A few points, however, can be made. First, the history of English encounters with Native Americans on the eastern seaboard, followed by a massive demographic, political and cultural expansion across the North American continent in the eighteenth and nineteenth centuries – the frontier legend, in short – is an incomplete history of Native America in this period. Many historians now think that early North American history should be examined from a broad continental perspective, with the focus being as much looking east from the west rather than the other way around, as is customary in accounts where English colonisation drives the historical agenda. The majority of Native Americans in 1700 lived well outside the realm of English colonisation. Of the 1.65 million people living in North America in 1700, about 300,000 were European, 250,000 of whom lived in the English colonies; another 300,000 Native Americans lived in or, more often, near the English in the greater north-east and greater south-east, while the remainder of Native Americans lived relatively distant from centres of European colonisation. The history of continental North America has thus to be detached from the history of English–Native American contacts in the seventeenth century.

Second, patterns of colonisation were highly influenced by Native Americans, both including those regions where Native Americans were a significant presence and those areas where Native Americans had disappeared after the early sixteenth-century onslaughts of disease from the Columbian encounter. The history of Barbados and the rapid deforestation of the island and quick conversion to plantation agriculture may have been different if Native Americans had been on the island and had got in settlers' way. Elsewhere, the presence of Native Americans was determinative of how settlement proceeded. In Virginia, for example, the English at Jamestown decided to settle among Native Americans in order to get them to be trading partners, influenced in this way from their understanding of Iberian colonisation and their experience of colonisation in Ireland. The idea made sense, but the reality of how the English acted towards the Powhatan Native Americans who controlled the area they moved to was very different: the English went out of their way on their first arrival to alienate Native Americans, even though they depended on them for their very survival. Their ethnocentrism and xenophobia made it impossible for them to think of Native Americans as equals, let alone superiors, and they refused to accommodate themselves to Native American values and customs, much to their disadvantage. Their attitude toward Native Americans was one reason why the colony struggled in its first decade and had to be put under martial law to stop settlers from rebelling. It was only the discovery that tobacco could be easily grown in the Virginia tidewater that saved the colony.

The process of interaction between the English and Native Americans quickly moved from settlers having relatively positive relations when the English first arrived and when they thought of Native Americans as sophisticated residents of lands they themselves had not mastered to increasingly hostile, even genocidal, opinions about Native Americans. Native Americans, in turn, lost their feelings of goodwill towards colonists as they noted that the English were not temporary but permanent visitors and that they lusted after the land that Native Americans thought was theirs, even if Native Americans had different conceptions of land ownership than did the English, placing less emphasis on private possession of land over collective occupation. They realised also that the English treated them with contempt and that they viewed the residents of the land they wanted as barbarians who did not use land properly and who should be rejected from the land they occupied so wastefully and be replaced by settlers with the 'improving spirit.' By the mid- to late seventeenth century, the attitude of Native Americans to the English was one of unremitting antagonism. These feelings of hatred were shared by the English, as they battled to transform Native American country into English and then British territory.

Settlers were aided in their efforts to make their societies English, rather than Native American, by the greatest weapon in the European colonisation arsenal – disease. It was the effects of demography, more than any other factor, which enabled the English to 'benefit from catastrophe.' Between 1500 and 1700, the Native American population in the east dropped from about 562,100 to 254,485. The decline was not uniform but resulted from frequent epidemics in which whole communities perished in attacks of smallpox, influenza, measles, scarlet fever and diphtheria.

The other weapon Europeans had was less obviously detrimental to Native American interest but which in the end proved just as dangerous to them as microbes. Native Americans fancied the goods that the English brought with them, like metal tools, some of which were used to replace indigenous good and thus change long-standing cultural practices. But overly avid Native American consumers of European goods risked becoming dependent on such goods. Some groups of Native Americans in the colony of New York were so interested in trade that they abandoned their traditional migratory ways and settled near the shore to participate in trade with the English. They quickly became entrapped in webs of dependency from which it was difficult to extract themselves.

Finally, it was not just Native Americans who were changed by their encounter with the English. The English were changed also, sometimes for the worse, as in their development of ever more pernicious forms of racism about people different from themselves but in other ways too. The English liked Native Americans as trading partners almost as much as Native Americans enjoyed access to European goods. This mutual appreciation of what each people had to offer each other was especially true in the Great Lakes region, where French and English colonists competed for control of the lucrative fur trade. It was in the area where what Richard White has described as a 'Middle Ground' occurred. Native Americans in this area knew that the English needed them to procure pelts and furs and conducted this trade with colonists in a posture of wary equality.[8] The 'Middle Ground' approach to Native American–English interactions shows that by 1700 English colonists were far from gaining control over eastern North America. How matters worked out depended mainly on local circumstances. Some areas saw ferocious warfare; other areas were relatively peaceful. And some Native Americans, like the Iroquois in New York and the Cherokee and Creeks in the south-east, were too powerful yet for the English to overcome them. Diplomacy mattered as much as war, even if it was diplomacy between peoples who eyed each other with suspicion and hostility.

What was most unfortunate for the Native Americans in English America circa 1700 was that, as Peter Mancall states, 'settlers increasingly devoted their attention to agriculture and the production of staple exports for the Atlantic commercial world.'[9] That orientation meant that the English, much more than the French in New France and the Spanish in New Mexico and Florida, were keen on acquiring Native American land and had less interest in trade over time. As settlement of the English and their descendants in eastern North America increased and the population started to expand westward, these trends only intensified.

African Americans and the plantation system

As Native Americans declined in numbers, African Americans became more numerous and conspicuous in New World labour forces. As latecomers to European colonisation in the Americas, the English were very aware that the Iberians had, from the mid-fifteenth century, engaged in a slave trade with West Africans, taking slaves to the Americas to serve as perpetually bonded chattel slaves. As early as 1555, a trader called John Lok travelled from England to West Africa and returned with five men, not intended as slaves but as people who would be trained in English commerce and returned to Africa to assist in future mercantile ventures. Other Englishmen were not so reticent about entering the transatlantic slave trade. John Hawkins engaged in three slaving voyages between 1564 and 1569. Nevertheless, most English voyages to West Africa before 1640 did not deal in slaves. The English were not averse to slave trading, but they were mostly interested in trading in gold and other goods. They were aware, however, of Iberian precedents and, when opportunity arose, turned quickly to slaving enterprises to West Africa.

What changed everything was the growth of the large integrated plantation system, first in Barbados, and then by 1700 throughout the British Atlantic world. The large integrated plantation was a self-contained economic unit with dozens to hundreds of enslaved labourers, on which all elements of population were combined in one place. It generated wealth for its owners to a greater extent than any other American or British institution prior to the Industrial Revolution. It was developed in Barbados in a rapid amount of time, in the two decades of the English Civil Wars. The spread of the transformation

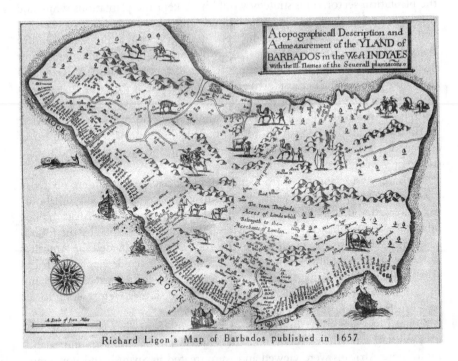

Richard Ligon's Map of Barbados published in 1657

Figure 2.1 Yland of Barbados, Plantations, Humphrey Moseley 1657

Source: Antiqua Print Gallery/Alamy Stock Photo.

suggested that it was a 'big bang' or 'sugar revolution,' but in fact, it was a process of change similar to what happened elsewhere, involving technological change (the introduction of sugar mills), investment by London merchants, the importation of African slaves who displaced white servants as the majority of labourers on plantations and the driving out of small farmers by large planters, whose great wealth from the profits of sugar gave them the ability to acquire land that was rapidly rising in value.

Why did the English choose to adopt such an unfamiliar new economic system when they had an institution – indentured servitude – that was familiar to them and that was already in place in the colonies from first settlement? Why did they invest heavily in a triangular trade between Britain, Africa and English America, sending English manufactured goods and Indian textiles to Africa in return for humans transported in the hellish conditions of the Middle Passage to serve as slaves on Caribbean plantations? Why did they bring to the Americas a group of alien and alienated people very different from themselves and neither Protestant or even Christian whom they hated and whom they feared would be a security threat unless kept down with ferocious brutality? The easiest thing for them to do would be to have continued with indentured servitude and increased the convict trade until it matched the labour needs of the plantation sector. This strategy would have kept the plantations white and Protestant rather than racially and religiously mixed.

The reasons behind the introduction of slavery into seventeenth-century Barbados and Virginia has been a topic of perennial historical interest, not just because of its massive importance to the history of British America and the United States but because evidence on motivation is so scarce that we can make several convincing explanations of this event that are hard to either prove entirely or disprove. Thus, it is an interesting case of historical detective work to find out why the English chose to introduce an especially severe form of unfreedom at the same time as republicans in England were claiming England as the home of liberty.

For some historians, the introduction of black slavery was a mere matter of economics. The number of white servants dried up just as the need for labourers increased and as planters sourced these labourers from West Africa, taking advantage of an enhanced English slave trade, which was helped by the founding of the Royal African Company in the 1660s, which provided the Americas with a regular, if not always enough to meet surging demand, supply of African slaves. The English could get access to African slaves because African merchants in societies with long experience of long-distance slavery were willing to sell slaves to Europeans in return for valuable goods.

Other historians trace the origins of slavery to racial doctrines about Africans existing since the early seventeenth century and shaped by an understanding of how Africans were viewed and were treated in Spanish and Portuguese America. The English placed Africans at the bottom of humankind, seeing them in ways that they did not see Native Americans or Irish Catholics, as outside the boundaries of civilisation and marked by a colour that signified barbarity, stupidity and a capacity to work hard in hot climates (the latter being a means of fulfilling self-interested ideas around climactic differences). Of course, we need to keep in mind that there was no uniform view of Africans in the Jacobean period. William Shakespeare, for example, portrays an African sympathetically in *Othello* while indulging in extreme racial bigotry towards an African, Aron, thought of as an implacable enemy, in *Titus Andronicus*. The blackness of African skins denoted for early seventeenth-century English people connotations of evil, sin, dirtiness and the devil himself, contrasting with whiteness, as a sign of purity and Christianity. There was a strand in sixteenth-century English writings about West Africans that doubted the very humanity of Africans, depicting Africans as cannibals and inclined to bestiality, living as pagans in unsophisticated societies. In effect, the English saw Africans as in every respect different from, and distinctly inferior to, themselves. As Africans were closer to beasts, in this view, than to humans, no thought needed to go into the unthinking decision, as historians have seen the introduction of slavery, to make Africans hereditary chattels with their children also being property for the owner of the mother of a slave child.

Arguments can be made for an economic or a racially ideological reading of the introduction of slavery. My own view tends towards the racial explanation.

Africans were always treated differently in English America to other people; were usually made slaves even before slave laws made the holding of enslaved people legally possible, with slaves in Virginia from as early as 1619; were given less rights and harsher treatment than any other peoples; and were subject to informal enslavement for themselves and their children. Whatever the cause for slavery becoming introduced, the result of the development of the plantation economy meant great wealth, the transformation of early America into a productive region suddenly very valuable to the English and to the massive importation over the next 150 years of African slaves into the colonies. As Barbara Solow argues,

> it was slavery that made the empty lands of the western hemisphere valuable producers of commodities and valuable markets for Europe and North America. What moved in the Atlantic in these centuries was predominantly slaves, the output of slaves, the inputs of slave societies, and the goods and services purchased with the earnings on slave products.[10]

One obvious result of slavery taking hold in plantation societies was an Africanisation of society and a blackening of the population. Hardly any Africans, perhaps 5,000, arrived in English America before 1640. The establishment of plantations increased migration dramatically so that 371,000 Africans arrived in English America between 1640 and 1700, a further 1,286,000 arrived between 1700 and 1760, and another 1,590,000 arrived between 1760 and 1820, with the major thrust of migration being before 1807, when the British Atlantic slave trade was abolished. If we look at migration patterns, 3,226,000 Africans came to British America, the vast majority (2,311,500) going to the West Indies, before 1820, as compared to 1,257,000 Europeans. In the seventeenth century, white and black migration was roughly equal, but in the eighteenth century, the ratio of whites to blacks dropped to around one in ten. The peak migration was to the Caribbean between 1751 and 1775, with 635,000 captive arrivals. By this time, the enslaved population in North America was enjoying natural increase, meaning that only 116,900 arrived in North America at this time, mostly to South Carolina and Georgia. The slave 'cargoes' were male-dominated but much less so than in European migration. In the slave trade, around two-thirds of African migrants were male, with more women and especially children than in the European migration. Before 1800, four-fifths of females and 90 per cent of children going to the Americas were African rather than European.

These Africans endured horrifying conditions in getting to America and matters did not improve greatly once they were transformed from captives to slaves and sent to work on plantations. The plantation was a terrible place to work. Planters, especially in the West Indies, devised the gang system of lockstep discipline and regimented labour to make slaves work hard and thus increase productivity. It was a terrific system for generating wealth but appalling for the health and welfare of slaves. The turmoil the gang system wrought on enslaved peoples' health can be seen in the dreadful mortality rates and low levels of reproduction experienced by enslaved people in the seventeenth century. In the last quarter of the seventeenth century, the annual rate of population decline in Barbados was 5.7 per cent and in Jamaica was 4.8 percent, almost all down to the arduous nature of sugar production. Making Africans do this work was very hard – the system was so psychologically oppressive and physically demanding that it was never tried with free labourers. As a seventeenth-century Barbadian slave about to be executed commented bitterly, '[T]he devil was in the Englishman that he makes everything work; he makes the Negro work; he makes the horse work, the ass work the wood work; the water work and the wind work.'

Violence was necessary to make enslaved people work in this soul-destroying environment. Antoine Biet, who visited Barbados in 1652 was shocked at the 'severity' of slavery and the frequent use of the lash against enslaved people, noting that masters could give slaves 'fifty blows with a cudgel; these often bruise them severely.' Ira Berlin summarises well the violence towards slaves in the seventeenth-century Chesapeake, probably the nadir of African American life in the Americas. 'Chesapeake slaves faced the pillory,' he noted, 'the whipping post, and gallows far more frequently and in far larger numbers than before.'[11] An example from Barbados illustrates just how violent and sadistic this world was. A failed slave revolt in 1675 resulted in six rebels burned alive; eleven beheaded and dragged through the streets, after which their heads were stuck on poles; and dozens of slaves castrated. As the most horrific forms of public punishment were disappearing in Britain as the Enlightenment became established, they were reappearing in new forms in the colonies but were being applied only to blacks. These medieval forms of punishment for enslaved people meant that the veneer of civilisation was very thin to non-existent when moving outside the confines of white polite society.

Anglicisation

What did English colonists want collectively when they crossed the Atlantic? What kind of social and political structures did they hope would emerge from their migration so far from home? Their ambitions can be seen in their naming practices, where they often renamed the Native American places they arrived in with names that reminded them of home – New York, New England, New Jersey – or to their allegiances to their rulers – Virginia, Maryland, Carolina – as much as they kept the original Native American names of places – Jamaica, Connecticut, Barbados. What they wanted was to transform their new homes through 'improvement,' a key early modern word, so that they resembled as much as possible the European worlds that they had left behind.

'Improvement' meant creating a society that was different from the savagery associated with Native Americans. It was not barbaric or wild but settled, cultivated and civilised. The model of civilised life was not some rural bliss but was the urban sophistication of seventeenth-century British towns. That was true even and perhaps especially in places where urbanisation failed to take hold. Paul Musselwhite shows how the eighteenth-century dream of a rural fastness in the Chesapeake, the one settled place in British America without a substantial urban dimension, came only after settlers failed to create functioning urban centres out of a long seventeenth-century process of colonisation in which settling around an urban nucleus was a central animating impulse. But even as repeated attempts to create towns failed, Chesapeake planters continued to try to introduce into their region the 'city commonwealths' that were the basis of civic government in English towns. These communities were made up, as Phil Withington shows, with active participants and officeholders working for the good of the whole through industrious commerce.[12]

Because Europeans associated autonomous urban communities with civic virtue, urban development was central to plans of settlement. As Paul Musselwhite argues, Chesapeake planters continued to try to develop towns and debate about the desirability of creating a civic urban culture in a new colonial society because

> towns and cities held the potential to generate new forms of local or imperial authority that could control markets, police trade, or generate revenue; they could help planters accumulate capital to trade independently; they could also offer the potential for new industries employing poor whites displaced by the consolidation of the plantation economy.[13]

Settlers thus wanted to re-create, not innovate, and to live in cultivated areas that resembled the small towns and rural villages of home. They wanted a fully developed market society, with credit, commercial agriculture, slavery and easy cultivation of money ad goods, all within a society in which English social hierarchies of gentility had become transplanted across the Atlantic. In short, they wanted to live in England but an England overseas – the aim was to extend England and then Britain spatially without creating new societies. It was for this reason that English settlers insistently reminded people back in Britain that they had never left England and the rights it gave to its inhabitants but that their societies were as much English as Kent, or, after 1707, Scotland.

The historical shorthand for the process is 'Anglicisation.' It was a process through which the English colonies of the Americas emerged from their diverse beginnings to become increasingly more alike in having shared values and social structures that linked them to English people and places. It was an expression of shared Britishness in common political and judicial systems, material culture, economies, religious patterns and engagements with the empire.

Anglicisation rested on two deep ironies. Anglo-America achieved a degree of Anglicisation only from the late seventeenth century and at a time when direct migration from England slowed to a halt. America became more English just at the time when individuals' links with the homeland became more distant and thus more idealised. It is not surprising, therefore, that the regions that probably most came to resemble England were New England and the

Chesapeake, which by the early eighteenth century had relations with England that mainly revolved around commerce and the transplantation of ideas derived from England into colonial culture. Second, what underpinned Anglicisation in the southern and mainland colonies was the alien institution of slavery. The introduction of slavery – something entirely new and unknown in Britain and without a clear British lineage outside dubious arguments later advanced in the late eighteenth century by proslavery advocates that it was somehow connected to the medieval practice of villeinage, provided the means whereby a settler in plantation America got rich enough to build houses on the English model, adopt English fashions and develop institutional frameworks that bore a close resemblance to what they remembered or imagined were English examples.

What a study of seventeenth-century English America shows us is that each colony was founded in some way as a religious or social experiment, meant, deliberately or not, to show England how good and decent people ought to act. Each of these colonies, except Barbados, which had its own developmental issues, failed spectacularly and nearly simultaneously to establish their utopian and improved societies effectively. The failure was most pronounced in New England, which was the colony that most purposefully followed the Puritan dream of creating a godly commonwealth in the New World. The failures of these societies at the end of the seventeenth century and the beginning of the eighteenth century brought each of them into crisis and chaos, echoing the crisis and chaos of Britain in the period of two seventeenth-century revolutions, described in the next two chapters. The Glorious Revolution thus arrived at an opportune time, as English America spun into crisis almost everywhere, with violent Native American wars, destructive servant rebellions, incipient slave revolts and constitutional uproar. That 1692 was the nadir of settler American experience was not coincidental.

We need to always consider colonial English America within the context of English and British history because the two histories cannot be understood apart from each other. As Andrew Shankman explains,

> all of these Anglophone societies experienced crisis nearly simultaneously. All grew ripe for new ideas and new processes of organisation at precisely the time when space opened in England for Whig ideas of governance and political economy to move from the margins and to make a new mainstream.

England itself became Anglicised and then became part of a larger British state in this period as it laid the foundation for a limited constitutional monarchy, a fiscal-military state of great geopolitical potential; and an Anglicised society that Shankman describes as 'polite, Protestant, self-confident to the point of smugness.'[14] The diversity between societies in Britain and its colonies diminished after 1707 as every place became similarly Anglicised. That Anglicisation was done initially to achieve the narrow but the important aim of solving the central conflicts that had dogged Britain in the seventeenth century. But it provided a blueprint for imperial success that lasted well and that was the foundation for eighteenth-century growth in British America. That stability and happiness within settler societies, a stability and happiness achieved, it has to be remembered, over and because of the suffering of African Americans and Native Americans, disrupted the 'harmony we are famous for,' as a South Carolinian politician put it, celebrating the rule of a native-born elite in his province, one that had been confirmed in power by the events of the late seventeenth and early eighteenth century.

Notes

1 Carla Gardner Pestana, *The English Atlantic in an Age of Revolution 1640–1660* (Cambridge. MA: Harvard University Press, 2004), 9.
2 Richard Dunn, 'The Glorious Revolution in America,' in Nicholas Canny, ed., *The Oxford History of the British Empire: The Origins of Empire* (Oxford: Oxford University Press, 2013), 455.
3 Bernard Bailyn, *The Barbarous Years: The Peopling of America – The Conflict of Civilizations, 1600–1675* (New York: Alfred A. Knopf, 2013).
4 Philip J. Stern, 'Company, State, and Empire: Governance and Regulatory Frameworks in Asia,' in H.V. Bowen, Elizabeth Mancke, and John G. Reid, eds., *Britain's Oceanic Empire: Atlantic and Indian Ocean Worlds, c. 1550–1850* (Cambridge: Cambridge University Press, 2012), 130–1.
5 D.W. Meinig, *The Shaping of America: A Geographical Perspective on 500 Years of History* vol. 1. *Atlantic America, 1492–1800* (New Haven: Yale University Press, 1986), 218.
6 John M. Murrin, *Beneficiaries of Catastrophe: The English Colonies in America* (Washington, DC: The American Historical Association, 1997).
7 For a more extensive treatment of Native Americans in the Atlantic, see Trevor Burnard, *The Atlantic in World History, 1492–1830* (London: Bloomsbury, 2020).
8 Richard White, *The Middle Ground: Indians, Empires, and Republics in the Great Lakes Region, 1650–1815* (Cambridge: Cambridge University Press, 1991).
9 Peter C. Mancall, 'Native Americans and Europeans in English America, 1500–1700,' in Canny, *Origins of Empire*, 349.
10 Barbara L. Solow, 'Slavery and Colonisation,' in Solow, ed., *Slavery and the Rise of the Atlantic System* (Cambridge: Cambridge University Press, 1991), 21–42.
11 Ira Berlin, *Many Thousands Gone: The First Two Centuries of Slavery in North America* (Cambridge, MA: Harvard University Press, 1998)
12 Phil Withington, *The Politics of Commonwealth: Citizens and Freemen in Early Modern America* (Cambridge: Cambridge University Press, 2005), 10.
13 Paul Musselwhite, *Urban Dreams, Rural Commonwealth: The Rise of Plantation Slavery in the Chesapeake* (Chicago: University of Chicago Press, 2018), 10.
14 Andrew Shankman, 'A Synthesis Useful and Compelling: Anglicization and the Achievement of John M. Murrin,' in Ignacio Gallup-Diaz, Andrew Shankman, and David J. Silverman, eds., *Anglicizing America: Empire, Revolution, Republic* (Philadelphia: University of Pennsylvania Press, 2015), 26.

Bibliography

Berlin, Ira, *Many Thousands Gone: The First Two Centuries of Slavery in North America* (Cambridge, MA: Harvard University Press, 1998).
Chaplin, Joyce, 'The British Atlantic,' in Nicholas Canny and Philip D. Morgan, eds., *The Oxford Handbook of the Atlantic World, 1450–1850* (Oxford: Oxford University Press, 2011), 219–34.

Countryman, Edward and Juliana Barr, eds., *Contested Spaces of Early America* (Philadelphia: University of Pennsylvania Press, 2014).

Gallup-Diaz, Ignacio, Andrew Shankman, and David J. Silverman, eds., *Anglicizing America: Empire, Revolution, Republic* (Philadelphia: University of Pennsylvania Press, 2015).

Horn, James and Philip D. Morgan, 'Settlers and Slaves: European and African Migration to Early Modern British America,' in Elizabeth Mancke and Carole Shammas, eds., *The Creation of the British Atlantic World* (Baltimore: Johns Hopkins University Press, 2005), 19–44.

Morgan, Edmund, *American Slavery, American Freedom: The Ordeal of Colonial Virginia* (New York: W.W. Norton, 1975).

Newman, Simon, *A New World of Labor: The Development of Plantation Slavery in the British Atlantic* (Philadelphia: University of Pennsylvania Press, 2013).

Richter, Daniel K., *Trade, Land, Power: The Struggle for Eastern North America* (Philadelphia: University of Pennsylvania Press, 2013).

Stern, Philip J., *The Company-state: Corporate Sovereignty and the Early Modern Foundations of the British Empire in India* (New York: Cambridge University Press, 2011).

Tomlins, Christopher, *Freedom Bound: Law, Labor, and Civic Identity in Colonising English America, 1580–1865* (Cambridge: Cambridge University Press, 2010).

3 British troubles, 1638–60

The British Civil Wars: interpretations

One event above all others defines Britain in the seventeenth century. That was the political upheaval between 1638 and 1660 in all three kingdoms of the British Isles, an upheaval which also had significant repercussions in the embryonic British Empire. It is the most far-reaching and violent convulsion in English history, except for the Norman Conquest of 1066, and equally traumatic for both Scotland and Ireland. It led above all to the execution in 1649 of Charles I, a death of a king ordained by the people of England (or at least its Parliament) through legal procedure rather than being the result, in the past, of skulduggery within oligarchical politics. That death showed that Charles I's belief that he ruled by divine right was severely contested by a population that believed that even the king had to be accountable to the laws of the nation – or at least he had to be accountable to the laws of England: that Scotland was not consulted about the English putting to death a Scottish monarch, following the execution of Mary by Elizabeth I in 1587, rankled greatly with people north of the English border.

The British Civil Wars led to the temporary abolishment of the monarchy and the House of Lords for eleven years and their replacement, under the protectorate of Oliver Cromwell, a previously little-known country squire who during the 1640s demonstrated military genius as the general in charge of the formidable New Model Army, the principal instrument through which Parliament exerted its will over the hapless Charles I. Cromwell was one of the more extraordinary figures in British history, loathed to this day in Ireland, as we will see in a later chapter, as a vicious religious zealot and war criminal, practising religious persecution and ethnic cleansing on a dramatic scale. In England, Cromwell has a more ambivalent reputation. The myth of him rising from obscurity to unparalleled power in Britain as a military dictator in the 1650s has some resilience. For mid-nineteenth-century Victorian defenders of Cromwell, such as Thomas Carlyle, Cromwell was a hero of the nonconforming Protestant tradition, the 'soul of the Puritan revolt' and the steadfast defender of religious and political liberties against the absolutism of Charles I. Carlyle went even further, seeing Cromwell as God's Englishman, the embodiment of the traits that were creating a worldwide empire – brave, resolute, godly and above all a teller of truths and not a man of falsehoods. Carlyle's rehabilitation of Cromwell went against a longer tradition of Cromwell as a bad man, a military dictator who did not respect parliamentary authority when he purged and dissolved Parliament on several occasions, a religious bigot and a tyrant. What remains accepted is that Cromwell was the English Napoleon, a man without military training but who had a rare ability in knowing how to win decisive battles. Cromwell attributed this skill to the intervention of God, making him convinced of the righteousness of his cause. As A.J.P. Taylor argued many years ago, 'God was for Cromwell what the general will was for Robespierre or the proletariat for Lenin: the justification for anything he wished to do.'[1] What was true for Cromwell was true also for many of his supporters. The Civil Wars were infused throughout by various varieties of religious Messianism.

The social effects of the Civil Wars were also many, although the basic structures of society in England, Wales and Scotland remained relatively unchanged. These countries remained places dominated by aristocrats, committed to local rule and deeply patriarchal in practice and principle. Historians nowadays are less inclined than in the past to see the Civil War period as a watershed in social relations in Britain, stressing that the capitalist transformation of the countryside had long roots and accompanied rather than caused political unrest They note also that the changing through the Reformation of England, Wales and Scotland from Catholic to Protestant countries had mainly occurred before the mid-seventeenth century and was often a halting as much as a revolutionary process. Constitutionally, however, the effects of the British Civil War were immense, even if also not perhaps as long-lasting as people of the time imagined. The government and the liturgy of the Church of England were briefly abandoned and even the unwritten constitution, an amalgam of evolving law and custom, customarily taken to be one the glories of England, was, for a period, put aside and replaced under Cromwell by two written constitutions.

As befits an event of such great historical importance, interpretations of how it came about and what it means have changed over time. From the Restoration of Charles II in 1660 until the nineteenth century, in other words, during the period that this book covers, the British Civil Wars and the rule of Cromwell were derided as a great disaster. It was considered a brief and unpleasant deviation from Britain's healthy devotion to limited monarchy. In the Victorian period, the mood changed, and the balance of sympathy swung from the king's cause to that of Parliament. Cromwell was hailed as a great, if not the greatest, Englishman. Instead of being an aberration, the British Civil Wars (usually reduced only to its English component) were viewed as a stage in the country's progress, and indeed the progress of the world, towards modernity and towards greater political liberty. It followed the thinking of the great Puritan poet John Milton, who in 1644 issued a plea for tolerance of religious expression in *Areopatigrica*, where he described his fellow Londoners as 'reading, trying all things, assenting to the force of reason and convincement.' For the Victorians, Milton's pleas were the first stirrings of toleration and of the British 'genius' for political liberty, Of course, Milton was not especially tolerant of other opinions. His advocacy of liberty did not extend to blasphemers, atheists, idolaters or Catholics, He was less concerned with justifying the human right to free belief and worship and was more interested in promoting the Gospel against its adversaries. It was to promote that cause that he welcomed the proliferation of unorthodox beliefs about religion and politics that flourished in the 1640s and 1650s.

The Victorians were also impressed with the religiosity of Cromwell and his supporters, calling the Civil Wars a 'Puritan Revolution.' The twentieth century was a more secular age and historians focused less on Puritans than on 'revolution,' casting the events of 1639–60 as the first modern revolution, the precursor of the French, Chinese and Russian revolutions. Predictably, the end of the Cold War and the start of a new phase in world history has led to further historiographical changes, one described by its practitioners as 'revisionism' and in the eyes of critics as amounting to an almost nihilistic view that the British Civil War was an event without real causes and with limited consequences except an unfortunate amount of pointless destruction. 'Revisionists' tend to see the British Civil Wars as emerging almost accidentally out of contingencies of government in the 1630s that a singularly unimpressive monarch was unable to deal with effectively.

Peter Lake even advises us not to look for long-term causes of the English Civil War, arguing that what occasioned the British Civil War was a certain kind of post-Reformation political culture that transformed relatively unimportant political events into a series of linked political crises in three kingdoms. He traces three kinds of political discourses – one against 'popery,' another against Puritanism and another that concerned 'evil counsel,' or the bad advice that monarchs received from ill-disposed Machiavellian ministers – that had their roots in the sixteenth century and that were the discourses, the interpretative modes and narrative tropes through which contemporaries view the political process. He argues that both sides shaped their attitudes to political events through a prism of political propaganda which led people to interpret the actions of opponents in the worst light. As he argues, Puritans and Parliamentarians before 1640, 'made their pitch for support against a popish conspiracy of evil counsel surrounding the king and argued for further reformation of both church and state to defeat that conspiracy and defend true religion.' Conversely, the king and his supporters 'appealed to a variety of constituencies by picturing central figures [in the opposition to Charles I] as, in effect, evil counsellors, machiavels and politiques, determined to undermine the powers of the monarch' and that they 'conjured a puritan threat to all order in church, state and society.'[2]

Similarly, the most dramatic event in the Civil War, the execution of Charles I on 30 January 1649 is not seen as being as consequential as once thought, neither the climax of a revolution nor the start of a revolutionary period that was either transformative or abortive, depending on perspective. Instead, it is seen by Philip Baker as 'marking the ultimate failure of the attempt to find a settlement in all three Stuart kingdoms following the parliamentarian victory in the first civil war,' with its major consequence being that military conflict continued for two years more than might have been otherwise the case. For Baker, the regicide had a 'surprisingly minimal' structural impact on the English state. Mark Knights reflects a growing consensus that the Civil Wars should be seen as part of a very long political process, spanning a long seventeenth century from around 1590 to about 1720, in which the major theme was the transformation of the state, more than a growth of political liberty or a resolution of the struggle over the identity of British Protestantism. As Jonathan Scott argues, because so much was left unsettled at the end of the Civil War and Commonwealth period, it was only during the second revolution of 1688 that the issues of the first revolution, such as the proper relationship between church and state, Parliament and monarchy and between the various regions that came to comprise Britain were worked out.[3]

European context

The revisionists have a strong point, even if the import of their argument is to drain much of the meaning of the British Civil Wars from historiographical consciousness and to make most of the event become seen as a sad example of pointless violence A point often made is that the Civil Wars saw the greatest numbers of deaths in Britain proportionately before World War I, with the implication being that we should equate the two events as being characterised more by meaningless death than by any real underlying important motivations. One of their strongest arguments is that we need to see the British Civil Wars in a wider European and global context. Britain was far from alone in experiencing unprecedented conflict in the early to mid-seventeenth century. Central Europe was torn apart by the Thirty Years' War (1618–1648), a monumental struggle that started off as a political crisis that turned into a clash of religions in areas still arguing about the sixteenth-century Reformation. In some places in Europe, nearly one-third of the population died in this conflict. Portugal, Catalonia and Naples experienced revolts against the oppressive rule of Spain as Britons were fighting in the 1640s. So, too, was France torn asunder by an aristocratic and constitutional rebellion of the Frondes. There were political upheavals in Sweden, Denmark and the Netherlands. Farther afield, China experienced one of its greatest periods of rebellion when the Ming dynasty fell in 1644, in a period of extreme bloodshed where perhaps millions died.

Peter Wilson shows that it is helpful to compare what was happening in Britain in this period with the much greater conflicts that erupted with the Bohemian Revolt and the subsequent Thirty Years' War as it shows that Britain was far from exceptional in what it experienced between 1640 and 1660. Both events are more characterised now than in the heyday of Marxist historical materialism in the 1960s and 1970s as wars of religion. As he notes, 'the fragmentation of western Christendom into distinct communities forged new connections across geographical, linguistic and social barriers, encouraging people to identify with others with whom they previously had little or no contact.' The major identification was between militants and moderates, the former believing that 'religious goals were within their grasp, regarded setbacks as tests of their faith, and were more likely to take risks in the conviction that God was on their side.'[4] They believed that they had to go to war because disputes were between good and evil, making the wars more violent than otherwise they might be. Moderates disagreed, being more pragmatic and flexible and 'saw conflicts as distinct, generally opposing calls to intervene elsewhere purely on religious grounds.' In addition, the British insistence on everyone having to agree with the monarch on matters he had decided on was not exceptional but common throughout Europe, as were increased debates about when the populace had a right of resistance. Thus, the British Civil Wars are hardly exceptional when looked at in a global context in an era of considerable social, political and military conflict.

The demands of Europe shaped the British civil wars in all sorts of ways. Charles I's decision to dispense with Parliament after 1629 was because he used a highly unpopular prerogative tax known as ship money to compel coastal communities to build a navy and to enforce Charles I's claims to lordship of 'British seas' as far as France and the Netherlands, ostensibly to rid England of pirates. He wanted to use the revenue to support his nephew Frederick V of Bohemia to recover the German Palatinate, a project that required Charles to enter a secret alliance with Catholic Spain. Despite Stuart assertions of rule over the sea, coastal communities feared foreign sea raids, such as one made by Barbary corsairs on the Irish town of Baltimore in 1631, during which more than two hundred Irish people were carried into slavery in North Africa. Projecting the power of the Crown outwards was always difficult.

A surprising event

Nevertheless, if the British Civil Wars are not exceptional, they are still surprising. The kingdoms of England/Wales and Scotland (not so much Ireland) were relatively peaceful in the early seventeenth century. Lake is correct to warn us against thinking that any sustained conflict in the 1640s in Britain was either inevitable or indeed likely. By comparison with much of continental Europe, Britain in 1637 did not look like a set of kingdoms in trouble – indeed England looked like an oasis of peace and order. Charles I's ability to remove his realms from European conflict in 1629 after involvement in war in Europe between 1624 and 1629 seemed to show he had some remarkable political skills. Indeed, Charles I was so confident that he ruled nations that were at peace that he decided not to call Parliament, an institution he found troublesome and irritating, and instead operated under what has been called Personal Rule – ruling through ministers rather than Parliament. By 1637, such Personal Rule had already lasted eight years and looked as if it could continue for many more years without major problems. His rule was not popular, but it was not disastrous, either. As Conrad Russell remarked, the primary state record of the period is 'not the record of a regime which was sitting on a powder keg.'[5] We can see how relatively peaceful England a few years before the outbreak of violence and civil war in Oliver Cromwell's willingness to be a justice of the peace. He was a Puritan and opposed to the Crown's policies but believed it was important for gentlemen to support the institutions of government.

On the face of it, Britain had navigated well a tricky succession transition in 1603 from the reign of Elizabeth to the rule of an experienced ruler in James VI of Scotland. This transition is covered in Chapter 1. There was no succession crisis in 1603, something which would have surprised Henry VIII, Mary I and Elizabeth I, all of whom had been preoccupied with whom would succeed them. Indeed, James VI and I brought England advantages which had been lacking under the Tudors. He had sons, meaning that no succession problem loomed. Joining Scotland to England and Wales meant that Scotland became less geographically problematic, both as a country with whom England had fought for centuries and as a back door through which continental powers such as France and Spain hoped to enter England. When James VI and I made peace with Spain in 1604, it meant that England and Scotland entered into greater security from attack from Europe than had been the case for over a century.

In addition, the tumults – social and political – of sixteenth-century England and Scotland reduced in the early seventeenth century. It seemed to many people that the disruptions of the Reformation had largely been settled by the early seventeenth century. Catholics were a despised and unimportant minority, demonised as eternal traitors after the Gunpowder Plot of 1605. The Protestant Church was full of factions and controversy, but a modus vivendi had been seemingly reached, with Calvinism dominant in Scotland and an uneasy truce existing in England between Puritanism and less Calvinist forms of Protestantism in England. It seemed less likely in 1630 than in, say, 1580 that a breakdown in political order was likely. England and Scotland were united, each under forms of Protestantism, and the powers of great noble magnates, especially in the English north and in the Scottish borders, which had made medieval kingship so difficult, were brought under control by Elizabeth I in England and James VI in Scotland. James was never going to meet the fate of his mother, betrayed by aristocratic rivals. In England, the north, where both aristocratic defiance and Catholic belief posed their largest danger to Tudor rule, were peaceful by the early seventeenth century.

Even Ireland was less problematic by the 1630s than it had been in the 1590s. Kingly rule was more secure than before, with fewer subjects than in the 1570s alarming their rulers by invoking the right or duty of subjects to rise against tyrannical or ungodly princes. Social disorder was also less pronounced than in the late sixteenth century, even if the demographic boom of that period still meant there were a multitude of masterless men on the roads, discontented and potentially rebellious. Recent research, moreover, has undermined what was a potent historical argument, conducted with huge polemical power in the 1940s and 1950s between R. H. Tawney, Hugh Trevor-Roper, Lawrence Stone and Christopher Hill. These historians described the early seventeenth century as a period of rapid economic transformation, with the English countryside moving towards a strongly capitalist orientation, with subsequent significant class conflict. For these historians, the English Civil War was based on this intense class antagonism, although each historian disagreed bitterly about whether the relevant classes who were fighting were between aristocracy and gentry, between rich and poor gentry or between a rising bourgeoisie and a declining feudal order.

The steam ran out of that argument a long time ago. Certainly, empirical research does not support a class-based interpretation of the conflict that emerged in England in the 1640s. If there was a difference between which side to support in the first English Civil War from 1642 to 1647, it was less based on class or even on region but on religion. The king's firm supporters were generally committed to the form of Anglicanism that Charles I supported while his opponents tended to be Puritans of some sort. Nevertheless, while for many people religion supplied the principal motive or impulse to arms, few felt that their religious beliefs permitted a resort to warfare in God's cause.

What is also increasingly clear is that the principal players in the revolt against the King were the nobility of all three kingdoms. Noble families in each kingdom saw it as their duty to end what they saw as Charles I's misgovernment, working with powerful groups of clergy, disaffected lawyers and aspiring politicians to put limits on the king's authority. The number of aristocrats was tiny, no more than three hundred in total, half of them barons and viscounts and thus in the lower ranks. The most senior nobles had titles in several kingdoms – there may have been no British state in this period, but a British aristocracy was rapidly emerging. One of the consequences of the period of rebellion was that it encouraged a speeding up of a long-term transformation of Britain's ruling elite. Relatively few nobles lost power during the Civil War, even those on the Royalist side. Most re-established their fortunes after 1660 and increased their political power. Between the early sixteenth century and the early eighteenth century, the nobility changed dramatically, from regional warlords with extensive semi-feudal power over men based on their ability to give favours and provide protection, to have great wealth but little military or regional power (outside the Scottish Highlands) but enormous powers under the Crown, essentially controlling an expanding central government. The Civil War thus did little to change essential ruling structures in Britain, with the landed nobility staying powerful throughout the period. In short, at the Restoration, the old ruling elite regained its power, which it used to promote its interests and to protect their property against both the Crown and the people.

Charles I and religious strife

Current research places a disproportionate amount of the blame for the crisis of the 1640s on Charles I, noting that his father, for all his unpopularity in England, was a far more astute monarch than his rigid, pious, uxorious and art-loving son. Charles I came to the throne accidentally. As a second son, he was not supposed to inherit the throne. Most of James VI and I's attention had been devoted to training, his eldest son, Henry, as an exemplary prince. The death of the Prince of Wales in 1612, aged eighteen, meant that Charles I took the throne aged 24 in 1625 as a second-best alternative.

Was he almost solely to blame for the conflicts of his reigns? Is that attributing too much influence on one individual and too little to the difficulties inherent in governing multiple kingdoms with multiple religions and several different legal regimes? The conduct and personality of Charles I must be counted as one of the major reasons why Britain exploded in the early 1640s. The evidence suggests that Charles I was a very flawed monarch, no matter how dutiful he was and how personally daring and brave and no matter that many of the provocative things he said and did about Parliament and Puritans had echoes in earlier reigns. Cromwell, for example, found Parliament just as troublesome as did Charles I, although he was better able to deal with this institution. Charles I exhibited three main flaws. The first was the policies he favoured and how he implemented these policies. These practical matters were much more important than any irritation faced by others about his personality, although his manner of dealing with the issues he favoured was almost certain to antagonise people who otherwise would have supported him.

Second, he was completely untrustworthy and a hopeless manager of people. He seemed incapable of understanding the viewpoints of his opponents and just kept on insisting about his rights and how everyone needed to show him obedience, perhaps due to a deeply felt insecurity that may have arisen from being the less favoured son of a powerful monarch. Finally, his political judgement was incredibly bad: it is difficult at times to fathom how he could have almost instinctively chosen the path most likely to antagonise, as was evident at his trial for treason, where he refused to take simple actions which may have preserved his head, such as showing some willingness to compromise with Parliament. He could never make a realistic assessment of the balance of political power and what would be the consequences arising from his actions. Nowhere was this more apparent than in 1648 when he restarted the English Civil War after having been roundly defeated in 1647. His chances of success in this second conflict were minimal and inflamed his opponents against him. It was even more evident in his trial in January 1649 when he essentially forced the English Parliament to try him for treason and then to execute him for refusing to agree to any terms acceptable to a body of legislators, very angry at his repeated bad behaviour, as they saw it. It made them determined to make the king, 'that man of blood, to account for the blood he had shed.'

The defects of Charles I played a very large role in creating crisis. But to blame him alone for the crisis of the 1640s is historically inaccurate. Charles I faced challenges that more skilled monarchs such as Elizabeth I and James VI and I would have found also very hard to solve, especially as the finances of the Crown were very problematic from the start of Charles I's reign. What was especially difficult for Charles I is that political conflict was managed through prisms of religious antagonism, making conflict both more common and more vicious, given how hard seventeenth-century people found it to compromise over religious faith.

The wars of the 1640s were fought in England, Wales and Scotland between alternative forms of the Protestant faith. For Calvinists, as opposed to the rival and less polemical strain of Protestantism, Anglicanism, the insistence by Charles I and Archbishop William Laud, an autocratic cleric accused of Arminian tendencies (Arminianism was a form of church governance that rejected predestination, which emphasised the power of bishops and church governors to determine church liturgy and which insisted on the importance of church hierarchy to determine forms of worship over congregational independence to worship freely) that the old Catholic structures of episcopacy (the rule of bishops) had to be maintained violated their deepest beliefs in authority resting in the participation of believers. They believed that what Charles I and William Laud, appointed archbishop in 1633 and executed in 1645 as being a hated opponent of Puritans and whom Charles I was powerless to keep from harm, were doing was transforming the Church of England into something akin to the Church of Rome, a religion imposed on people of faith from above.

Puritans were vehemently opposed to the Laudian program of liturgical reform, such as imposing a new Anglican prayer book on Presbyterian Scotland in 1638, the event that precipitated the Civil War. That event ultimately left Charles I with no alternative but to summon Parliament and end his Personal Rule. Charles I badly misread Scottish opinion by introducing this prayer book. The leaders of Scottish were Covenanters, who had signed a National Covenant in Greyfriars' Church in Edinburgh on 28 February 1638, committing the signatories to maintaining true religion and resisting anyone, even the king, who tried to change what they considered agreements made about Presbyterianism as long ago as 1581 and 1590. It was thus a constitutionalist, anti-absolutist movement that Charles I should have recognised as a real challenge to his authority. He did do so, in part, realising that what the Covenanters were agreeing to was more than just preserving the religious status quo but an argument about 'freedom' and who was to rule Scotland. Covenanters' opposition to episcopacy was combined with an objection to the royal supremacy over the church. It is not surprising that war resulted from such a direct challenge to Charles I's authority. It was a war that might have been prevented if Charles I had been less stubborn and had not refused to acknowledge that there was anything in the prayer book that was contrary to 'true religion.' This intransigence meant that compromise proved impossible to broker. His political incompetence is shown perfectly in how he allowed a small difference of opinion to turn into a full-blown war. In February 1638, for example, Charles I issued a proclamation that it was he, not his bishops or councillors, who was responsible for the prayer book and that anyone who opposed it would be regarded as a traitor. The result of this provocation was the National Covenant. Its signatories realised that Charles I's statement meant that they now had to challenge their king directly and that to save themselves from retribution that they needed to unite the Scottish nation behind them – which is one reason why the campaign by the Covenanters quickly moved beyond religious to economic grievances, such as antagonism to politically influenced monopolies in trade and, to some extent, dissatisfaction with taxation. Thus, the consequence of Charles I's interventions was to turn a limited protest into a full-blown rebellion.

Central to Puritan conceptions of religion was millenarianism: Puritans were people who looked at current events through a world view that saw Christ's kingdom on earth as always imminent. For them, the Reformation had not gone far enough to create a godly Britain. They placed more stress than did Anglicans on the power of sermons and upon individual readings of Christ's messages while Anglicans placed more attention on the observations of the sacraments. The sacraments were Protestant modifications of rituals inherited from Catholicism and gave meaning, it was believed, not just to prayer and worship but also to the major social events of baptism, marriage and burial.

Much of the antagonism between Anglicans and Puritans in the 1620s and 1630s came out of the difficulties of foreign policy in a calamitous period for European Protestantism. Puritans saw Catholic attacks on Protestants in Europe and interpreted those attacks to be signs that Protestantism was imperilled. They never believed that Charles I did enough to protect what was called 'the Protestant international' from assaults by Catholic rulers who were intent on establishing autocratic rule and in enforcing a Catholic religious orthodoxy. It is important to note that the two eras of crisis in Charles I's relations with Parliament, 1628–29 and 1640–42, both came after England had been defeated in battle and when Englishmen felt humiliated by how poorly its affairs in Europe were managed. Those wars compounded Charles I's eternal monetary problems, forcing him to depend on the goodwill of a hostile Parliament to give him enough revenue to allow the Crown to function.

Outside entanglements in Europe also made parliamentarians and Puritans convinced that popery from the Vatican was making inroads into English society. Fear of popery was always more popular among the British people than was the Puritan idea of establishing a godly global commonwealth. Anti-Catholicism was always a potent force in seventeenth-century Britain. That Charles I had married a Catholic princess from France one year after he ascended the throne only heightened popular suspicions that Charles I's religious policies and family behaviour were disturbingly crypto-Catholic. His appointment of William Laud as archbishop of Canterbury, as noted earlier, seemed to confirm that tendency to Catholicism. Laud was a radical conservative, aiming to return the Church of England back to its political and social pre-eminence that had slipped since the mid-sixteenth century. Laud was also not reluctant to use the church courts, especially the Court of High Commission, to crush dissenting views among clergy and laity alike. It was largely opposition to Laud's vision of the Anglican Church that encouraged thousands of hard-line Puritans to cross the Atlantic and to establish in the 1630s the early Congregationalist Commonwealth of New England.

Scotland and London

Opposition to the king's policies in the late 1630s and early 1640s was strongest in Scotland and in London. It was in Scotland where Charles I committed political suicide in 1637 and 1638, as discussed earlier. The impasse between Charles I and the Covenanters led to the Scots sending an army into northern England and defeating the English at Newburn. The royal defeat was comprehensive and had two important consequences. First, it showed that Charles I could be challenged and that rebels could get away with not submitting to royal authority. Second, the Scottish invasion had not been met by significant English resistance. The English had not flocked to the support of the Crown just because Scots were on their territory. The Covenanters proved a formidable force – united over the twin principles of Presbyterianism and parliamentary government. Indeed, the Scots were welcomed by the English as their natural supporters. When a Scottish army crossed the River Tweed in 1644, it did so at the explicit invitation of the English. It provided the English Parliament with support at a time when Charles I seemed to be in the ascendant with twenty thousand Scottish troops, paid for by the English Parliament, that could be used to harass the royalists. In return, the English Parliament promised the Scots that it would reform both the English and Irish religions to make them like Scottish Presbyterianism.

The power of the Covenanters eventually faltered, just as did the importance of its army, which failed to deliver the knock-out blow to the king it was expected to do. It was withdrawn to Scotland in January 1647, though not before having orchestrated Charles I handing himself over to the Scottish army in 1646, with Charles I hoping, wrongly, that this action would divide the parliamentarian allies. Charles I was not invited, however, to travel back to Scotland with the army and was left with limited forces to deal with English opponents. When Charles I was executed without Scottish consultation, the Covenanters declared as king of Scotland his son Charles II. That declaration helped encourage royalists in the far north of Scotland to revolt against covenanted Scotland in February 1649 and Cromwell to invade in the Northern Hemisphere spring of 1649. Cromwell's defeat of the Scottish army at the Battle of Dunbar on 2 September 1649 ended up with four thousand Scottish deaths and ten thousand Scots captured. A year to the day later, the remains of the Scottish army was destroyed at Worcester, in the English midlands. The Covenanted state ended at the same time. That defeat explains why for many historians the 'covenanting moment' was a failure. Nevertheless, the influence of Covenantors on Scottish society was long-lasting. Its brief ascendancy entrenched the distinctive Presbyterian religious culture that continues to shape the country.

By November 1641, Charles I found revolt everywhere, with events in England starting to run out of control because of pressures from the Irish and Scots who were fighting against the imposition in their kingdoms of alien priorities from England. In England, his major problem was in London. The city accounted for nearly 10 per cent of the English population and was famously restive. It was full of opponents to the king in its churches, in the trading companies and in the streets. The leaders of London, its overseas commercial merchants, remained resolutely opposed to the king throughout the 1640s. Their opposition forced the king to leave the capital early in the Civil War, not returning until he was tried and executed in 1649.

Parliament received a major advantage through its control of London and East Anglia, the richest and most populous parts of Britain. The support of London brought Parliament administrative, economic and military advantages. It could exploit the industrial capacity of the city to make its resource base to fight more secure. Meanwhile, London's vibrant press produced masses of pro-Parliament propaganda that brought supporters over to the parliamentary cause. Merchant wealth underpinned Parliament's ability to control the navy and to develop a formidable military fighting machine, the New Model Army, eventually led by Oliver Cromwell. The royal capital of Oxford could not match London's power.

The first Civil War between 1641 and 1647 was immensely destructive, especially in Ireland, where perhaps one-third of the population is estimated to have died, a rate like that of Germany on the Thirty Years' War but also in England, where death was often accompanied by terror and war crimes. The death rate was high, with disease aggravating battle casualties. It has been estimated that some eighty thousand were killed because of the fighting over the whole course of the Civil Wars with another one hundred thousand dying from disease. There was also a sudden increase in emigration from Britain to the Americas and elsewhere, plus the start of convict transportation, which reached a peak of seventy thousand between 1650 and 1659. Death and migration on this scale had significant demographic effects, making it harder for women to find husbands and meaning that the proportion of unmarried women in their early forties rose to one-quarter by the 1690s. The loss of so many men also weakened the labour force and towns other than London were disproportion- ately affected by sieges and wanton destruction of buildings and businesses. For most of the civilian population, the war brought extreme deprivation. Taxation to pay for the war greatly increased, collected by hated county committees, staffed by social upstarts willing to enforce unpopular actions and to under- mine the traditional rulers of the shires. One of the great strengths of English governance, the local administration in counties, largely broke down under the pressure of both sides seeking to set taxes to fund their armies.

The English Civil War was one of many battles, small and large. The most important of the first Civil War were at Marston Moor in Yorkshire in 1644 and at Naseby in Leicestershire in 1645, both massive defeats for the Royalists. The latter battle was ferociously fought between armies that together con- tained thirty thousand men. That battle was the making of the New Model Army, an army in which officers and men had an unusually close association, formed over a combined commitment to Puritan religion, formidable fight- ing strategies and a determination to exert its will over politics in the country.

It was at Naseby where Cromwell's military genius and his impressive cavalry forces came to the fore and where violence and death were most apparent. One thousand royalists died, and four thousand prisoners were taken, as well as large amounts of artillery and supplies. In the following months, the New Model Army was unstoppable. By the winter of 1645–46, royalist prospects were bleak. In April, the royalist cause ended in ignominy after Charles I left Oxford in disguise and after aimlessly, it seems, wandering around, surrendered, as noted earlier, to the Scottish army. Oxford surrendered in June; the final castles held by the royalists fell in August 1646, except for Harlech which incongruously held on until March 1647. It was the New Model Army, more than anything else, which won both Civil Wars in England and which triumphed in an epic and brutal campaign in Ireland and Scotland between 1644 and 1652. Its triumphs were due to its discipline, the leadership of Cromwell and Henry Fairfax, and the courage inspired by the discipline of the troops as well as extraordinary administrative competence, keeping the army continuously in the field and its soldiers fed and paid.

Regicide and the Commonwealth

The regicide of the king on 30 January 1649 led to a momentous constitutional change, the beginnings of eleven years of various forms of republican government. The execution of the king was contentious at the time and remained so after the war was completed. A few people talked about putting Charles I to death for treason against his people right from the start of the conflict in England, but most people wanted him to reform his ways and continue to rule. The driving force behind the regicide was the New Model Army which turned decisively against this 'man of blood' soon after negotiations with him failed in 1647. When the king started a second Civil War in 1648, it lost its patience with this untrustworthy monarch. The army decided to write what it called a *Remonstrance*, written mainly by Commissary-General Henry Ireton, Fairfax's son-in-law. It made several accusations against Charles I and demanded both a reformed Parliament that was to meet regularly and a form of elective monarchy, in which it would play a leading role in determining who would be elected king. The traditional view is that *The Remonstrance* was a clarion call for Charles I's execution, but a close reading of the document fails to see a direct call for execution.

But the army was intent on moving forward with some punishment of Charles I, with troops led by Colonel Thomas Pride invading Parliament in December 1648 and turning away or arresting members of Parliament it disliked. Pride's Purge paved the way for the House of Commons to agree to a trial of the king, which took place between 20 and 27 January. Charles could have preserved his throne, if not his dignity, by pleading guilty but Charles refused to recognise the validity of the court. In reality, Charles had little choice but to do what he did – we cannot really say he threw away his life and the Stuart monarchy by his actions, given that for a decade he had exhibited an

Figure 3.1 The execution of Charles I in Whitehall on 30 January 1649

Source: From a contemporary German engraving, Pictorial Press Ltd/Alamy Stock Photo.

absolute commitment to the notion of a divinely ordained monarchy and thus to the belief that he could never give up his political power without offending God. The impasse in views between King and Parliament virtually ensured his execution. But if Charles I had been less dogmatic in his views and in his 'rights,' then a Parliament reluctant to kill him may have come up with another option rather than execution.

It was a revolutionary act by any standard, condemned throughout monarchical Europe and greatly resented by the people of Scotland and Ireland, who were given no choice in the fate a man who was their rightful ruler. Scotland replied immediately that Charles II was the king of their country, proclaiming him indeed king of Great Britain, not just Scotland. For Scotland, the Union of the Crowns since 1603 had been a mitigated disaster, as policy was increasingly made in England for Scotland without Scottish input. The execution of the king without asking Scots for their opinion only confirmed their lowly status in English eyes. The execution thus exacerbated rather than solved the problem of composite monarchies which had bedevilled Britain for two generations. As John Morrill comments, 'the instabilities of the Stuart dynastic agglomerate were replaced by the instabilities of a militarised tripartite Commonwealth which could command obedience but not sufficient loyalty or support.' By 1660, it was clear that 'England's attempt to solve the British problem by incorporating the awkward neighbours had been a failure.'[6]

European monarchs had looked on at horror at the English willingness to kill its king. They were no happier to see Britain turn into what they considered an illegitimate and lawless republican regime, existing uncomfortably in a world of monarchical rule. It was probably only because France was weakened by its own internal revolution, the Fronde, and through fighting a war against Spain, that it did not give Charles II the help he requested to invade England. It did, however, provide indirect support. European hostility meant that that the Commonwealth was diplomatically isolated in the 1650s.

Regicide also helped unleash forms of political radicalism, with religious dissenters rejoicing at how regicide seemed to justify thinking anew about all political matters. The 1650s saw the emergence of a range of stridently radical Protestant sects, such as the millenarian Fifth Monarchy men, the egalitarian Levellers under Gerrard Winstanley and the pacifist Quakers. The latter was the largest and most enduring sect and was much more assertive and challenging than it was to become in the late seventeenth century. Quakers from 1652 under George Fox were religious activists wanting to awaken the world to the inner light of the spirit of God. They disrupted church services, haranguing clergy and congregations to debate with them and refused to accept conventional marks of social respect, such as taking oaths or raising their hats to superiors.

What is most impressive today about policy in the Commonwealth period is the determined efforts of Cromwell to institute an imperial expansion of English rule. He accompanied military intervention in Scotland and Ireland with the 'incorporation' of both kingdoms into the English Commonwealth, on terms which weakened their national identities and institutions and which included their representation in the English parliament. Cromwell also made direct interventions into European politics, mainly through his belligerent and ideologically based opposition to Catholic Spain. One of his boldest acts was to send an embassy to the Netherlands, proposing that it and Britain combine, as two Protestant republics opposed to Spanish rule in Europe and the Americas.

When the Dutch turned the proposed union down, England reacted badly. It passed a protectionist Navigation Act in 1651, aimed mainly at the Dutch, which restricted the import of goods into England to English ships or ships from the country of origin (mostly English colonies). The Navigation Act, however, had lasting consequences, establishing a mercantilist framework within which English and then British commerce operated for the next century. London merchants were highly enthusiastic about this new commercial regime, this arrangement being their reward for their support of Parliament in the 1640s. The merchant group also changed, with new men, many from lower social background than the oligarchy of state-backed monopolies, the Levant Company and the East India Company, which had previously run the City of London. These merchants, led by the entrepreneurial Maurice Thomson, the premier Atlantic and Africa merchant of the first half of the seventeenth century, used its ability to enter into the relatively open Atlantic trade, especially into the emerging plantation colonies such as Barbados and Virginia to gain money for themselves and to promote greater government involvement with the British Atlantic colonies. As Blair Worden summarises,

> in the commercial initiatives of the early 1650s, and in the flexing of the Commonwealth's muscles in its relations with its neighbours, the joint pursuit of gain and godliness produced, in devout and hard-headed merchants and in idealist thinkers, intoxicating visions of a newly prosperous society whose wealth, no less than the might of the army and navy of the infant Commonwealth, would be an instrument for the Puritanization of Europe.[7]

A singular development in this period was the strengthening of the Navy. Between 1649 and 1660, 216 ships were added to the navy, half as prizes and the remainder newly built. It was a remarkably effective fleet, doing well in wars against the Dutch and, unlike the army, distinguishing itself in the capture of Jamaica (if not Hispaniola, the original objective of the Western Design). The navy became during the Commonwealth period a great support for the defence of trade with Europe and in the Atlantic world, supplanting what merchants had usually been forced to do themselves. The navy became more professional in this period, both in its manning and in how it was supplied, with towns on the south coast of England increasingly oriented around the navy's extensive provisioning demands. It is important not to attribute the growth of the navy entirely to Cromwell. The separation of the merchant fleet and the Royal Navy was long-standing but had come under strain in the 1620s, when merchants became more reluctant than before to lend ships to the Crown, even when given a bounty. Technology made a difference too. Changes in ship design in the early seventeenth century encouraged a specialisation of function, making merchant ships not suitable for naval warfare. The result was a shift in the composition of the English navy towards custom-built royal ships. In 1627, there were ten royal ships and ninety private vessels in Île de Rhé. By 1645, the summer guard had thirty-six royal ships and sixteen private vessels while by 1673 at Schoonveldt in the Anglo-Dutch War all forty-nine vessels were royal vessels. Privateering was similarly reduced so that 1660 the divorce between the merchant fleet and the Royal Navy was complete. Nevertheless, the navy remained crucially dependent on seamen from the merchant marine in times of crisis, recruiting them either by enticement or by press-ganging.

Over the seventeenth century, the navy came to play a much more prominent role in the life of England and then Britain. Its growth required the development of new fiscal resources, as navies ate up money. Charles I started the development of such new resources in his ship-money levies of the 1630s, allowing for some shipbuilding and regular patrols of the English Channel. But the English navy did not keep pace with the building programs of its European rivals and

England was humiliated as a result in 1639 when a squadron meant to protect Spanish troops going to Flanders was forced to watch while the Dutch attacked this squadron in supposedly English waters. The Commonwealth governments devoted much more money to the navy, and it gradually became established as a vital part of English military strategy. There was never much public opposition to a standing navy, unlike the ideological opposition to standing armies. From the 1660s, Parliament became increasingly accustomed to voting large sums to the navy, although the public and Parliament depended on more accountability from 'its' navy as it spent more money on maintaining it. We should not think that the rise of the navy to worldwide prominence was uninterrupted progress of naval glory. Major advances, such as the gaining of the upper hand in the seas around England against the Dutch in the First Anglo-Dutch War of 1652–54, were matched by setbacks such as the humiliation of 1667, when in the Second Dutch war a Dutch fleet under M. A. de Ruyter sailed up the River Medway, burning several large naval vessels, and cruised almost at will on the southern and eastern coasts, disrupting commercial and naval convoys.

Overall, however, it became clear to other European states that England was a developing imperial power that needed close watching. Its newly acquired (but contested) naval superiority in Europe and its footholds in the Caribbean, which with the birth of a distinctive form of plantation agriculture in Barbados were becoming increasingly profitable, caused surprise and alarm in the capitals of continental Europe. The marriage of Charles II to Catherine de Braganza of Portugal in 1662, because of which England gained crucial new territories in North Africa (Tangier) and India (Bombay), showed that England had a formidable capacity to subjugate and colonise lands outside Europe. These developments, as Jonathan Israel argues, fundamentally altered European perceptions of England's overseas empire. He notes that

> where previously she had been a secondary power, and her colonies in Ireland and North America had appeared marginal, suddenly fear of English mastery of the seas and of the Indies, East and West, and therefore of the trade of the world, became a pervasive reality influencing the thinking of statesmen and diplomats throughout western Europe. Nor were these anxieties of the 1650s and early 1660s in any way eased during subsequent decades. On the contrary, they tended to intensify throughout the crucially formative period down to the Peace of Utrecht in 1713.[8]

Cromwell, foreign policy and the Civil War in the Atlantic

Oliver Cromwell played an important but not overwhelming role in the Commonwealth. He was always a realist and willing to be flexible in his policy, especially regarding allowing Anglicans to worship as they pleased. He kept the more zealous Puritans under control through an emphasis on political stability. He had indeed an iron fist, as his often-brutal treatment of Parliament showed, and he demonstrated ruthlessness that amounted to tyranny. He seldom justified his actions except that he was being guided by a God who was Himself a breaker of rules, and indifferent to human laws and institutions. But he had to negotiate always with contending forces and did so with conspicuous success, compared to the rigid and untrustworthy Charles I. We do not get far if we insist on seeing Cromwell as polarised between the God-driven man of principle and the duplicitous calculating politician. He saw himself as a man always struggling for religious and civil liberty, but these causes were always intertwined and always subjects for negotiation, a form of collaboration and accommodation which Cromwell frequently found intensely frustrating. Looking at how Cromwell had to negotiate between competing factions brings us to the hard truths of politics in the early modern state – one that James VI and I and Charles II recognised but which Charles I and James VII and II did not. The first truth is that religion and politics were inextricably linked and thus a political decision had religious implications (and vice versa) which tended to lead quickly to politics being tied up with faith, making it hard for people to compromise without giving up their commitment to what they considered was God's will. A wise politician had to make sure that he did not make policy which forced people to have to decide whether they would abide by their understanding of what God wanted or give in to earthly politics. Cromwell was able to do this, as seen in his many accommodations with different Calvinist sects and even with Anglicans and, remarkably, de facto with Catholics. Second, as J. C. Davis notes,

> the dispersed nature of the distribution of authority, responsibility and decision-taking in the early modern state meant that authority was always mediated, brokered and subject to the complicity (or its absence) of unpaid office-holders and high rates of participation by heads of household in office-holding.[9]

Without a permanent civil service or political parties and virtually no means of easy coercion through police or military or even through law, any politics had to be done through making loose coalitions of supporters, using a limited amount of patronage and by negotiating between strong-minded and independently minded men of means.

Cromwell, however, was a man devoted to reform and the reforms he made were significant and were not entirely turned back by the Restoration, even if his principal objective, to make England permanently Puritan, failed in the long-term. As Lord Chancellor of Oxford University, for example, the redoubt of Arminianism, he made sure that Puritans were appointed as heads of college and that priests in training were exposed to Puritan teaching. Where he was particularly decisive and influential was in foreign policy. We can detect a real shift In England's relationship to the wider world from his reign. What was less important than the results of Cromwell's aggressive attitude to overseas expansion, which underlay his war with first the Netherlands and then with Spain between 1655 and 1660, which were mixed and uncertain, was the changes in attitude toward Britain's overseas involvement at both the state and public levels.

Cromwell directed public consciousness of empire more effectively than had been the case with earlier polemicists for English overseas expansion, such as Samuel Purchas and Richard Hakluyt from the late sixteenth and early seventeenth centuries. He emphasised the economic as much as the moral imperatives of overseas expansion and how expansion in the Atlantic would aid England in becoming the most stridently Protestant power in Europe. Most important, the serendipitous and unplanned acquisitions of overseas territory, mostly coming out of private initiative, were now allied to state policy and the empire asserted as a matter of national honour, as well as good for national economic well-being. In addition, Cromwell's aggressive and militaristic foreign policy made it clear that the English government believed it legitimate to seize the overseas territories of other European empires by force and to use colonies as counters in treaty negotiations. Ironically, considering Cromwell's strongly religious motivations, the result of Cromwell's attitude to the Atlantic was to reduce arguments that colonisation had a spiritual motivation but that it was a secular enterprise. After all, the targets for acquisition or for trade between empires were the islands of the Caribbean, which were valuable because they produced the highly desirable crop of sugar and which facilitated trade in African slaves.

Initially, Cromwell's attention was in securing Scotland and Ireland for the Commonwealth and the creation of a Protestant international with the Dutch and Sweden, though neither of these fellow Protestant regimes agreed with the Commonwealth (both before and after Cromwell's rule) as they did not see themselves as natural allies of the English. Cromwell's main target was Spain, which he thought potentially vulnerable in its American colonies to invasion and conquest. In 1655, Cromwell launched an ambitious war against Spain in the Caribbean, called the Western Design. It was a disaster, perhaps the greatest military failure of Cromwell's career. It was appallingly organised, badly led (except in the navy) and quickly subject to the dreadful demography of disease that always greeted soldiers not immune to tropical diseases when they campaigned in the Caribbean. The Western Design failed in its major objective, which was to take Hispaniola, and the English were forced to take the barely inhabited island of Jamaica as an unsatisfactory consolation prize. That island did not prove to be valuable until well into the 1660s and probably into the 1670s, when it was an important privateering base through which to raid the Spanish Main.

Cromwell took the news of defeat very badly. His reaction to the setback in the Caribbean was instrumental in his reorganisation of England into twelve military zones, each with a major-general in charge. It was during this reorganisation that the notorious mid-1650s 'war on sin' emerged. Cromwell believed that one reason for his failure in the West Indies was the continued sinfulness of the English population – God was thus taking revenge against a sinful people by allowing for military defeat. This 'war on sin' led to laws being passed that punished people for offences against godly moral order, as the Presbyterians in Parliament saw it, and, most shockingly in the views of most of the populace, for people engaging in simple pleasures, such as going to alehouses, dancing around maypoles and even celebrating Christmas. Cromwell's encouragement of the worst tendencies of his moralistic supporters went a long way to undermining the moral authority of the Commonwealth and making people eager for his rule to finish. In addition to the domestic effects of the failure of the Western Design on public morale, the failure of Cromwell to inflict damage on Spain in the New World and in Europe (although he did achieve an impressive naval victory off the Canary Islands in 1657), meant that he could not count any more on England rallying around him against traditional Catholic armies, an attitude that had largely sustained him in his brutal campaign in Ireland in 1649–51, as it became quickly clear that Cromwell's plan that the great costs of war would not be met by acquiring cheaply Spanish New World territory but would have to be met by increased domestic taxation.

Almost all the conflicts of the Civil War period were fought in the British Isles, although one exception was a naval expedition to the Americas led by Sir George Ayscue in 1651–52 which brought the key colonies of Virginia and Barbados, royalist colonies that had revolted after the regicide, under parliamentarian control. The Puritan colony of New England, unsurprisingly, was strongly in favour of the parliamentarian cause. The main effect of the Civil War period was to loosen the ties between England its colonies, as metropolitan implosion both distracted attention in England from the colonies and reduced the ability of the centre to intrude into the affairs of the periphery. Perhaps the area of empire most affected by the empire was in India where the infant East India Company was seriously harmed by events in Britain. War made it difficult to raise money for trade and disrupted the sale of Company cargoes. The Company struggled not to become bankrupt during the 1640s and 1650s. It also exposed the state-controlled monopoly to new threats. Charles I had never been very supportive anyway, and the East India Company felt itself forced in 1640 to lend him what was for it the massive sum of £50,000.

That gift backfired because it alienated Parliament from the company. In any event, Parliament, supported by independent new merchants trading to the Atlantic, such as the indefatigable Maurice Thomson, who resented the monopoly power of Indian merchants, worked hard to try to undermine it. The company could operate, but it had to compete with rival and better politically supported groups, such as a syndicate led by Thomson, who could now send ships freely to Asia. Cromwell, however, reversed to an extent the policies of the Rump government in the early 1650s, and in 1657, he and his ministers rejected Thomson's plea for the creation of a regulated company, under which members would have been free to trade under their own account under common rules. Instead, he decided to create another joint-stock company to be managed as a single body with a monopoly of English trade in Asia. It was under this agreement that the East India Company operated until his dissolution in 1858. Cromwell believed that a monopoly suited English state interests best and returned the East India Company to the privileges that it had been given at its first establishment under Elizabeth I in 1600 and which had been whittled away during the reigns of the early Stuarts. Both James VI and I and Charles I had been unable to resist the temptation to raise money by selling permission to trade against the company's monopoly.

In British America, the main effect of the Civil War was to reinforce the loose control of the Crown on colonial development, as explained in chapter two, and to encourage the colonies to replicate England in asserting the power of local representative bodies modelled on Parliament and which quickly came to be identified with the preservation of English liberties. The development of colonial assemblies coincided with a time when some of the most influential leaders of the opposition to Charles I, such as the Earl of Warwick, were involved in colonial ventures (Warwick was a member of the Virginia Company and a principal coloniser of the briefly successful Providence Island settlement in the Caribbean in the 1640s) and when the very existence of Parliament was itself under threat from the Crown. Colonists believed that the creation of parliamentary-like assemblies was a guarantee that their move to the New World did not mean they had lost any of their much-loved English liberties, the ones that their compatriots in Britain were fighting for. The outbreak of civil war raised major questions about the relationship of the colonies to the mother country, questions that were made more urgent by the sudden end of English involvement or interest in colonial affairs. The start of conflict in Britain sharply reduced inflows of capital and people to the colonies – in many ways the colonies were left alone to develop as they wished for nearly 20 years and especially in the 1640s. It created problems over the exact location of imperial authority – in England or Britain alone or shared between metropolis and colonies – that would persist until the American Revolution.

In a comparative sense, English America suffered (or enjoyed) the kind of metropolitan implosion that would only happen in French America in the 1790s and in Spanish America after 1808. The colonies reached the Restoration of 1660, even after the shock of regicide and the imposition of the Navigation Act by the Commonwealth, relatively unscathed. Indeed, the effects of the Civil War period was to leave them with an enhanced sense of their ability to govern themselves. What was happening, in fact, was that alongside the implosion of royal authority in the Americas came an expansion of the economic activities of the colonies, led by the West Indies. That meant that, sooner or later, a restored royal government would turn its attention to the colonies and try and assert its control over its imperial possessions.

Moreover, while the Civil War had left the colonies to develop on their own, leading to both diverse political institutions but a common political ideology, based on an insistence that Englishmen overseas remained English subjects with all the rights inherent in English subjects, the civil war had also exposed a fissure between different groups propounding an interest in English colonisation. One side favoured a forceful assertion of the royal prerogative in English America. The other was inclined to support a strong Parliament and to side with dissenters, who were numerous in America, not just in New England but in William Penn's 1681 establishment of the Quaker province of Pennsylvania. As J. H. Elliott declares,

> such political and religious divisions militated against the formulation and pursuit of a coherent policy designed to enhance royal control over the colonies, and gave the representative bodies already well entrenched in America room to manoeuvre when they felt themselves threatened by the power of the crown.

In addition, 'some ministers and officials in London spoke the language of prerogative while others spoke the language of liberty and consent.' It made impossible any scheme to have one form of government in America and the West Indies. The Civil War meant that the colonies would always be politically diverse and religiously plural in ways that distinguished them from societies in Britain, where pluralism either did not exist or, as in Ireland, was not acceptable to people in power.

Restoration

The principal weakness of the Commonwealth was the lack of support in England and even more in Scotland and Wales for republicanism. In 1657 under the leadership of the Anglo-Irish nobleman, Roger Boyle, Lord Broghill, a man who had previously run the government of Scotland, parliamentary opponents of military rule and the 'tyranny' of the major-generals offered Cromwell the opportunity to be made king. They did so in a petition to him, called the Humble Petition and Advice, Broghill saw a Cromwellian dynasty (Cromwell had a son, Richard, who briefly succeeded him as Protector in 1658) as the practical solution to widespread popular discontent with military rule. When Cromwell rejected this offer and was reinstated in great pomp in June 1657 for a further term as Lord Protector, the pomp contrasting markedly with the simple ceremony when he first became Lord Protector in 1653, it was clear that republican rule rested entirely on him alone. He died on 3 September 1658 and although his son ostensibly succeeded him, it was clear from Cromwell's death that the Commonwealth was dead. Richard Cromwell was forced to abdicate in May 1659.

Once again, events in Scotland determined the end of the Civil War, just as events had precipitated its beginning. It was the actions of the commander of English forces in Scotland, George Monck, that enabled the Restoration of the Stuart monarchy to occur without bloodshed. Monck was horrified by a major uprising against parliamentary rule in the north-west of England in October 1659 and brought his army into England to keep order. Soon, he set about purging parliament, with army support, of its most radical MPs. Popular opinion supported Monck against increasingly resented Puritan rule and the navy clinched the issue, by giving, under Edward Montagu, soon to be created

Earl of Sandwich, its support to Charles II. Charles II became king officially in May 1660, although he always dated his reign from the death of his father on 30 January 1649.

In some ways, the Civil War did not result in enduring change. The sweeping reforms of the 1650s to entrench Puritanism were quickly reversed after 1660. The sweeping reforms of the 1650s to entrench Puritanism were quickly reversed after 1660. And the concerns that had led to Civil War from 1638, notably worries over Catholicism, remained central to British political identity. If James VII and II had not been a self-declared Catholic, it is hard to imagine that the Glorious Revolution would have occurred, no matter how troubling James VII and II's authoritarian tendencies were.

The most lasting result of the Civil War period was an awareness that the state needed more money to support it and that without such money there would always be antagonism between the Crown and Parliament. Indeed, Patrick O'Brien connects the rise of the British fiscal–military state with conflict in the English Civil War. He insists that Britain in the eighteenth century came to be a high-taxing, fiscally powerful state because wealthy elites were so devastated by the destruction of the Civil War that they were willing to make government fiscally powerful in order that this government would pass legislation that secured individual property rights. Thus, England was able to develop a fiscal–military state in which revenue from taxation was much higher than anywhere else in Europe. As O'Brien comments, it was fortunate that this domestic reconstruction of the state occurred 'when England's domestic economy began to generate the kind of accelerated commercialisation, colonisation, urban concentration, and proto-industrialisation that facilitated the collection of duties on domestic production and imports.'[10]

The result was that government income in 1700 was ten times as great as in 1600. It is ironic that the resistance to Charles I eventually strengthened the government, partially the monarchy but more explicitly the state. Thus, the big winner of the Civil War was the English state that achieved an increase in state revenue from which a standing army and a strong navy would be built, enabling England to become an imperial power. The Civil War did not result in England or Scotland becoming godly nations, but they did become greater players on the world stage. It meant that while in the seventeenth century the political quarrel was over whether it was the monarch or parliament which exercised sovereignty, the lesser quarrels of the eighteenth century would be over the shared power of monarch and Parliament over the people. The people's interests were less threatened by the royal prerogative than by corruption occasioned by the improper exercise of state patronage.

The great loser in the conflict in England, although not in Scotland, was Presbyterianism, the motor of the Puritan movement. It was caught between the residual Royalism of conservative Britain and the incipient radicalism unleashed by republicanism in the 1650s. Charles II and his Parliament moved from 1662 with the act of uniformity to force from office Dissenting ministers and make England under the Church of England an Anglican redoubt while allowing Scotland to continue as Presbyterian and leaving Ireland divided between Anglicans and Presbyterians in a country where Catholics were still the dominant majority of the population. Significantly, however, the Anglican establishment sided with Parliament rather than with the Crown in 1688, making that event work out quite differently than in 1640 as the Church of England stood with the English nation rather than against it. Compared to the French Revolution of 1780, the Civil War and the English Revolution that arose from these wars was an ambivalent affair, between sectarians committing to uprooting the old order and republican pragmatists who wanted to preserve as much of England's ancient constitution as possible.

In the long run, the pragmatists won, although their adherence to republicanism did not survive. Charles I may have been unpopular; the monarchy was not. Only Ireland of the four nations of the British Isles in which war raged in the 1640s and where republicanism was established in the 1650s has renounced monarchical rule since the Restoration in 1660 and of the British Empire that existed in the seventeenth century, only the Thirteen Colonies that became the United States, from 1776, and India, from 1950, have been prepared to do what Parliament did by force in 1649, which is to get rid of a legitimate monarch. And, within Britain, Scotland has never in its long history willingly given up monarchical rule. The radicalism of the Civil Wars in Britain is that it resulted in a brief period of significant religious and political reform. The conservatism of the period is that such reform was temporary and must be put up against the fact that monarchy has been by any margin the longest-lived institution in British history.

Notes

1 A.J.P. Taylor, *Essays in English History* (London: Hamish Hamilton Ltd: 1976), 23–6.
2 Peter Lake, 'Post-reformation Politics, Or on Not Looking for the Long-term Causes of the English Civil War,' in Michael J. Braddick, ed., *The Oxford Handbook of the English Revolution* (Oxford: Oxford University Press, 2015), 34.
3 Philip Baker, 'The Regicide,' and Mark Knights, 'The Long-Term Consequences of the English Revolution: State Formation, Political Culture and Ideology,' in Braddick, *Oxford Handbook of the English Revolution*, 154, 166, 519 and Jonathan Scott, *England's Troubles: Seventeenth-Century Political Instability in European Context* (Cambridge: Cambridge University Press, 2000).
4 Peter Wilson, 'Kingdom Divided: The British and Continental European Conflicts Compared,' in Braddick, *Oxford Handbook of the English Revolution*, 586–7.
5 Conrad Russell, *The Fall of the British Monarchies, 1637–1642* (Oxford: Oxford University Press, 1991), 1.
6 John Morrill, 'The English Revolution in British and Irish Context,' in Braddick, *Oxford Handbook of the English Revolution*, 573.
7 Blair Worden, *The English Civil Wars 1640–1660* (London: Weidenfeld and Nicholson, 2009), 120.
8 Jonathan Israel, 'The Emerging Empire: The Continental Perspective, 1650–1713,' in Nicholas Canny, ed. *The Oxford History of the British Empire: The Origins of Empire* (Oxford: Oxford University Press, 1988), 423.

9 J.C. Davis, 'Oliver Cromwell,' in Braddick, *Oxford Handbook of the English Revolution*, 227.
10 P.K. O'Brien, 'The Nature and Historical Evolution of an Exceptional Fiscal State . . .', *Economic History Review* 64 (2011), 435–6.

Bibliography

Braddick, Michael J., *God's Fury, England's Fire: A New History of the English Civil Wars* (London: Penguin, 2008).

Braddick, Michael, ed., *The Oxford Handbook of the English Revolution* (Oxford: Oxford University Press, 2015).

Cust, Richard, *Charles I and the Aristocracy, 1625–1642* (Cambridge: Cambridge University Press, 2013).

Davis, J.C., *Oliver Cromwell* (London: Arnold, 2001).

Elliott, J.H., *Empires of the Atlantic World: Britain and Spain in America 1492–1830* (New Haven: Yale University Press, 2006), 151–2.

Harris, Tim, *Rebellion: Britain's First Stuart Kings, 1547–1642* (Oxford: Oxford University Press, 2014).

Macinnes, Allan I., 'The "Scottish Moment", 1638–1645,' in J.S.A. Adamson, ed., *The English Civil War: Conflict and Contexts, 1640–1649* (Basingstoke: Palgrave Macmillan, 2009), 125–52.

Pestana, Carla, *The English Atlantic in an Age of Revolution* (Cambridge, MA: Harvard University Press, 2007).

Woolrych, Austin, *Britain in Revolution, 1625–1660* (Oxford: Oxford University Press, 2005).

Worden, Blair, *The English Civil Wars, 1640–1660* (London: Phoenix, 2009).

Worden, Blair, *God's Instruments: Political Conduct in the England of Oliver Cromwell* (Oxford: Oxford University Press, 2012).

4   Making Britain, 1660–1707

The Civil War and demography

It is always hard to determine in history to what extent things would have happened without a major event occurring and the extent to which that event shaped all that followed, changing the historical trajectory of a country. Social historians are more resistant than political historians to attribute social and economic change to political events alone and instead stress long term developments, such as changes in patterns of population change or alterations in economic orientation, rather than the circumstances of certain event, which may have high profile but may not have had as lasting an effect on underlying social and economic patterns as contemporaries claimed. Thus, current historical orthodoxy suggests that the major social changes that occurred in seventeenth-century Britain were largely independent of the conflict in mid-century which led to the execution of a king, the rule of Oliver Cromwell in the new political formation of a military-controlled republic and savage conflict between his opponents and supporters in a calamitous set of civil wars. The fundamental features of British life – considerable class differences, patriarchal government at the level of the household, racist assumptions about Africans, Native Americans and foreigners of all kinds – remained relatively constant and unchanged throughout the turmoil of this period and indeed well into the nineteenth century. The biggest social changes were demographic, and these changes do not seem to have been especially influenced by mid-century political conflict.

Indeed, the 1640s were as important demographically as they were politically. The balance between population and resources altered, which in the sixteenth and early seventeenth century seemed to be pointing England and Scotland towards a Malthusian crisis of overpopulation in lands where resources were not increasing relative to the population at a commensurate rate. It indicated that eventually these countries would not have the ability to feed and maintain their growing populations. This situation shifted after 1660, especially in England, so that the relationship between resources and population became more balanced. A proportion of this drop in the rate of population growth might be attributed to the extremely high death rates of marriageable men in the Civil Wars and outmigration in the 1630s and 1640s to British America. Many women could not marry and have children because there was a shortage of men available to marry in the decades around mid-century. And migration to the Americas, particularly from southern England, declined considerably after 1660, when the opportunities in England and to an extent Scotland seemed more favourable for young men than did possibilities in the Americas. In the Americas, the advent of plantation agriculture based on the exploitation of ordinary workers (starting with white indentured servants before the labour force became mainly black slaves), the inability of settlers to entirely deprive Native Americans of their land and the growth of class-based tensions made migration less appealing. The increased death rates in England in the second half of the seventeenth century also resulted from factors largely out of human control, such as some exceptionally cold winters and increased mortality from infectious diseases, such as smallpox and typhus.

The main reason for the significant slowing of population after 1640 after 150 years of near-constant, markedly upward growth was not increased numbers of people dying before they could marry and have children (infant and child mortality remained high but not increasing in incidence) but was a decline in birth rates, as measured in baptisms recorded in Church of England parishes. In 1660, the population of England was 5.03 million, probably falling to under 5 million in both the 1670s and 1690s. It was 70 years before the peak post-Restoration population of 5.3 million attained in the 1660s happened again. Births declined primarily because more people than before chose not to marry and because those who did marry married later, meaning that in a society in which forms of preventative contraception of births were largely absent that couples had fewer children than when they married at younger ages (illegitimacy rates were very low, making marriage crucial to the formation of families). Demographic decline was most conspicuous in the ranks of the nobility, where an unprecedented number of peerages failed in the late seventeenth and early eighteenth century for lack of heirs. This winnowing of the aristocracy led to the aristocracy, paradoxically, becoming stronger than it was, as those nobles who survived and reproduced tended to inherit wealth from those families that failed to prosper. This was the period of heiresses, of rich families having but a single female heir, who conveyed wealth on marriage, usually to a high-born young man, in ways that concentrated wealth among those who were already wealthy.

Scotland had a much lower population than England and Wales, with around 1.25 million people in 1691, just before nearly a decade of poor harvests and subsequent famine set in, leading to a population decline over a decade of between 10 and 15 percent. In England, by contrast, population decline came from mostly beneficial circumstances, reflecting easier economic circumstances after 1660. Population decline was beneficial in England, as there was a small but crucial easing of the population-induced pressures on the necessities of life between 1660 and 1720.

Within this overall picture of slight population decline in Britain, there were two exceptions. The population of Ireland increased to nearly 2 million by

1687, recovering some of the losses it had incurred in the catastrophes of the Civil War period. And the town of London grew at a fantastic rate. The 'great wen' of London grew rapidly throughout the seventeenth century, especially after 1660, until by 1700 it had perhaps five hundred thousand people, or one in ten of the inhabitants of England and Wales. It was by that date as large as Paris, even though France had four times the number of inhabitants as did England and Wales. Its rate of growth is even more remarkable given London's notoriously unhealthy demography, which itself was a major contributor to stagnant population levels in the country at large. The ratio of births to deaths in London was too low to generate positive demographic growth and without substantial in-migration would have led to a collapse in the population of the city over time. But migration into the city was constant and substantial, as young adults sought to take advantage of London's booming economy to find well-paying jobs. It was also the location of the large Huguenot migration of Protestant refugees from France who fled to London after the Edict of Nantes of 1598, making Protestantism legal, was revoked by Louis XIV in 1685, making it clear there was little future for them in France. It was from this period that London's overwhelming and irresistible rise as the centre of British political, cultural and economic life began. London had always had an outsize importance in England, but from around 1680 onwards, its wealth and size meant that what happened in London had a disproportionate effect on the life of the rest of the country, a reality of British life that has continued until the present.

A growing economy

London was the dynamic motor of a growing economy. Although poverty had far from disappeared, it seems that, on average, people had more money to spend from the 1660s on items other than mere sustenance, including increasing amounts of disposable money spent on 'luxuries,' some of which, such as tea and sugar consumption, soon became not so much luxuries but necessities. Increasingly, as discussed in a later chapter, people began to buy goods not because they needed them but because they wanted them. Crucially, more goods were becoming available to purchase in an economy where manufacturing was expanding beyond the traditional artisan-shopkeeper of household manufacture. Now, manufacturers made goods in larger workshops, employing more people than under household production, producing specialist goods to precise specifications. These changes in purchasing patterns began what historians call a 'consumer revolution.'

Joan Thirsk notes that 'by the end of the seventeenth century, people had a choice of so many different qualities of linen for domestic use and personal wear that it was impossible to count them' with the new invention of shops with windows full of goods on display presented a 'magnificent range of choice.'[1] Carole Shammas's extensive study of the pre-modern consumer in Britain and British America adds to this picture the growth of Atlantic and Asian goods – tobacco and sugar from the Americas and tea and above textiles from Asia.[2] The increase of these commodities was astounding. Tobacco imports from the Chesapeake were less than 15,000 pounds in 1615 but 13 million pounds by 1700 while sugar from the West Indies more than doubled from the 1660s to 1700 and then doubled again from 1700 and 1730, when the average person ate 15 pounds of sugar a year, with the rich undoubtedly consuming a great deal than that, as poor people consuming less – sugar may have become cheap, but the products that were made with sugar, such as puddings and cakes, remained expensive and for special occasions.

Producers did not do as well as consumers. They received less money from what they grew than they had done before, with grain and wool prices edging downwards. Farmers responded by increasing agricultural productivity through improving the soil with fertilisers, nitrogen-fixing clovers and new crops, including potatoes from the New World. Agricultural prices were low or stagnating, with the prices of most grains dropping between the 1680s and the 1740s, although wartime pressures between 1688 and 1714 led to some increase in demand and an improvement in prices. Stable or falling prices resulted from weakened demand from a stagnant or declining population. Some of the resulting slack was taken up with exporting to Ireland and the continent. But the biggest problem that farmers faced, especially in the 1690s, a decade of relative cold in a century termed the 'Little Ice Age,' was that prices and productivity fluctuated in unexpected ways. Prices in over half the years between 1690 and 1715 were either unusually high or unusually low, providing a very unsatisfactory and unsettling environment for farmers, labourers and landowners.

These variations in agriculture are important because the domestic economy was always much the largest sector of the economy. Nevertheless, overseas trade, especially in the Americas was a very dynamic part of the economy. It was from the late seventeenth century that England began to take advantage of the European 'discoveries' of 'new' lands and sea routes. Overall, trade did not grow very fast, with imports from the Atlantic, Asia and Africa growing sixfold and exports a bit more during the seventeenth century – impressive figures but from a low base. What was most important was a shift in the location of trade, from Europe to the Atlantic. By 1700, 30 per cent of imports and 15 per cent of exports came from Asia or America, with sugar, tobacco and calicoes the most important imported commodities, adding to traditional exports, such as wool, to make overseas trade very profitable to the well-placed overseas merchants in London and Bristol engaged in such activities.

Another, more problematic, commodity was African slaves, transported from West Africa to the plantations of the New World, to grow other commodities, such as sugar, rice and tobacco. Atlantic trade proved a godsend for England and later Britain, as its expansion occurred just as most branches of England's commerce with Europe was flagging. The trade was conducted within a mercantilist framework, whereby all goods traded with the colonies had to be transported by English carrier. Mercantilist legislation, of course, was often evaded – the early eighteenth century was the great period of smuggling in both Britain and in the Americas. It was a widespread practice that authorities, especially in British America, usually winked at, as colonists appreciated access to cheaper goods and welcomed the chance to trade illegally but profitably with Spanish America.

Trade with India was not as important as trade in the Atlantic, but it grew rapidly after the Restoration, with imports increasing nearly sixfold and exports eightfold from the 1660s to the 1680s, albeit, as noted earlier, from a low starting base. What was most attractive to Britons were Indian textiles. European consumers (re-exports of Indian cloth to Europe also happened) were excited by the stunning range of colours and designs in calicoes that India provided to them. Indians, however, were less enamoured about European goods, meaning that goods from Asia were bought through bullion obtained mostly in exchange with Spanish America. It linked trading relationships between East and West in an interlocking, mutually dependent system. It also meant that bullion that might have otherwise gone to Europe flowed to China and Asia, a cause of considerable complaint among political economists who thought, probably wrongly, that, in the long run, this transfer would cause great economic problems in a Europe denuded of specie.

Just as important as the volume in trade was who benefitted from it. Colonial trade quickly became concentrated in relatively few hands, Nuala Zahedieh shows that in 1686, twenty-two London merchants exported goods worth more than £1,000 to the West Indies, and nineteen did the same to North America, with twenty-eight merchants receiving more than £5,000 in that year from the West Indies, or more than 50 per cent of the total imports from the region.[3] These overseas merchants became influential in post-Restoration politics, providing the impetus for ending the monopoly of the Royal African Company, so that they could enter the slave trade, and providing crucial support as Whigs for William III in the Glorious Revolution of 1688.

Transoceanic trade played an important role in one of the most significant developments in the 1690s, the so-called financial revolution, leading to the fiscal-military state, as explained elsewhere in this book. Colonial expansion provided new opportunities for mercantile investment, including capital acquired from foreign lands. New groups, notably Quakers and Jews, used the opportunities available in overseas trade to secure a foothold in English commercial trade.

We can see how well new groups did in overseas trade in the late seventeenth century by studying a small group of Sephardic Jews in Jamaica. They came to Jamaica in the 1660s and 1670s and engaged mostly in illegal trade with Spanish America with some involvement in the local leg of the Atlantic slave trade, after Africans had arrived in Jamaica and before they were distributed to Jamaican plantations or sent to Spanish America. Despite being involved in Jamaica's riskiest trade, Zahedieh shows, Jews prospered. How did they do so in a culture peppered with anti-Semitism? Envious rivals denounced them for acting in concert and in conspiring against Christians. There is not much evidence of such conspiracies, but what seems to have been true is that Jews in Jamaica, just like private traders in the East India Company after 1660, maintained 'high levels of individual autonomy and flexible, fluid organisation within a decentralised network with thick horizontal links.' They drew as much on social capital from within the Jewish diaspora of the seventeenth century as on actual capital. Their critics were right to see Jews as sticking together but wrong in seeing them as a cabal of entirely self-interested agents. As Zahedieh comments, 'in forging solidarity and social discipline, the Sephardim deployed strategies common to the associational culture which flourished throughout early modern Europe as the growing bourgeoisie struggled to adjust to rapid economic and social change . . . cement [in] group commitment with mutuality.' In short, the Sephardim, a traditional communitarian group with 'strong private-order institutions,' used their 'high levels of trustworthiness to gain 'a competitive advantage which not only stimulated envy and retaliation but also allowed the Sephardim to combine with the Christian elite to capture rent-seeking opportunities and obtain political protections.'[4]

Rent-seeking or trying to take advantage of special connections with government or other institutions to gain a step on other rivals that were not derived from better abilities in the marketplace, was a feature of commercial life in late-seventeenth century London. As Zahedieh notes,

> in allowing a small elite to use political power to secure rent-seeking enterprises and engross the fruits of empire, the Revolution of 1689 was far less glorious than the Whiggish myth-makers would have us believe and did, in fact deliver sustained damage to growth.[5]

Merchants used the language of the ancient constitution to protest Crown 'tyranny,' but that language often was used to mask the relentless pursuit of self-advantage through the manipulation of political interest groups to favour one group of merchants over another. Merchants tended to oppose Charles II and James VII and II less from ideological opposition to their centralising aims but because the Crown undermined vested interests within colonial trade in the late Stuart Atlantic world. The Glorious Revolution enhanced the power of larger merchants trading in the Atlantic who used their support of the winning side in that conflict to get personal and collective advantages by such things as attacking and destroying the monopoly of the Royal African Company over trade with Africa and especially in the Atlantic slave trade. The ending of that monopoly allowed more enslaved people to be brought to the Americas but at greater cost to consumers and with London and African merchants taking a much bigger cut of profits than previously.

The Glorious Revolution also ushered in a lengthy period of war, which proved a bonanza for many well-placed merchants able to get lucrative government contracts to supply troops. One result of the Glorious Revolution was that small planters in the Americas and smaller merchants in the capital were largely driven out of business, unable to compete with the economic and especially political advantages that the richest merchants had in London. The career of Gilbert Heathcote, who died in 1733 as probably the richest commoner in Britain and who started out as a merchant in the 1670s in Baltic trade before moving profitably into Atlantic commerce in the 1680s, illustrates how well rich merchants did under William III and Anne. He was an enthusiastic supporter of both the Glorious Revolution and the campaign against the Royal African Company. He was a major player in Jamaican trade and in the Atlantic slave trade, trading on his account. The end of the Royal African Company's monopoly brought him many commercial benefits. His attention to commerce was matched by his attention to politics. He became the member of Parliament for the City of London in 1701 and served as an agent for the Jamaican governor, allowing him access to the Spanish slave trade and to wartime contracting. His access to large amounts of capital proved very beneficial to a cash-strapped wartime government. As a major lender of funds to government, he had a firm interest in ensuring that government credit was sound. He advocated for the chartering of the Bank of England, of which he soon became a director and a major customer. He seems to have earned £60,000 between 1697 and 1700 alone from his investments in this relatively new institution. His support helped the Bank survive, but he did extremely well himself from his calculated support of this principal support of the Whig regime that was in power in the 1690s and 1700s.

He was thus part of a small commercial elite, as Zahedieh argues, who

> was able with Crown collusion, to secure rent-seeking enterprises and fight expensive wars, while with higher input prices and risky trading conditions, plantation production stalled, the volume of Atlantic trade stagnated, the number of participants in colonial commerce contracted, and European rivals began a process of rapid growth,

which enabled them to match Britain in overseas expansion until growth in the British Atlantic economy resumed in the 1740s. Although 'England's extensive growth in the New World can be viewed as bringing windfall profits that did much to explain the long period of increasing commercialisation and Smithian growth which culminated in the industrial revolution,' that growth might have been greater if the majority of windfall profits had not been accumulated by a small group of well-placed rent-seeking merchants who were more interested in personal profit than the long-term development of a dynamic overseas trading sector.

Thus, 'close examination of the interests at play in England's Atlantic world does not support the Whiggish view that the Glorious Revolution changed institutions in ways that were better for growth than those that prevailed in an earlier period.' What the Crown and its merchant supporters did in the Atlantic world after 1700 (and probably in Asia as well, although this part of overseas trade is less well documented than Atlantic trade) was 'to manipulate and manage the imperial economy in its own interests and ushered in a long period of slow growth.'[6]

Long-distance trade stimulated changes in credit practices, necessary given the complicated nature and heavy credit demands of the Atlantic slave trade. It also stimulated innovations in insurance and in mercantile practice generally, as Atlantic and East India trade put a premium on gaining commercially sensitive information that gave a merchant an advantage over competitors and which he and competitors used to subvert governmental restrictions on trade – trade is always, as Adam Smith reminded us in *The Wealth of Nations*, a mixture of competition, cooperation and conspiracy. Merchants needed to be highly skilled individuals, able to carefully manage and juggle between multiple and sometimes competing commercial activities. One of the first things they needed to do to succeed in business was to develop more systematic accounting practices, especially in the complicated plantation trade and the slave trade: the origins of modern accounting are closely tied to Britain's involvement in slavery and the plantation economy. These overseas merchants became the most sophisticated traders in Britain by 1700 and the best at what they did in Europe, eclipsing by the early eighteenth century the previous predominance of the Dutch in transnational commerce. As Zahedieh concludes, 'by the end of the seventeenth century, the accumulation and refinement of commercial skills in London made it look set to overtake Amsterdam as Europe's major entrepot, shipping centre, commodity market and market for capital.'[7]

London was well suited to be the hub of the developing commercial system. It was located near the mouth of a major river and able to host ocean-going vessels. It dominated England's overseas trade and was the centre of the law, Parliament, finance and industry. It had a relatively open and flexible institutional framework that encouraged lots of aspiring merchants to enter overseas trade. London merchants played a crucial role in creating the necessary commercial networks and became ever more efficient, reducing costs so that they became as productive as their principal European competitors. The creation of a workable Atlantic system posed complex problems and raised solutions which relied on the capital, skill and ingenuity which London possessed in much greater capacities than anywhere else in the Atlantic world and which to an extent it retains today.

Late seventeenth-century politics

Increasingly historians do not see the Civil Wars of the mid-seventeenth century in Britain as initiating a break in political culture as much as being the backdrop shaping how that political culture evolved in the second half of the seventeenth century. In short, the Civil Wars of the 1640s was an unfinished revolution, and its principal themes were only completed after a second revolution, the Glorious Revolution of 1688. As Mark Knights argues,

> seeing the two seventeenth-century revolutions as a part of a revolutionary process, rather than as two separate "events," has the advantage not only of analysing themes across the two revolutions – such as partisan divisions, print culture, state formation, and religious toleration – but also of seeing

the second revolution through contemporary eyes, since those living in 1688 never forgot the precedent and lessons of the earlier revolution.[8]

The reinterpretation of this period as one continuous revolution makes it similar to other major historical events, like the Reformation or even the Enlightenment, as having both long-term causes and long-term consequences.

As noted in the previous chapter, the big winner from the Civil War was the state. But the transformation of the state did not happen immediately. The English Civil War placed great demands on the customary system of English governance, which was highly participatory, very localised and dispersed, both because the activities of the state were so expensive and because each locality was influenced by the sudden infusion of the central government into settled local areas of outsiders to that locality, be they the arrival of Irish in Cheshire, the Scots in Northumberland or Londoners into Essex. In some ways, what is remarkable about a period in which the state became more important in everyday life is that the traditional reliance in England on governing being largely done by men holding voluntary office lasted until the eighteenth century. But the existing system faced great pressures in the mid-seventeenth century, pressures which greatly shaped politics in the late Stuart period. Just because the mid-seventeenth-century Commonwealth regime solved the state's central problem of finance through the successful introduction of the excise, allowing for indirect taxation of good consumed by the populace, does not mean that the problems of a powerful state in a political system marked by volunteerism were solved by the 1670s and 1680s.

The Glorious Revolution solved the problem that vexed Britons from the 1630s to the 1680s by changing the focus. Changing ideas about what 'corruption' was shows how the focus changed. Until the 1660s, corruption was defined in largely religious terms – corruption in politics occurred when people adhered to illegitimate faiths or, as William Laud was argued to have done, transformed legitimate faiths into something illegitimate. From the Restoration, however, corruption in public life was increasingly seen as fiscal rather than religious corruption (a way of thinking about corruption that has lengthy echoes in Anglo-American life until the present) and as arising from rent-seeking behaviour, as done by people such as Gilbert Heathcote, as described earlier, who used their access to state power to avoid the self-regulating voluntary office-holding model of public duty. As Knights argues,

> one legacy of the revolutions was thus the oppressive, tax-levying state that favoured a group of parasites who fed off it; another was a tradition of protest against this that championed the ideal of participatory, self-governing communities resting on an ideal of disinterested officeholding.[9]

Both of these reactions reflected a state that had enhanced powers from the late seventeenth century onwards and which was more active than before, a trend that started with Cromwell in the 1650s in such things as the Western Design and which continued under Charles II and James VII and II until the Glorious Revolution.

The period between the two seventeenth-century revolutions saw religion continue to be a matter dividing more than uniting society. Anglicans and Dissenters tussled throughout the second half of the seventeenth century because the Restoration of the monarchy was not accompanied by a religious settlement. It seemed to contemporaries that one form of intolerance had just been replaced by another form of intolerance. Debates about the boundaries between church and state were shaped by the continuing demand for some toleration for the Protestant sects that had been in power in the 1650s or some relaxation of Anglican doctrine to allow moderate Dissenters to be included, or, in the language of the time, to be 'comprehended,' into the established church. Anglicans fiercely resisted such efforts at toleration until after the Glorious Revolution. It took that event to make a Toleration Act in possible in 1689, which gave some recognition to Dissenters, although not to Jews or Catholics. It was not an uncontested development, however. The Anglican church turned militant under Anne in the first decade of the eighteenth century, especially when a High Tory cleric, Henry Sachaverell, preached in 1709 against tolerating Dissenters and was impeached by Parliament for his troubles. The rare militancy of the Anglican Church after the Glorious Revolution, as seen in Sachaverell's intemperate outbursts, was not successful in reversing a trend towards greater

Figure 4.1 The Landing of William of Orange, 1688, also known as the Glorious Revolution

Source: William of Orange, later William III of England, Lebrecht Music & Arts/Alamy Stock Photo.

religious toleration of people not in the Church of England in England. The Toleration Act was not repealed in 1709, and eventually, the extreme religious language that marked the seventeenth century was toned down. Britons after 1689, not just in England but in Scotland and Wales also, gave up, after 1689, the idea that a godly reformation of society was either possible or desirable. In this respect, the long-term effect of the Glorious Revolution was to set aside one abiding theme arising out of the Reformation, which had been behind many of the convulsions of the sixteenth and seventeenth centuries.

Other struggles that had been part of the Civil War period also continued up until the Glorious Revolution, as both Robert Brenner and Steven Pincus have argued in contentious viewpoints which not everyone accepts. For Brenner, writing from a Marxist perspective, it took two revolutions for the dominance of overseas merchants and a capitalist aristocracy to become entrenched in English power structures.[10] Pincus suggests that throughout the late seventeenth century, debates in Britain, especially in England, centred on rival visions of political economy as much as on religion, with Whigs believing in manufacturing, rather than land, as he argues Tories believed, as the way in which Britain could become rich and happy (the term *Whig* was a pejorative name given to one faction in the Exclusion Crisis of 1678–81 over whether James VII and II could be heir to Charles II that was derived from Scottish cattle rustlers; the other faction, named Tories, also was given a pejorative name, derived from medieval depictions of Irish brigands. Both sides took the names with pride, and their original meanings soon faded.) Pincus argues that it was the Whig vision that prevailed, in ways that unleashed British interest in involving itself in the wider world.[11]

Moreover, Pincus suggests, it was only with the second seventeenth-century revolution that British foreign policy became clear, with antagonism towards Spain and the Netherlands being replaced by hostility towards France, under its highly capable and to British eyes terrifying monarch, Louis XIV. In many ways, of course, the slowness by which France came to be identified as Britain's principal rival was less due to British than to French objectives. Louis XIV's basic strategy in Europe, at least before his dreaded rival, William III, became king of the three kingdoms of Britain, was to build French supremacy by attacking Spain and by acquiring the Spanish Netherlands. Louis XIV was generally friendly towards Charles II and James VII and II, a friendliness which did not play well in Britain among a largely Francophobe population, who were bolstered in that anti-French feelings by what they heard from Huguenot Protestant refugees who flocked to England after the revocation of the Edict of Nantes in 1685 in what was an even bigger, if not so consequential, influx of French migrants since the Norman Conquest. Louis XIV's support of the Stuart monarchs was less due to their crypto-Catholicism (Charles II) and real Catholicism (James VII and II) but because their hostility towards Spain and the Dutch in the 1660s through 1680s suited him geopolitically. What Louis XIV did not realise, however, until the Glorious Revolution was that his relative friendliness towards England gave England a chance to achieve colonial and maritime expansion without significant French opposition. In retrospect, pro-French government policy before 1689 allowed Britain to move ahead in its Atlantic, African and Asian strategies in ways that became more difficult in the early eighteenth century, even though by that latter period Britain's overseas empire was immensely stronger than it had been half a century previously.

The Glorious Revolution saw British foreign policy reverse. The Dutch realised in 1687, when Louis XIV resumed economic warfare with them, that their best chance of survival lay in allying themselves with Britain. The Glorious Revolution was thus a marvellous piece of luck for the Dutch, putting William III on the throne and uniting the Dutch with the English in a war with the French, greatly weakening the strategic position of France in both America and the West Indies. Ironically, the move of both France and Britain to focus on antagonisms between each other rather than on mutual antagonism to Spain in the Americas, proved a boon to that latter empire at a time it was especially vulnerable. The Dutch started war with France from May 1689. It was the English who most benefitted from Dutch action, as they fought France where England was strongest at sea and outside Europe, as well as in Europe itself, where France had advantages over Britain. The 1690s was a decade when the English achieved great ground against both the Dutch and the French in the Caribbean, West Africa and India. The English were also more comfortable fighting their traditional foe, the French, in a Second Hundred Years' War, than they were at challenging their fellow Protestants in the United Province. It meant that it was easier to create a British identity after the Glorious Revolution, founded on Protestantism and a commitment to commerce, than in the messier world of the four male Stuart kings and their less-than-fervent support of either central tenet of eighteenth-century Britishness.

What also connected the two revolutions together was ideological divisions within the British population. In both revolutions, a key area of dispute was the doctrine of popular sovereignty and the right of resistance. The Whig triumph in 1689 established that a right of resistance existed, something both the royalist heirs of the 1640s, the Tories and Charles II and James VII and II, both denied in ways reminiscent of the views of Charles I. To an extent we can see how the debates over the Civil War continued into the Glorious Revolution through an examination of the works of John Locke, the pre-eminent thinker of the Glorious Revolution, in the way that his principal ideological target, Thomas Hobbes, had been in the Civil War. Locke was greatly concerned in his political theory masterpiece, *The Two Treatises of Government* (1689), in which he established a theoretical basis upon which rights of resistance theories could be justified, in countering the authoritarian ideas of Robert Filmer in his posthumous *Patriacha* (1680), originally written in the 1630s, and Hobbes's *Leviathan* (1651). Locke argued, in part from doctrines derived from the radical Levellers during the Commonwealth, that in certain circumscribed circumstances the governed might legitimately resist or even withdraw their allegiance from a despot. Locke is considered the avatar of liberalism, but it is important to remember that he was a man of the late seventeenth century, not the twenty-first century, as important in providing a reason for why African chattel slavery in the plantation colonies of English America is lawful as in establishing the ideological basis for a liberal state. We can see the two revolutions as having not only enabled a transformation of the public sphere, one in which print was central, but also leaving behind for eighteenth-century commentators a complex, rich and contested ideological heritage that celebrated revolutionary and counter-revolutionary sets of ideas and languages.

Charles II

To understand the political context of these wider changes, we need to examine the rules of the two sons of Charles I who became rulers of the three kingdoms of Britain. Charles II was not a reforming monarch. In the immediate aftermath of the Restoration he was determined to turn the clock back to 1641. His only major act of retribution was to pursue and execute as many people who had signed the document to kill the king and to restore back to eight hundred English royalist landowners their confiscated estates and allow another three thousand royalist families to buy back their sequestered estates. Otherwise, retribution against Parliament and their supporters was limited and war crimes (of which there were many, including many rapes) were left unpunished. In both Scotland and Ireland, Charles II did very little and even less in Atlantic America. His reign was significant in continuing the Commonwealth's policy of populating the colonies with African slaves and British criminals. It is during Charles II's reign that plantation slavery became truly established in British America, not least in Jamaica, the Commonwealth's sole Caribbean conquest, which he encouraged to be developed by both planters and pirates.

His rule was always precarious, however. Charles II never forgot the desperate days of his exile and, unlike his father and brother, was unwilling to test the patience of Parliament too unnecessarily. The 1660s saw his monarchy under threat. In 1661–62, deaths rose, and marriages and baptisms fell under the stress of a poor harvest; plague tested London in 1665, where perhaps a quarter of the population died; the Great Fire of London destroyed much of the capital's historic buildings in 1666; and in 1667, the Dutch, upon whom Charles II had rashly declared war, sailed up the Thames, nearly to London itself.

His major crisis came between 1679 and 1681 in the Exclusion Crisis when part of England's political elite tried repeatedly to persuade Parliament to exclude from the succession Charles II's brother and heir James, an open and devout Catholic) because James was suspected of wanting to turn England into an absolute monarchy like France. Yet despite three general elections in two years (still unmatched in British history), Charles II triumphed over his enemies in the crisis, managing to avoid signing any Exclusion Bill and thus preserving the inheritance of his brother as a Catholic king of Britain. The episode soured Charles II permanently from Parliament, and between 1681 and his premature death in 1685, he ruled without Parliament. If he had lived longer or had had a legitimate heir to go with his brood of illegitimate children, who have filled the ranks of the upper aristocracy ever since, then his attempt to pretend that the Civil Wars had not happened and that English demands for liberty could be ignored may have succeeded.

Indeed, Tim Harris concludes that Charles II was not just a bad man of tyrannical habits but also a very successful ruler. He survived the Exclusion Crisis and rebuilt the authority and prestige of the Crown, so much so that in the final four years of his reign, England appeared to be moving towards a style of monarchical absolutism like that which had developed on the continent, especially in France. He had consolidated royal authority over Scotland, while Ireland was more peaceful, prosperous and stable than ever before under English rule. Indeed, Harris argues, 'such was the nature of royal recovery, that when James II came to the throne, in 1685, he enjoyed the strongest position of any monarch, certainly since the accession of the Stuarts in 1603 and arguably since the accession of Henry VIII.'[12]

Charles II had restored not just the monarchy as a physical reality but had also done a brilliant job in rallying public opinion behind that monarchy and against its parliamentary Whig opposition. Royal recovery in the early 1680s was tied up with the Crown's ability to win back public opinion, which had been largely lost during the 1670s, when too many people became alienated from Charles II's overly authoritarian regime. The period was one of dramatic expansion in the printed press, with wide circulation and an even wider ability to provoke political controversy in a society where in London – always a centre of what the government thought of as sedition – perhaps 80 per cent of the adult male population was literate and where everywhere all except most women and landless labourers had some attachment to literacy.

What is unclear is the extent to which the strengthening of the regime under Charles II was due to the monarch himself. Charles II does deserve some credit for managing a composite monarchy in difficult circumstances. Although most people in England, Wales and Scotland welcomed the Restoration in 1660, they wanted different and mutually incompatible things. In England, for example, the political nation was divided between those people who wanted the monarchy to be more accountable to Parliament (these people becoming Whigs) and others who thought that Parliament was abusing its powers (these people becoming Tories). In Scotland, conflict between Presbyterians and Episcopalians raged without cease, and Catholics in Ireland found little ground with Protestants of any denomination. What was important was that Charles II never lost control of the situation, as his father had done and as his brother was to do. He retained his freedom to determine when and for how long Parliament should sit and what it should talk about. He used his prerogative to prorogue and dissolve Parliament when he felt that Whigs were challenging him again.

But the relative peace of the 1660–85 period was not entirely due to Charles II's skills in keeping the monarchy in control. The Scots were less united in 1679 than in 1637 and so could not mount the significant challenge to the Stuart regime as they had done forty-two years earlier. And the Irish never rebelled in 1679 as they had done in 1641. Public opinion was favourable to Charles II and was crucial to the maintenance of his power. The key to this powerful public support was the rise of Tories as a distinct faction within British politics. Tories felt that the greatest threat to English liberties and the Protestant religion was not the monarch and the hint of absolutism in Charles II's position (an absolutism they did not entirely object to, in any case, believing resistance to legitimate authority unlawful and, more important, that confronting a monarch would only restart conflict that might lead again to the horrors of death, destruction and republicanism that they saw as the legacy of the Civil Wars). They feared Charles II's opponents more than Charles II, hating what they saw as an unreasonable and intransigent Whig grouping and their non-conformist allies, whose motivations they thought were self-interested and corrupt, in both the older and newer understandings of the word. To prevent turmoil such as in the 1640s and 1650s re-emerging, Tory supporters of Charles II believed it imperative to stick to the existing church–state arrangement, as by law established.

Where Charles II showed brilliance was in understanding that the composite monarchy problem could be used to his advantage. He self-consciously, Tim Harris suggests, 'developed a British solution to defeat the challenge posed by the Whigs in England.'[13] Charles II, in short, did exactly the opposite to what Charles I did, which was to let problems in one kingdom exacerbate tensions in the other kingdoms. When things went wrong in England, Charles II turned to affairs in Scotland, as in 1681, when in the heights of the turmoil that was the Exclusion Crisis, he got the Scottish Parliament to affirm that Parliament could not exclude the heir to the throne in Scotland. That achievement blunted efforts in England to pass an exclusion bill because to do so would heighten the likelihood of a new three-kingdom civil war.

Charles II's success was deeply ironic insofar as what he did best was to mobilise public opinion to his side – a mobilisation that was very important because if the masses showed genuine disaffection with a regime's policies, then Britain became impossible to rule, as James VII and II was to discover. The irony was that Charles II was far from being a monarch who encouraged a flourishing of the public sphere and the debates that took place in it. He did his best to shut down debate when it occurred by using laws of seditious libel against Whig polemicists, by using the authority of Oxford to censure certain offensive doctrines, by using laws against non-conformity to silence preachers and by filling up Anglican churches with loyal government men. He would even issue orders to stop bonfires – immensely popular but dangerous occasions where people gathered – on Whig anniversaries in the name of preserving public order. As Harris wryly concludes, we see 'a government which realised it had been unable to contain the public sphere, which recognised that it temporarily needed to engage with it, at which, having successfully done so, then sought to control it again.'[14] Harris warns us against the traditional view of Charles II as the 'merry monarch' with loose sexual mores, who turned the country from austere Puritanism to a place of fun once again, with Christmas celebrated and Restoration rakes writing some decent poetry and great theatre. The biographer of Charles II calls him 'the most savage persecutor' in English history, throwing thousands of English non-conformists out of their jobs into prison – this was the time in which John Bunyan's *Pilgrim Progress* (1678) was written to immediate acclaim and which was composed when Bunyan was imprisoned for twelve years for his dissenting beliefs. His theme of Christian tribulations in a time of persecution struck a chord for radical Protestants suffering under Charles II. Historians no longer describe this period as essentially peaceful until James VII and II disturbed good order through his foolishness.

Charles II and his supporters saw themselves in what in modern parlance we would describe as a 'war against terror,' beset on all sides by enemies of the established order in church and state. They looked backwards to the 1640s and 1650s and feared a repeat of what they had convinced themselves were assaults by a small minority against an oppressed majority. Like everyone that makes such an argument about 'silent' and patriotic majorities harassed by unrepresentative minorities, the truth was very different. Britain and Ireland in the 1670s and 1680s were bitterly divided places, where political and religious tensions were deep and hard to resolve. If Charles II had devised a workable system of control by his death in 1685 that did not mean that he had created a happy realm under his merry rule. Four years after he died, the problems his strong rule had covered up re-emerged in a Glorious Revolution, which was much more divisive and bloodier then depicted in the past. It may have been 'glorious,' but it was not peaceful.

The Glorious Revolution and its interpretation

In four short years after his election in 1685, the seemingly impenetrable position of James VII and II disintegrated. James VII and II quickly overcame an attempted coup by the eldest illegitimate son of Charles II, the Duke of Monmouth. James VII and II was vengeful against these 'traitors.' At a battle in the south-west, James VII and II's troops captured 1,300 men of a force of 7,500, butchered some immediately, executed another 300 (including the duke) and sentenced 850 men to paid servitude in the Americas.

James VII and II was encouraged by his success against Monmouth and by the loyalty of the population to him to continue his brother's decision to reduce the size of the electorate to the English House of Commons to create a more pliable assembly. He also revoked charters of boroughs before reissuing them so that he had more control over them. His main ambition was religious, repealing legislation in England called the Test Acts that confined all government posts to members of the Church of England. He dismissed anyone who refused to agree to his policies of repeal and replaced them with those who were more compliant, often either Catholics or dissenters. It led to many prominent men losing offices they and their families had possessed for generations. Sir John Plumb notes that 'not since the Norman Conquest had the crown developed so sustained an attack on the established political power of the aristocracy and major gentry.'[15]

James VII and II went further on the attack against the established church in April 1688, when he used his prerogative powers to issue a 'Declaration of Indulgence,' where he recommended toleration of religion and required all Anglican clergy to read out his declaration from his pulpit on two successive Sundays. Seven bishops revolted, and James VII and II responded by charging them with 'seditious laws.' It was a disastrous mistake on James VII and II's part as it led to a public trial and discussions of to what extent people could refuse to obey a king on grounds of religious conscience. A judge made the stakes clear:

> I can see no difference, nor know of one in law, between the king's power to dispense with laws ecclesiastical and his power to dispense with any laws whatsoever. If this be once allowed of, there will need no Parliament; all the legislative will be in the King.

Not surprisingly, the judges declared the bishops 'not guilty' on 10 July 1688.

Meanwhile, a more consequential crisis had emerged. In June 1688, Mary of Modena, James VII and II's wife, gave birth to James Stuart, Prince of Wales and heir to the three thrones of England/Wales, Scotland and Ireland. This baby would be raised a Catholic, and everyone knew that this meant that he could continue James VII and II's policy of toleration to Catholics and possibly turn Britain into a Catholic nation. Given that James Stuart, the Old Pretender, did not die until 1766 and his second son lived until 1807, the risks of the Reformation being overturned were very real. Generally, a nation followed the faith of its ruler, which is why when Henri IV became king of France in 1594, he gave up his Protestant faith to take up the Catholic faith of his country people. As the later Jacobite *Life of James II* put it, 'the birth of the Prince gave the greatest joy to the King and Queen, and all those who wished them well' while it 'gave the greatest agonys imaginable to the generality of the Kingdom.'

Twenty days after the birth of the Prince of Wales and one day after the case against the seven bishops had been dismissed, seven highly placed people from the upper reaches of Whig aristocracy, the army, navy and the church, wrote a letter to William of Orange, inviting him to invade. As Tim Harris notes, 'it was an incredible letter – an invitation from a foreign power from high-ranking and religious figures to invade their own country' and led to

> an incredible series of events, which would result in what has become to be known to English history not as 'the Dutch Conquest' but 'the Glorious Revolution' – a revolution seen as glorious, that is, because it rescued England from a popish despot and secured Protestant liberties through a Declaration of Rights.[16]

The Glorious Revolution used to be thought of as a largely bloodless coup, based on events in England alone. That characterisation was not correct, because in both Scotland and, especially, Ireland, the revolution was very violent. William III's army was large and professional. He took over England with relative ease. His fleet arrived in Devon on 5 November, under what was later termed 'the Protestant wind.' William III subdued the west quickly, as few people flocked to James VII and II's standard, and by 18 December 1688, he was in London and effectively in control of the government. By 13 February 1689, James VII and II had fled England, and William became William III and his wife, James's daughter, became Mary II. It was a regime change that was achieved in England with remarkably little bloodshed. William III's role was crucial. Jonathan Israel concludes that it was William alone who 'shattered James' power and destroyed his previously considerable might.'[17] Thus, as Jeremy Black argues, 'James's fall occurred as the result of an external invasion of England';[18] it should be seen not as being caused by domestic issues but 'as an instance of what had last been seriously attempted a century earlier,' by the Spanish Armada of 1588. In short, this interpretation suggests that the Glorious Revolution was an example of an invasion rather than a rebellion, the most significant example of the wider world having an impact on Britain in our period, rather than the other way around.

The immediate results of the Glorious Revolution were far-reaching. William and Mary rewarded Parliament and the Whigs for their audacity in inviting William III to Britain. The Mutiny Act left the Crown in charge of armed forces but only for six months, after which it would need to convene Parliament to have this act renewed. A Toleration Act was passed, which abolished the rights of bishops and the courts to enforce conformity and left religious matters in the hands of Parliament. Most important, Parliament insisted that it was Parliament, not the Crown, that could levy customs and excise. Parliament agreed to a bargain, granting the king a substantial civil list but keeping the power over money distribution firmly to itself. The reduction of Parliament from 1660 was now reversed and, so far, permanently.

For later commentators, the result was almost miraculous. Edmund Burke, in 1791, as a new revolution started in France, saw the Glorious Revolution as a pre-emptive counter-revolution, solving contentious issues in the country before unhappiness with James VII and II would have led to a real revolution: 'what we did then was in truth and substance, and in a conditional light, a revolution not made but prevented.' For Thomas Babington Macaulay, the great Whig historian, working in the climactic year of 1848 and among many revolutionary convulsions in Europe, the Glorious Revolution was so soberly done as not to merit 'the terrible name of Revolution.' But, he continued, the Glorious Revolution 'of all revolutions, the least violent' had been 'of all revolutions the most beneficent' because it brought to an end a century of inadequate monarchs without money and always given bad advice, had furnished a long period of unresolvable clashes between Parliament and the Crown and had stopped the monarchy being seen as a source of evil. Instead, Macaulay argued, the Glorious Revolution ushered in a state dedicated to the vigorous promotion of commerce, broad religious tolerance, free competition among political interests and an institutional framework of beneficial regulations which all together formed the bedrock for the formation of liberal democracy. For Macaulay, the Glorious

Revolution was Britain's '*last* revolution,' as it led to the modern state.[19] For Macaulay, the Revolution was Glorious because it was bloodless, consensual, aristocratic, sensible and non-transformative – an unrevolutionary revolution, in short, that kept Britain Protestant and showed, moreover, that Britain was an exceptional nation, committed to political liberty but so moderate that the excesses of political conflict that were common on continental Europe – which veered in this view between anarchy and absolutism – were absent. Of course, he dealt only with England: the Revolution Settlement in Scotland and Ireland involved great violence and much material suffering.

Steven Pincus, in the most radical recent retelling of the meaning of the Glorious Revolution (which he does not term *Glorious* but 'the first modern revolution') argues that Macaulay's Whiggish interpretation has shaped scholarship until very recently, with scholars seeing the revolution both as restorative, rather than innovative, and not as a break in British history as much as part of a long period in continuity in British politics. The Glorious Revolution was glorious because it was mostly conservative. As Jonathan Scott opines, 'the Revolution was a "glorious revolution" – in the seventeenth-century sense of that word – because at last it restored and secured, after a century of troubles, what remained salvageable of the Elizabethan church and state.'[20]

Pincus has advanced a dramatically new interpretation of the Glorious Revolution. For him, Macaulay's neglect of social history, because for Macaulay and later historians, the period was not one of rapid social change, was wrong. Pincus sees late seventeenth-century England as a society on the cusp of radical social and economic change, some of which are canvassed in later chapters in this book on war and society, gender and the Industrial Revolution. He sees England as the first modern society, with a booming economy, flourishing overseas trade, and increasing urbanisation, especially in London, whose growth made it world-historically exceptional. What James VII and II was doing, he argues, was acknowledging this modernisation by creating a centralising, bureaucratic state, professional standing army, a world-class navy, absolute sovereignty like what Louis XIV was doing in France and a move away from a confessional Protestant state to one where toleration of religion was automatic and subsidiary to considerations of commerce and governance. James VII and II was not a fool but a reformer, whose reforms were too much for contemporaries, who had to use violence against him. Pincus argues that

> it was precisely because James VII and II had been able to create such a powerful state that many of James's opponents realised that it could only be resisted with violence and that only a revolutionary transformation could prevent a future English monarch from re-creating his modern absolutist state.[21]

Thus, the Glorious Revolution, in Pincus's view, created a new kind of English state after 1680, one that was not absolutist as in France but which was still very strong and designed to help England (and then Britain) transition from an agrarian into a manufacturing society and into a state capable of fighting great wars without bankrupting itself. Perhaps reacting against an American scholarship from the 1960s and 1970s which saw the British imperial state as weak and ineffective in governing its worldwide empire, Pincus sees the development of a powerful liberal state coming out of revolutionary transformations in England as the first modern society. The philosopher John Locke was the avatar of this modern, liberal and activist state, as seen in his theoretical arguments in *The Two Treatises*.

A modern revolution and the making of Britain in 1707

Like all powerful reinterpretations of a familiar event, Pincus's new view on the Glorious Revolution has provoked as much opposition as agreement. Some critics object to the method of argumentation Pincus adopts, which is that if the historians he opposes see the Glorious Revolution as conservative and non-violence then he must take the other extreme, that it was radical and violent. The starkness in having one side being modernisers who wanted to see England become a centralised bureaucratic state on the French model and the other wanting England to become a Dutch replica, as a vibrant commercial society based on toleration and strong representative government seems to other critics as lacking nuance. It joins everyone, so the argument against Pincus goes, into a rigid schema whereby modernisation explains everything. Pincus downplays religion as a motivating cause, which is rather strange, given the explicit comments from contemporaries, many of whom would not have seen themselves as modernisers, that anti-Catholicism and confessional motivations were important in shaping opposition to the Catholic and pro-Toleration James VII and II, And Pincus struggles to find the smoking gun that suggests that James VII and II or his advisors had a pre-prepared Gallic blueprint for a new kind of English state. He also must inflate the number of deaths in the conflict by including deaths in wars that followed the Glorious Revolution. That 1688 was more violent than often depicted in older literature does not mean that it was comparatively violent in a Europe in which great episodes of violence were frequent. In short, critics argue that Pincus's view of 1688 as a battle between Francophobes and Francophiles is reductive when most evidence suggests that people were less interested in France than in what was happening around them, in Britain.

Where Pincus's account is most helpful is in how he shows that the revolution of 1688, while connected inherently to the British Civil Wars in conception, pointed to a different kind of politics in its resulting implications. That kind of politics was one that looked forward to the eighteenth-century world of interests, in which political economy was very prominent. He shows that the Glorious Revolution was important and that it was more than just the last invasion of England or a shabby coup d'etat. Real concerns were at stake in a highly politicised and partisan state. Moreover, he helps move us away from a revisionist historiography in which a concentration on motives alone has made it impossible to identify a common set of motivations for any significant group.

This approach makes it hard to allow any event to have causation outside the complicated and confused set of motives that individuals agonised over.

Not surprisingly, this has led to accounts that over-emphasise the stubbornness of Charles I as a cause of the Civil Wars and the lack of intelligence and political understanding of James VII and II. Both Catherine Sedley and his cynical brother, Charles II, attributed James VII and II's problems to his intellectual shortcomings and his stubborn attachment to the Catholic faith. Insisting on being a Catholic in late seventeenth-century Protestant England and Scotland was akin to a member of the royal family in the 1950s adopting communism, or, as was a bit more likely given the history of Edward VIII, fascism. Sedley quipped of James's mistresses. 'We are none of us handsome, and if we had wit, he has not enough to discover it.' Charles II predicted what would happen to his brother: 'my brother will lose his kingdom by his bigotry and his soul for a lot of ugly trollops.'

Certainly, anti-Catholicism is as potent an explanation for the Glorious Revolution as contests over modernisation, an anti-Catholicism provoked almost unnecessarily by a foolish king. A thought experiment in imagining James VII and II as Protestant rather than Catholic suggests that no matter how unhappy his subjects were with him, he would have survived. Most Protestants seem to have viewed James VII and II as a threat to national security, though this happened very late into his reign, around mid-November 1688, after William III had landed. William III did not get the support he wanted until James VII and II had shown himself to be an incapable leader in battle, breaking down unmanfully and experiencing massive nosebleeds brought on, it appears, by nervous tension. His natural supporters, the landed gentry and the Anglican clergy, found that they had pressing matters elsewhere when called on to show their loyalty to him. He chief soldiers, Henry Fitzroy, Duke of Grafton, and John Churchill, made Earl and later Duke of Marlborough by William III as a reward for his treachery, deserted James VII and II only three days after James had joined his army in Salisbury.

The English, whatever their view on the legitimacy of overthrowing a monarch, had certain views on what an English monarch ought to be – he had to be Protestant, employ the prerogative sparingly, and govern through Parliament. There was, by 1689, and because of 1649 and Charles I's execution, a recognition that monarchical power was fundamentally consensual at its base. That James VII and II fled the country and his people rather than stayed and fought proved the prejudices of the population – his cowardice showed his evil nature and resulted from his aggressive Catholicism. What James VII and II did, or more precisely failed to do, was what one would expect from a Catholic. For just about every Protestant in the late seventeenth century, Catholicism was the handmaiden of arbitrary government, and a Catholic ruler would, in his commitment to 'popery,' reduce the nation to 'slavery.' To prevent such tyranny, revolution was acceptable and the rule of Parliament through an idealised 'ancient constitution' was to most a miraculous result – hence a revolt or invasion being termed 'Glorious.' The main result of this miracle was that 'the subjects ought to be governed by laws enacted in parliament, and not by the mere pleasure of the king.'[22]

James VII and II's failure also shows, Tim Harris argues, how difficult it was to rule three kingdoms, when subjects refused to cooperate with what a king wanted. James VII and II was not a natural absolutist – he was forced into this position when people refused to comply or passively resisted the laws he insisted on being passed and obeyed. His regime was collapsing from within even before the birth of his Catholic son. The invasion followed an internal rebellion; it did not provoke it. James VII and II's failure also showed how bitter the divisions of the seventeenth century in Britain were and how the differences varied from kingdom to kingdom.

The results of the Glorious Revolution also have an important British dimension that led to the creation of a British nation after the Union of Scotland with England and Wales in 1707. England did not fall apart after 1689 (the opposite, in fact, occurred, even given the outbreak of war with France). Scotland, on the contrary, did fall apart. Its harvests failed every year between 1688 and 1698 in the worst decade of the Little Ice Age. The result was famine and population decline of 10 per cent overall in a decade and perhaps one-third in the Highlands. Its troubles were compounded by the disaster at Darien, covered elsewhere in this book. In addition, the accession of Anne in 1702 caused a further problem, as the English had manoeuvred this result without consulting Scotland. England has also included clauses in the Act of Settlement that showed that the Scots were bound by English dynastic solutions and that, therefore, the English Parliament could legislate for Scotland. Scotland was furious and passed a law that provided that the next Scottish monarch had to be different from that of England unless 'there be such conditions of Government settled and enacted as may secure the honour and sovereignty' of Scotland.

For the English, this attitude made them seek union between the two kingdoms, something they had been reluctant to do a century earlier. They forced through union in 1707, threatening Scots that if it did not happen, they would be treated as aliens in England and that they could not send goods southwards. They succeeded through these threats, adroit political management and the bribery of leading Scottish nobles to get their way. The Scottish Parliament agreed to a union on 16 January 1707 with England agreeing on 1 March 1707 and the union coming into force on 1 May 1707. Britain now existed. Protestants in England, Wales and Ireland welcomed it. Scots were less happy, especially Presbyterians, who feared an Episcopalian takeover now Scotland was allied to a powerful Anglican state where their enemies, the bishops, sat in the House of Lords. Subsequent events showed that this fear, at least, was not to be realised. Eventually, the Union proved to be very successful for Scotland – and for Britain.

Notes

1 Joan Thirsk, *Economic Policy and Projects: The Development of Consumer Society in Early Modern England* (Oxford: Clarendon Press, 1988), 106.

2 Carole Shammas, *The Pre-industrial Consumer in England and America* (Oxford: Clarendon Press, 1990), chapter 4.

3 Nuala Zahedieh, *The Capital and the Colonies: London and the Atlantic Economy 1660–1700* (Cambridge: Cambridge University Press, 2010), 58.

4 Nuala Zahedieh, 'Defying Mercantilism: Illicit Trade, Trust, and the Jamaican Sephardim, 1660–1730,' *Historical Journal* 61 (2018), 94–6, 101–2.

5 Nuala Zahedieh, 'Regulation, Rent-seeking, and the Glorious Revolution in the English Atlantic Economy,' *Economic History Review* 63 (2010), 890.

6 Ibid.

7 Nuala Zahedieh, 'Overseas Expansion and Trade,' in Nicholas Canny, ed., *The Oxford History of the British Empire: The Origins of Empire* (Oxford: Oxford University Press, 1988), 420.

8 Mark Knights, 'The Long-term Consequences of the English Revolution: State Formation, Political Culture, and Ideology,' in Michael J. Braddick, ed., *The Oxford Handbook of the English Revolution* (Oxford: Oxford University Press, 2015), 519.

9 Ibid., 521.

10 Robert Brenner, *Merchants and Revolution: Commercial Change, Political Conflict, and London's Overseas Traders, 1550–1653* (Cambridge: Cambridge University Press, 1993).

11 Steven Pincus, *1688: The First Modern Revolution* (New Haven: Yale University Press, 2009).

12 Tim Harris, *Restoration: Charles II and His Kingdoms 1660–1685* (London: Allen Lane, 2005), 7.

13 Ibid., 413.

14 Ibid., 419.

15 J.H. Plumb, *The Growth of Political Stability in England, 1675–1725* (London: Penguin, 1967), 60.

16 Tim Harris, *Revolution: The Great Crisis of the British Monarchy, 1685–1720* (London: Penguin, 2006), 3–4.

17 Jonathan Israel, *The Anglo-Dutch Moment: Essays on the Glorious Revolution and its World Impact* (Cambridge: Cambridge University Press, 1991), 5.

18 Jeremy Black, *A System of Ambition? British Foreign Policy 1660–1722* (Harlow: Longman, 1991), 135.

19 Cited in Geoffrey Parker, *Global Crisis; War, Climate Change & Catastrophe in the Seventeenth Century* New Haven: Yale University Press, 2013), 394–5.

20 Jonathan Scott, *Algernon Sidney and the Restoration Crisis, 1677–1683* (Cambridge: Cambridge University Press, 1991), 27.

21 Pincus, *1688*, 7.

22 Julian Hoppit, *A Land of Liberty? England 1689–1727* (Oxford: Oxford University Press, 2000), 50.

Bibliography

Armitage, David. 'Making the Empire British: Scotland in the Atlantic World,' *Past & Present* 155 (1997), 34–63.

Harris, Tim, *Restoration: Charles II and His Kingdoms 1660–1685* (London: Allen Lane, 2005).

Harris, Tim, *Revolution: The Great Crisis of the British Monarchy, 1685–1720* (London: Penguin, 2006).

Hoppit, Julian, *A Land of Liberty? England 1689–1727* (Oxford: Oxford University Press, 2000).

Pincus, Steven, *1688: The First Modern Revolution* (New Haven: Yale University Press, 2009).

Prest, Wilfrid, *Albion Ascendant: English History, 1660–1815* (Oxford: Oxford University Press, 1998).

Scott, Jonathan, *England's Troubles: Seventeenth-Century English Political Insecurity in European Context* (Cambridge: Cambridge University Press, 2000).

Stanwood, Owen, *The Empire Reformed: English America in the Age of the Glorious Revolution* (Philadelphia: University of Pennsylvania, 2011).

Wrightson, Keith, *Earthly Necessities: Economic Lives in Early Modern Britain, 1470–1750* (London, 2002).

Zahedieh, Nuala, *The Capital and the Colonies: London and the Atlantic Economy 1660–1700* (Cambridge: Cambridge University Press, 2010).

5   Ireland

Introduction

The accession of James VI of Scotland to the throne of England in 1603 also meant that he became king of Ireland. His accession followed by a few days the English victory over the native Irish of Ulster in the Nine Years' War (1594–1603), an event allowing England control for the first time over the whole island and signalling the final collapse of the old Gaelic order. James quickly consolidated his power over a diverse and not especially prosperous island. Most Irish were peasants living in small, clustered rural settlements, without much leadership possible from the great Gaelic families, such as the O'Neills, the Maccarthys and the O'Briens.

The island was a patchwork of competing religious and ethnic groups, each vying for political and economic power. Increasingly, the major divisions came over religion, with the native Irish and the Old English combining as Catholics against aggressively Protestant new elites, both English and Scottish. Historians do not see the outbreak of rebellion in 1641 as due to irreconcilable internal tensions – it was mostly connected to objections to Charles I's rule under Stafford and was, at least initially, localised and specific in nature. The internal tensions in Ireland, however, contributed to the extreme violence that occurred in 1641, violence that was not surprising in an island in a state of constant conflict for the previous hundred years. From the 1540s, indeed, government-sponsored slaughter was an endemic part of Ireland's colonial experience. The combination of heavy-handed military tactics combined with Catholic resentment meant it took little to spark a fire of dissent and rebellion in an explosive colony.

Ireland in the early seventeenth century

Ireland was thus a powder keg, even though it was relatively peaceful between 1603, when James VI and I became king and at the end of an especially brutal war that had extended the English state's power across the island, and 1641, and the start of a long, bloody, near-genocidal civil war. Ireland had a mix of three internally divided groups – the Gaelic Irish, the aboriginal inhabitants of the island who, alone in Britain, had developed outside of being incorporated into the Roman Empire. They were subjects of the English Crown from 1541, with their leaders having accepted English noble titles. They presided over a mass of peasants, oppressed by both their leaders and by the English, who derided them in explicitly racist terms as uncivilised barbarians. The experience of English conquest of the Gaelic Irish in the sixteenth century proved crucial in creating a colonial understanding of the 'other' which was extended in the late sixteenth and early seventeenth centuries across the Atlantic to English views about the capacities of Native Americans. What the English did and felt in sixteenth-century Ireland and their recent experience in putting down very violently a revolt begun in 1595 by the Gaelic lords of Ulster had massive long-term impacts on English colonisation, shaping the distinctive and bluntly ethnocentric English colonising ethos for the whole of its imperial history.

The second group were termed Old English, well-heeled (in the main) descendants of medieval settlers from England to Ireland. They were concentrated in some of Ireland's most profitable lands, owning perhaps one-third of good land in 1641, focused on Dublin and its surrounding counties (the Pale), with some settlement in Galway and Mayo. That region was the base of the most influential Old English leader, the Earl of Clanricard, a major power broker in Ireland under Charles I.

The third group were recent settlers from the sixteenth century onwards, the New English. These were colonial adventurers and risk-takers. For some, the risks paid off marvellously. Richard Boyle, the younger son of an obscure gentry family from Kent, went to Ireland in 1588 as a minor administrator. He plunged, not always legally, into the Irish land market and eventually became the Earl of Cork, Ireland's chief justice and probably Ireland's richest man. In Ulster, a similar tale is attached to the Devon migrant Arthur Chichester, who, by his death in 1625, had established a huge estate in Carrickfergus and Belfast. He served as Lord Deputy of Ireland from 1605 to 1616 and was ennobled as Lord Chichester.

Into this mix came in the early seventeenth century a radically new group, whose presence has proved enduringly important in keeping Ireland a divided and contentious island. Between 1603 and 1641, seventy thousand England and thirty thousand Scots moved to Ireland as ordinary settlers, seeking opportunities in its formal plantation schemes. There were major settlements of the English in Munster, in the south-west, and, most important, in the northern province of Ulster. In Ulster, forty thousand migrants had settled by 1641, two-thirds of whom were Presbyterian Scots. It is hardly a surprise that this unprecedented movement of Protestants into the most Gaelic and Catholic of Ireland's provinces proved combustible. It was not an accident that the revolt of 1641 started, as in 1595, among the Gaelic lords of Ulster, in a last-ditch effort to prevent the radical transformation of their region. To put the Ulster migration in perspective, it was the biggest migration of Britons outside of mainland

Britain anywhere in the Atlantic world, including the substantial migrations of population to Virginia and Barbados.

The Ulster plantation scheme is worth noting in detail not just because of its political importance in Irish history but also because of its ideological importance as the most significant example of how a certain conception of 'British colonisation' came into practice. Ulster was the primary area where the three peoples of the British Isles (excepting the Welsh who were relatively little involved in Ireland) cohabited uneasily together and where they clashed incessantly. The virtues of diversity, so endlessly trumpeted today as a fundamental human value, were not values that appealed to people in the seventeenth century: racial purity and ethnocentric localism were much more lauded as desirable attributes for any society. Yet the reality of the expansion of the British world in the seventeenth and eighteenth centuries was one where different cultures came up against each other and had to perforce manage to live with each other, even when each culture wanted to either keep to itself or else deal with another culture only in a superior and domineering position. James VI and I's plan was that Scots and English settlers should function as equal partners in a civilising and reforming endeavour, mixing together as tenants of landlords called 'undertakers' who had each been allocated relatively small (1,000–2,000 acres) properties, seized from vanquished Irish nobles. James VI and I also set aside acres to endow key 'civilising' institutions, such as the Protestant Church of Ireland and Trinity College, Dublin. In addition, he forced merchants in London to take on the entire costs of founding the town of Londonderry (local Irish call it Derry to this day) to bring capital and economic prosperity to a commercial backwater. It was, in part, wrangling over how this plantation should be run that directly contributed to the outbreak of rebellion in 1641.

As in Scotland, this 'civilising' mission had as many successes as failures. Irish chieftains quickly realised the reality on the ground – they needed to assimilate in everything except religion (usually a non-negotiable fact that proved impossible to compromise over, in ways everything else was capable of compromise) so that they could exploit the economic advantages for them of the adoption of the English system of landlord–tenant relations and of a commercial economy. Losses in autonomy as the English asserted ever greater control over Irish affairs were, to an extent, compensated by elite access to English ideas of agricultural improvement and to the customs of a bigger and more modern country. The Gaelic and Catholic earls of Antrim, for example, became 'improving' landlords in Ulster, boasting by the late 1630s that they had more than three hundred Protestant families living as tenants on their large estates. The second earl reported proudly in 1637, 'I have compounded my affairs here with my tenants wherein I was not so inward to my [own] profit as to the general good and settlement by binding them to plant [trees] and husband their holdings so near as may bee to the manner of England.'

Their actions show a truth about colonisation. Even small numbers of intruders into a traditional society can quickly initiate profound and systematic changes through the introduction of material goods and new cultural practices. This was true both in Ireland and in contact with Native Americans in North

America. These introductions caused intense competition among elite members in the societies being invaded to control and monopolise such goods and practices, damaging in the process the livelihoods and traditions of less favoured indigenous inhabitants. That process certainly happened in early seventeenth-century Ireland, where regional power brokers adopted English dress, spoke in English rather than Gaelic and built grand houses in the English manner. The earls of Clanricard, Kildare and Antrim, for example, all built great houses in an English style in this period to demonstrate their conversion both to 'Englishness' and to the 'civilising' colonising policies insistently foisted on Ireland by English imperialists. Colonisation was accompanied by consent as much as by coercion from strategic elites to the policies of colonisation. We need to note the extent to which certain Irish leaders welcomed, for their own reasons, aspects of colonisation at the same time as they resisted, often violently, those aspects of the colonisation process, such as the forced seizure of land, that they did not like. The result of these housebuilding activities, sadly, was the incurring of massive debts and dependence upon London moneylenders. By the late 1630s, the Earl of Antrim owed £42,000 to London merchants. He and other Catholic nobles soon found their power slipping away into financial dependence.

Adaptation to Ireland happened on all sides, with Scottish settlers in Ulster becoming frontiersmen, having to navigate between their richer and more powerful English planter neighbours and their impoverished Gaelic Irish sub-tenants. They could not forge an exclusively Scottish world in Ireland, try as much as they wanted. What the Ulster experience in the first half of the seventeenth century showed was that the Scots and English were not, as James VI and I had intended, equals, as the English retained most of the power in the island, leading to considerable tensions, especially in Ulster. The English were powerful in Ulster but not always happy. London merchants found that the money they expended on developing towns in the province and in recruiting settlers to go there was the single most expensive contribution made by the City of London to British imperialism. The returns, however, were disappointing, which may be one reason why many established London merchants did not invest in transoceanic colonial commerce and preferred to stick to investment in the Levant and in Asia. At the same time, colonisation in Ireland was an activity that was almost entirely English in planning and financing, even though it had a government in London which was self-consciously British. Moreover, Scottish involvement in Ulster took up Scottish colonisation efforts in the seventeenth century to such an extent that they were seldom otherwise involved with Atlantic, Asian or African ventures until well after 1707. The Irish were even less involved in empire, with the only significant Irish involvement in overseas colonisation being their migration to the tiny Caribbean island of Montserrat.

Ireland and the Civil War

There is still resistance to considering Ireland as significant within the English Civil Wars, or, more precisely, in seeing its role as determinative in that conflict rather than just a component and mostly separate part of a largely English event. For Blair Worden for example, the term *British Civil Wars* seems mostly a reaction to Anglo-centricity, less than a better way to see these conflicts in larger contexts. He argues that replacing the term *the English Civil War* with the more all-encompassing term *British Civil Wars* risks exaggerating 'the extent to which English events interacted with events elsewhere' and 'can obscure the distinctiveness of each of the three conflicts.' Indeed, he asserts, 'the Irish and Scottish Wars broke less constitutional or ideological ground than England.'[1]

Nevertheless, as Worden admits, the crisis of 1640–42 in the three kingdoms ruled (badly) by Charles I was a British crisis, as the authority of Charles II in 1640 was tested by, first, events in Scotland and, then, war in Ireland. If we look at these events from the perspective of Ireland, then it was England and to a lesser extent Scotland that were the predatory powers, posing an existential threat to Irish autonomy and well-being through their actions in the early seventeenth century. But Ireland was also a threat to England, if only because it promised to explode into violence at any time. It was the most contentious part of the British Empire – the closest place to England, apart from Scotland and Wales; the most obviously contentious; and the place that could always host a rebellion that European powers might take advantage of to challenge Britain within its own heartland. It is for this reason that Ireland deserves a chapter of its own in this book, alone of any of Britain's possessions in the Atlantic world. Because it was so close to England, Ireland needed, English rulers believed, closer management and more vigorous treatment than anywhere else. And Ireland posed a special threat to English self-conceptions of themselves as a peaceful, although conquering, nation insofar as the Reformation was especially incomplete on the island, making claims that Britain was Protestant always illusory, if Ireland was part of the British mix. England tried to change Ireland through the grand social and economic policy of establishing plantations in Ulster, but that policy was a mixed success.

The use of the word *plantation* to describe colonisation efforts in Ireland is interesting in two ways. First, it was an attempt to soften linguistically what the English government was trying to do in Ireland, which was to conquer it and colonise it according to practices within Europe with great historical precedents, not just from medieval times with the Anglo-Normans in Ireland and Wales but also from the precedent of ancient Romans, who adopted colonisation as a means of spreading their authority and their notions of civility throughout much of Europe, including England. The Roman precedent meant that *colony* always was a word with a sharp edge. *Plantation* was a gentler word, with horticultural associations that John Milton later associated in the 1650s with God, whom he described as 'the sovereign Planter' who had 'framed all things to man's delightful use.' Second, the word *plantation* proved to be applicable to other kinds of colonisation rather than that specifically designed for the Irish. The English used the word *plantation* to describe the social and economic character of their settlements in America and the West Indies and even used the word *plantation* as part of its major seventeenth-century institution controlling colonial policy, the Council of Trade and Plantations, created in 1660. To 'plant' was something different than to conquer or to colonise. It implied a real commitment to settlement by people of British descent in new places – to 'plant' meant to 'put down roots' and to agree to transform the landscape in which 'planting' was taken place so that civil society and improved agriculture could lead to the Anglicisation of foreign places. That 'planting' was done by 'settlers' was ideologically crucial in determining that English colonisation in places such as Ireland and North America was conceptually different from what was done in Africa or Asia, where little effort was ever made to trying to transform people or landscape. What made Ireland especially interesting as a colonisation project was not that it involved Europeans colonising other Europeans – that was common throughout Europe since the days of Rome and, as in Spain, with the fifteenth-century *Reconquista* provided models for colonisation in the Americas. Its distinctiveness is that the English never pretended, as they did to justify their colonisation efforts in the Americas from the seventeenth century and in Australia from 1788, that the land they were colonising in Ireland was somehow uninhabited and the land uncultivated (terra nullius). That myth was never possible in a land where the native Irish population could not be dispersed out of sight and thus out of mind. The English tried to displace the Native Irish as much as they could, moving them into the west of the island, but the numbers of Gaels was, from the start of colonisation in the sixteenth century, always far too large to adopt any strategy of terra nullius.

The heavy-handedness of this unusual social experimentation in colonial transformation in seventeenth-century Ireland was matched under the rule of Charles I by draconian and incompetent government. Unlike England, the 1630s saw government intervention peak in Ireland. It did so under the rule of Thomas Wentworth, Earl of Strafford, who was Charles I's minister in Ireland from 1633. He adopted brisk methods to reconstruct royal authority and break its critics. He achieved in some ways his aim, as in the 1630s Crown power was strengthened and revenues increased. But in the process, he alienated every section of Irish society, Protestant and Catholic.

Ironically, it was not his rule but his fall that made tensions in Ireland boil over. Stafford was executed in May 1641, after a highly political trial for treason, where he was abandoned by his master to satisfy parliamentary bloodlust. Strafford was accused by Parliament of both supporting the hated Archbishop Laud and in promoting Arminianism (which many Protestants thought both crypto-Catholic and perilously close to European-style absolutism) and of promoting a trend to autocracy throughout Britain. His fall led to the Catholic realisation that the Crown was enabling the entrenched forms of Protestantism in Ulster and elsewhere to become a dominant force in the island. It encouraged Catholic leaders to take their chances in a Catholic rebellion. They understood that Parliament was becoming increasingly anti-Catholic and wanted to take pre-emptive actions to stop this development. Irish Catholics leaders were aristocrats mostly loyal to the Crown but who hoped to increase their own influence in it and were anxious that their long-held fear that an assertive English Protestant desire to drive Catholics out of Ireland was about to be realised. They took advantage of the weakening of the government's authority in Dublin to stage a pre-emptive uprising.

It went badly wrong. The Catholic leaders' desire for a small concentrated rebellion soon failed in the light of massive popular Catholic support for widespread revolt, intended to end English rule over the island. The result was catastrophic for Ireland's future. Religious and economic distress from Catholics dispossessed of their land allied with violent repression of the rising from Dublin led to the killing of at least two thousand Protestants, and perhaps to as many as one in five of the Ulster Protestant population (propaganda makes establishing firm numbers impossible). These deaths were covered extensively in English propaganda of the period, with Catholic butcheries of innocent Protestants being a principal theme and one that shocked an easily alarmed Protestant population in England and Scotland. The undoubted excesses of the 1641 uprising were massively and luridly exaggerated in accounts brought by refugees and spread in print, souring relations between England and Ireland for a generation.

During the first Civil War, however, Ireland's wars were not especially brutal. The butchery of the first few months of the rebellion in 1641 subsided as conflict operated more or less under established principles of war. Increasing moderation on the battlefield gave a space for negotiation, which proceeded in fits and starts until 1644. England re-entered the war in that year and returned the brutality of 1641 with interest. Throughout the 1640s, a significant proportion of the documented massacres in the English Civil War had a direct or indirect Irish connection, The English tended to view the Irish in highly negative terms and as deserving bad treatment more than was allowable for English opponents. In December 1645, for example, the Scottish Parliament ordered that Irish prisoners 'be executed without any further assize or process,' as granting such prisoners quarter was considered under Protestant doctrine to be a sin.

One Englishman hangs hugely over the history of Ireland as the most polarising person in its history. Oliver Cromwell, who was voted in by Britons in 2000 as one of the greatest Britons of the millennium, is uniquely reviled in Ireland as the worst Englishman to come to that island. That accolade comes among heavy competition from villains such as Sir Humphrey Gilbert in the 1570s, Sir Robert Peel of Great Famine infamy in the 1840s and David Lloyd George and Winston Churchill in the 1910s and 1920s. It has to be placed, moreover, within a story of Anglo-Irish relations in the sixteenth and seventeenth centuries that is a near-relentless tale of bloody tragic episodes, ending in the nearly permanent disenfranchisement and impoverishment of the native Irish within their own land by a colonial power with greater resources than were available to the Gaels and who were determined to impose their colonialist will on a people they thought barbaric and uncivilised. But Cromwell, even though he spent just nine months of his full life in Ireland, is seen there as a pre-eminent war criminal. When the Irish Taoiseach, Bertie Ahern, himself not of blameless character, visited the British Houses of Parliament in 1997 and saw a painting of Cromwell hung prominently in the office of the foreign secretary, Robin Cook, he walked out, refusing to return until the picture 'of that murdering bastard' was removed.

What did Cromwell do to provoke this everlasting ire? He came to Ireland in late July 1649. His words on arrival set the tone for what was to follow at Drogheda and Wexford. He promised rewards for all those carrying on 'that great work against the barbarous and bloodthirsty Irish,' inflammatory words encouraging Protestant brutality as revenge. for Catholic atrocities committed against Protestants in 1641–42. The storming of Drogheda on 11 September and Wexford on 11 October 1649 established Cromwell's reputation for cruelty and savagery, a reputation, as we have seen, which persists. Much remains unclear about what exactly happened at these sieges but even Cromwell recognised that dreadful things happened at both places, stating that the scale of the slaughter could not 'but work remorse and regret.' It was an unprecedented amount of killing for no reason other than revenge. Cromwell's message was that his opponents could expect little mercy in what amounted to a war of extermination. Cromwell justified what had happened in religious terms, the massacres being 'the righteous judgement of God upon these barbarous wretches, who have imbrued their hands in so much innocent blood.'

The war in Ireland continued until 1653. The leader of the rebels from 1641, Sir Phelim O'Neill, was executed on 10 March 1653, and the war ended on 27 April 1653 with the surrender of Irish forces at Cloughoughter, Co. Cavan. It was a devastating war, a 'demographic catastrophe,' in which about

Figure 5.1 Cromwell taking Drogheda by Storm

Source: Chronicle/Alamy Stock Photo.

20 per cent of the population died from deaths in battle and from disease. The countryside was ravaged by the systematic destruction of its agricultural system, leading to famine and misery. As Micheál ó Siochrú argues, by 1653 'defeated, exhausted and defenceless, the Catholic Irish faced an uncertain future at the hands of an unforgiving and rapacious parliamentary regime.'[2]

Irish fates had been decided earlier, in the Act of Settlement, passed in August 1652. It condemned all Catholic landowners in full or partial confiscation of the estates, while the execution of hundreds of rebel leaders, mostly ordinary people, took place. As many as forty thousand Catholics sailed for the continent, to escape persecution and punishment. The Catholic clergy were completely emasculated and rendered unable to provide much service except clandestinely to its Catholic congregation. Thousands of Catholic rebels were sent as indentured servants to Barbados, where most perished from tropical disease and over-work. Within Ireland, Catholic landowners were transported to the Gaelic west of Ireland and their lands elsewhere were distributed among English and Scottish settlers in the Cromwellian Settlement.

Matters did not really look up with the Restoration, as Charles II in his 'Gracious Declaration of November 1660' accepted 1659, not 1641, as the benchmark for all future land claims. Thus, the Cromwellian land settlement was confirmed, and Irish Catholic hopes that their estates would be returned to them were dashed. The impoverishment and discrimination against Catholics were enshrined in parliamentary legislation resulting from Cromwell's invasion. An embittered cleric reflected how all the 'towns, cities, free towns, and market towns in which the Catholic faith had sat as if on a royal throne, became sewers, sinks and dung pits of English heresies.' The appropriation of Catholic lands was the single largest shift in landownership anywhere in the early modern period and was Cromwell's lasting legacy in Ireland. A lethal combination of racial superiority and racial bigotry had led to catastrophic loss of life, the destruction of much of Irish infrastructure and economy, and the permanent creation of a Catholic underclass and a dominant Protestant minority, who would rule Ireland unchallenged, even after Catholic political emancipation and land reforms in the nineteenth century.

Ireland after Cromwell

Disillusionment with profits from Irish colonisation, continuing worries over the threats to security that Protestant settlers faced from hostile and 'barbaric' Irish Catholics, and better opportunities elsewhere meant that Commonwealth plans for a new plantation scheme, bringing thirty-six thousand settlers to Ulster and to midland counties never achieved their purpose. The idea was that Irish lands would be used to pay off an English army, thus presumably solving several government problems all at once. It was a policy adopted by Britain throughout the seventeenth and eighteenth centuries, working especially well in British North America after the Seven Years' War, when Highland troops received confiscated Native American lands in places such as the colony of New York.

De-mobbed English soldiers from Cromwell's army, however, tended to return to England, where in better economic conditions in the 1650s and 1660s, their skills gave them access to good jobs. Many soldiers also had experienced the horror of the Irish Civil War when they been taught to fear and despise Irish Gaels. It was hard to persuade such soldiers to settle among a people they hated. Thus, the confiscation of Gaelic land in the 1650s did not lead to the hoped-for results. Irish land had lost most of its charm by then and propaganda about seemingly paradisiacal plenty failed to match a reality of a place that was wet, poor, inaccessible and full of enemies. Careful investigation of who gained what in the Cromwellian settlement in the three west Ulster counties of Donegal, Londonderry (Derry) and Tyrone shows that 91 per cent of the land intended for new settlers fell to those already settled before 1641. Even those who succeeded in Ireland, such as the bureaucrat, political economist and land speculator William Petty, complained that '[o]ur estates here are mere visions and delusions and require more attendance than a retail shop.' The one modest success was urban settlement. By the 1670s, Petty guessed, 20 per cent of Ireland's population lived in towns, but in these towns, most obviously in Dublin, Protestants were numerous. Over half the island's Protestant population were urban-dwelling.

Nevertheless, while the English and Scottish settlement of the first half of the seventeenth century may have been disappointing, it led to a large increase in the Protestant population of Ireland, almost all of which occurred through natural increase rather than immigration. By 1687, Protestants accounted for 20 to 25 per cent of Ireland's growing population of nearly 2 million people. The English gave up migrating to Ireland from the 1650s but that was not the case for Scotland. Ulster continued to draw Scots and some northern English until the early eighteenth century, when migration turned towards North America. By 1733, Ulster had 62,624 Protestant families, and probably 300,000 Protestant people, which was 60 per cent of the Protestants of Ireland, a remarkable increase since 1630. That province was thus the Protestant redoubt in Ireland, as it remains.

Meanwhile, the Gaelic Irish suffered. William Petty, in 1672, described their standard of living as follows: 'six out of eight of all the Irish live in a brutish, nasty condition, in cabins with neither chimney, door, stairs or window.' They sustained themselves on a monotonous diet of milk and potatoes, with oats and barley eaten as cakes, rather than as bread. Their poor standard of living made them always vulnerable to famine when there was bad weather or poor harvests, as in 1673–74. Real hardship hit the Irish much later. The famine in 1728–9 inspired the Dublin cleric, Jonathan Swift, to write his most notorious pamphlet, *A Modest Proposal for Preventing the Children of Poor People from being a Burthen to their Parents or Country* (1729) in which he set out in elaborate style how the poor could breed and fatten their children as food for the rich. It was a biting satire against English oppression and indifference to Irish humanity.

The economic miseries of post-Revolution Ireland reached a nadir in 1740–41, when a cold winter devastated the potato crop, the sustenance of the rural poor. Low rainfall in the spring and summer led to livestock dying. By the winter of 1740–41, famine had set in, with typhus, smallpox and dysentery adding to malnutrition to result in dramatic rates of mortality. Perhaps 310,000 to 480,000 people, or between 13 and 20 per cent of the population, over-whelmingly poor rural Catholics, died in a catastrophe almost equal to the more famous Great Famine of 1845–50. Contemporaries blamed mercantilism, which stopped most Irish trade to England and its colonies, and the rapacity of its often-absent landowner class, whose sole interest seemed to be in extract-ing rents from their tenants and then spending that money on luxury goods rather than on improving their estates. Such accusations were not entirely fair. Some estates of absentees, especially well-resourced ones like those owned by the dukes of Devonshire, who inherited much of the estates of the Boyle fam-ily, the earls of Cork, adopted modern English agricultural methods quickly and effectively. It was often not the rich absentee but the impoverished resi-dent landlord who was least likely to adopt methods of agricultural innovation which might have aided their tenants. The earls of Donegal, for example, were debt-ridden descendants of Arthur Chichester and were landlords with large acreages but little capital and even less expertise. Their tenants suffered more than did those of the Devonshire estates.

The economic problems Ireland faced in the early to mid-eighteenth cen-tury were connected less to commercial restrictions and a weak landlord class than to their starting position as a thinly populated and undeveloped periphery of western Europe in the early seventeenth century. This low starting point, S. J. Connolly asserts, would have made economic growth in Ireland over the next century unlikely, even without the pressures added by war, oppressive colonisation and competition from an economically stronger and aggressive neighbour.[3] It had an inherently unequal pattern of trade in which it exchanged finished and half-finished products, such as beef, butter and yarn, for manufac-tured goods. Of course, this situation was also true for all Atlantic colonies, but in the case of American and West Indian colonies, the unfinished products they grew, such as sugar and tobacco, were highly desirable and thus very profitable.

Ireland, by contrast, had little that Europe wanted and was in direct com-petition with farmers elsewhere, not just in England but also in France. Con-sequently, the main reasons for Ireland's low level of eighteenth-century economic development are located in geography and market conditions rather than in the political behaviour of its ruling class. Inequality, with most of the population living at the barest subsistence, even in good times, compounded the problem. Ireland faced the worst of colonisation in a society in which even before English colonisation the interests of the Irish peasant were ignored. But the imposition of English rule was not accompanied by the introduction of the system of poor relief and customary entitlements that protected the position of the rural poor. The Catholic Irish were not African slaves working in the West Indies – they always maintained their independence and their work was much less arduous, while their diet, while boring, was seldom so bad as to stop demographic increase (quite the opposite, in fact – one problem the Gaelic

Irish always had was a high birth rate). But they were similar in one way, which was that they were largely excluded from a rights-based culture and from entitlements to a limited form of social welfare. Instead, the rural Irish poor were left remarkably exposed to the full pressures of a rapidly developing market economy.

The second half of the eighteenth century saw considerable economic improvements in Ireland. The main contribution was the expansion of a new manufacturing industry, the spinning and weaving of linen from flax fibre. Ireland also became from mid-century more included in the growing transatlantic economy, providing preserved beef, pork, butter and fish to feed growing numbers of West Indian enslaved persons Its lower cost of labour made its manufactured goods attractive to American consumers, and from 1717 and even more so from 1733, Irish merchants were finally allowed to trade linen with America, as long as they departed with their goods from an English port. Thus, the improvement in Ireland's economy was facilitated by the wider framework and remarkable growth of Britain's Atlantic economy.

Irish merchants became notably cosmopolitan in the middle of the eighteenth century, establishing cadet branches of merchant firms in the Caribbean, in Philadelphia, in New York and in southern Europe. The Irish today sometimes forget they were involved in the ramifications of slavery, seeing the slave trade as entirely British, not Irish. But the island was by the end of the Seven Years' War, the larder for the Caribbean, especially Ireland's grazing heartland of southern Ireland, around Cork. William Petty had been prescient in 1672 when he saw Ireland's future in Atlantic commerce: the island 'lieth commodiously for the Trade of the new American world, which we see everyday to Grow and Flourish.'

Another commodity important for the Irish in the Atlantic world was the Irish people themselves. In total, the net migration from Ireland to British North America and the West Indies between 1630 and 1775 was around 165,000, with anything up to one hundred thousand making the journey between 1700 and 1775 and perhaps as many again between 1775 and 1800. The Irish sometimes went voluntarily but were more likely than other people in the British orbit to migrate as indentured servants or as convicts. The most notorious such convicts were rebels from the Cromwellian campaign. These convicts were worked excessively hard, put to work doing activities that slaves did, in the broiling sun of Barbados. They complained bitterly about how close their treatment was to that of slaves though this sort of statement was wildly over-exaggerated. Convict Irishmen never faced the same sorts of social, economic and constitutional boundaries as did enslaved Africans, contrary to a discourse that they did that now exists within contemporary Irish politics. Unlike later Irish migration to the nineteenth-century United States, most Irish migrants were Protestants, especially from Ulster.

They were encouraged to go to North America by news of good conditions in the colonies but there were also pressures coming from uncertain economic conditions in the Ulster linen industry. During the height of Ulster migration to the frontier regions of the American South between 1770 and 1775, a severe recession in the linen industry put about one-third of Ulster weavers out of work. In addition, the rapid commercialisation after 1750 of Ulster's economy made the most vulnerable members of Protestant communities jobless and desperate, meaning that many of these migrants were forced to travel to America as indentured servants. Catholics also migrated, although in proportionately fewer numbers than Protestants. Perhaps one-quarter of migrants to North America (and fewer to the Caribbean) were Catholics from southern Ireland. These migrants, of course, moved from one colonial society anxious about the dangers of 'popery' to another also characterised by periodic bouts of anti-Catholicism.

Ireland and Britishness

It might be thought that Ireland was immune to the mid-eighteenth-century surge of patriotism throughout the British Empire that led to the development of a popular commitment to Britain and its national symbols, embraced increasingly and fervently during the Seven Years' War. Most Irish people tended to have local loyalties, if they had any loyalties at all, especially as large areas of the country were run by great magnates without much recourse to central authority, narrowing the spatial boundaries of ordinary Irish people to the area presided over by a landowner. In such circumstances, it was difficult to think more broadly about national or global concerns. In 1746, for example, the Earl of Kerry was described as 'a kind of sovereign in the wild country' of south-west Ireland, from which he took his title. This nobility was ideally placed during the Seven Years' War, according to the Lord Lieutenant of Ireland, the Duke of Bedford, to prevail on their tenants and dependents to enter into the army and thereby 'bring into it a better class and rank of people than would otherwise exist.' Their loyalty, however, stayed with their patrons rather than extended to the British nation.

It was less class than religion which determined loyalty to Britain. Irish Protestants were more fervent than the Catholic elite in declaring their affection for Britain. The Catholic elite tended to display loyalty to Britain for determinedly self-interested reasons, as a means of sharing the privileges of the English and as a lever for securing the repeal of anti-Catholic legislation that especially affected them and their interests. Irish Protestants were British in inclination and saw themselves as part of a British world, just like that occupied by British North Americans. Anglican landowners and merchants looked to London for political and cultural models, while Ulster Presbyterians gravitated towards ancestral Scottish homelands. This devotion to Britain, however, did not mean a reflexive acceptance of the policies put forward by British governments. The Irish Ascendancy's patriotism (the name given to the local Protestant ruling elite) was therefore intended to promote and protect their sense of themselves as entitled to the rights and privileges of subjects of the British Crown.

That sense of Britishness was not shared by Ireland's Catholic peasantry. These downtrodden people had a deep commitment to Jacobitism, even if there was no Jacobite rebellion in the island, unlike Scotland. But some degree of commitment to the larger British project started to emerge even among poor Irish Catholics during the Seven Years' War when Irishmen started to serve in the ranks of the British army. By the American Revolution, Irish soldiers were prominent in the army's rank and file, alongside Scottish Highlanders. Soldiering tended to widen horizons and promote a sense of allegiance to Britain as well as to Ireland itself. Nevertheless, Irish Protestants were hesitant about allowing Catholics to serve in the army, seeing them as a potential fifth column and worrying about the risks to safety if their enemies were trained in military matters. It was a similar concern to that expressed by white settlers in the West Indies and in the American South to the idea of arming enslaved people or free people of colour in the same period. What is interesting is that in both Ireland and the Caribbean, the exigencies of manpower demand overcame ideological hesitation about arming potential internal enemies. The advantages that using the large reserves of Irish Catholic manpower gave to an imperial state involved in a worldwide conflict and needing an expansion of its armed forces to police this growing global empire were too great to be ignored. Resistance to Irish Catholics serving in the army soon disappeared by mid-century. By 1757, near the start of the Seven Years' War, 28 per cent of rank and file serving in the British army in North America were Irish. During the Napoleonic War, Ireland became a major source for British infantry. In one study of twenty-two British unit rosters in this war, only one (the Royal Dragoon Guards) contained no Irish Catholic surnames. Peter Karsten argues that these volunteers did not see themselves as joining the British army as much as joining 'the army' and that, by doing so, they were giving tacit support to the reality of the Irish situation as members of a larger British whole. He describes the Irish soldier as 'Catholic, poor, sometimes of an adventurous, bellicose sort, apolitical, and he saw himself as a soldier by occupation.'[4] In short, the Irish soldier was an attractive candidate for recruitment into a uniform military system, where he literally disappeared into the uniform itself. He was, by the 1790s, a 'subject' who could be incorporated into the army like any other subject of the Crown. The Irish soldier may have been apolitical, but his extensive recruitment had political consequences. It made calls for Catholic emancipation more compelling. Many members of William Pitt's administration in the 1790s believed that the urgent need that Britain had to recruit more Irish soldiers made making concessions to the Catholic majority in Ireland seem prudent as well as the right thing to do. This growing sympathy for Catholic emancipation, however, met with a violent backlash among poorer Protestants, especially in Ireland where the ultra-Protestant Orange Order either initiated or inflamed simmering sectarian violence in 1795–96.

The Seven Years' War encouraged the Irish to feel British, but this greater sympathy for British values did not stop occasional protests against British rule, as happened at the end of the war when there were significant outbreaks of rural unrest in Ireland, There was a riot in Munster in 1761 against landlord-ism and the practice of enclosure of common land, and soon after rural Ireland saw the rise of a vigilante group, 'Whiteboys,' who wore coarse linen as a form of uniform and were not reluctant to use violence against their opponents in order to destabilise rural society. Opposition to the Whiteboys tended to be based on a fear that they were part of a popish plot – always a potent concern among Irish Protestants who tended to see the hand of Rome in any political or social disturbance. The second conflict in the 1760s involved a group called the Hearts of Oak in Ulster, a socio-economic revolt by mainly Protestant ten-ants, angry at excessive tithes levied by county magistrates, who tended to be landlords. The revolt was quickly and violently put down, but it had a larger legacy, forming precedents for the future, as also did the Whiteboy episode in a somewhat different context, for mass marches of discontented Protestant ten-ants. Violent repression led to violent resistance, making the management of Irish affairs always central to British imperial affairs. The close relationship of many members of the British ruling class to Irish matters, often with leading ministers, as with the Earl of Shelburne in the 1770s and 1780s, themselves Irish landowners, meant that Britain was always determined to use whatever means possible in order to quell potential popular uprisings. Britain made sure, for example, that it always kept large numbers of troops stationed in the island, ostensibly to protect the island from foreign invasion, but with a larger primary objective in keeping Protestant rule safe from attacks from below and in stop-ping Catholics from putting their discontent into political action.

The Irish occupied a strange position within the eighteenth-century British Empire, as Irish Protestants recognised. These Protestant patriots saw Ireland as a sister kingdom to Britain, with the same rights to liberty and autonomy as Scotland and England. British politicians insisted that Ireland's constitutional position was either that of a dependent kingdom or a foreign country or a child colony. Equality between Ireland and Britain was thus never considered possible, and the Irish suffered constantly throughout the relatively calm years of the eighteenth century from metropolitan condescension. In short, Britain never took Irish concerns seriously, although they took the possibility of dis-turbance in Ireland which might affect British security very seriously indeed. Even though patriotic Irish Protestants had their own Parliament and seemed to be managing the economy well, that condescension and contempt for Irish domestic concerns remained. The result was continuing tension on the island. Irish Protestants resented how they were treated as second-class subjects by Britain and complained that they 'were never thanked for venturing our lives and fortunes at the Revolution [of 1688] for making so brave a stand at Lon-donderry and Iniskilling' (the latter being battles in which the Irish forces loyal to William III confronted and defeated the Catholic forces of James VII and II). But Irish Protestant resentment was limited to whingeing about how little respect they received. They were unable to complain too much when they were so dependent on British armed support and when they faced a dominant Irish Catholic majority, which was always a threat to Protestant security, even during the eighteenth century when Protestant rule in Ireland was strongest and least contested.

It is hard to fit eighteenth-century Ireland into existing imperial paradigms, such as core versus periphery or mother–child metaphors. For S. J. Connolly, the peculiarity of the Irish situation means that Ireland is best viewed outside the colonial lens and instead seen as an ancien régime society, as in provincial France, more than like an American colony. He argues that the eighteenth-century Irish Parliament had more in common with the Parlement of Bordeaux than with the Virginia House of Burgesses.[5] Of course, Ireland could be both an ancien régime society and an imperial colony, a combination increasingly clear after the end of the Seven Years' War, when Ireland was drawn increasingly into the affairs of the empire. After 1763, during the viceroyalty of George, viscount Townshend, the colonial status of Ireland was made clear. Townshend broke the control of local power brokers – the aforementioned 'undertakers' – in order to assert more forcefully royal prerogatives. He decided, for example, against considerable popular opposition, to replace indirect with direct rule by a resident chief governor, supported in the Irish Parliament by his own faction. It was a profound change in the method of governing Ireland.

Townshend's actions did not just threaten the power base of Protestant Ireland and alienate him and the Crown from a generation of ambitious members of the Irish elite, it seemed to be an example in Ireland of the ministerial tyranny perceived in Britain in respect to the closely followed decision of the freeholders of Middlesex to elect the radical John Wilkes as member of Parliament (MP) over the determined opposition of the government and similar to the disagreeable acts that Townshend's brother, Charles Townshend, was afflicting on the British American colonists. For Irish patriots, Townshend's actions in Ireland were an example of despotism and violations of the settlement of the Glorious Revolution. Ironically, as James Kelly notes, 'political activists took full advantage of the increased freedom of political expression that flowed from the diminution in the closeness with which the authorities monitored print to articulate a distinctly more radical message.' In general, however, the radical Whig position common in British America about ministerial tyranny and the need to resist such tyranny was not dominant in Ireland in the late 1760s until Townshend's recall as viceroy, his recall being on other matters, in 1772. Kelly notes that 'the traditional caution that guided Irish peers and MPs when constitutional and electoral matters were at issue continued to act as a brake on their ability to press successfully for change.'[6]

Ireland and the American Revolution

As we have seen, Ireland was always a political problem for the British government. Its fears about the Irish propensity for rebellion came to the fore in the American Revolution and even more so in the 1790s when revolutionary fervour in France contributed to a major uprising in 1798, brutally put down by the imperial troubleshooter Charles, Marquess Cornwallis, who was more successful in Ireland, as was also the case in India, than he had been at Yorktown in Virginia in 1781. The 1798 rebellion had some similarity to the War of American Independence as being dissent-led secessionist movements within the empire, which faced ferocious opposition from Loyalists and which relied ultimately on French intervention for success (which occurred in the Thirteen Colonies in rebellion in North America but not in Ireland). They were, however, quite different events in conception, implementation and, most of all, context, a context in which the value of Ireland to British security was always considered more important than maintaining an imperial presence in North America. One sign of Ireland's continuing importance to Britain is that when rebellion erupted in 1798, it encouraged William Pitt the younger, the British prime minister, to put through a legislative union, connecting Ireland officially with Great Britain from 1800 in a new configuration called the United Kingdom, from which southern Ireland eventually extricated itself in 1922.

Ireland was not directly involved in the earlier rebellion of 1776 in America. But it was at the top of British officials' attention. It was at the top of attention for traditional reasons relating to the possibility of trouble in Ireland causing problems domestically in England. Initially, Ireland was sympathetic to its American cousins, as in the Stamp Act controversy, which elicited much support of the American position in the Irish press. America tried to keep Ireland onside by excluding them from colonial non-importation agreements in the 1760s. After 1770, however, attitudes hardened in Ireland against America, increasing as the troubles in America had an impact on the Irish economy and as Ireland was given no special consideration by Americans. That change in attitude came about mainly because Americans came to see Ireland as constitutionally subordinate to Britain. The Irish quickly understood that the point in contention in the Thirteen Colonies – the right to continue to legislate for themselves – was a right that Ireland did not even possess to have it taken away. The American Revolution provoked a considerable amount of soul-searching among Irish leaders, which eventually led in 1782 to significant constitutional changes in the kingdom/colony.

Britain was suspicious of Irish opinion and Irish behaviour during the American Revolution, knowing that probably most of the Irish were sympathetic to the American position and that they related what the British were doing in America unfavourably to the Irish situation. Nevertheless, there was never any chance that Irish Protestants would have translated their warm feelings into action, given what they perceived as the constant Catholic threat to their dominance. That threat also focused the attention of the British. They were more prepared than elsewhere in the empire to counter any local discontent through strategic concession to Irish opinion. That strategy became more urgent after France entered the war in 1778. Britain feared that the French would foster a Catholic uprising in order to attack Britain from the West. Indeed, they were more worried about this hypothetical possibility than about real French invasions, such as that planned for Jamaica in 1782.

Consequently, Ireland was granted several concessions during the American Revolution, all of which helped counter some long-standing Irish resentment against Britain. It repealed the 1720 Declaratory Act which asserted British parliamentary sovereignty over Ireland and made the Irish Parliament merely advisory. The effect was to give Ireland something akin to the dominion status of white settler colonies in the twentieth century. Thus, Ireland achieved without much effort what America had to fight for and separate themselves from the British Empire to obtain. From 1782, Ireland was a distinct kingdom within a composite monarchy. Only the king and the Irish Parliament could make laws, and the hated Poynings' Law was repealed so that the Privy Council no longer had the power to suppress or alter Irish bills. Most important, Britain gave its total support to Irish Protestants, even those such as the Irish Volunteers, who had the potential to use violence against British rule. The Volunteers were a defence force of part-time predominantly Presbyterian soldiers with significant Anglican support outside Ulster which, at its peak, numbered around sixty thousand men, formed to combat the potential French invasion threat but, after it became clear that this threat would not eventuate, soon turned its attention (and its guns) to demanding redress for Ireland's grievances, as Protestants saw them. They were remarkably successful in focusing the attention of Lord North and his government in London. North received reports in 1779 of a government out of control, with a rebellious Irish Parliament and paramilitary demonstrations by armed men committed to getting action in response to their demands for constitutional reform. North decided that caution was the better part of wisdom and agreed to give the Irish sweeping concessions to avoid confrontation in Ireland when he was facing unprecedented problems in the Americas.

North's original concessions related mostly to trade. He agreed that Ireland could enter equally into colonial trade with Britain, except where the monopoly of the East India Company pertained. He agreed to regularising trade between Ireland and Britain and, last of all, allowed Irish merchants into the Levant trade. These actions were welcomed in Ireland as a first step, but they were naïve concessions insofar as constitutional questions of the legislative power of Britain to regulate Irish life remained unchanged. By the end of February 1780, the major symbols of Irish colonial dependency had been raised in the Irish Parliament, such as the tenure of Irish judges and the absence of an Irish habeas corpus legislation. By 1782, these issues were largely resolved. North's defeat in America in November 1781 led to a new government under the Anglo-Irish aristocrat, the Earl of Shelburne (later the Marquess of Lansdowne), a descendant of the seventeenth-century political economist William Petty. This government quickly moved to meet Irish demands for an Irish constitution, passed in 1782 to great acclamation in Ireland. It marked the high point of Protestant Nationalism in Ireland, although the opportunistic way in which the gains had been won – it never would have happened without events in America and Europe intruding – and the paramilitary agency of the Volunteers, a group claiming to speak for 'the people' and threatening and enacting violence if their demands were not met introduced a worrying new development in Irish history, one that has bedevilled the politics of the island until today. These were cautionary notes for the future.

1798 and Union

Thus, much in Ireland and its relationship with Britain remained unsatisfactory. Irish representation remained unchanged with three-quarters of the Irish Parliament elected as members of rotten boroughs, controlled by British landlords. The failure to reform Parliament meant that the new Declaratory Act of 1778, which guaranteed colonial assemblies, including Ireland, the exclusive power of internal taxation, merely transferred arbitrary power overseas to aristocracy at home. And some of this local aristocracy, such as the Earl of Shelburne, was indistinguishable from the British aristocrats whom the Irish thought their special oppressors.

For Irish Protestants, the 1780s seemed to be golden years. But, in addition to how their constitutional achievements had been won in 1782, there were concerns that this 'golden age' was temporary. British leaders showed, by Irish Protestant standards, a disturbing tendency to want to grant Catholics rights that protestants thought they were not entitled to and which might undermine the Ascendancy. Irish Protestants believed that any concession to Catholics was the thin edge of the wedge, leading to Catholics getting the vote and using their numerical dominance to overturn the Cromwellian land settlement. The 1780s, therefore, was good times for the ruling protestant Irish elite but also saw the beginnings of a division between Britain and Irish Protestants. The former, according to the latter, were allowing Catholics to be, step by step, incorporated into the political nation. They condemned the British as naïfs, meddling in matters they did not properly understand. Protestants argued that Catholics were inherently ungrateful people (although why they should be grateful to the people who had deprived them of land, rights and wealth is hard to comprehend) and would not see the concession of the British government as gracious gifts but as signs of imperial weakness that they would exploit given any opportunity.

Perhaps the most important result of renewed imperial attention to Ireland in the 1780s was to cement Ireland as being central to British thinking about the wider world, a process that coincided with the rise of the empire to match the importance of Europe in British policy making. Unlike earlier times, however, the Irish elite could not claim to be able to deal themselves with Irish concerns – that had to be left to the notably more interventionist and authoritarian, if more humanitarian, British imperial government. The difference can be seen most dramatically in how the 1740–41 famine was dealt with compared to the more famous Great Famine of 1845–50. The former is not as well known as the latter, mainly because few people outside Ireland became aware of it. The little action that was taken to counter it and deal with the misery it occasioned was done entirely within Ireland and by the Irish themselves. Such a result was predictable, given Irish insistence on their right to self-rule, even given the constraints of legislation like the Declaratory Act of 1720 and Poynings' Law. By the 1780s, Britain was determined to make its presence felt in Ireland as much as in other parts of the empire.

Ireland, however, was a weak link in the developing empire. The outbreak of the French Revolution led almost immediately to another upsurge in disaffected groups in Ireland conspiring (as the British saw it) against the empire. As R. B. McDowell comments, the French Revolution gave would-be reformers an uplifting sense of participation 'in a great drive against tyranny and anachronistic privilege.'[7] The strongest manifestation of this sense of uplift was the founding of the Society of United Irishmen in Belfast on October 1790. This society was singular in that it mixed liberal Protestant Dissenters and middle-class Catholics, many of whom were self-professedly enlightened merchants or professionals. They agitated for Catholic emancipation and constitutional political reform. Their actions, unsurprisingly, led to a lower-class Protestant backlash, especially in Ulster.

By 1795–96, sectarian violence and gang warfare had emerged, providing an incentive for France to try to invade Britain through Ireland, which it attempted four times starting at the end of 1796. The French threat forced Britain to increase its military presence so that by 1798, there were one hundred thousand British soldiers there and naval squadrons stationed off the Irish coasts. This large military presence meant that when rebellion occurred in 1798, led by dissident elements within the Protestant governing elite – Arthur O'Connor, Lord Edward Fitzgerald, and Theobold Wolfe Tone – it was able to be put down with relative ease, if with maximum violence. The rebellion itself was unlikely to succeed being an uncoordinated mass rising-cum-sectarian civil war which happened before a French army had appeared to support the rebels. The climax came in what Roy Foster calls 'probably the most concentrated episode of violence in Irish history' with the British army defeating the rebels at Wexford on 21 June 1798 at the Battle of Vinegar Hill.[8] Foster's assessment is an overstatement, as Irish deaths were, at one thousand, fewer than in mid-seventeenth conflicts. But its consequences were considerable. The main effect of the rebellion was to show just how strong was British determination to keep Ireland under its dominion, at whatever cost.

It also was a rebellion which led, as noted earlier, to the Irish Union, debated and agreed in the Irish and British Parliaments in 1799 and 1800. The importance of adding an Irish dimension to British overseas expansion was vital in having the Union Act passed in 1801. This was to be a Union for Empire, with the voice of Irishmen 'heard not only in Europe, but in Asia, Africa and America.' It showed how things had changed in half a century. In 1750, empire in Ireland meant little beyond trade, migrants and convicts. Irish involvement in the empire from 1763 onwards had become substantial. Empire was also conceived as a means of solving the eternal problem of accommodating Catholics and Protestants. Pitt's message was clear, as Thomas Bartlett argues: it was only in a 'Protestant Empire' – that is, an Empire in which Protestants were a majority, at least at the metropolitan centre – that Catholic emancipation be contemplated with equanimity.'[9] It did not work as intended. Sectarianism only increased in the nineteenth century, and Ireland did not prosper after Union as Scotland had done after its Union in 1707. It did mean, however, that Ireland became part of an imperial nation, as seen in becoming settlers in Canada, Australia and New Zealand and in serving as soldiers almost everywhere.

What did the Union of 1801 do for Ireland? It terminated Ireland's formal status as a dependent kingdom, or colony, and confirmed the independence tentatively given to Ireland in 1782 while taking away the mechanism (the Irish Parliament) through which that independence was meant to be secured. It gave instead of its own Parliament substantial representation to Ireland in the Houses of Parliament, especially in the House of Lords, where twenty-eight Irish peers were joined by many peers with English titles but Irish lands. In the House of Commons, Ireland had one hundred MPs. What it did not do was allow for any economic or administrative integration with Britain, Free trade between Ireland and Britain only started in 1824, and the customs and excises regimes of the two countries were not put into unison until 1853. For Ireland, this was not an entirely bad result, as it was, by some measures, undertaxed until the late nineteenth century. The Union, moreover, did not end Irish colonialism. Like India, Ireland was governed by a viceroy who was ostensibly titular with ill-defined powers but who exercised considerable if ceremonial powers and reminded Irish people daily of their continuing dependence on British symbols and customs. In sum, despite continual demands on both sides of the Irish Sea for Irish and British laws and institutions to be reconciled, no government before the Union collapsed during warfare, in 1922 could bring itself to accept what had meant to happen in 1801 – a new country being created in which Ireland was an equal partner with England and Scotland. It might be argued that this unwillingness to see Ireland as worthy of the same consideration as Britons has been a feature of British, especially English, involvement with Ireland right up to the present day. Thus, the continuation of this essentially colonial view of Ireland from the British mainland means that Ireland deserves attention more in this book than any other part of Britain and its empire as the oldest, longest-lived and most contentious of all English and British involvement with the wider world.

Notes

1 Blair Worden, *The English Civil Wars, 1640–1660* (London: Weidenfeld and Nicholson, 2009), 2–3.
2 Micheál ó Siochrú, *God's Executioner: Oliver Cromwell and the Conquest of Ireland* (London: Faber and Faber, 2008), 224.
3 S.J. Connolly, *Divided Kingdom: Ireland, 1630–1800* (Oxford: Oxford University Press, 2008), 348.
4 Peter Karsten, 'Irish Soldiers in the British Army, 1792–1922: Suborned or Subordinate?,' in Karsten, ed., *Motivating Soldiers: Morale or Mutiny* (New York: Routledge, 1998), 57.
5 S.J. Connolly, *Religion, Law and Power: The Making of Protestant Ireland, 1660–1760* (Oxford: Oxford University Press, 1992), 2–3.

6 James Kelly, "'Era of Liberty": The Politics of Civil and Political Rights in Eighteenth-century Ireland,' in Jack P. Greene, ed., *Exclusionary Empire: English Liberty Overseas, 1600–1900* (Cambridge: Cambridge University Press, 2010), 98–9.
7 R.B. McDowell, *Ireland in the Age of Imperialism and Revolution, 1760–1801* (Oxford: Clarendon Press, 1979), 363.
8 Roy Foster, *Modern Ireland, 1600–1972* (1988), 280.
9 Thomas Bartlett, *The Fall and Rise of the Irish Nation: The Catholic Question, 1690–1830* (Dublin, 1992), 244–67.

Bibliography

Barnard, Toby, 'Crises of Identity among Irish Protestants, 1641–1685,' *Past and Present* 127 (1990), 39–85.

Bric, Maurice, 'Ireland and the Atlantic World, 1690–1840,' in S.J. Connolly, ed., *The Oxford Companion to Irish History* (Oxford: Oxford University Press, 2011), 462–78.

Canny, Nicholas, *Making Ireland British, 1580–1630* (Oxford: Oxford University Press, 2001).

Connolly, S.J., *Divided Kingdom: Ireland, 1630–1800* (Oxford: Oxford University Press, 2008).

Kelly, James, ed., *The Cambridge History of Ireland*, vol. III. *1730–1880* (Cambridge: Cambridge University Press, 2018).

Ohlmeyer, Jane, 'A Laboratory for Empire? Early Modern Ireland and English Imperialism,' in Kevin Kenny, ed., *Oxford History of the British Empire: Ireland and the British Empire* (Oxford: Oxford University Press, 2004).

Ohlmeyer, Jane, ed. *The Cambridge History of Ireland*, vol. II. *1550–1830* (Cambridge: Cambridge University Press, 2018).

ó Siochrú, Micheál, *God's Executioner: Oliver Cromwell and the Conquest of Ireland* (London: Faber and Faber, 2008).

6 Imperial Britain, 1688–1763

Introduction

The first British Empire was acquired in a decidedly ad hoc fashion. Beginning in the sixteenth century, the Crown added to the remnants of its medieval territories several previously independent kingdoms. It acquired Wales and Ireland by conquest, incorporating the former into the realm in 1536 and leaving the latter hanging between being an independent kingdom and a dependent colony, an uncertain constitutional status not resolved until 1801, when it was incorporated within the United Kingdom. James VI and I of Scotland when he ascended the English throne in 1603 brought Scotland into this composite monarchy with a full political union between Scotland and England only achieved from 1707. Before that date, Scotland and England were two different countries with a common king.

Meanwhile, the English Crown allowed private initiatives to establish English colonies on the eastern seaboard of North America and on several Caribbean islands, starting with Barbados in 1624. This process was covered in Chapter 2 but bears a summary to put eighteenth-century developments into context. At the same time as England started its American Empire, it involved itself in slave trading and gold trading in West Africa and in 1600 set up a chartered company, the East India Company, which, by the end of the seventeenth century, was on the verge of major economic expansion. It also had some military outposts by the mid-seventeenth century in Tangier in North Africa and Bombay in India.

This chaotic and ill-defined empire was mostly left to develop through the efforts of private investors with relatively little state involvement until 1655, when Oliver Cromwell, as part of an aggressive pro-Protestant protectorate foreign policy, organised an ambitious Western Design in the Greater Antilles region of the Spanish-controlled Caribbean. This initiative represented the first serious deployment of the military resources of the English state overseas and outside Ireland. It was not very successful, although it resulted in the conquest of the barely settled Jamaica, as a consolation prize for English failure to take the valuable island of Hispaniola. It did, however, result in one lasting alteration of English foreign policy priorities. As Nicholas Canny notes, 'the maintenance of those colonies and trading positions that had been acquired in almost serendipitous fashion during the first half of the seventeenth century now came to be considered a matter of national interest as well as pride.'[1]

We can trace the ideology of English and then British imperialism (Scotland, Ireland and Wales were not officially involved in much colonisation overseas in the seventeenth century save for the disastrous Darien expedition undertaken by the Scots in the 1690s) to roughly this period, with a ramping up of interest in empire from the Restoration of 1660 and especially from the 1670s through 1680s. From this time onwards, it was widely accepted that colonies were essential to the economic well-being of the community, besides what sort of national pride having colonies entailed. As Canny also notes,

> by the end of the seventeenth century, a new concept of Empire had been established, which involved the assertion of dominion over foreign places and peoples, the introduction of white, and also black settlement in these areas, and the monopolization of trade with these newly acquired territories.[2]

Expansion of the empire

From the late seventeenth century, Britain's empire, and the role of the state in that empire, expanded rapidly. Before the split of the British Empire with the creation of the United States of America in 1783, there were thirty-four parts of the Atlantic Empire: one in Ireland, eighteen in North America, eleven in the Caribbean, three in the Western Atlantic and one (Senegambia) in West Africa. In addition, there was the possessions controlled by the East India Company in South Asia and tentative claims to possessions charted by James Cook in the Pacific, as well as Minorca and Gibraltar, as imperial gains in 1782 from Spain because of the Peace of Paris (Minorca lasting only as a British possession until 1802). In the Atlantic, all these possessions were settler-dominated (settlers being permanent residents of British or Irish heritage), with ostensible control of their activities located in London. These colonies were generally free to trade with each other and were allowed by the imperial government a considerable amount of self-government.

Of course, the verb used earlier, *to allow*, was fiercely contested in the colonies. Even though metropolitan Britain tried periodically to make colonies confirm to imperial authority, most forcefully in the late 1670s and symbolically in grand plans made by imperial bureaucrats that were put forward but never seriously considered likely to be implemented, in 1701 by the leading imperial official of the late seventeenth century, William Blathwayt, and in 1721 and again in 1731 by Martin Bladen, Blathwayt's principal successor as colonial supremo, elites in Atlantic colonies maintained until the 1760s a firm insistence about colonial rights to govern themselves. Central to settler self-conceptions of their political rights was their insistence that they gained these rights by inheritance. Settlers, according to colonial political theory, were all equally freeborn English subjects, who had left their native country to establish

English hegemony over New World lands. They denied that this move overseas to lands controlled by the English, then the British, made any difference to the political status they had within England. They refused to accept that they could lose any inherited rights simply by moving across the Atlantic. Their right to self-government derived, they insisted, not from imperial pleasure but from their basic English rights of political inclusion in the nation guaranteed to them by the Magna Carta of 1215 and continually reinforced by parliamentary decree ever since that date.

Daniel Dulany of Maryland put the colonial position most vividly, He did not accept that Maryland was 'a Conquered Country.' He argued that such a claim was 'false' because if there had been a conquest,

> the Indians must be the Vanquish'd, and the English the Victors, and con-
> sequently, the Indians would be liable to the Miseries, in which a Conquered
> People are involved. Otherwise the Conquerors themselves must be Loos-
> ers [sic] by their Courage and Success which would be but a poor Reward
> of their Valour.

He argued in 1728 that

> [t]he First Settlers of Maryland, were a Colony of English Subjects, who
> left their Native Country, with the Assent and Approbation of their Prince;
> to enlarge his Empire in a remote Part of the World, destitute of almost all
> the Necessaries of Life, and inhabited by a People, savage, cruel, and inhos-
> pitable. To which Place they (the first Settlers) transported themselves, at a
> great expence; ran all the Hazards, and underwent all the Fatigues incident
> to so dangerous and daring an Undertaking, in which Many perished, and
> Those that survived, suffered All the Extremities of Hunger, Cold and
> Disease.

These original settlers to Maryland 'were not banished from their Native Country, nor did they adjure it' but going to this strange and difficult land 'met with such Success, as to raise a Subsistence for Themselves, and to become very beneficial to their Mother-Country by greatly increasing its Trade and Wealth.' In short, '[t]hey have been as advantageous to England, as any of Her Sons, that never went from their own Homes. or underwent any Hardships.' They had a charter which guaranteed their rights, but those rights existed anyway 'had the Charter never been made; as were the Rights of English Men, to all the Liber-ties, confirmed by Magna Charta, and other subsequent Statutes, before they were Made,' these rights being 'antient or common-law Rights' that all Eng-lishmen held, wherever they resided. He concluded his peroration by insisting that the Crown and his subjects had reciprocal rights, 'for as the Subject is bound to obey the King, so is the King bound to protect the Subject.' What 'is necessarily followed' is 'that the greatest Advantage, which the Subject can possibly derive, from the Royal Protection, is the Benefit of the Laws' while '[t]his Subjection, and this Protection, are not bounded by Space, less extensive than the British Dominions.'

Britain never accepted the entirety of Dulany's position, believing that settler insistence on their right to self-government violated a central premise of the constitutional settlement of 1689, the primacy of the sovereignty of parliament. Indeed, in 1729, just after Dulany had written his stirring defence of settler rights, the attorney general, Sir Philip Yorke, countered Dulany's contentions by declaring that 'such general statutes as have been made since the settlement of Maryland and are not by express words located either to the plantations in general or to the provinces, are not of force there.' Nevertheless, despite these lasting differences over the constitutional status of settler colonies, during the long period between the Glorious Revolution of 1680 and the 1760s, the relationship between most colonials in the Atlantic World and the British government was positive. Settlers were bound to Britain by commercial ties, cultural attachments and by a common need to defend themselves against threats emanating from France and Spain. Jack Greene summarises how the first half of the eighteenth century in British America 'was a period of extraordinary growth . . . in terms of the volume and value of all colonial trades and in the territorial, demographic, economic, social, political, and cultural development of the American colonies.' New colonies were established in Georgia, the Virgin Islands and at the end of the period in Novia Scotia while Britain 'consolidated and extended [its] areas of effective occupation in all the older colonies.' Metropolitan writers started to take notice of this growth and how valuable the colonies were becoming to Britain, and 'their welfare became a prime consideration in the state's decision to invest heavily in imperial conflicts with France and Spain between 1739 and 1763.' British victory in the Seven Years' War just reinforced the value of this area of the world to Britain, with nine new American and one African colonies being added to the British Empire from 1763.[3]

The Glorious Revolution

The battle between competing visions of imperial control was joined by the late 1670s, coming out of determined resistance to Stuart centralisation in many parts of the empire, notably Jamaica, Virginia, New York and Massachusetts. The settler argument was clear and never wavered until 1776. Settlers rejected, as we have seen with Dulany, that they were beneficiaries of conquest; they denied that their rights relied on royal prerogative; they insisted instead that their rights came to them as the birthright of English subjects gone overseas and that wherever English people and, after 1707, Britons moved within the empire, they retained the rights of fellow subjects who stayed home. They argued, in addition, that without that protection of being fully invested English subjects they would not have moved overseas and undertaken what they insisted was the arduous task of settlement in hostile and ill-governed Native American lands, all to the benefit of the Stuart monarchs. Their argument went hand in hand with a determined belief in Protestant liberty – settlers were necessary bulwarks to the twin perils of popery and arbitrary government. Settlers were proud of what they had done by crossing the Atlantic, transforming what they saw as 'wilderness,' occupied badly by Native Americans, into recognisably British landscapes. That the Atlantic was full of settler communities underwritten by a flourishing and, from 1698, largely privately controlled, Atlantic slave trade showed that settlers in creating successful civil societies were doing things that benefitted Britain. The settler argument was that they should be left alone to do as they liked, as this was both a privilege given to people of British descent, wherever they were, and an option that made the empire great.

This view was maintained by settlers, notably in North America, until the American Revolution. It was not just Dulany (whose family became Loyalists) but the oldest founding father, Benjamin Franklin, born in 1706, so a young man when Dulany made his statement, who adhered to such views. Franklin's views are worth recording in-depth as they show concisely the lineaments of one view of what should be the imperial relationship between the state and settlers that pertained in the British Empire before the 1760s. He argued for an empire based on common interest, a common interest based on ethnicity, as he saw it, or race, as we might see it today, not economics. Colonists and Englishmen as white Britons deserved preferment over those of a darker hue. If far-sighted British politicians (William Pitt the Elder comes to mind, as this was his position during the Seven Years' War) adopted policies that recognised the shared Britishness of white settlers, whether born in Britain or raised in the Americas, a bright imperial future beckoned. As Franklin insisted, the links connecting Britain to British settlers in places such as Pennsylvania, where Franklin lived in his increasingly rare periods spent outside Europe, were those of fraternal affection and a shared sense that they were members of a common enterprise. He told Peter Collinson,

> We are in your Hands as Clay in the Hands of a Potter and as the Potter cannot waste or spoilt his Clay without injuring himself; so I think that there is scarce anything that you could do that may be hurtful to us, but which will be as much or more so to you.

British vitriol against their fellow country people left him bemused. He could only resort to sarcasm:

> The gentle terms of republican race, mixed rabble of Scotch, Irish and foreign vagabonds, descendants of convicts, ungrateful rebels etc, are some of the sweet flowers of English rhetoric with which our colonists have of late been regaled. Surely if we are so much their superiors, we should show the superiority of our breeding by our better manners!

Asked by friends in 1766 what made Americans loyal before 1763, he told them: 'They were governed by this country at the expence only of a little pen ink, and paper. They were led by a thread. They had not only a respect, but an affection for Great Britain.' Once the bonds that linked Britons in America with Britons in Britons in America were dissolved, then the British Empire, as he knew it, would also be dissolved. America, he told David Hartley, a British parliamentarian, 'will not be destroyed: God will protect and prosper it: You will only exclude yourself from any share of it.'

Franklin predicted in 1760 that in a few generations, white settlers in British North America would eventually outnumber the number of people in the metropolis, to the mutual benefit, he thought, of both areas, adding to the great glory of a glorious empire. He crowed in *Observations on the Increase of Mankind* that rapid population increase in North America will mean that there

> will in another Century be more than the People of England, the greatest Number of *Englishmen* will be on this Side of the Water. What an Accession of Power to the *British* Empire by Sea as well as Land! What Increase of Trade and Navigation! What Numbers of Ships and Seamen!

Britain had to do nothing to maintain that affection. There was no danger, he thought, of America 'uniting against their own nation, which protects and encourages them, with which they have so many connections and ties of blood, interest and affection and which 'tis well known they all love more than they love one another.' Indeed, Franklin continued, 'I will venture to say, a union amongst them for such a purpose is not merely improbable, it is impossible.'

The Glorious Revolution of 1688–89 solidified settlers' opinions about their rights, leading to celebrations in the colonies of the event as a principled victory of Protestant parliamentary government over Catholic absolutism, ignoring other interpretations of it as a shabby Dutch coup d'état led by self-interested London merchants out for rent-seeking advantages in an empire reshaped around their interests and by avaricious power-hungry aristocrats eager to replace monarchical tyranny with oligarchical injustice. The latter interpretation is possible when one looks at one of the major imperial actions that followed the Glorious Revolution, the confirmation of the East India Company charter in 1700 after the company had secretly given William III a large sum with which to fight wars against his hated enemy, the French under Louis XIV. By contrast, the Royal African Company, which had a monopoly over trade with Africa, including trade in slaves was out of favour with William III, as it had been very much associated as the creature of James II. When a select group of London merchants attacked it in order, mainly, to capture the profits from the slave trade for themselves, no royal protection of the monopoly followed. Private traders could compete with the state monopoly in 1698, and in 1708 the Royal African Company was reduced by parliamentary fiat to a shell of its former self, mainly in charge of maintaining government forts in West Africa and removed from direct involvement in most trading activities with African merchants.

The Glorious Revolution was a genuinely transatlantic phenomenon that was a climactic event in seventeenth-century Anglo-America. It paved the way for new and more powerful local ruling elites to emerge in the colonies from Barbados to Maryland to Massachusetts – planters in the former, merchants and planters in the middle, merchants in the latter. It galvanised American society in some of the same ways as the revolution at home galvanised the British state, although the colonial state was always much smaller and less intrusive into local autonomy than in Britain, especially in the loosely governed Middle Atlantic states and in the Chesapeake. More important, it exposed a fundamental and permanent rift in outlook between the two major sections of Atlantic America, the mainland colonies in North America and the island colonies in the Caribbean. To these two models of imperial governance can be added three others – Scotland, Ireland and India.

One of the ironies of the Glorious Revolution's settlement is that the greatest imperial beneficiaries were white settlers in the Caribbean, men who had shown little willingness to get involved in 1688 on behalf of William III and Mary. Throughout the 1690s, William III gave special favour to the West Indian sugar interest, implicitly accepting the argument made in 1689 by Barbados absentee planter Edward Littleton, in *The Groans of the Plantations*, that the sugar colonies were ruinously overtaxed and mismanaged. William III gave the West Indian settlers their fondest request, the end of the Royal African Company's monopoly, which led almost immediately to a doubling of the volume of slave imports into the Caribbean and to a rapid rise in the price of African slaves. That price increase was not unwelcome to rich planters, as its main effect was to drive small planters from the slave markets, allowing richer men freedom to buy enough slaves so as to implement the large integrated plantation that had large economies of scale, making sugar planting very profitable. This wealth consolidated the wealthy planter elite in power in the islands for the next century and made them the richest people of the enemy, except for a few nabobs (European employees of the East India Company, returning like Robert Clive in splendour to Britain where they bought up large country houses and engaged in politics). William III and his ministers also supported much greater military aid to the West Indies than they allowed for North America and, from 1696, supported planters in attacks on privateering antagonists, with privateers now renamed as pirates and thus subject to imperial repression and to gruesome rituals of capital punishment if caught. From 1696, the privateering option in the Caribbean, with economic activity being oriented towards commandeering through plunder the wealth of Spanish America, was thrown over to full-heartedly supporting planting interests.

Settlers in North America got fewer direct benefits from the Glorious Revolution than did their compatriots in the Caribbean, but, as Richard Dunn argues, 'the Revolution made it obvious that the North American colonists, for better or worse, must operate within a transatlantic system, with London as the metropolitan core.'[4] The same process of elite consolidation that took place in the West Indies also occurred, with an even more telling effect, in North America, notably in the Chesapeake, where a Creole landed elite formulated

Figure 6.1 Pierre Mignard, Louise de Keroualle, Duchess of Portsmouth, with an unidentified servant.

Source: Art Collection 3/Alamy Stock Photo.

an ideological political consensus that kept wealthy planters in charge of social, political and economic affairs until well after the American Revolution.

The main result of the Glorious Revolution in the Americas was an emergence from the 1690s of two varieties of colonial relationship. The West India relationship was tailored to suit big sugar planters, who had been severely challenged politically under the late Stuarts. They could rule only with strong support from a powerful and intrusive imperial state, whose strictures they largely supported, not surprisingly as the imperial state gave them so much help – reduced Crown taxes, more slave imports, considerable military assistance against both other European empires and from their numerically dominant but hugely oppressed enslaved populations and full protection from foreign competition for their tropical commodities shipped to Britain through generous tariffs. As Dunn argues, 'the revolutionary settlement gave them these things, crystallizing their dependent colonial status.'[5]

In North America, by contrast, settlers there also got what they wanted but in different ways. What they wanted, and got, was a looser relationship with the Crown, which Franklin later lauded as the basis of imperial harmony in North America. They essentially broke through from imperial control, if they did so only in fact but not in theory. The threat that Britain could change the nature of the relationship because it did not accept settler arguments about the virtues of colonial autonomy always hovered in the background of otherwise satisfactory relations between the North American colonies and Britain between 1688 and 1763. The principal result of the Glorious Revolution in North America was to broaden the realities of American self-government and to validate in practice local self-determination within an economy and society that was almost as dynamic and expansive as in eighteenth-century Britain itself. North America attracted more white settlers than in the malign disease environment of the West Indies, and many of these settlers came not from England but from Ulster and from Germany. North American society in the first quarter of the eighteenth century thus became relatively heterogeneous in ethnicity; a pluralistic society in places such as Pennsylvania and New York; and economically diverse, with a large amount of participatory politics in which more people than in Britain were able to take part, and a significant urban sector in the American North, where models of Anglicisation, or conformity to British norms of behaviour, became more possible than could ever have been imagined in the rudimentary social structures of seventeenth-century America.

British views of sovereignty

But we should not just accept the American view of the imperial relationship as axiomatic. In many ways, it was North America which was anomalous, not the other parts of the empire, let alone Britain. North American colonists might have been left alone in a policy of 'salutary neglect,' to use a phrase used at the time that suggested there was an unofficial policy of not enforcing parliamentary laws in North America in case it angered colonial opinion, although historians now are dubious about whether the actual policies of the British government towards North America, even during the long peace between 1713 and 1739, could be characterised by that perceived policy. But 'salutary neglect' certainly never operated in any other parts of empire at any time in the eighteenth century. Empire was often on the minds of Britons, both ordinary Britons and members of the political nation. Steven Pincus argues that between 1680 and 1784, nearly 70 per cent of parliamentary days were spent in discussing imperial issues. And outside Parliament, imperial matters were widely canvassed. The widely circulated *Gentleman's Magazine* and the *London Magazine* covered imperial affairs in every issue from April 1732 to the end of 1784, ranging from the South Sea Company to Native American policies to debates over tariffs on sugar, tobacco, silk and tea to local issues in Scotland, Ireland or Bengal.[6] Pincus insists that recent scholarship on Britain in the eighteenth century shows that after the Glorious Revolution, Britain and its empire were connected by an increasingly active, powerful and interventionist imperial government in Britain.[7]

His arguments are supported by the detailed analysis of parliamentary legislation on economic matters recently undertaken by Julian Hoppit. Hoppit notes, as outlined in the next chapter in this book, that the British state was a complex one – a powerful fiscal-military state modified by local pressure that made it an entity that tended to proclaim without being able to implement its rulings. But despite these structural weaknesses, the British state in the early eighteenth century was a very active state, with large numbers of bills – more than two hundred per session from 1763 – put forward by members of Parliament, a large percentage of which failed to make it into legislation and many of the remainder being highly specific acts tied to individuals or localities. Parliament handled revolutionary levels of legislation in the eighteenth century, with most of the more consequential dealing with economic and imperial matters. It also began, after the Glorious Revolution, to meet every year, a practice that continues to the present day.[8] As noted subsequently in this book, Britain was committed to a strong fiscal-military state which spent funds not just on preparing for war but on developing national and especially imperial infrastructure. The British state was most active in its empire, from building forts in West Africa, rearranging the highways of Scotland, establishing new Atlantic colonies and recompensing colonists when they suffered from natural disasters.

The view from London about settler pretensions as to their supposed rights was based on its transformation after 1689 into a powerful, though not uncontested state. From the perspective of London, the importance of the Glorious Revolution was that it formed part of a long-term crisis in European interstate rivalry, largely prompted in Britain by fears of the absolutist government of Louis XIV. Britain was a prize jewel in that competition, won by William III and then, from 1714, by the Hanoverian George I. Quite remarkably, over the course of the next quarter century, Britain managed to transform itself from an object of desire into a great power. Second, the Glorious Revolution was a further painful consequence of the sixteenth-century Reformation. It showed that Britain as a Protestant nation would only countenance Protestant monarchs and, as in the Jacobite Rebellions of 1715 and 1745, would defend its rights to select such Protestant monarchs even against candidates for monarchy with better hereditary claims but the wrong religious affiliation. Monarchy was strongly and permanently put in its place in Britain's constitutional system.

Finally, the Glorious Revolution was a critical stage by which an increasingly complex society that was rapidly modernising circumvented the structural limitations of hereditary monarchy as the mainspring of government through the institutionalisation and regularisation of parliament. The rise of Parliament to sovereign authority was a momentous outcome of the Glorious Revolution, providing how its main causes were addressed in the new order.

Colonial obsessions, thus, came low down the pecking order in the wider meaning of the Glorious Revolution, William III and his officials maintained that the limits placed on the royal prerogative because of the revolutionary settlement did not extend to the colonies. For example, the eternally troublesome colony of Massachusetts had to accept a new charter in 1691, with a governor appointed by the Crown who could veto legislation and with Massachusetts required to submit its laws for review in London and open its franchise beyond members of the Congregational churches. Nevertheless, most colonists welcomed the revolutionary settlement, for, in practice, William III and his successors tolerated settler representative government (although this does not amount to 'salutary neglect') and significant local control over the justice system. Moreover, the bonds of empire were strengthened by an increasingly vibrant Atlantic world in which goods, ideas and people moved freely.

Because the empire brought so many obvious economic benefits to Britain, there was an enormous incentive for all sides to try and make it work, often through increasingly important transatlantic lobbying and interest groups. Nevertheless, William III's refusal to budge on accepting limits on his royal prerogative outside England, Wales, and Scotland meant that while the eighteenth-century empire was more integrated than the Stuarts' scattered and highly autonomous plantations and with a considerable acceptance of local self-control, it was an empire whose inhabitants were subject to royal authority in a way that was no longer the constitutional norm within the British archipelago.

The Board of Trade

In addition, from 1696, a new imperial infrastructure emerged with a replacement of the old and now ineffectual Lords of Trade established under Charles II. The new institution was the Board of Trade. Unlike the Lords of Trade, which was a subset of the Privy Council and had some power to implement policy, the Board of Trade was a purely advisory body except for a brief time in the 1750s under the assertive rule of the Earl of Halifax. Despite this lack of a role within cabinet and despite the small size of the colonial bureaucracy it controlled (it had 98 officials in 1730, 95 in 1760–61, before a sizeable increase to 225 in 1780–81), its lack of influence in the imperial administration in Britain was noticeable, especially when contrasted with the importance of ministers responsible for Britain's military activities and its overall weakness on the ground in the colonies, where governors and other officials were routinely ignored when they were personally unpopular or put forward unpopular policies. Nevertheless, the Board of Trade had a profound influence on the culture of the empire. The main reason behind this lasting influence was that the board made the agenda that governed imperial policy and it stuck to that agenda rigidly at least until 1763.

Its creation in 1696 points to that year as being one of enormous significance in British imperial history, followed as it was closely by restrictions on the Royal African Company in 1698 and expansion within the East India Company as it got a new charter in 1700. A new Navigation Act was passed in 1696, so, too, was a crackdown on piracy initiated by Edward Randolph, a tireless proselytiser for imperial integration, and vice-admiralty courts were established to govern lawlessness and smuggling on the sea. As Michael Hall argues, the creation of vice-admiralty courts and the Navigation Act revision, in general, 'struck so closely at the government of the colonies as to alter fundamentally their relationship to the Crown.'[9]

The Board of Trade was a centralising force, signalling a shift in thinking about empire in the late seventeenth- and early eighteenth-centuries in which trade was increasingly seen as crucial to the building of a strong metropolitan state and the projection of imperial power. It started with a bang, orchestrating in its first four years a series of policies designed to increase royal authority in the colonies. Its most important policy, however, was very contested. It insisted on making governors' instructions issued to them on royal appointment binding on colonial assemblies. To an extent, this policy was an admission that self-government by settlers was irrevocable – the Hanoverians may have wanted to increase the Crown's executive and judicial power in the Empire, but it never tried, as James II had done in the 1680s, to govern colonies without assemblies. As Craig Yirush argues, 'following the Glorious Revolution, political debate in the empire centered on how far royal (and later parliamentary) authority could be extended before it violated what the settlers considered to be the rights of Englishmen outside the realm.'[10]

There was always a fatal flaw in the empire's political structure – the uncertain relationship between parliamentary sovereignty and colonial rights. Colonists agreed with the British government on one point – their right to self-government based on their inheritances as English-born subjects. Imperial officials, no matter whether they were Tories or Whigs and no matter their fierce arguments over aspects of imperial policy, all agreed on the privileges of parliamentary sovereignty and the right of Parliament to revoke colonial charters and restructure the internal constitutions of the colonies. This delicate and uncertain balance that emerged in the crucial years between the Glorious Revolution and imperial consolidation in the 1720s shaped the politics of empire right up to the era of the American Revolution.

The Board of Trade never gave up its claims, as can be seen in the most comprehensive report on the colonies done before the 1760s, by Martin Bladen in 1721. Bladen was a long-serving Board of Trade official, serving between 1717 and 1741, and a disciple of both Randolph and Blathwayt. He had excellent experience of imperial matters, especially on determining the borders Britain was contesting with France and Spain in the St. Lawrence Valley of present-day Canada. He also, in customary eighteenth-century fashion, placed relatives into colonial governorships, such as in Maryland. The 1721 Board of Trade report was highly critical about the weaknesses of royal authority in the colonies, especially outside royal colonies. Private colonies such as Pennsylvania were lambasted as disloyal: Pennsylvania apparently had a charter which gave it five years to send its laws to London, during which time these laws were in force, and just five months for the Crown to review them. They decried how little revenue they received from the colonies, especially in North America, where the colonists seemed to be getting rich without paying any taxes; how Crown privileges were extended corruptly to individuals (although Bladen himself was hardly an innocent in this respect); that individuals were cutting down royal woods to the detriment of the Royal Navy, which relied on such timber for shipbuilding, and concluded that the weakness of royal authority in the empire was detrimental to Britain's wealth and, by extension, to its military and strategic power.

It urged the king to revoke colonial charters to private colonies; reduce the patchwork of colonial institutions so that there could be a single approach to Native American problems; and place all of the colonies in the jurisdiction of one person, a captain-general with a fixed salary out of a permanent revenue act (the granting of a permanent revenue was constantly refused in the colonies, except, and for unusual and particular reasons, in Jamaica in 1723). Unsurprisingly, it recommended that the Board of Trade be the principal location of imperial jurisdiction. Its vision was the common one that thinkers on imperialism kept advancing and which kept getting ignored by key decision makers. It was an argument for political centralisation, which seemed obvious to men in Whitehall but less so to merchants in Calcutta or Kingston or to fur traders in the American interior, that would allow for a more effective enforcement of the empire's commercial regulations. It would render the colonies economically beneficial to Britain, plus strengthen the British Empire against French competition. Britain might not be at war with France in 1721, but France remained a central threat to British ambitions in India, the West Indies and North America. The demand for political reform in the empire was thus driven by both commercial and geopolitical considerations.

The next decade saw a few movements in the direction of greater centralisation, but that movement was not pronounced. The Crown showed little interest in spending more money on the colonies, especially in North America. Britain was, as always, more interested in Europe than in empire, especially with the accession to the throne of George II in 1727, a man hugely invested in his homeland of Hanover in Germany. Indeed, Hanover occupied much more attention in the government of Robert Walpole than did any part of empire. Moreover, what Walpole and later the Newcastle-Pelham ministry was most interested in was the maintenance of their power at home, and for them, the main purpose of empire was to give sinecures that gave colonial income to their supporters in Parliament.

Above all, Walpole thought that a light hand rather than a heavy touch worked best in the empire, especially in North America, a region less important to him than the revenue-producing West Indies. Overall, it was a policy that worked well, making the ambitions of the Board of Trade seem overstated. Outside of Highland Scotland, support for the Hanoverian monarchy – a central plank of the Walpolean Whig consensus – grew stronger over time, with Britons, Irish, Americans and West Indians alike seeing the Protestant George II as a liberty-loving ruler who provided protection in return for allegiance. The British constitution was venerated not just by Britons but also by philosophers such as Montesquieu and Voltaire as the best in Europe in the way that it balanced democracy, aristocracy and monarchy in ways that led to the advancement of liberty and the promotion of commerce. As David Armitage has argued, this was the peak period when the ideology of the British Empire was 'Protestant, commercial, maritime and free.'[11] When Martin Bladen put forward a revised plan from the one ignored in 1721 in 1739, taking advantage of what he thought were the new conditions of war with Spain in the War of Jenkins' Ear, it fell on deaf ears, once again. Walpole was more interested in getting the cooperation of the colonies for wars against Spain (from 1739) and, under the Duke of Newcastle, against France (1744–48) than in entertaining Bladen's centralising tendencies.

The result, as Bladen might have predicted, was a disturbing breakdown of authority in the empire from the 1740s. That breakdown led to worries that France would take advantage of eroded royal authority in the empire and to a reinvigorated Board of Trade from 1748 under the leadership of the Earl of Halifax. What was mostly different in 1748 was that a powerful aristocrat with ministerial and perhaps prime ministerial ambitions decided that the usually unimportant area of imperial affairs (at least for highly placed young men on the make) was a place to make his name. The new assertiveness under Halifax encouraged some royal governors, such as Robert Dinwiddie, lieutenant governor of Virginia between 1751 and 1758, who had been frustrated by what they considered were continual colonial affronts to royal authority, to support Halifax in creating a unitary empire on the 1721 model, with the colonies subordinate to the king in Parliament.

Managing the empire

Where the Board of Trade was important before 1748 was in the formulation rather than the implementation of imperial policy. As can be seen in how its proposals for greater centralisation were generally ignored, the Board of Trade spoke mainly for itself when it sought greater powers before the Seven Years' War. Halifax's efforts to give the Board of Trade a more decisive role in making imperial rules and in using the Board of Trade in a concerted plan to implement its vision for establishing metropolitan supremacy in imperial government was almost wholly unsuccessful, something understood by Charles Townshend, a leading imperial politician of the 1760s who cut his teeth in government under Halifax, but which was not appreciated by Townshend's political rival and sometimes ally, George Grenville, architect of the Stamp Act.

What Townshend was able to do under Halifax was to look at the empire as being an empire that was moving from an assemblage of regions and societies into a coherent and consolidated system. He had to deal with the management of a commercial empire in an Atlantic world increasingly defined by imperial competition, with wars as one result of competition becoming too intense. It was a world in which the colonies were becoming settled societies and producing ever more goods, snapped up in a Britain being transformed by a consumer revolution and the development of homegrown industries that manufactured goods to sell to the Americas and by the rise of enlightened and ambitious merchants in London intent in improving Britain's fortunes, and their own, through trade in the Atlantic. Thus, by the time that Townshend, a member of Parliament (MP), sat on the board from 1747 (having failed to gain what he most wanted, which was a seat on the Admiralty), centre and metropole were increasingly tied together by dense networks that gradually became an integrated part of broader global patterns that themselves were in the process of becoming integrated.

The reality of this integrated system leapt ahead of the bureaucratic structures designed to keep this system under control. As Patrick Griffin argues, 'the empire resembled a rabbit warren of differing arrangements passed under different monarchs all for different reasons to address different problems.'[12] New levels of trade started to eclipse older constitutional apparatuses. Charles Townshend dealt mainly with the Atlantic but also had a purview over the Levant, the East India Company and the rapidly growing Atlantic slave trade. As was true for most statesmen involved in advancing British interests through imperial adventuring, Townshend appreciated that the West Indies and their plantations linked the whole imperial system together. He intervened in the slave trade regularly, as he knew that places such as Jamaica depended, in large part, on the policies of the Board of Trade and that Britain's future, he suspected, rose and fell as the islands prospered or suffered. Townshend made a report in 1751 on whether Georgia, founded without slaves, should become a slave society on the model of its neighbour, South Carolina. He thought that slavery was essential for colonial prosperity because 'in almost every colony where the use of slaves has been introduced, laws have been passed for the well-ordering and governing them.' Georgia thus became transformed in the 1750s into a fully functioning slave society. Townshend thus contributed to the creation of a British Atlantic commercial system largely from his desk at Whitehall and from his home in Mayfair.

He became part of a new and more aggressive generation of imperial statesmen, willing to follow Halifax in believing that Parliament should assert more control over colonial affairs. Where Townshend differed from George Grenville, another of Halifax's acolytes, was that he was less convinced that a recognition of parliamentary supremacy in Britain meant that any assertion of its authority over the colonies and that their assemblies did not have to result in a constitutional crisis. Grenville's understanding of imperial rule was one of imperial grandeur, like centralised visions held on the continent, and expressed without attention to a system of thought or a thought of system as a concept that might be of use. Townshend, by contrast, thought that once parliamentary authority in the empire had been established (here he agreed with Grenville) that each constituent part of the empire could serve the specific good for which it was best suited. Thus, the Caribbean should be opened to measures of free trade that was not allowed in North America and should even be allowed to be an exception to mercantilist theory, with slaves being able to be shipped from the West Indies to foreign colonies.

Metropolitan authorities from 1715 to 1756, however, did not hold to Grenville or Halifax's later ideas about the importance of colonial submission to imperial authority. They seldom pushed measures that would cause trouble in their Atlantic empire or which interfered with colonial cooperation during the many periods of warfare after 1739 that Britain was engaged in. In the same way, settlers did not insist that they would influence the external affairs of Britain or, until the Seven Years' war changed things, be involved in the empire's policies towards Native Americans. They did, however, insist on autonomy in internal affairs, a feat which they largely achieved, due to the British government thinking that stopping such autonomy a low priority. Governors continually complained that when they raised issues of concern which showed colonial violations of the royal prerogative, the British government either undermined them with limited support or allowed settlers to get their own way. Even when the imperial government was minded to take a position in colonial disputes, as in the prolonged battle between Governor Charles Knowles and the Jamaican Assembly in the 1750s, when Britain sided with Knowles, at least initially, and censured Jamaica in the only formal censure of a colonial assembly made by Parliament, governors never got full support from the imperial centre – Knowles, for example, was eventually sent home in some disgrace.

By the early 1760s, however, when the Jamaican Assembly had an altercation with a colonial governor, these transgressions by local leaders from the mid-1750s had been largely forgotten. Just as in 1758, when the Assembly forced Knowles from office and the British government acquiesced in that expulsion, an almighty row over the exercise of the royal prerogative between Governor William Henry Lyttleton and the Jamaican Assembly ended in a comprehensive victory in 1764 to local Jamaican politicians. Lyttleton's defeat was not surprising in a period after 1750 when governors were less likely than before to be attuned to local concerns, were more obviously politicised and were more expected to follow the party line of the administration which appointed them.

One major reason why tension between settlers and the British government increased in the 1760s was that colonial governors were less impressive than before and not as able to accommodate themselves to both settler and metropolitan demands. Successful governors usually walked this balance, doing so by paying attention to the interests and wishes of settler politicians in a system of imperial governance accurately described by Jack Greene as 'negotiated authority.' By 'negotiated authority' Greene meant that governors maintained a delicate and internally contradictory balance of power through the careful cultivation of the interests of well-placed and well-connected settlers while insisting on the authority that the Crown assigned to itself.[13] Usually, they managed this negotiated settlement only by keeping their metropolitan superiors in the dark about violations they were meant to report about. When a governor had to complain about colonial violations of imperial authority, it was usually too late – he had lost the confidence of the people he was ruling, and governance then became close to impossible. That opening of colonial politics to the imperial gaze was relatively infrequent in the 1730s and 1740s, when British America was fortunate in having several successful and long-serving royal governors, such as Edward Trelawney in Jamaica, William Gooch and Francis Fauquier in Virginia, James Glen in South Carolina and Jonathan Belcher and William Shirley in Massachusetts. These governors tended to see themselves as part of the colonial establishment rather than opposed to local elites. As a result, they avoided confrontation, engendering lots of goodwill which was used to reinforce the charisma of metropolitan rule, especially that of British monarchs, in the colonies.

But by the 1760s, the quality of colonial governors notably declined, just as the problems of imperial governance became more urgent. William Burke complained in September 1776 that 'these gentlemen who held American employments had been the most zealous of all the others against . . . the claims of the colonists.' Governors such as Sir Francis Bernard and Thomas Hutchinson of Massachusetts, who could not walk a steady line between upholding royal authority and evincing a commitment to settler interests and mores, became inadequate defenders of metropolitan goals whenever those goals differed from local opinion, By contrast, the relatively little known Sir Henry Moore, governor of New York just after the Stamp Act was put in place in 1765 and previously a Jamaican governor of great distinction who was given a baronetcy for the skill by which he managed an imperial crisis, the massive slave revolt led by Tackey and Wager in Jamaica in 1760, pursued policies that alternated imperial firmness with political reconciliation.

His skill in maintaining his authority while being popular with settlers prevented the most volatile of Britain's American colonies from exploding into revolt in the ways that happened in Boston. Most important, Moore governed as Walpole did – with a light touch, respecting the rights of colonists to have a voice in how they were governed and agreeing to consensual governance, just as was fundamental within local politics in seventeenth- and eighteenth-century England, with policy based on a flexible interpretation of the English common law. Some contemporaries were convinced that consensual government worked. Adam Smith argued in 1776 that the success of the British in America was due to having lots of available land taken from Native Americans and to colonists having 'the liberty to manage their own affairs their own way.' In this respect, he echoed very closely the claims made by Daniel Dulany nearly half a century earlier.

Interregional connections

Imperial Britain worked in two ways, only one of which statesmen in London recognised. One relationship was between individual parts of the empire and the imperial centre – a relationship which was manifested in formal institutions such as colonial governorships and imperial legislation, such as the Navigation Acts from 1651, often revisited, which regulated colonial trade within a broadly mercantilist framework. But there was another sort of imperial relationship, one which became increasingly important from the mid-eighteenth century where the relations between colonies mattered. It is going too far to say that by the 1740s, the British Empire formed a unified 'system' in which the commerce of one section fed into that of another, but the trend was moving that way, especially in the most economically dynamic parts of the empire, such as the West Indies, the Middle Atlantic colonies of New York and Pennsylvania, the slave forts of West Africa and the trading enclaves of South Asia.

The dependence of one part of the empire on other parts was made dramatically clear in the last stages of the crisis that led to the War of American Independence. Caribbean planters realised with a jolt that if revolution came to the Thirteen Colonies, then the West Indies would be badly affected. George Walker, a Barbadian planter, told the House of Commons about the 'absolute dependence of the West Indies upon North America for subsistence and for lumber.' The Caribbean was provided with salted fish from Newfoundland and New England, timber from New England and the Middle Atlantic and flour, livestock and grains from New York and Pennsylvania. It meant that 'North America is truly the granary of the West Indies.' Rice came from South Carolina, ships from Bermuda and, although Walker did not mention it, labour in the form of enslaved Africans from West Africa. These Africans, moreover, were purchased in West Africa using textiles from India as a principal form of exchange. The imperial economy, at least in the Caribbean, although considerably less so in other places, such as the Chesapeake and the American interior, was linked in multiple ways that made the parts that made the empire seem, by the 1740s, greater than the whole.

Walker's views were quickly realised from 1776. In Jamaica, planters operated a just-in-time plantation management system, where they devoted all their good land to growing sugar for export, mainly to Britain, neglecting food crops in the hope that they could buy imported supplies from North America and Ireland. The stopping of supplies from America caused famine and thousands of deaths among the enslaved. The imperial economy, it became clear, was a delicate mechanism, easily disrupted by war and geopolitical competition.

We can see the extent of the interdependence of colonies in the British Empire in the mid-eighteenth century in looking at Jamaican commerce, as outlined in shipping list records. These records show that nearly as many ships were registered in North America (3,179 ships) as from Britain (3,885 ships) and more than from the Caribbean (2,245 ships). Of these ships, most (2,060) were owned by people in New York, Pennsylvania and Massachusetts, with few registered in the Chesapeake. The total value of goods entering Jamaica from North America was very large, about £400,000 per annum (when exports to Britain were not much more than double that amount and when Jamaica was a colony particularly oriented around exports), with £125,000 per annum sent Jamaica to the mainland. Pennsylvania was easily the biggest market for Jamaican exports, with £100,185 per annum, with Massachusetts with £58,495, New York with £37,996 and South Carolina with £34,405. The trade with the Chesapeake, the most populous plantation region of America, was much smaller, at £24,028 per annum.

Philadelphia, as Jamaica's largest market, sent to Jamaica one-third of the colony's beer, beef, pork and bricks; half of its bread, wine, butter and cheese; almost all its flour; three-quarters of its tallow, soap and candles; and 80 per cent of Jamaica's ham. Jamaica also received lots of beef, pork, butter and fish from Ireland and logwood from Honduras. Probably the most important market, however, was West Africa, from which Jamaica received 5,367 enslaved captives per annum between 1752 and 1769. In short, Jamaica was a central node in the mid-eighteenth-century British Atlantic world, as connected to North America and West Africa as to Britain and Ireland. Other colonies were less outward-directed than Jamaica, but in almost all colonies, except for Maryland and Virginia, inter-imperial trade was significant throughout the eighteenth century.

Imperial agendas

The Board of Trade excelled not in management but in giving overall direction to imperial policy. It is important to note that this overall direction was never a clearly enunciated policy and happened by contingency as much as by design. As William Burke wrote in a pioneering transnational imperial comparison in 1757, European colonisation was 'not pursued upon any regular plan, but . . . were formed, grew, and flourished, as accidents, the nature of the climate, or the dispositions of private men happened to operate.'

But we can elucidate dominant trends. First, the interests of the empire were always to be subordinated to the interests of Britain, either economically or geopolitically. There was never any real suggestion that in any dispute between Britain and settlers, settler interests should prevail. Occasionally, voices were heard that Britons should listen more to its subjects overseas and that the colonists were correct in thinking that the empire was an extension of, rather than different from, metropolitan Britain. But the overwhelming tendency was to always put Britain first, the empire second. The primacy of British interests was expressed as early as 1651 in the Navigation Acts, by which colonial commerce was forced to travel within boundaries determined by the English Crown.

The second objective was to get rid of private colonies and separate sovereignties rather than Parliament. That effort was largely successful. In Britain, a crackdown in the Highlands after 1746 reduced some of the powers of Highland chieftains, notably their ability to raise private armies, bound by feudal obligations. In the Americas, the number of royal colonies increased from just seven in 1675 to fourteen in 1730 and to twenty-four by 1763. Only the charter colonies of Rhode Island and Connecticut and the proprietary colonies of Maryland, Pennsylvania and Delaware stayed outside royal jurisdiction. The relationship between proprietary colonies and the imperial government was not always harmonious, notably in Pennsylvania when disputes between the proprietors, the Penn family; the local government; and the British state were endemic. In India, of course, a quite different arrangement obtained. Philip Stern describes the arrangement as a distinct 'company state,' where British interests were managed by the East India Company. In Stern's view, this mode of government ended after the Battle of Plassey, when the expanding British imperial state hijacked this semi-private mode of governance. Recent work on eighteenth-century British involvement in India suggests that Stern may have overstated his case. Britain gave considerable aid to the East India Company before 1757 for infrastructure requests, following what they also did in West Africa with the Royal African Company. Britain thought these expenditures did not belong to the East India Company but came under their jurisdiction.[14]

A third objective was less successful, which was exercising political control and financial power over colonial legislatures. As noted earlier, only Jamaica was willing to grant royal governors a perpetual revenue act, guaranteeing an annual sum of money to the imperial government. It did so for specific reasons to do with the nature of its settlement as a conquest in 1655 from the Spanish. The Crown had to agree that free white Jamaicans were entitled to the benefit of English laws. The result was that Britain was the overlord of multiple overseas polities with little in common with each other except that settlers were emotionally connected to Britain and that each place was obedient to a common monarch. Thus, the constitutional situation of these polities was that they were composite monarchies, similar to other emerging European state. As C. A. Bayly notes, what Britain aspired to but never achieved until the early nineteenth century, and then only in some places, was a means whereby their expanding state power was used in 'a systemic attempt to centralise power within colonial territories, to exalt the executive above local liberties and to remove non-European and non-British from positions of all but marginal political authority.' Bayly believes that these measures represented an 'attempt to establish overseas despotisms which mirrored in many ways the polities of neo-absolutism and the Holy Alliance of contemporary Europe.'[15]

Ireland was different. It was close to Britain, full of potentially rebellious Catholics (who, unlike African slaves, Native Americans and Bengalis, could not be easily distinguished from the rest of the white population) and was a logical place from which a European nation, probably France, could launch an invasion of Britain, as had been made manifest in James VII and II resistance to William III in Ulster during the Glorious Revolution. Consequently, Ireland was tightly ruled, as we saw in a previous chapter. In addition to being more firmly connected to metropolitan power, it was thoroughly drawn into the metropolitan patronage network – its viceroys were leading English aristocrats, often with substantial landholdings in Ireland. It also had lots of British troops on the island. Political matters were governed by Poyning's Law, a late medieval holdover under which every piece of Irish legislation was vetted and re-vetted by the British-appointed Irish Privy Council.

Finally, the Board of Trade attempted to regulate ever more fully the activities of royal governors through very detailed royal instructions given to governors at the time of appointment. It also tried to get ever more information out of their gubernatorial representatives, insisting on more frequent reports on a wide range of activities and wanting more frequent reports on a wide range of activities and wanting more frequent submission of journals, laws and accounts for the benefit of the board. Once again, Jamaica is a good example of how after 1748 bureaucratic interference from the imperial centre became more intrusive. When Governor Knowles clashed with the Jamaican Assembly over the largely symbolic issue of moving the island's capital from planter-dominated Spanishtown to merchant-controlled Kingston, the Board of Trade asked for and partially received a whole series of information about social and economic conditions in the island that today provides lots of information for social historians.

The ironic result of increased information gathering from the 1740s and a more determined stance to impose order on recalcitrant colonial subjects was that a system of colonial management that, overall, had served Britain well since the Glorious Revolution was discarded with disastrous results after the Seven Years' War. By 1780, Edmund Burke could declare that 'the board of trade and plantations has not been of any use to the colonies.' All the successful American colonies preceded in date of creation the start of the Board of Trade in 1696 and subsequent colonies such as Georgia and Nova Scotia were mostly failures, the former having, in Burke's view, 'a dead political visage' and the latter being an 'ill-thriven, hard-visaged, and ill-formed brat, that cost a fortune and returned little profit'. What Burke did not appreciate, however, was what the dynamic and growing imperial state of the early to mid-eighteenth century had done through using money in reshaping the development of imperial infrastructure, from ports to forts to roads and to buildings of all kinds. Many of these activities occurred under the guise of military expenditure, such as provisioning Native American roads, building roads in the interior and promoting the Post Office and various communication networks. What Burke also failed to understand, as was true in the case of most North Americans as well, is that the relative indifference of Britain to its overseas empire in North America was not replicated in other polities attached to England. The most conspicuous example of how the British government between 1680 and 1756 cared deeply about and interfered regularly in the affairs of a place on the peripheries was its attitude to Scotland, although we could also look at India, Ireland or the West Indies for examples of greater British intervention into local matters than was the case in North America.

Scotland

Scottish participation in Britain's eighteenth-century overseas expansion is peculiar, reflecting its status as not only a region colonised by England but also a colonising region itself – perhaps even before the creation of the United States, the first post-colonial state. Scotland penetrated the British Empire from early in the seventeenth century as setters, indentured labourers and traders. In this way, they were building on a long-standing tradition of trading, sojourning and settling in the Baltic, in Scandinavia and in the Low Countries. They were also soldiers, famous as mercenaries in European wars, including the Wars of Religion in the sixteenth century and the Thirty Years' War in central Europe in the seventeenth century.

All these characteristics continued after Scotland had joined England in the new polity of Great Britain in 1707. But even before then, Scotland was central to English overseas expansion, as noted in Chapter 5, through their extensive emigration to the Ulster plantations from 1600 onwards. The Scottish view of the world was always outward-looking. In part, this outward orientation reflected the nature of its society, which made thinking out of Scotland a necessity for much of its population. Scotland was a land of relatively few people, fewer than 1 million in the late seventeenth century, and had lands that were often marginal and of poor quality. Famine was never far away from Scottish life, notably after 1693, when repeated bad harvests in the Highlands spread to the Lowlands three years later, creating crippling food shortages and untold misery that was not relieved until the better harvest of 1700. Migration was a means of keeping the Scottish population from starvation. During the seventeenth century, population depletion from migration might have been as high as 250,000 people, helping keep the total population relatively static, not only acting as a constraint on manpower but also lessening the impact of Malthusian disasters as in the 1693–1700 period.

Seventeenth-century migration also meant that Scottish opportunities for colonisation further afield than Ulster were seriously limited because Scottish resources were too limited and scattered to provide any other colony with a supply of artisans and agricultural workers. Scotland drifted in the seventeenth century into a form of economic dependence on England. Scottish leaders resisted this seemingly inexorable shift to dependency, looking as early as 1680 for ways to overcome the looming balance of trade disaster they saw in having their trade confined to England while their ability to trade beyond Europe was hindered by protectionist English legislation in the form of the Navigation Acts. The Crown was also unhelpful, favouring its English rather than its Scottish side in the late seventeenth century. It was only in 1695 that William III finally conceded a charter to the Company of Scotland to allow Scotland to trade with America, Africa, India and China.

It encouraged the Company of Scotland to embark on one of the great tragedies of imperialism in Britain, the Darien scheme. It was a fiasco of remarkable proportions which came close to bankrupting Scotland and which led

Scotland closer to the Union of 1707 than might otherwise have been the case. The aim was to access Spanish trade through establishing a Scottish colony in the Spanish territory of Panama. Between 1698 and 1700, vast sums of money were sunk into this scheme, one put forward by William Paterson, a financial entrepreneur who, like his compatriot, John Law, who nearly bank-rupted France in the early eighteenth century, was addicted to big risks. He had won big through creating the Bank of England in 1694. He believed he would continue his success in Darien, describing his project as 'one of the most beneficial and best-grounded pieces of Trade at this day in Christendom.' Excessive advertising encouraged migrants to move to Darien and investors to invest heavily in the project. The latter lost their money; the former lost their lives, dying in droves in the malign tropical environment of Panama. As T. M. Devine and Philipp R. Rössner conclude,

> managerial incompetence, the hostility of Spain, and lack of support from England ensured that the venture collapsed in national humiliation and financial disaster. But the sheer scale of the endeavour and the huge invest-ment it attracted from Scottish society in general confirmed the aspiration of the nation to seek its economic future in the New World.[16]

The latter qualification is important to note. By most reckonings, Scottish involvement in empire in the eighteenth century brought great benefits to the country, which recovered well from the travails of the 1690s to be a lead-ing centre of Enlightenment culture, with an economy increasingly oriented around overseas trade with the British Empire. It was, after England, Europe's second-largest importer of Chesapeake tobacco which made up to 40 per cent of total imports and exports by 1760. The Atlantic colonial trades, including sugar as well as tobacco, underpinned Scotland's remarkable commercial success before further transformations because of the Industrial Revolution. Scotland was especially important in the East India Company, not just as merchants but also as administrators and perhaps most of all as soldiers. They evinced a degree of curiosity about foreign cultures – they were noted 'Orientalists,' establishing the contours of Western investigations of Indian religions and cultures – and were markedly partial to favouring their own country people in their financial dealings as particularly adept bankers. To critics, this Scottish version of mutu-ality led to accusations of clannishness and exclusivity. Overall, however, Scot-tish involvement in empire was impressive. Andrew Thompson, looking at the nineteenth century as much as the eighteenth century, notes that

> of all the peoples of the United Kingdom, it is the Scots' contribution to the British Empire that stands out as disproportionate. They were the first peoples of the British Isles to take on an imperial mentality, and possibly the longest to sustain one. In the spheres of education, engineering, explo-ration, medicine, commerce, and shipping the Scots earned a particularly strong reputation for empire building.[17]

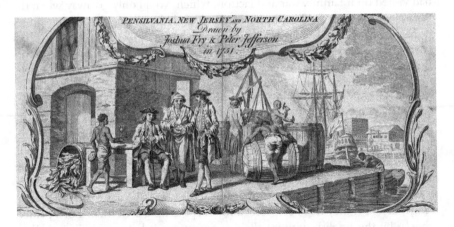

Figure 6.2 The tobacco trade, Merchants relax while slaves load barrels with tobacco bound for export, Joshua Fry and Peter Jefferson, 1751

Source: Everett Collection Inc/Alamy Stock Photo.

This tale of success would have seemed surprising to contemporaries in the early eighteenth century. Scotland, even as a constituent part of Britain, was the most troublesome region for the English to control. Of course, English disputes with Scotland go far back in time, to medieval and early modern wars. But conflict continued into the eighteenth century with two major Jacobite rebellions against Hanoverian rule in 1715–16 and 1745–46. It was clear from the Glorious Revolution onwards that Scotland was resolved to maintain its own identity and not be swallowed into England. The Scots, unlike the English, did not hold to the fiction that James VII and II had abdicated. Instead, they insisted that monarchical government had always been limited and that the people had the right to get rid of a monarch if they believed he was acting illegally. They argued, therefore, that the Glorious Revolution was a restoration of the Scottish 'legal limited monarchy.' They argued that the Glorious Revolution was not a change in constitutional arrangements but a continuation of existing practice and that their religious and political independence was enhanced but not altered by the events of 1688–89. Their main response to the Glorious Revolution was to increase the powers of the Scottish parliament, with firm notice to London that they considered they were self-governed and that they need not abide by the idea of the parliamentary sovereignty of the British Parliament – one seen as mostly English in composition and influence.

Scots disagreed fiercely among themselves about the future direction of their country. The majority Presbyterian population believed that they had the right to rule Scotland as they pleased. A minority and heartily disliked (by Presbyterians) Scottish Episcopalian group, concentrated in the north-east and in the Jacobite Highlands, objected to the Hanoverian regime on religious grounds. They argued that when Scotland spurned indefeasible hereditary right, God had visited on it famine, war and faction, which would only go away when the Stuarts were restored. Hostility to England tended to come from other directions, however. The Union of 1707 was widely unpopular, seen correctly as a corrupt bargain entered into by avaricious and self-interested aristocrats. Scotland was even more oligarchical in its politics than England or Ireland. A central plank of British policy towards Scotland under George I and II, therefore, was to cultivate the support of leading Scottish noblemen. What they needed and got was people like the best colonial governors, men who could navigate between supporting the Hanoverian regime and securing Scottish interests. They found what they wanted and needed in John and Archibald Campbell, Second and Third Dukes of Argyll, respectively, who controlled Scotland from 1708 to 1761, virtually as a personal fiefdom.

What irked Scots most was that with the death of the last Stuart monarch, Anne, in 1714, they had been forced to accept as king a German-born prince, chosen by the English without their consultation. It led to a major rebellion against George I, led by the embittered and self-seeking Earl of Mar and supported belatedly by James, the Old Pretender, who was twenty-seven in 1715. The Pretender proved to be as ineffectual a leader as his father, deserting his people at the time of their greatest need and returning in humiliation to the continent, leaving his supporters to face the wrath of the British government. The rebellion failed for purely military reasons, Mar was an inferior soldier to Argyll who occupied the strategic lynchpin of Scotland at Stirling, ensuring Mar's defeat. Nevertheless, this was still the most serious major challenge to Hanoverian rule that this family (still in power today) ever faced. The Pretender had foreign support from France and Spain, although the death of Louis XIV in September 1715 was a setback. And the Royal Navy stayed firm in support of the Hanoverians. If it had wavered, then the West Indies might have been lost to France. The rebellion could have succeeded. If the Scots Jacobites had linked up with potential rebels in the strategically important north-east of England, cut off London from its fuel supplies, then mobilised the large Catholic population of Lancashire and taken advantage of Tory discontent with the Whig coup d'état of 1715 which put them in power for decades, then George I would have been forced to fight for his crown probably just north of London. Having stated that, support for the Jacobites in Scotland was always uncertain, despite discontent with the Union. George I was probably not in any real danger, which may have one reason why in 1716, just after the rebellion had been put down, he left for a five-month trip to Hanover.

The result of the 1715 rebellion was the solidification of the Hanoverians in power. Unsuccessful rebellion strengthens a challenged regime. Debate within the Scottish elites between Jacobite nationalists and unionists moved decisively in favour of the latter by 1720, purely on grounds of practicality, Scottish support for the Union thus remained firm until the 2010s. For British rulers after 1715, Scotland seemed manageable except in the Highlands, which was thought to be uncivilised, barbaric and militaristic. Britain tried to subdue the region by a mixture of rewards and coercion. It sent General George Wade to be military supremo in the Highlands, made examples of anyone showing incipient Jacobitism, tried to disarm the clans and established an effective chain of military barracks linked to a system of new roads. In addition, they established many schools of religious instruction, although teachers were not allowed to teach in Gaelic, making many of the schools largely redundant. In 1727, they also raised £30,000 to stimulate the Scottish economy. Their efforts were relatively successful. When a new Jacobite rebellion occurred in 1745–56, led by the twenty-five-year-old Charles Stuart, the Young Pretender, taking advantage of the end of the War of the Austrian Succession as a pretext to involve Britain in another war of royal succession, only eighteen clans joined him, down from the twenty-four that had supported his father thirty years earlier.

The 1745 rebellion was not as dangerous as in 1715, although it caused major alarms among an anxious ruling class and was only ended when the Royal Duke of Cumberland defeated the Jacobites at the Battle of Culloden in April 1746. Cumberland took strong revenge against his defeated enemies, giving him the nickname of 'Butcher,' a nickname which followed him ever after, sullying his reputation permanently. The consequences of rebellion were that it showed to Britons that 'British' identity was a fragile thing and that the Highlands was full of 'Robbers and Banditti.' But the long-term effects of the putting down of the 1745 rebellion was to end forever the threat of Jacobitism. It destroyed Highland autonomy by dragging a reluctant and uninterested Hanoverian Crown into the clans' mountain fastness. Thus, British victory at Culloden gave the government carte blanche to reform Highland society.

Argyll's representative in London, Andrew Fletcher, Lord Milton, was especially keen on the political emasculation of the Highlands and in changing their cultural traits. He advocated policies that combined commercial progress with political stability. His plan for the Highlands was that his policies were intended to 'civilize them by introducing Agriculture, Fisherys, and manufactures, and thereby by degrees extirpating their barbarity, with their chief marks of distinction, their language and dress, and preventing their idleness, the present source of their poverty, Theift, and Rebellion.' The policies he advocated, and which were advanced by the Newcastle–Pelham government, were numerous, but the most important act put forward was the ending of hereditary judicial rights attached to landownership, which rights were the cornerstone of clan chieftains' power. In a precursor to what George Grenville and Lord North tried to do in North America in the 1760s and 1770s, the Earl of Hardwick used legal radicalism to effect a 'Scotch Reformation.' He abolished ancient Scottish acts at a stroke and insisted on vesting judicial power fully in the Crown as the ultimate representative of the public, without which, he argued, guarantees of individual liberty were impossible. The political effects on the Highlands of the failed 1745 rebellion were thus considerable.

These acts were important but what really changed the Highlands after 1750 was economic modernisation by improving landlords who used enclosure to drive tenants off the land and into migration and the raising of new regiments to serve in the British army in the Seven Years' War, thus acclimating Highlanders to imperialism. The government, against the advice of hardliners such as Hardwicke, who thought that the Highlands was an unacceptable state-within-a-state and needed to be brought into line, practised a form of 'negotiated authority', as in North America, in which they used the power of clan chiefs to mobilise significant levels of Highlands' manpower but under the aegis of the state. Clan chiefs were happy, as they got money for their efforts, which they spent on agricultural modernisation. Meanwhile, ordinary Highlanders found serving in the British army a safety valve from the oppressions they suffered from their lairds. These lairds were now owners of estates rather than feudal lords, and their relationship to their tenants gradually came to resemble similar relationships elsewhere in Britain. By the 1770s, the Highlands was no longer a place apart, although ironically this was the time when the Highlands became valorised as a place of romanticism and military heroism. A 'patriotic partnership' between Highland elites and the British state was organised to the benefit of each. Ordinary Highlanders also benefitted from their service abroad, being awarded land in America seized from Native Americans. In short, the Highlands moved from being a colonised state into being themselves at the vanguard of colonisation efforts in North America and India. Thus, as Matthew Dziennik argues,

> the disproportionate level of Highland mobilization cannot be explained by state interest, economic necessity or defeatism alone; it can be explained by the coincidence of Gaelic self-interest and the interests of empire, an intersect that made many Highlanders politically patriotic even as they pursued their own advancement.[18]

Empire and performance

The maintenance of British authority overseas and within Britain depended on force, as the next chapter details. But force, as this chapter has revealed, was not enough to keep order in societies which did not have the coercive mechanisms of the modern state. State formation arose as much out of culture as out of politics and bureaucracy, and thus had an intrinsic performative character. Empire was sustained as much through theatrical displays and through day-to-day practices that enacted hierarchies of class, authority and race. Through ceremonies, the singing of such things as national anthems and the acceptance of cultural norms of Britishness in overseas locations, including areas such as India that were very different in climate and culture from anything to be found in Britain, Britain exercised a state power through day-to-day performative practices that legitimised European authority (and, by extension, the authority of white men) across the globe. Central to the performative nature of the imperial state was the promotion of civility and social and economic reform. That promotion was associated with the concept of the 'family'. As William Blackstone argued, by public police and economy, I mean the due regulation and domestic order of the Kingdom, whereby the individuals of the state, like members of a well-governed family, are bound to conform their general behaviour to the rule of propriety, good neighbourhood and good manners; to be decent, industrious, and inoffensive in their respective stations.

Kathleen Wilson interprets Blackstone as follows:

In other words, it was the regulation of individual and collective behavior that polity depended upon, rendering 'domestic order' within and without the state possible. In colonies, such regulation was taken on by masters and mistresses as well as governors and councillors, upon whose ability to 'see like a state' depended the reproduction of coercive labor regimes, the exertion of moral and intellectual suasion, and the imposition of social hierarchies among their various charges.[19]

Jamaica, again, is a key place where concerns about the family were evident. It was a society with a well-deserved reputation for demographic disaster, random cruelty and extreme racial division. Colonial rule was presaged on theatrical performances of privilege and terror with spectacularly violent punishments of enslaved persons. But white Jamaicans were vulnerable to attack for other reasons than for their failure to conform to British models of domesticity as outlined by Blackstone. Their infatuation with 'rioting in the goatish embraces' of black women, as historian Edward Long put it, resulted in a 'mongrel' population that seemed to contemporaries more Spanish American, and thus inferior, than British. Claims to Britishness required more than the political rhetoric of Daniel Dulany about colonial rights as inheritors of English liberty through birthright. If settlers in Jamaica and the white community in Bengal failed to create families that seemed recognisably British within societies that were grossly disordered, then it was hard to justify that they were contributing to a viable body politic no matter how much wealth these societies produced. It reminds us that we can think of the imperial state in different ways, as being as much performative as institutional. It was often in the margins of empire – Jamaica, the Scottish Highlands, Calcutta – where the contours of political and social order were thrown into sharpest relief. Those contours showed that increasingly Britain was an imperial nation and that their advances in imperialism between 1689 and 1763 were overwhelmingly successful.

Notes

1 Nicholas Canny, 'The Origins of Empire: An Introduction,' in Canny, ed., *The Oxford History of the British Empire: The Origins of Empire* (Oxford: Oxford University Press, 1988), 21.

2 Ibid., 22.

3 Jack P. Greene, 'Britain's Overseas Empire before 1780: Overwhelmingly Successful and Bureaucratically Challenged,' in Greene, ed., *Creating the British Atlantic: Essays on*

Transplantation, Adaptation, and Continuity (Charlottesville: University of Virginia, 2013), 116.

4 Richard S. Dunn, 'The Glorious Revolution,' in Canny, *Origins of Empire*, 463–4.

5 Ibid., 465.

6 Steven Pincus, 'Thinking the Empire Whole,' *History Australia* (forthcoming).

7 Steven C.A. Pincus and James A. Robinson, 'What Really Happened During the Glorious Revolution,' in Sebastian Galiari and Itai Sened, eds., *Institutions, Property Rights, and Economic Growth: The Legacy of Douglass North* (New York: Cambridge University Press, 2014), 192–222.

8 Julian Hoppit, *Britain's Political Economies: Parliament and Economic Life, 1660–1800* (Cambridge: Cambridge University Press, 2017), 25.

9 Michael Hall, 'The House of Lords, Edward Randolph, and the Navigation Act of 1696,' *William and Mary Quarterly*, 3rd ser. 14 (1957), 502.

10 Craig Yirush, *Settlers, Liberty, and Empire: The Roots of Early American Political Theory, 1675–1775* (Cambridge: Cambridge University Press, 2011), 90.

11 David Armitage, *Ideological Origins of the British Empire* (Cambridge: Cambridge University Press, 2000), 182.

12 Patrick Griffin, *The Townshend Moment: The Making of Empire and Revolution in the Eighteenth Century* (New Haven: Yale University Press, 2017), 25.

13 Greene, 'Britain's Overseas Empire before 1780,' 134.

14 Philip Stern, *The Company State: Corporate Sovereignty and the Early Modern Foundations of the British Empire in India* (New York: Oxford University Press, 2012); James Vaughn, *The Politics of Empire at the Accession of George III: The East India Company and the Crisis and Transformation of Britain's Imperial State* (New Haven: Yale University Press, 2019).

15 C.A. Bayly, *Imperial Meridian: The British Empire and the World, 1780–1830* (London: Longman, 1989), 8.

16 T.M. Devine and Philipp R. Rössner, 'Scots in the Atlantic Economy, 1600–1800,' in John M. Mackenzie and Devine, eds., *Oxford History of the British Empire: Scotland and the British Empire* (Oxford: Oxford University Press, 2011), 38.

17 Andrew Thompson, 'Empire and the British State,' in Sarah Stockwell, ed., *The British Empire: Themes and Perspectives* (Oxford: Oxford University Press, 2008), 52.

18 Matthew P. Dziennik, *The Fatal Land: War, Empire, and the Highland Soldier in British America* (New Haven: Yale University Press, 2015), 16.

19 Kathleen Wilson, 'Rethinking the Colonial State: Family, Gender, and Governmentality in Eighteenth-Century British Frontiers,' *American Historical Review* 116 (2011), 1300.

Bibliography

Armitage, David, *Ideological Origins of the British Empire* (Cambridge: Cambridge University Press, 2000).

Greene, Jack P., *Negotiated Authorities: Essays in Colonial Political and Constitutional History* (Charlottesville: University of Virginia Press, 1994).

Griffin, Patrick, *The Townshend Moment: The Making of Empire and Revolution in the Eighteenth Century* (New Haven: Yale University Press, 2017).

Hoppit, Julian, 'Patterns of Parliamentary Legislation, 1660–1800,' *Historical Journal* 39 (1996), 109–31.

Mulford, Carla J., *Benjamin Franklin and the Ends of Empire* (New York: Oxford University Press, 2015).

Pincus, Steven, 'Rethinking Mercantilism: Political Economy, the British Empire, and the Atlantic World in the Seventeenth and Eighteenth Centuries,' *William and Mary Quarterly* 69 (2012), 3–34.

Stern, Philip, *The Company State: Corporate Sovereignty and the Early Modern Foundations of the British Empire in India* (New York: Oxford University Press, 2011).

Vaughn, James, *The Politics of Empire at the Accession of George III: The East India Company and the Crisis and Transformation of Britain's Imperial State* (New Haven: Yale University Press, 2019).

Wilson, Kathleen, 'Rethinking the Colonial State: Family, Gender, and Governmentality in Eighteenth-Century British Frontiers,' *American Historical Review* 116 (2011), 1294–322.

Yirush, Craig, *Settlers, Liberty, and Empire: The Roots of Early American Political Theory, 1675– 1775* (Cambridge: Cambridge University Press, 2011).

7   War and society, 1689–1756

Introduction

The most enduring images of Hanoverian society are those created by London engraver and artist, William Hogarth. Some of his main concerns were about the excesses and hypocrisies of high life and the vulgarity and brutishness of low life. His most famous series of prints were composed early in his career, in 1732 and 1733, when he titillated his large audience with *A Harlot's Progress* and *A Rake's Progress*. His greatest triumph, *Marriage à la Mode*, appeared in 1745 and was a complex narrative composition, depicting a hostile world that in its essence was degraded and futile and in which city, court, and commerce had combined to destroy the moral foundations of the ruling elite.

At first glance, Hogarth seems an entirely domestic artist. Born in 1697 at Bartholomew Close, Southfields, London, the son of a migrant from Westmoreland in the north-west of England, Hogarth was proudly British, indeed English, in outlook. He was determined to establish an English art rooted in English social mores and manners and mocked the pretensions of artists imitating what they had seen in Europe, laughing at young men who 'by studying in Italy have seldom learnt much more than the names of the painters.'

Yet even some of his most celebrated engravings, such as twinned prints that were depictions of life in London – *Gin Lane* and *Beer Lane* (1751) – and which lambasted the evils of gin as somewhat foreign while praising the good honest regenerative qualities of English beer, are commentaries on wider issues, dealing with Britain's increasing involvement with the wider world from the second quarter of the eighteenth century. The pairing of these prints suggests that Hogarth was more than just a spectator in the long-lasting eighteenth-century debate over Britain's future and its capacity to marshal its resources in a future war with France. The problem with gin, Hogarth argued, was that it debilitated the nation. In an initial print of *Beer Lane*, Hogarth included a miserable Frenchman hoisted high by a strong blacksmith. Other prints also depicted feeble Frenchmen, such as emaciated men near Calais who did not get the caloric benefits of beer and beef. His most anti-French print came out in 1756 and was called *The Invasion*. The French are drawn as cruel torturers, religious fanatics and half-starved soldiers who emerged from an inn with the sign 'Soup meagre a la Sabat Royal.' Drawing home the point, a better-dressed French officer points to the flag behind him that contains the words 'Vengeance et le Bon Bier et Bon Boeuf de Angleterre.' In the bottom corner, Hogarth's friend, David Garrick, wrote verses against strutting 'half-starved Frenchmen,' opining that the English will 'teach these bragging Foes/that Beef and Beer give heavier Blows/than Soup and Roasted Frogs.'

Hogarth came of age during the 'long peace' between 1713 and 1739. That experience of peace made him unusual for people living in Britain in the eighteenth century, where war was otherwise nearly constant. Hogarth and his contemporaries saw war only in middle or old age, meaning that they enjoyed adolescence and early manhood unmarked by the experience of war, a singular experience for the generations born between the beginning of Charles I's reign and the end of George III's reign. Thus, Hogarth's protection from the pity of war was unusual, as Hogarth himself realised in his anti-French satires. The normal experience for eighteenth-century Britons was to be war with France and often also with Spain.

When we think of the eighteenth century, we tend to see it in peaceful terms, as a time of commerce and improvement, of toleration and reason and of patriotism and politeness. It was shaped, moreover, by the reality of frequent, if usually inconclusive, warfare. This warfare was generally favourable for Britain, which may be one reason it engaged in it so regularly. Britain entered war in 1689 as a junior power and left in 1713 as a great power, a position it maintained for the next two centuries. Such an achievement came at considerable cost in terms of lives lost and resources diverted but 'war did not overrun England.' 'Rather,' Julian Hoppit notes,

> it enabled her to confirm the Revolution settlement, further develop some of its consequences, enhance her international status, and underscore her colonial prospects and pretensions. Together the Glorious Revolution and the wars that followed took England out of a dark age of civil strife and, for better and for worse, set her on a course toward her imperial meridian.[1]

The fiscal-military state

The frequency of British involvement in war after 1689 meant a profound reorientation of ordinary Britons' relationship with the state as Britain struggled to find ways of paying for waging war, the most expensive thing a state did. The state itself grew considerably in this period, meaning that connections with the state by individuals were much greater in the eighteenth century than they had been a century earlier, even if a great deal of what we would consider today the proper functions of the state were still carried out at the local level by unpaid volunteers. That relationship was marked by increased taxation and larger amounts of parliamentary activity. British, and to an extent Irish, involvement with a relatively activist state separated residents of the British archipelago out from other Europeans and also from Britons abroad, notably in

British North America, where rates of taxation were notoriously small, a fact that became quickly apparent in the controversy over the passing of the Stamp Act in 1765, which caused such controversy in British North America, in part, because North Americans were not used to such taxation from the central state.

Many Britons shared American concerns about the growing power of 'Leviathan,' or an intrusive state controlled by Parliament, cherishing a limited executive, a balanced constitution, cheap government, local autonomy over administration and individual liberty. But the need to wage frequent wars not only meant that the British state had to collect plenty of taxes to pay for it and, in the course of fighting such wars, build up what contemporaries feared was a gigantic debt, it also expanded its tentacles of control into the community in ways that had not been possible in the seventeenth century and which never quite occurred in Britain's wider empire, except to a limited extent in the British West Indies and more extensively in British India. Increased state activity was especially apparent in the economic sector. Julian Hoppit notes that after the Glorious Revolution of 1689, the British Parliament increasingly intervened in regulating and directing Britain's economic life through taxation and legislation, creating a new political order through government activity that allowed Britain to become a major European power and a significant global empire and which led to a 'significantly heightened role for Westminster's legislation in both national government and local life.' This legislation enabled Britain to fight repeated wars and made real what was only theoretical before – the idea of a sovereign state based on principles of political economy. 'Political economy' had been coined in France in the early seventeenth century but only became a term that came into common use in Britain in the 1760s. Adam Smith in *The Wealth of Nations* (1776) described political economy succinctly as 'a branch of the science of a statesman or legislator' which gave 'a plentiful revenue or subsistence for the people' and which supplied 'the state or commonwealth with a revenue sufficient for the public service,' meaning that political economy done correctly 'proposes to enrich both the people and the sovereign.' That enrichment was mainly to be spent on waging war without bankrupting the state or the people within a state.[2]

The state before 1800 primarily did one thing: it waged war against other states and raised revenues to pay for this activity. It also engaged in the redistribution of wealth and income. The British state in this century was a mechanism of rent-seeking in which powerful people used the power of the state to gain privileges and exclusionary rights, such as monopolies, tariff restrictions and acts designed to benefit themselves. The purpose of such legislative activity was mainly to generate income for the few at the expense of the many. This was true in eighteenth-century Britain as much as ancient regime France. Nevertheless, Britain never quite became an oligarchic kleptocracy, as in some parts of Europe and the world where the ruling elites were both closed and united, stealing the money of the less powerful to fund the lifestyles of the powerful. What balanced the rent-seeking nature of the elite's relationship with the state was the elite's reluctant but important recognition that it had to pay the

majority of the taxes so that it allowed the state to become sufficiently hege-
monic to protect elite interests and to fight wars that protected British trade,
not least colonial trade, from which most of these increases in taxes emanated.
That the British elite was relatively highly taxed meant that they had the moral
authority that encouraged the general populace to obey the law (even if smuggling and flouting laws that provided revenue to the state was widespread and a
significant, if unknowable, part of the national economy).

Patrick O'Brien, one of the most important chroniclers of the beginning of
the fiscal–military state in England – an institutional evolution that distinguished
Britain from every other state in Europe and which gave Britain's government
the ability to increase its tax take sufficiently to meet the costs of frequent and
increasingly expensive wars – connects the rise of this fiscal–military state with
conflict in the British Civil Wars of the 1640s. He insists that Britain came to
be a high-taxing, fiscally powerful state because its elite was so devastated by
the destruction they faced in the Civil War that they were willing to make a
government fiscally powerful in order that this government would pass legislation that secured individual property rights. The British did not have low
taxes but rather they had higher taxes than anyone else in the world except the
Dutch (a nation that was rich and prosperous in this period – high taxation and
prosperity do seem to be linked). Ostensibly, the wealthy paid most of these
taxes as land taxes, but most taxes were indirect levies, two-thirds coming from
customs revenue and excise taxes. These sorts of taxes are highly regressive,
thus lessening the burden of taxation on the landed gentry and aristocracy and
increasing it on the general population. That moving of the burden of taxation
away from the landed elite occurred most noticeably in the long premiership
of Robert Walpole, in the 1720s, when the land tax was kept deliberately low,
thus ensuring parliamentary support for this powerful prime minister. Yet the
key point is that the landed gentry and aristocracy, unlike their counterparts in
France and Spain, shared in the patriotic duty of paying taxes to keep the state
fiscally buoyant and to fund the navy and the army to defeat Britain's enemies,
those continental powers where the wealthy avoided most taxation.

The land tax was not minimal. It could be an important part of the state's
fiscal armoury, especially in wartime. Nevertheless, the rates on which taxes
were levied on land declined during the long peace between 1713 and 1739.
The fiscal slack was taken up by customs and excise taxes which provided
between 60 and 70 per cent of government revenues. The overall tax rate went
up considerably in the eighteenth century, especially after mid-century, from
about 3 to 4 per cent of income in 1689 to 10 to 11 per cent by 1715. It stayed
at roughly that level until about 1759 when it increased to 12 percent, reaching
a peak of 18 per cent in 1810, before reducing to around 13 per cent by 1815.
Another way of calculating the incidence of taxation is that it rose by a factor
of 16 or over 6 times if corrected for inflation over the long eighteenth century.
Julian Hoppit summarises the rise in various factors of British economic and
state growth in the eighteenth century as follows. The population rose between
the 1700s and the 1790s (both periods of intense warfare) by 67 percent, with

gross domestic product (GDP) rising by 98 percent. Taxes increased more rapidly still, rising by 134 percent, while government expenditure outstripped revenue collection, increasing by 185 percent. The result was a massive rise of 430 per cent in British debt. The state became much more active in these years in managing the economy, with acts from Parliament on finance increasing by 413 percent, meaning that the legislative edifice that supported the fiscal-military state grew much rapidly than did the population or the economy. The increase was especially rapid after 1760, leading Hoppit to conclude that in respect of the money raised per public finance act, peak 'productivity' occurred between 1730 and 1750, making these years the period in which the fiscal-military state was most effective.[3]

The great majority of tax monies raised was spent on the navy and the army, even in peacetime, and in servicing government debt, usually acquired during wartime. In peacetime, spending on civil government by the national state was usually about 15 per cent of total government expenditure. It suggests that from an expenditure point of view that the British government ran a military state. To an extent, this was true, although we must keep in mind that many key government activities, including the management of an extensive poor-relief system, were carried out at the local level, administered by unpaid local leaders. There is no doubt, however, that the state became larger and taxes became greater in the eighteenth century.

Fortunately, Britain was able to afford such expenditure. As O'Brien notes, it was lucky that the domestic reconstruction of the state began when England's domestic economy began to generate 'the kind of accelerated commercialization, colonization, urban concentration, and proto-industrialization that facilitated the collection of duties on domestic production and imports.'[4] Economic growth, while low by modern standards, was generally constant in the period. Between 1650 and 1760, GDP growth was 0.61 per cent per annum, although population growth meant that GDP per capita wealth between 1700 and 1780 was a less impressive 0.23 per cent per annum.

A good deal of this rising wealth and growing revenues is attributable to the wealth of Britain's plantation colonies, which already in 1688 may have been part of overseas trade that accounted for 20 per cent of national income. The plantation sector was an especially dynamic part of the economy. Nuala Zahedieh has looked at the copper business as a specific example of how colonial trade facilitated improvements in England's technological capabilities in the late seventeenth century. She shows that colonial demand for mundane copper vessels helped foster inventive mentalities, uniting interest in natural knowledge with craft skills. These actions provided the means whereby a once-moribund industry was able to attract the human and financial investment necessary for applying major technological breakthroughs in industries such as mining and smelting. She concludes that

> endogenous responses to the market opportunities created by imperial
> encounters created by imperial expansion stimulated adaptive innovations

on several main fronts; the accumulation and enhancement of transport networks to create an increasingly integrated and commercialized national economy; and a major investment in the mathematical and mechanical skills which raised England to technological leadership in Europe.[5]

Plantation profits played a crucial role in making the fiscal–military state a success. Pat Hudson notes that the fiscal–military state gave a great stimulus to growth and innovation, with plantation produce, which was liable to consumption taxes, which were important in redistributing wealth from taxpayers and government creditors to merchants and manufacturers, especially in emerging industrial regions such as Lancashire, where exports accounted for up to 80 per cent of some firms and industrial sectors. As a result, much capital found its way across the Atlantic or to Africa. She emphasises how plantation trade had strong multiplier effects, stimulating process, product and financial innovations and generating institutional provisions that affected wide areas of the economy. In short, the effect of the plantation goods coming into Britain from the late seventeenth century led to hothouse conditions conducive to technological and organisational innovations, in response to accelerating demand for exotic crops. Recent research into the value of plantation produce to Britain's GDP supports Hudson's contention. Plantation trade, Klas Rönnbäck concludes, including production on American plantations and industries dependent on the American plantation complex, accounted for an annual value-added average of 3.5 per cent of GDP between 1700 and 10 to 11 per cent of GDP between 1800 and 1810.[6]

The Glorious Revolution and institutional stability

The start of the fiscal–military state was closely connected to the Glorious Revolution of 1688–89. Historians have been impressed by how Britain, after 1689, was able to levy taxes, raise loans, gather military supplies and mobilise soldiers and sailors on an unprecedented scale. They did such things so effectively that the state advanced its finances and geopolitical position in this position rather than moving towards bankruptcy. That it showed it could manage this transition to becoming a state where short-term loans based on the word of the monarch were replaced by a long-term national debt service by parliamentary taxes and underwritten by the wealth of the nation so easily in a short period in the early eighteenth century when monarchs from Henry VIII in the 1530s to Charles II and James II in the 1680s had come unstuck when they tried to wage war with inadequate resources has been the subject of intensive investigation.

One explanation was provided by the 'new institutional economics' of the 1960s, which has been taken up recently by historians with a conservative orientation to claim that Britain had, in David Landes's words, an ideal institutional framework following reforms in the 1690s that secured property rights and contracts with an 'honest government' that economic actors could not exploit for private advantage (or for rent-seeking, to use economic language).

For Niall Ferguson, 'it was in the eighteenth century that the British state developed the peculiar institutional innovations . . . that enabled Britain at once to empire-build and to industrialize.' Daron Acemoglu and James Robinson have argued that the events of the late seventeenth century in Britain brought about a significant redistribution in political power that 'brought about major changes in economic institutions, strengthening the property rights of both land and capital owners and which spurred a process of financial and commercial expansion. The consequence was rapid economic growth, culminating in the Industrial Revolution.'[7]

These comments are serious statements from serious historians and follow the argument in a much-cited article by Douglass North and Barry G. Weingast from 1989 that was as much a commentary on neoclassical economic assumptions about market efficiency as it was about institutional change in England in the 1690s. North and Weingast insisted that institutions and political systems influenced market conditions and questioned the paradigm then current within the economics of the 'perfect market,' in which institutions could be largely ignored. Some polities, the institutional economists argued, were better than other in producing economic growth and early eighteenth-century Britain was one such efficient polity.[8] By using the Bank of England as a means of managing the national debt, Britain was able to borrow and spend out of all proportion to its population. Moreover, the establishment of this bank had constitutional implications which in themselves had positive economic implications, in what amounted to a virtuous feedback loop. The main constitutional implication of the 'financial revolution' of the 1690s was to institutionalise William III's dependence on parliamentary supply. This dependence at once reduced the monarch's fiscal autonomy (while allowing him with the support of Parliament to have access to much greater resources than James II had ever enjoyed). It also ensured that Parliament became a permanent feature of government, acting formally in concert with the monarchy. No year in Britain has passed since 1689 when Parliament has not met, a great contrast to previous centuries when monarchs, most famously Charles I during his period of 'personal rule' in the 1630s, often governed for years without Parliament meeting.

To an extent, this argument reflects the disciplinary priorities of economics and is part of an ongoing argument in that discipline over the role of institutions in shaping market behaviour that is applied to historical situations and to present-day conditions far removed from late seventeenth-century Britain. These themes are less important in the discipline of history as historians are more resistant than economists to teleological explanations of events in which features of the past are used to explain contemporary issues. Historians expert in the economic history of this period tend to stress that rent-seeking was rife in the 1690s and 1700s and that property rights in Britain were far from secure in the aftermath of the Glorious Revolution, especially in a period of constant warfare and with an insecure and contested succession to the throne arising from the lack of heirs that William III, Mary II and Anne had to enable a Protestant monarchy.

One example of rent-seeking in this period which led to economic advantages for the nation was the ending of the monopoly of the Royal African Company, an action that entailed considerable debate. Parliamentary legislation weakened it in 1698 and effectively destroyed the company's monopoly in 1708 in African commerce (primarily comprising captive Africans sold into enslavement in the Americas). It is hard to lament the end of an institution such as the company which was based on trading in human flesh, but its end did not diminish, but rather increased, the volume of captives transported in the Atlantic slave trade. Proponents of ending its monopoly were convinced that their attacks on the company's monopoly were an ideological vindication of the virtues of free trade and open competition, and to an extent, they were supported by a considerable expansion in the numbers of Africans able to be supplied to colonies desperate for fresh inputs of labour. Yet the opening of the trade to independent merchants caused the prices of enslaved Africans in both Africa and the Americas to rise so that poorer men were kept out of Atlantic slave markets. The great majority of the benefits of increased trade in African slaves went to wealthy London merchants and to a rising class of great planters in British North America. Moreover, the philosophical arguments made in favour of free trade by the supporters of breaking the African Company's monopoly seem self-serving when we consider that the monopoly of the East India Company was preserved at the same time as the African Company's monopoly was ended. The East India Company was an organisation better connected to the Whigs, who came into power with William III, than to the Tories, who were associated with James II, the main supporter in the 1680s of the African Company. The different trajectories of these two monopolies undermine arguments in which the Glorious Revolution is seen as creating a system of stable politics in which strategies of economic growth could be put forward which reduced rent-seeking and corruption, Indeed, the 1700s and 1710s were among the decades in British history in which political corruption and economic self-seeking were most frequent, or at least most self-evident.

In short, the development of the fiscal-military state in the eighteenth century does not necessarily prove much about British exceptionalism – the idea that Britain was somehow the fount of liberty and that this unique devotion to liberty largely explains its great geopolitical successes of the eighteenth century. Even in the eighteenth century, as Mark Knights has told us, Whig views of Britain having a perfect constitution which allowed for perpetual improvements in a discourse dominated by notions of continual progress was contested by Tory historians such as David Hume, who saw the constitutional battles of the previous century not as the preordained victory of the forces of good over the forces of Stuart tyranny but as merely the temporary dominance of one faction within British politics over a vanquished faction.[9] Historians in the 1930s such as Herbert Butterfield (theoretically) and Lewis Namier (practically) demolished the eighteenth and nineteenth-century Whig version of history, as enthusiastically promulgated by Thomas Babington Macaulay and others, showing that people in the eighteenth century were less concerned about abstract notions of liberty and that history could be written (by the winners) as a single line to greater freedom, prosperity and progress than they were consumed by personal ambition, focused on gaining patronage and wealth, were as selfish and as unprincipled as in any other age and that the Hanoverian regimes were conspicuous for ideological complexity and for being both exclusive and oppressive.

Financial successes and failures

We can see the complexity of the period in one of its great successes – the creation of the Bank of England in 1694 – and the 'financial revolution' which accompanied it – and in one of its great failures – the South Sea 'bubble' of 1720 where another financial institution, the South Sea Company, collapsed in dramatic fashion. The first institution was set up to deal with waging war and worked very well. In 1692, the government backed a City of London syndicate, headed by the Scottish entrepreneur, William Paterson (who later came badly unstuck in the Darien scheme of the late 1690s) to create a national bank, funded to the amount of £1.2 million from 1,268 investors, who got 8 per cent interest guaranteed by Parliament. Suddenly, the government could make long-term public borrowings – by 1713 the government had raised nearly £16 million on long-term loans with guaranteed interest. As well as giving Britain the means to confront Louis XIV without the crushing taxation which Louis put on his subjects, it enlisted the material self-interest of the City of London in supporting in financial ways 'Revolution principles' and allowed for ongoing war. By 1710, British taxpayers and the Bank of England supported a land force of nearly 171,000 men and 48,000 sailors. A large proportion of soldiers were foreign nationals fighting under allied command but the number of Englishmen in these armies was considerable, at fifty to sixty thousand men.

But credit schemes did not always work. The South Sea Company had been funded in 1711 by Tories (as a counterpoint to the Whig-controlled Bank of England and East India Company) and was intended to take advantage of increased access to the lucrative Spanish American trade – access which never eventuated, in part, due to Spanish hostility to Britain coming out of the Treaty of Utrecht in 1713 which established peace after the War of the Spanish Succession. The South Sea Company's directors want for broke in the late 1710s and formulated an ambitious and, in retrospect, foolhardy plan to take over the national debt to trade with Spain in the Americas. It seemed for a time that this scheme would work, although most of the justification for its success came from misleading and wildly optimistic propaganda from the company itself. Shares in the company rose to unheard-of heights, and all of London became obsessed with the profits that could be made in Britain taking over profits from the legendarily wealthy silver mines in Potosi (in northern Peru, now Bolivia). But it was all smoke and mirrors. There was no substance in the South Seas Company's claims, and by September 1720, the price of shares in the company dropped very fast, leading many people into ruin, including some of the greatest nobles in the realm, such as the Duke of Chandos and the Duke of Portland. Both grandees had to turn to investments in Jamaica to try to recoup their losses: the Duke of Portland became a highly popular governor of the island before succumbing to Jamaica's malign tropical climate in 1726.

One consequence of the establishment of the fiscal-military state was deeply ironic. It was central to British ideology in the eighteenth century that France was dangerous and had to be combatted unless it took over Europe and threatened Britain in the wider world. Louis XIV's shadow remained large even after his death in 1715. He was widely believed by Britons to want to establish a 'universal monarchy' in Europe and to import absolutist government everywhere in the continent. Britain's role was asserted to be the champions of a balance of power between European states, defending the liberties of Europe against Bourbon 'universal monarchy.' As Colin Jones notes, this belief was 'a familiar British fantasy.'[10] But French absolutism, much feared, was also much overstated. As in Britain, Louis XIV, XV and XVI had to rule through cooperation and conciliation with an often-truculent aristocracy and a famously restive population. And France by no means had its own way in Europe, as new states, such as Russia and especially Prussia, emerged to challenge it. France, moreover, feared Britain as much as Britain worried about France. Its fears about Britain were very similar to those that existed in Britain about France. The French thought Britain overly aggressive and inclined to tyranny, especially with its oft-professed desire to establish a 'universal monarchy of the sea.' They remembered Britain as a pariah state as it had been in the sixteenth and seventeenth centuries and as a haven for lawless pirates and predatory soldiers and sailors that were a primordial threat to European civilisation, a civilisation which France thought it exemplified and defended. In many ways, moreover, it was the French state that was weak, not the British one. France could not collect the taxes that the British could – if it had been able to do so, France's much greater wealth and larger population would have enabled it to fund large armies and a big navy that would have crushed British military pretensions quite easily.

A weak state?

The strength of the eighteenth-century British state is a subject of considerable debate. The rise of the notion that Britain created a viable fiscal-military state in the aftermath of the 'financial revolution' of 1689 and the end of the American war on 1783 has put paid to earlier assumptions by theorists of state formation that England's distinctive parliamentary system and extensive amateur volunteer administration at county and especially parish levels meant that it avoided the absolutism, strong central bureaucracy and large standing armies characteristic of many eighteenth-century European states. Few historians cleave to that view now.

For example, Britain has been shown to have had a steady and expanding central bureaucracy from 1689 that was larger and more effective than similar civil services in Europe. Of course, by modern standards the size of the British civil service was tiny. The British government employed perhaps eight thousand people in 1750 and spent only 9 per cent of its revenue on civil administration. As Jacob Viner wittily puts it, Britain 'was something like a police state without official policemen, a meddlesome government without a bureaucracy.'[11] The number of staff in the Treasury, the most important branch of the administration, was just fifty-three. When George III ascended to the throne in 1760, the Admiralty had just sixty people, while the Board of Trade was staffed by twenty-three people.

Nevertheless, just concentrating on the number of officials in the civil service is misleading. What is important is the trend, and that trend was always upwards, especially in the customs and excise sector, where most government employees worked and where, for the most part, they acted with a professionalism and dispassionate objectivity uncommon in a European state. Britain's government bureaucracy was increasing, was larger than it had been in the seventeenth century and was significantly more effective and efficient than its counterparts in France and Spain.

Moreover, it was augmented by quasi-governmental bodies that involved themselves in raising and funding military manpower. The extent to which military recruitment was based on individuals or corporate bodies remote from government could cause problems. Volunteer forces in mid-century wars and privateering vessels under license from the government saw themselves outside state control. London could not just tell these forces to do what it wanted, especially in America, where provincial troops believed that they were responsible to colonial assemblies, not to British officers. The mixed private-state nature of the British military was most evident in India, where fighting was conducted by the forces of the East India Company, mostly sepoys or native Indians, rather than by the British army. When Colonel William Draper, conquered Manila in the Philippines in 1762, a significant proportion of his army was made up of sepoys and European troops in the pay of the East India Company. Even in Britain, the state depended on the willingness of large landowners to allow the army to recruit soldiers from among their tenantry.

The state managed to get around such problems, however, even if it remained dependent on contractors who did not always share the imperative of central government. The clearest example of how the state increased its ability to recruit soldiers and expand its armed forces was in the Highlands of Scotland. The Highlands had been a centre of opposition to British power, being the locus of the Jacobite rebellion in 1745. Matthew Dziennik has shown that the empire did not enter the Highlands through the barrel of a musket and the brutality that accompanied the collapse of the last Jacobite rebellion in 1746 but through the state's demand for military manpower and through accepting these needs by Gaels to advance local, although not parochial, political and social agendas. A 'patriotic partnership' between Highland elites and the British government allowed both to benefit from the consolidation of the fiscal–military state.

As Dziennik argues, by 'embracing imperial connections, especially with North America, Highland people sought to interpret the empire in ways that would empower themselves in their communities.' The result was the mobilisation of about twenty thousand men for Highland regiments (one in eight eligible males) fighting in colonial wars compared to the situation before 1756 when just one Highland battalion, the Forty-second foot, was raised in 1739. The Highlands became one of the most heavily mobilised areas in Western Europe and became a principal strength of the British Empire. The fiscal-military state offered much-needed revenue to the Highlands, partially countering the enclosing actions of large landowners, such as the Duke and Countess of Sutherland, that led to extensive Gaelic depopulation in the Highlands from the late eighteenth century onwards. Dziennik concludes that the

> disproportionate level of Highland mobilization [after 1756] cannot be explained by state interest, economic necessity or defeatism alone; it can be explained by the coincidence of Gaelic self-interest and the interests of empire, an intersect that made many Highlanders politically patriotic, even as they pursued their own advancement.[12]

The state's ability to mobilise Highland soldiers to fight in foreign lands is one indication of its crucial role in being able to successfully mobilise resources for war. Stephen Conway notes just how agile the state was in the mid-eighteenth century in relation to public finance. It was able, in the face of sometimes fierce public opposition, to expand the British armed forces enormously, especially after 1757. It reformed and modernised local militias at home and paid foreign auxiliaries from Europe and India and even mixed-race volunteers in the Caribbean on a large scale, with 30 per cent of money that the army had in the Seven Years' War being spent on foreign troops. The British government also reimbursed colonial American governments for some of their expenses with perhaps half of military costs in the Seven Years' War being covered by the British government. These contributions to colonial coffers in that conflict was one reason why the British government, after 1763, felt that Americans had a debt that they owed to Britain for gains achieved in the just-finished war. As Conway notes, 'vast sums, in short, were found to pay for a global war effort, and this must surely be counted as a substantial achievement.' The government found little problem in borrowing, getting £12 million in 1763 at just 4.8 per cent interest and £2 million in 1756 at only 3.4 per cent interest. Conway suggests we should discard old views that the post-war failure to tax the American colonies shows the weakness of the American state and instead should see this post-war drive to tax America

> as a symptom of great confidence on the part of British government, the British parliament, and the whole state machine . . . After having emerged triumphant in a titanic struggle with France and Spain, British ministers were prepared to address what they saw as the flaws in the imperial system – flaws that had been recognised for many generations but had been left unremedied for fear of provoking trouble. . . . A ramshackle and

loose-reined empire was to be transformed, by greater central control, into a more cohesive and sustainable whole.[13]

Imperial wars, 1689–1756

Between 1689 and 1756, England and then Britain was frequently at war with either Spain or France or sometimes both. These wars deserve some brief attention. The first war involving Britain against France arose out of long-term tensions between France, England and the Dutch Republic from the 1670s and 1680s. Louis XIV provoked the Dutch into war in the mid-1680s by making aggressive attacks on Dutch commerce as a means of trying to reduce Dutch power. When William III became king of England as well as ruling over the Dutch Republic, in part doing so to increase support for his military campaigns against France, European war became inevitable. The Nine Years' War lasted from 7 May 1689 until the Treaty of Ryswick in 1697. It was mainly a war of attrition designed to stop France from altering the balance of power in Europe, but to insular Englishmen, it seemed a fight in favour of Protestant liberty. Louis XIV's Catholicism, absolutism and quest for glory showed France to be the home of tyranny, a tyranny that the English thought they had ended with the abdication of James II, although warfare in Ireland continued for a few years after William III took the throne. This war, like all wars fought before the climatic Seven Years' War, was indecisive in its results, with no side winning a complete victory. Nevertheless, France lost more than other countries did. The conclusion of the war showed that concerted allied power was able to contain France. Louis XIV had made only limited gains and did so at great cost.

War broke out again on 4 May 1702 because of great power disputes over who was to rule Spain following the death without heirs of the Habsburg Charles II. Louis XIV had angered the English by adding to the issue of Spanish inheritance that of the British succession when he recognised as king of Great Britain and Ireland, James Stuart, the son of James II and after James's death on 16 September 1701, James II's heir. Thus, the causes of the War of Spanish Succession appeared to the English to be the same as in 1689: the preservation of the nation (which from 1707 with the union with Scotland became Britain) from 'Popery, Tyranny, and Universal Monarchy.'

It was a hard-fought and long war, ending only with the Treaty of Utrecht in 1713. It was also inconclusive in its results. Nevertheless, Britain did best of all powers involved in the war. It was the war which established firmly Britain as a great power in Europe and a rising power in the world. England's greatest triumph came on 13 August 1704 at Blenheim in the Low Countries under the Duke of Marlborough, a deeply unattractive character as a man, with limitless ambition and equally limitless avarice. He was, however, an inspiring military leader, brave in battle and talented and fearless as a strategist with superior political abilities, able to get his way in a complicated set of European alliances with a non-always reliable monarch and often-hostile government. He became as celebrated during the war as his descendant, Winston Churchill, was to become during the 1940s. Marlborough's wife was nearly as important as he was: it was one of the more remarkable marital partnerships in British history, akin perhaps to Tony and Cherie Blair's duopoly in the 1990s and 2000s. Sarah Churchill was the best friend of Anne until displaced by the lowly born Abigail Masham after 1708. Masham represented the views of Marlborough's enemy, the Tory leader, Robert Harley, and persuaded the queen to move towards peace rather than continue fighting, as the Marlboroughs wished.

Britain did well out the peace that emerged in 1713, gaining territory in Europe and America, and the *asiento* contract to supply Spanish America with slaves. The peace also secured European support for the succession of the Protestant George I in 1714. The rest of Britain's European allies, however, were displeased as Britain preferred self-interest in the negotiations to keeping promises it had made with its allies. It was this betrayal that led to the lasting nickname of 'perfidious Albion' and gave some force to French claims that it was Britain, not France, which acted with peremptory aggression in disrupting global balances of power. Spain was the big loser in 1713 – being required to front many of the costs arising from prolonged warfare – while France was hated for its dreams of European dominance and global territorial expansion.

The balance of power established at Utrecht in 1713 lasted with only two brief conflicts between Britain and Spain until 1739. From 1739 to 1763, Britain was engaged in almost continual war. The most important of these wars was the Seven Years' War, which will be largely dealt with in the next chapter. Unlike earlier wars, these mid-century conflicts were global affairs, especially the Seven Years' War. By 1762, nearly one-third of the British army was based outside Europe. The first war with Spain from October 1739 arose from tensions over illegal commerce in the Caribbean and was fought mainly in the American colonies, with triumph at Porto-Bello in 1738 balanced by disaster at Cartagena in 1741. It merged after October 1740 into the European-wide War of the Austrian Succession after the death of another Hapsburg monarch without heirs, the Holy Roman Emperor Charles VI. Once again, British troops fought in Germany and the Low Countries. In America, the great event was the fall of Louisburg in French Canada in 1744, an event which shook French confidence in the stability of its American empire.

Because it contained the last internal rebellion in Britain, 1745 was different. Charles Edward Stuart, the son of the Jacobite claimant to the throne, organised an army in the Highlands and defeated a British army on 17 September 1745 before marching into northern England. The Hanoverian regime was in real danger of being overthrown, with London in uproar and France massing troops for an invasion of southern England. Internal dissension and a lack of English support made the Jacobites retreat. On 16 April 1746, the Jacobites were soundly defeated in brutal fashion at Culloden by the Duke of Cumberland, George II's younger son, The Highlands were pacified and crushed by determined British attacks on the clan structure which sustained the Highland military and social culture. Meanwhile, war in Europe and India meandered indecisively, leading to a formal peace at Aix-la-Chapelle in 1748 when France regained Louisburg and soon after took Minorca.

The peace that emerged in 1748 was hardly peace at all, except a little in Europe. In North America, continuing Anglo-French conflict simmered constantly, meaning that when war between France and Britain was officially declared in 1756 conflict had well and truly begin in the Ohio Valley between the British, the French, Native Americans and colonial Americans, such as George Washington, It was Washington's raid with his Virginia soldiers in Jumonville on a small French Canadian force in May 1754 which sparked the larger global conflict, one greatly advanced by the crushing defeat suffered by General Edward Braddock at the Battle of the Monongahela near Fort Duquesne in the Ohio Valley in July 1755.

The ending of war usually caused domestic turmoil, especially when, as after the end of the War of the Austrian Succession in 1748, eighty thousand soldiers and sailors were demobilised, plunged into unemployment and cast adrift to fend for themselves, often in London, where the result was a predictable rise in crime and social disorder. The brief period of peace between 1749 and 1753 created a crisis in social relations in Britain that was greater than in 1713, when a larger body of men (157,000) were demobilised and in 1763, when nearly 200,000 men were demobilised. The main reason was probably that in the other years political crisis attracted attention more than did rising rates of crime. The rise in crime after 1749 was especially great, however, creating a social panic about increasing class tensions, concern about the degeneration and moral decline of the working population on whom Britain relied for protection against France in warfare and a gin craze that seemed to be unstoppable. It is in this context that we ought to read William Hogarth's excoriating *Gin Lane* (1751). Gin impaired British military might and commercial power, it was argued in the press and Parliament. It led ordinary people to crime and aggravated the dislocations that emanated from demobilisation. It made the lives of the wealthy vulnerable – leading aristocrats were frequently held up by highwaymen, had their houses robbed and faced derision from common people when they ventured out in public. The gin craze and crime wave of this period led to feverish reports in the increasingly vocal press; a series of government inquiries led by the novelist and London magistrate, Henry Fielding; and an escalation in executions.

The end of war thus provoked, as it always does, notably after the end of twentieth-century World Wars, considerable examinations of class relations, thoughts on the role of the state in preserving good order, and concerns about national morality and degeneracy. Then as now, people worried about the social effects of training men in violence and then letting them loose to exercise these skills in chaotic and uncertain urban settings. Demobilisation scares showed that mid-eighteenth-century Britain was not an oasis of patrician calm but was riven with domestic conflict and fears about the future. While we know that British fears that they could defeat France in future wars were misplaced due to the virtues that the establishment of the fiscal-military state imposed on the government, people around 1750 did not have our historical hindsight. They worried that they had entered peace without the capacity to wage war if war once again returned, as was likely and indeed as happened.

The old understanding of the 1750s as a period of stability within a cohesive oligarchical order has broken down as scholars recognise the stresses that were in public life in this decade. Oligarchy coexisted with carefully nurtured local concerns and within a series of overlapping and interlocking special interest groups, such as the powerful West Indian lobby. Whig leaders were not just concerned, as Lewis Namier believed, writing in the 1930s, with the spoils of office but wanted to maintain the Hanoverian Protestant succession. Britain's rulers had considerable fears about Jacobitism re-emerging after 1745 and in a landed elite with divided political loyalties, Whigs had many doubts about Tory allegiances. Their doubts encouraged them to keep their political faith, even in major crises in 1745–46 and 1756–57. Bob Harris notes that

> Hanoverian stability was on occasion based on nothing more than the realization that the alternative – Stuart restoration – promised less and threatened more, especially to the Anglican Church and to Protestant religion. Only spectacular and unforeseen military victories [after 1759] and buoyant overseas trade brought popularity and most of this was focused on Pitt, an outsider.[14]

In short, the so-called Whig oligarchy that ruled Britain between 1714 and 1760 was not as stable as historians such as J. H. Plumb writing in the 1960s argued. Harris concludes that 'if the pulse of the political nation beat slower in many places in the 1750s, this was a consequence of the weakness of the opposition at the national level, and the entrenchment of Whig supremacy at a local level.'[15] Moreover, it was a decade when Britain experienced one of its periodic moral panics, possibly due to growing prosperity in the 'industrious revolution' (as described in Chapter 11) giving poor people more money, some of which was spent on leisure and entertainment and in greater consumption of things that wealthier people thought of as unnecessary luxuries. It is noticeable, for example, that this decade saw both a broader drive to eliminate London's culture of criminality and an increased hostility towards making provision for the poor.

The Royal Navy and command of the seas

Scholars have transformed our view of the eighteenth-century British state by seeing it as a 'fiscal-military state,' but it might be more accurately termed a 'fiscal-naval state.' The Royal Navy absorbed a massive proportion of the resources of the state and was key to British military strategy and economic expansion, not least in its expanding empire. The extensive infrastructure of dockyards, ordnance, victualling and hospitals meant that the navy accounted for at least 20 per cent of annual peacetime public expenditure and well over 30 per cent of warfare expenditure. The navy grew rapidly in size over the eighteenth century, expanding from 173 to 313 vessels between 1688 and 1713, within that latter year having 40,000 sailors and 1,000 officers, with a total tonnage twice that of France. The officer class was more socially diverse than in the army, as naval commissions were not available for purchase. Most admirals, however, had some connection to nobility. George Anson, for example, who served in all the wars of the eighteenth century until he was First Lord of the Admiralty in the Seven Years' War, was a kinsman of the Earl of Macclesfield, a relation which he used to his benefit. Young gentlemen of respectable family liked the navy as it gave them opportunities for honour and for profit when enemy ships were captured, as officers were entitled to prize money from such captures. Service in the Caribbean was especially desirable for ambitious and avaricious officers, as this was the region where prize money was most abundant, as Admiral George Rodney made clear in his remarkable career, as the naval officer most prominent in the service after the death of Lord Anson in 1762. Rodney's prize money in the 1740s enabled him to purchase both a country estate and a seat in Parliament.

Having noted that, it is indisputable that the major role of the navy was not in supporting overseas expansion and in defending overseas trade but

Figure 7.1 The Invasion, plate 1, William Hogarth, 8 March 1756

Source: Artokoloro Quint Lox Limited/Alamy Stock Photo.

in guarding Britain from the threat of invasion. This threat was always real, especially from France which could always easily pin down large naval forces merely by assembling troops on its side of the English Channel. The solution which Britain developed to deal with the threat of foreign invasion was to establish in the 1740s the Western Squadron. This major strategic decision in the 'blue water' policy of the British government in this period was part of several changes in the 1740s that saw a change of direction in British attitudes to the wider world. The 1740s was a key decade in the reformulation of foreign and imperial policy, when we see a united British Empire coalescing out of as a series of different empires in different regions and when we start to see Britons envisaging their nation as part of an empire of the seas (or even an empire of goods) in which there was a sense of a shared 'Britishness' uniting Protestant Britons in the British archipelago and British America. As Kathleen Wilson has argued, it was in this decade that we see the emergence of an aggressive popular imperialism, driven by an expanding commercial 'middling sort,' often involved in colonial trade. A manifestation of this popular imperialism was the lionification of Admiral Edward Vernon as a daring military hero following his successful assault on Porto Bello on the Spanish Main in 1740. Even if the widespread and excited celebration of Vernon's exploits was at least partly attributable to the contrast between Vernon's daring and bravery and the seeming reluctance of Robert Walpole – well known as a man who wanted to avoid rather than prosecute war – to attack Spain with proper enthusiasm, it also showed how, by the 1740s the navy had come to attain a special position in British sense of themselves as an imperial and maritime people.[16]

The Western Squadron was intended to defend the home waters of Britain, its establishment showing that 'Vernon-mania' did not yet signify an enthusiasm for extending the physical boundaries of empire. When it came to determining where national priorities were, it was Europe, as Brendan Simms and Marie Peters have insisted, that took precedence over empire until at least the late eighteenth century.[17] Its purpose was to have a force of ships easily able to cruise the waters westward from the mouth of the English Channel. It was well placed, as its chief architect, Admiral George Anson argued in 1746 and 1747, years following the 1745 Jacobite rebellion when fears of French invasion of Britain were especially intense, to cover travelling convoys, to watch the main French naval base at Brest and to block enemy fleets. It stayed the core of Britain's naval strategy for the next century and longer. Most of the fleet was kept at home in port rather than afloat at sea. Anson argued that 'the French can never be so much annoy'd nor this kingdom so well secured as by keeping a strong Squadron at home, sufficient to make detachment, whenever we have good intelligence that the French are sending ships either to the East or West Indies.' Between 1757 and 1762, 64 per cent of the 'ship-days' of the navy were served in home waters or in the Mediterranean. N.A.M. Rodger argues that it was superiority in European waters that made possible successful operations overseas.[18]

The British navy was a formidable fighting force in this period, although this did not mean that it did not face sharp criticism, often from former admirals turned parliamentary opponents of the government, notably Vernon, who used his status as a national here to condemn government corruption. And admirals were celebrated only when they showed themselves to be fearless and successful in battle. When Admiral John Byng decided not to fight a superior French force in 1757 and thus allowed, as the popular press contended, for the French to seize Minorca in the Mediterranean, he was court-martialled and executed by firing squad on his ship. This shocking display of official vengeance prompted Voltaire to famously quip that the British sometimes executed an admiral 'to encourage the others.'

But the navy's strengths were many. It received substantial government funding, even if it always spent that money and more each year and complained incessantly about how little money it received. It also had a strong centralised administration, with the First Lord of the Admiralty being a member of the cabinet, thus allowing the navy a direct say in national decision making, a great advantage when the cabinet member was someone who was politically influential, as was the Earl of Sandwich, first lord of the admiralty between 1748 and 1751, again in 1763 and between 1771 and 1782. During the Seven Years' War, under the leadership of George Anson, the navy not only added considerably to its fleet numbers but built durable ships that in the hands of a skilled crew could catch a technically faster French ship. Its naval successes in this war provoked the French to respond with a massive naval-building campaign so that by the time of the War of American Independence, the French, for the first time, nearly reached parity with the British navy in the size of its fleet. Otherwise, the British navy always had more ships than the French peaking in the last years of the Seven Years' Wat. The building of such a large and impressive fleet met with little public opposition – the public supported a 'standing navy' in ways it was reluctant to do with a 'standing army.' By 1762, the navy had eighty-two thousand men under arms, a manpower figure it did not match again until the Napoleonic Wars.

Traditionally, the Royal Navy is seen as a place of great oppression and harshness for ordinary sailors, governed in popular imagination by the trinity of rum, sodomy and the lash. It was undoubtedly true that life in naval vessels was rigorous and that the discipline of the navy was brutal, although if we compare the life of a naval sailor with that of a sailor in one of Britain's most important maritime trades, the slaving business and the Middle Passage, the comparison is not always favourable to the merchant marine. Guarding African captives was as physically dangerous as serving in the navy in wartime and more dangerous than the navy in peacetime. It was more likely to lead to death from disease and involved ordinary sailors in gruesome and unpleasant shipboard duties. And one advantage of serving as an ordinary sailor in the Royal Navy was that it was a multi-ethnic and even multiracial workplace, with perhaps nearly 10 per cent of seamen not being British and only about half being English. Some seamen were even Africans. The Royal Navy provided better working conditions than plantation slavery and could protect a runaway slave from being reclaimed by his owner. Olaudah Equiano, the author of one of the first black autobiographies in English and which gave a disturbing account of being a captive on a slave ship during the Middle Passage, spoke warmly of how serving in the Royal Navy during the early years of the Seven Years' War gave him a different and more pleasant perspective on how working-class white seamen could interact with Africans. For some historians, the experience of being a seaman made the eighteenth-century navy and merchant marine the birth site of a self-conscious international working class, with recruits experiencing the 'shock of proletarianization at sea.'[19]

Recent research suggests that the image of pressgangs seizing drunken men and forcing them into a hellish life in the navy – a staple of popular images of the Royal Navy in this period, usually accompanied by Samuel Johnson's quip that serving at sea was akin to being in prison with the added risk of drowning – is largely a misimpression. Impressment did occur, mainly because the merchant marine paid higher wages to seamen in wartime, making it harder to man naval vessels just when manpower was most needed. When it did occur, however, it could provoke opposition. We can see this in examining impressment in the life of Admiral Charles Knowles, a controversial naval officer who was a rare hero of the otherwise failed expedition to Cartagena in 1741. He became an experienced and skilled sailor in the Caribbean and in the 1750s served as a combative governor of Jamaica. He was a man who seemed to attract tumult wherever he went and who loved contention of all kinds. He was also involved in impressment when in Boston in 1747. On his arrival in the town, he advertised for a privateer crew and when men congregated at the port to enlist, he swept them up, claiming that he was looking for thirty seamen who had previously deserted from his squadron.

Bostonians were outraged at this sharp practice, which fuelled their sense of injustice over impressment, which they considered to be contrary to British legal opinion, A mob of three hundred privateers and slave-ship sailors mobilised with arms, marched on the port, took one of Knowles's officers as a hostage and threatened to burn Knowles's boats which he used to get from his ship to shore. Governor William Shirley found the mob so intimidating that he retreated to his home. Knowles was not similarly cowed. He acted by also taking men hostage and threatened to bombard the town if his men were not returned. That action – which Knowles was quite prepared to do and which would have caused a major imperial incident if it had happened – proved impossible due to unfavourable winds preventing Knowles from approaching the town. It did give him, however, a deserved reputation in the empire for intemperate arrogance combined with reckless bravery. The point of retailing this minor episode is to show that impressment was highly unpopular and was usually resisted, mostly successfully. Knowles went on from Boston to raid ships in the Caribbean, clearing perhaps as much as £100,000 in prize money, some of which he used, like Anson, to buy a house in the country and fund a successful but costly parliamentary campaign. His election as a member of

Parliament in 1750 gave him some protection from his many enemies, several of whom challenged him to duels,

Most of the prize money, of course, went to the leading naval officers but even ordinary seamen were entitled to shares of money gained through the capture of enemy ships. This fact might have been a factor in encouraging men to enlist – the navy did not have significant problems in getting recruits except, as noted earlier, at the start of wars. We only have records from the Napoleonic period as to how sailors were recruited but it appears that between 1793 and 1802 that of twenty-seven thousand seamen, 16 per cent were impressed and more than 80 per cent volunteered.[20] Naval sailors were paid less than merchant seamen but did not lose their wages when shipwrecked or captured. They probably ate better and had better medical treatment than other seamen, helped by officers' general fanaticism about keeping ships clean, thus helping to stop the spread of diseases which could often sweep through merchants' ships. And if seamen were injured, they had some possibility of getting a pension from money that sailors themselves paid in regularly from their wages into superannuation funds. The navy also provided men (and the occasional woman by the end of the eighteenth century) with some adventure in foreign lands that may have appealed to people who would otherwise have been stuck with the drudgery of life as an agricultural labourer or the uncertainty of life on the margins in London or Liverpool.

The most skilled of these seamen could even rise in the ranks. James Cook is the most famous example of a man from very humble origins attaining lasting fame in the navy through using his exceptional skills as a navigator to become the great explorer of his age. Cook's rise is remarkable but not in itself utterly surprising. Contrary to long-term assumptions that sailors in the navy came from the dregs of British society, they tended, by contrast to be skilled men, not society's outcasts. Even if they had been pressed, they were likely to be experienced boatmen working on river barges or seamen forcibly removed from the merchant marine.

Welfare and warfare

Much of the literature on the fiscal-military state has concentrated on money as to how Britain could wage war efficiently and effectively across four continents by the time of the Seven Years' War was a major achievement in the period and placed Britain at an advantage to its imperial competitors. Lawrence Stone, for example, declared that British victories over France came not from 'military prowess, technological innovation or diplomatic skill' but from its 'overwhelming financial superiority.' His hard-headed conclusion was that military victory was 'a question of money, not men, since money could always be used to hire men and Europe was full of mercenaries willing to serve a reliable paymaster.'[21] Making war in the eighteenth century was incredibly expensive. William Pitt the Elder declared that it was fighting by guineas – guineas being expensive coins. It was something Britain was very good at doing.

It was not just money that mattered, however. Men were important if wars to be won. They were not just interchangeable pieces on strategic chessboards where the more of them that were there, the more certain was the result. If they were not cared for properly, this lack of concern could affect popular support for wars and could harm recruitment, as well as jeopardise military success. Caring for men was important because disease was so virulent among soldiers that armies could be destroyed by fever rather than by fighting. Campaigns in the Caribbean, for example, were notoriously affected by disease. Yellow fever raged in the Caribbean from the early 1690s, coinciding with large British forces confronting French and Spanish forces in the region. Soldiers were perfect victims for mosquitoes brought on slave ships from Africa. They were not immune to yellow fever and malaria and were hemmed into tightly packed camps where fever could spread rapidly once established. The effects of mosquito-borne disease on American geopolitics were immense. As John McNeill explains,

> without continued and reliable assistance from tropical disease, Spain would have lost its Caribbean holdings to Britain . . . the Spanish won their New World empire in the sixteenth century with decisive help from Eurasian diseases; they kept it in the eighteenth century with the help of African ones.[22]

One example of how sickness led to military disaster came in the disastrous Cartagena campaign of 1741 when an armed force of 11,000 men was reduced in weeks to 2,200 British regulars and 900 provincial Americans. Military commanders soon learned that to win battles, troops had to be deployed rapidly and that if invasions were prolonged, then campaigns would be unsuccessful. The brilliant campaign the British waged to capture Havana in 1762 was only partly due to successful military tactics and was more the result of careful planning where British leaders learnt lessons from failures during the 1740s. They learnt from Cartagena that resource provisioning needed to be improved and that a siege would only work if considerable time went into preparing a quick assault and a rapid departure. By this time, military commanders had come to appreciate the difficulties inherent in West Indian amphibious assaults and adjusted their tactics accordingly. Even with these preparations, Havana was a costly victory in respect to troop lives lost. Between 17 July and 11 October 1762, nearly 5,000 men died from a force of 11,203 and a further 5,713 were sick, leaving just 880 men of a final force of 7,225 men fit for duty.

British leaders were careful to obscure in the popular press the sickliness of the campaign in Cuba, meaning that British success in Havana was highly heralded at home. The colonial American press was less easily fooled. They reported extensively on the poor health of American troops in Cuba and linked this fact to other imperial actions in 1762–63 that they disliked, such as British inability to curb Native American hostilities in Pontiac's War. It was not a coincidence that American resistance to British actions in the mid-1760s was centred in New England from where most of the soldiers who died in Cuba had originated.

The Havana expedition was interpreted by Americans as a sign of its willingness, especially in New England, to make wartime sacrifices for the advancement of the British Empire. What they did in Havana and in other colonial conflicts made them think that their contributions to the Seven Years' War should have led them to have had a larger role within the empire. Thus, they were very angry when Britain seemed to downplay America's wartime contribution and instead harangued them for their propensity to engage in illicit smuggling with the French and for not paying, in British eyes, their fair share of the massive costs of warfare in this conflict. As P.J. Marshall notes, 'British opinion seems to have interpreted the American response to the war not as generous contributions by dutiful fellow subjects but as generally pusillanimous attempts to evade what was necessary for their own survival.'[23]

The American response to the loss of manpower from disease at Havana illustrates how Britain could get into trouble if it thought, as Stone argues and as George Grenville seems to have believed when instituting the Stamp Act in 1765, that winning wars was just a question of money. Soldiers needed to be looked after and the state had to show that it cared about the people who fought for it. One reason for the state to do this was that theories of political arithmetic linked a nation's strength to its military manpower: sickness was thus a national concern and if troops were dying then this was problematic. Ironically, it was continental campaigns that elicited the most concern, even though military deaths from disease in the Caribbean and in India were far more extensive than in Europe. The issue for the public was that troops in Germany were neither labouring at home nor protecting vital colonial commerce but, it was suspected, fighting mainly to serve George II's vanity as Elector of Hanover and thus dying for nothing. That they were dying from common diseases such as typhus and dysentery rather than from exotic tropical fevers only compounded the problem.

Such deaths from disease, common in the War of the Austrian Succession in the 1740s, suggested ill management and a lack of care and compassion towards ordinary soldiers. As Erica Charters argues, 'sickness among soldiers was seen as evidence of physical, political and moral disorder, because it reflected ill-discipline among the ranks, ill-administration and corruption among officials and the declining strength of the British state.'[24] It was for this reason that military leaders such as the Marquess of Granby, whose name decorates pubs today all over England, in recognition of how he combined valour with humanitarianism, were depicted frequently by painters during the Seven Years' War in ways that showed their benevolence. Edward Penny's *The Marquess of Granby Relieving a Sick Soldier* (1764) was immensely popular, with the marquess shown as giving a small gift of alms to a soldier, through which we see the general and the man of feeling united in one person.

The death of James Wolfe

By the end of the Seven Years' War, the militarisation of British society by its constant involvement in global wars since 1739 and, even since 1689, made painters such as Penny and even more the American Benjamin West find military heroes suitable subjects for large epic paintings. As Linda Colley notes, this cult of heroism was very attractive to an aristocratic elite, to whom the protracted warfare of the period (including the wars following the Seven Years' War) was a 'godsend.' 'It gave them,' she acidly comments, 'a job and, more importantly, a purpose, an opportunity to carry out what they had been trained to do since childhood: ride horses, fire guns, exercise their undoubted physical courage and tell other people what to do.' West was important, however, in encouraging well-born Britons 'to see themselves as heroes of a national and imperial epic.'[25]

West's most important history painting was *The Death of General Wolfe* (1771) which Colley calls a 'splendid fraud' as it made a Christian martyr and British hero of one of those characteristically problematic imperial heroes, such as Admiral Lord Nelson and the Victorian George Gordon, whose heroic death was in reality not especially heroic and whose desire for immortality through sacrifice, duty done, raised as many issues as it satisfied. It was an extraordinarily popular painting, then and now, and established Wolfe in the pantheon of great British military heroes. He was the opposite in the public imagination to the executed Admiral Byng, whose cosmopolitan manners and love for polite society marked him as effeminate, and Lord George Sackville, court-martialled for cowardice at the Battle of Minden in Germany in 1759 and widely and probably correctly thought to be homosexual, or at least an aristocratic fop, who got his offices through his rank. Sackville survived his court-martial, becoming a major politician under Lord North, but he never shook his reputation as 'the coward of Minden.' Despite his continuing ill health and sexless bachelorhood (not dissimilar to William Pitt the Younger), he was the antidote to effeminate aristocratic leadership that made the aristocratic critics of Sackville protest when he was ennobled by George III in 1781 as Viscount Sackville that he was 'the greatest criminal his country had ever known.'

Wolfe, by contrast, represented the professional soldier, rising through the ranks by merit until he was general aged just thirty-two. Moreover, his life was remarkable for his devotion to upright discipline and he was conspicuously, indeed rashly, brave on the battlefield. At Quebec, he established a reputation as the consummate patriot – indeed his death, which opponents thought cruelly he had engineered to become a martyr to British imperialism unleashed enormous grief among the British public when they heard about it. As Nicolas Rogers contends, 'to the British and American public, the sheer intrepidity of his ascent at Foulon, the brief but dramatic battle on the Plains [of Abraham], the manner of this dying, all redounded to his honor and fame.' It was a death with direct political implications. Wolfe's valour and death reinforced the hawkish claims of [William] Pitt's allies that hard-won victories on the field of battle should not be abandoned in any peace negotiations and that the immense cost of Pitt's grand strategy was justifiable by the conquests made and by the deaths of brave British heroes. Wolfe became the instrument of an interpretation of British history that signalled a new engagement with the world and a fresh excitement about imperialism and Britain's greater role in the world in the early 1760s. As Rogers concludes, Wolfe

> epitomised the fusion of libertarian and imperial goals that were the hallmark of British national aggrandizement in this period, a coupling that elaborated the emergent British empire of the Atlantic as Protestant, commercial, maritime, and free. In effect, Wolfe, by capturing he headquarters of New France, had helped liberate North America from French religious bigotry and absolutist rule, and paved the way for a new era of commercial expansion under British auspices.[26]

Benjamin West recognised how Wolfe's apotheosis fit with contemporary concerns over Protestant providentialism and commercial optimism and that it had a grandeur that enabled direct comparisons with other times. His innovation was to clothe his subjects not in classical or biblical garb, making them seem separate from their times, but in modern military costume while including in his painting references to history. The most obvious reference was to Van Dyck's portrait of Christ taken from the cross, which itself would direct viewers to Van Dyck's portraits of Charles I, another martyr to British liberty in Tory minds. More important, his inclusion of colonial Americans and native Americans, all subservient visually to the dominant figures in the painting, British officers, including a brigadier-general, Robert Monckton. Wolfe's critic, the well-born George Townshend, brother of Charles, author of the Townshend Acts in 1768 and later promoted to be marquess Townshend, was explicitly excluded from the tableau. Townshend, second in command at Quebec and as involved as Wolfe in the victory and demonstrating obvious bravery in battle, thought Wolfe petty and vindictive, comparing him not to Charles I but to Oliver Cromwell as a man who would bring the empire low through corrupting pride and unchecked self-regard (although Townshend also thought Wolfe a poor general, making the comparison fraught, given Cromwell's military genius).

The version of history that was being advanced by West and accepted by most Britons, however, did not allow for nuance. If Wolfe was a hero, then his opponents had to be knaves. Britain was taking up Rome's mantle as a great empire. Such a great ambition required great sacrifices, such as an utterly heroic, uncomplicated and brave soldier like Wolfe. Wolfe, according to Townshend, wanted to ruin and destroy French Canada, just as the Duke of Cumberland had wreaked revenge on the Highlands at Culloden. The quest for glory led to cruelty, in Townshend's view. In some respects, the death of Wolfe was fortunate as it allowed Townshend, as the new commander after Wolfe's death, to countermand his superior's orders to decimate the French Canadian

Figure 7.2 Robert Clive and Mir Jafar after the Battle of Plassey, 1757 (1760)

Source: Steve Vidler/Alamy Stock Photo.

countryside and break the French army. But few people were listening to such voices of calm, not least the aristocratic leaders who George III put in charge in the 1760s.

West's painting was a brilliant evocation of new ideas of a united Britain and a subservient empire. Wolfe stands for the glories of Britain and is supported by three officers, representing the three constituent kingdoms of Britain – England, Scotland and Ireland – while Americans watch reverently, suggesting that one day (but not quite yet) they will be also included in an expansive vision of Britain. Ironically, while Townshend, the grandson of Walpole's most important advisor and a bona fide member of a cosmopolitan Whig aristocracy who had upheld the rule of George I and II, was displaced from West's painting, the artist found room for Simon Fraser, the son of Lord Lovat, executed as a Jacobite traitor in 1747. The son of a rebellious Highland chieftain was now a mainstay of the empire, and in this period in which the cult of military heroism was paramount, the memory of men like Wolfe and the simplified vision of British Empire he was thought to have represented was inviolable.

Notes

1 Julian Hoppit, *Britain's Political Economies: Parliament and Economic Life, 1660–1800* (Cambridge: Cambridge University Press, 2017).

2 Ibid., xiii, 3–4.

3 Ibid., 77–9.

4 Patrick K. O'Brien, 'The Nature and Historical Evolution of an Exceptional Fiscal State . . .,' *Economic History Review* 64 (2011), 435–6.

5 Nuala Zahedieh, 'Colonies, coppers, and the market for inventive activity in England and Wales, 1680–1730,' *Economic History Review* 66 (2013), 805–25; idem, *The Capital and the Colonies: London and the Atlantic Economy, 1660–1760* (Cambridge: Cambridge University Press, 2010), 285.

6 Pat Hudson, 'Slavery, the Slave Trade and Economic Growth: A Contribution to the Debate,' in Catherine Hall et al., eds., *Emancipation and the Making of the British Imperial World* (Manchester: Manchester University Press, 2014), 36–59; Klas Rönnbäck, 'On the Economic Importance of the Slave Plantation Complex to the British Economy during the Eighteenth Century: A Value-added Approach,' *Journal of Global History* 13 (2018), 308–27.

7 Cited in Hoppit, *Britain's Political Economies*, 31.

8 Douglass C. North and Barry G. Weingast, 'Constitutions and Commitment: The Evolution of Institutions Governing Public Choice in Seventeenth-century England,' *Journal of Economic History* 49 (1989), 803–32.

9 Mark Knights, 'The Tory Interpretation of History in the Rage of Parties,' *Huntington Library Quarterly* 68 (2005), 353–73.

10 Colin Jones, *The Great Nation: France from Louis XV to Napoleon* (London: Allen Lane, 2002), 589.

11 Jacob Viner, *Essays on the intellectual history of economics*, ed., Douglas A. Irwin (Princeton: Princeton University Press, 1991), 51.

12 Matthew P. Dziennek, *The Fatal Land: War, Empire, and the Highland Soldier in British America* (New Haven: Yale University Press, 2015), 3–4, 16.

13 Stephen Conway, *War, State, and Society in Mid-Eighteenth Century Britain and Ireland* (Oxford: Oxford University Press, 2006), 50.

14 Bob Harris, *Politics and the Nation: Britain in the Mid-eighteenth Century* (Oxford: Oxford University Press, 2002), 64.

15 Ibid., 65.

16 Kathleen Wilson, 'Empire, Trade and Popular Politics in Mid-Hanoverian Britain: The Case of Admiral Vernon,' *Past and Present* 121 (1988), 74–109.

17 Brendan Simms, *Three Victories and a Defeat: The Rise and Fall of the First British Empire, 1714–1783* (London: Allen Lane, 2007); Marie Peters, 'Early Hanoverian Consciousness: Empire or Europe,' *English Historical Review* 122 (2007), 632–68.

18 N.A.M. Rodger, 'Sea-Power and Empire, 1688–1793,' in P.J. Marshall, ed., *The Oxford History of the British Empire: The Eighteenth Century* (Oxford: Oxford University, 1998), 179.

19 Niklas Frykman, 'Seamen on Late Eighteenth-Century European Warships,' *International Review of Social History* 54 (2009), 67–93.

20 Anthony Page, *Britain and the Seventy Years War, 1744–1815: Enlightenment, Revolution and Empire* (Basingstoke: Palgrave Macmillan, 2015), 109.

21 Lawrence Stone, 'Introduction' to Stone, ed., *An Imperial State at War: Britain from 1689 to 1815* (London: Routledge, 1993), 5–6.

22 J.R. McNeill, 'The Ecological Basis of Warfare in the Caribbean, 1700–1804,' in Maarten Ultee, ed., *Adapting to Conditions: War and Society in the Eighteenth Century* (Tuscaloosa: University of Alabama Press, 1986) 27.

23 P.J. Marshall, 'The Thirteen Colonies in the Seven Years War: The View from London,' in Julie Flavell and Stephen Conway, eds., *Britain and America Go to War: The Impact of War and Warfare, 1754–1815* (Gainesville: University of Florida Press, 2004), 72.

24 Erica Charters, 'The caring Fiscal-Military State during the Seven Years War,' *Historical Journal*, 52 (2009), 940.

25 Linda Colley, *Britons: Forging the Nation 1707–1837* (New Haven: Yale University Press, 1992), 178.

26 Nicholas Rogers, 'Brave Wolfe: The Making of a Hero,' in Kathleen Wilson, ed., *A New Imperial History: Culture, Identity and Modernity in Britain and the Empire 1660–1840* (Cambridge: Cambridge University Press, 204), 241–2, 245.

Bibliography

Bowen, H.V., *War and British Society, 1688–1815* (Cambridge: Cambridge University Press, 1998).

Brewer, John, *The Sinews of Power: War, Money, and the English State, 1688–1763* (New York, 1989).

Charters, Erica, *Disease, War, and the Imperial State: The Welfare of the British Armed Forces during the Seven Years' War* (Chicago: University of Chicago Press, 2014).

Conway, Stephen, *War, State, and Society in Mid-Eighteenth Century Britain and Ireland* (Oxford: Oxford University Press, 2006).

Dziennek, Matthew P., *The Fatal Land: War, Empire, and the Highland Soldier in British America* (New Haven: Yale University Press, 2015).

Hoppit, Julian, *Britain's Political Economies: Parliament and Economic Life, 1660–1800* (Cambridge: Cambridge University Press, 2017).

North, Douglass and Barry G. Weingast, 'Constitutions and Commitment: The Evolution of Institutions Governing Public Choice in Seventeenth-century England,' *Journal of Economic History* 49 (1989), 803–32.

O'Brien, Patrick K., 'The Nature and Historical Evolution of an Exceptional Fiscal State . . .,' *Economic History Review* 64 (2011), 408–46.

Rogers, Nicholas, *Mayhem: Post-War Crime and Violence in Britain, 1748–53* (New Haven: Yale University Press, 2012).

Simms, Brendan, *Three Victories and a Defeat: The Rise and Fall of the First British Empire, 1714–1783* (London: Allen Lane, 2007).

8 Britain at the accession of George III, 1760

Introduction

The accession of a new monarch is a good time to take stock of a nation's progress, even if such an event generally means more for a royal family than for the rest of the population. What the accession of a new monarch in the seventeenth and eighteenth centuries allowed was an opportunity to evaluate what the nation stood for. Such evaluations were made in the various symbolic ceremonies that were associated with the ascent on the throne of a new monarch. If the monarch was young, as was the case with George III when he became king on 25 October 1760, then the evaluations mixed statements about where people thought the country was presently at with an anticipation of things that were to come. The coronation of a new monarch was the single biggest symbolic expression of Britain's hopes and fears in the mid-eighteenth century and bears a little examination. George's coronation was held, as was customary for English monarchs, in Westminster Abbey on 22 September 1761, nearly a year after he had become king on the death of his grandfather, George II, the second Hanoverian monarch. George III proceeded with his teenage queen, Charlotte, in two sedan chairs to the abbey. Charlotte was pregnant soon after, giving birth to a son and heir, George, on 22 August 1762, thus fulfilling her main duty, which was to provide the Crown with people who could inherit the throne. She well and truly exceeded her royal duties, producing fifteen children between 1762 and 1783, thirteen of whom survived into childhood, including seven rather troublesome sons. George and Charlotte went the abbey in comparatively modest fashion, carried in sedan chairs rather than the newly commissioned but not-yet-finished Gold State Coach. This vehicle was last used by Elizabeth II in 2002 for her Golden Jubilee and will probably not be used again. The last two monarchs have called it 'horrid' and 'uncomfortable,' and a new state coach commissioned for Elizabeth's diamond jubilee will probably be used.

George III made a point, both at his coronation and in his first address to Parliament, of emphasising that unlike his German-born grandfather and great-grandfather, he had been born in Britain and 'gloried' in the 'name of Briton.' The coronation was an eagerly awaited event, attended by the great and good of the nation, which in 1761 meant in the main the British aristocracy. The grandest aristocrats were in the procession, and the rest strained to get a ticket for attendance. The coronation was full of symbolism, involving one climactic moment after another, from Handel's 'Zadok the Priest,' as the musical centrepiece (as it has been at every coronation since 1727) to the crowning of the king to the singing of a bathetic 'God Save the King' and the 'Te Deum.'

What distinguished this coronation from previous ones was its iconography, which was more imperial and grandiloquent than was customary. War motifs were prominent, as befitted a nation still embroiled in a major conflict with France. Some military men were fearful about George III becoming king, especially those involved in warfare in Europe. George II had had a wealth of European military and diplomatic experience dating back to the early eighteenth century. His grandson was not similarly experienced, and indeed, his attitude towards Europe at this stage of his reign was one of almost contrived truculence. He was so determined to be 'British' that he was contemptuous of George II's beloved Hanover, declaring that the current war difficulties in Germany were 'entirely owing to the partiality [George II] had for that horrid Electorate which has always lived upon the very vitals of this poor country.' There were more references in the coronation ceremony to imperial themes than even to war, indicating just how central empire had become to Britain's conception of itself. As Holger Hoock notes, 'at the height of the first truly global war, there were rich opportunities to convey a confident, patriotic message of British imperial triumph under a reinvigorated monarchy.'[1]

How George III's accession was commemorated in 1760–61 was a radical departure from the royal coronation a century earlier, at a time of much greater tension in the British Isles. Charles II's coronation on 23 April 1661 had been preceded by a grisly settling of scores on 15 October 1660 when ten men who had signed the death warrant of Charles I were executed, nine by the punishment for treason, which was hanging, drawing and quartering. That act of horrific vengeance against republican opponents of the monarchy was followed by the posthumous execution of the long-dead Oliver Cromwell, John Bradshaw and Henry Ireton and by another execution by hanging, drawing and quartering of two more regicides in 1662. The difference in tone and conduct between 1660 and 1760 not only reflected a nation that was demonstrably more 'polite' and 'enlightened' than it had been under the Stuarts but also a nation that, despite being at war, was more united, much happier and domestically more stable.

The personality of George III

George III has attracted an enormous amount of scholarly attention, which is itself somewhat surprising given how ordinary, dutiful, unexciting and plodding he was in a reign that is third to only those of Elizabeth II and Victoria in its longevity. He emulated Charles II in the number of children he had but, unlike Charles II, produced all these children with his wife – unkindly characterised by waspish commentators as decidedly plain and boring. Some of this attention from historians has been to show that he was 'bad' as well as 'mad,' but most historians have seen him less as a person of importance than as a manifestation in royal form of changes that were occurring in mid-century Britain. It is especially tempting to see his accession as the end of a long period of political division and the coming together of a coherent ruling class that was to rule relatively unchallenged until the end of the period of this study. George III's accession was welcomed enthusiastically, indeed euphorically, because it seemed to people at the time to suggest that Britain was henceforth to prosper in patriotic harmony. George III did place a lot of importance on extinguishing ancient animosities, ending the proscription of Tory families and allowing adherents of High Church principles more room within an expansive Anglican Church. Such hopes were not untrue – Britain was relatively harmonious from the 1760s to the 1780s, especially when compared to other European nations – but a little misplaced. Political division hardly disappeared: there were forty-eight county election contests (the political bellwethers of major ideological conflict) in the twenty years after George III's accession compared to twenty-eight in the previous twenty years.

Historians are interested in George III primarily for two events in his reign, both of which he was partially responsible for: the loss of the Thirteen Colonies of British North America and the establishment of the United States of America in 1787–88, and the surprising revival of monarchy in the latter part of his reign, ironically after the loss of America and as his medical health became problematic. Abolition and the tumults of the French Revolution and Napoleonic War also occurred under his reign, but as these mainly occurred after he had a bout of insanity in 1788, from which he recovered but which returned in 1804, leading in 1810 to his son, George IV, being appointed regent and effective monarch, these seem less obviously connected to him. George III was in many ways an accidental monarch or, at least, one, who if he had succeeded his father rather than his grandfather, whose reign would have been less obviously a break from previous regal patterns. His father, Frederick Lewis, was meant to be king after George II but died in 1751. Like George, Frederick was a devoted family man, with nine children, although, unlike his son, Frederick had also had a period as a conventionally promiscuous bachelor prince. Nevertheless, Frederick adopted new methods of child management in which principles of sensibility predominated rather than the harsh parental controls that Frederick himself experienced from his father, leading to one of the most famously contentious relationships between monarch and heir in British history. One of Frederick's distinctions is that he was probably the only Hanoverian until the twentieth century who did not incur the hatred of his eldest son and heir. Frederick was responsible for a more sympathetic impression of the Hanoverian dynasty, one devoted to the arts as much as to war and with much better gender and family relations. As Linda Colley argues, 'much of George III's reign would be a reprise in more favourable circumstances of what Frederick attempted to do before his early death in 1751. Frederick had wanted to extirpate traditional party divisions; George presided over their dissolution.'[2]

By 1760, the Hanoverian monarchy was secure enough to focus on matters other than survival, which had been what the first two Georges had been required to attend to. Indeed, George III was confident enough in the future of his rule that he even allowed himself an admiration for the much-hated Stuart monarchs. When Johan Zoffany painted the two eldest sons of George III as infants in 1764, he posed them under Van Dyck's portrait of Charles I's children. He would have done so surely only with the permission of George III. By 1760, George III did not fear a resurgence of Jacobitism. Nevertheless, his reign never saw him try to emulate either Charles I or James II. He had less power than virtually any monarch in Europe. He retained the power to appoint the government, but in practice, he could only appoint as prime minister men who had support in the House of Commons. He ruled always as a constitutional monarch dependent on the advice of his ministers. He was quite prepared to dismiss ministers he disapproved of but had to do so with the support of leading politicians. There was never any serious attempt in his reign to follow other European monarchs and make royal power more absolute. His constitutional restraint encouraged the British to consider their country a bastion of liberty, especially in contrast to France, Spain and Prussia.

His rectitude, love of domesticity and even his mental troubles and his difficulties with his rambunctious sons tended to endear him to his people rather than the opposite. Colley argues that after twenty years on the throne, the image of the monarchy had been transformed since George's coronation into a much more respected and popular institution than it had been for several hundred years, probably since the death of Henry V in 1422. One example of this greater regard for the monarchy was that the turgid 'God Save the King' anthem started to be played regularly at theatres and on ceremonial occasions while cartoons of the monarch which had been often savage in the 1760s and 1770s became much milder by the 1780s. Indeed, by the time of the French Revolution, cartoons of George III became affectionate and patriotic, even in the hands of otherwise vicious masters of visual satire, such as James Gillray and George Cruickshanks. As Colley argues, 'the shift in criticism of the monarchy which first became apparent in the 1780s, a shift away from anger at the institution to mockery of individual royals and their foibles helped – as it still helps – to preserve it.'[3]

She attributes the popularity of George III in the latter part of his reign to his ability to project the image of an ordinary gentleman of private virtue. Other historians, by contrast, argue that people were disturbed by George's 'madness,' by his departures from regal demeanour and by his manic affability. These personal foibles, oddly, contributed to increasing depictions of George III by loyal Britons from the 1790s as a genial father-figure, menaced by bloodthirsty Jacobins at home and abroad, with the image of the king being an effective weapon against proponents of parliamentary reform. His personal vulnerability and reputation as a good man made radical republicanism seem even more dangerous to worried conservatives, making reformers become careful not to show any personal animus against the king. Not everyone agreed, but George III's ideals of domestic probity, private virtue and self-restraint were eagerly adopted by Anglican evangelicals who were prominent in the regimes led by William Pitt the Younger, the dominant political figure of the last twenty years of George III's active reign. As Marilyn Morris notes,

> George III's public displays of marital devotion and the unmarried Pitt's apparent sexual continence seem to represent a sea change from the openly adulterous George II and [Robert] Walpole. Walpole's adeptness at amassing huge amounts of wealth and spending it lavishly bordered on the marvellous, whereas Pitt's personal finances fostered a stunning combination of abstemiousness and perennial debts.[4]

One positive result of George III's accession was that the hitherto divisive conflict between British and Hanoverian national interests disappeared. George III could not be thought of as an alien ruler, more committed to Germany than to Britain, depriving Tories and Jacobites of a major tenet of their ideology. As Lewis Namier wrote a long time ago in a groundbreaking book on the structure of British politics around 1760, the two-party pattern of parliamentary divisions that had existed since the early 1700s ended in the 1760s and politics tended to reflect temporary alignments of individual politicians and their factional or personal followings. Namier mistakenly thought that what he found for the 1760s was not new but part of longer-standing patterns, so he underestimated that extent to which parties still were powerful even after their influence had diminished once George III came on the throne. He also unstressed the extent to which ideological difference underpinned national politics – politics was not just a matter of who knew whom and how personal connections could bring about personal advantage; differences of opinion rooted in varying conceptions about social order and direction existed and led to fierce contestation within the narrow political elite that governed the nation. But certainly, the 1760s saw politics become transformed from the divisive party politics that existed through the 1750s.

Some areas of previous contention in respect to Britain's connections with the outside world subsided in importance as George III took control of ministerial appointments. Scotland, for example, became a loyal province of Britain, and the former Jacobite stronghold of the Highlands became a supplier of soldiers for the British Empire. George III's relations with Scotland were generally good, although his choice of the unpopular Scottish noble, the Earl of Bute, raised a predictable wave of Scotophobia in England. The appointment of the Oxford magnate, Lord North, son and heir of the Earl of Guildford, produced stability in Scotland. The American Revolution harmed that stability, as Scottish opposition to British policy in the Americas was considerable. But, in general, Scotland became a bastion of the empire during George III's reign. The appointment of Henry Dundas in 1794 as chief minister for Scotland by

Pitt turned the country into essentially a benevolent dictatorship. Dundas, later Viscount Melville, used Pitt's India Act of 1784 as a mechanism of patronage, rewarding Scots with posts in India on an unprecedented scale. His power grew until he became the indispensable person in Scotland. He fell from power in 1806 but only so far as that power was passed onto his son, Robert, who himself retained overwhelming political power in Scotland until resigning over the issue of Catholic emancipation in 1827. The rule of the two Dundas men was powerful but not despotic. As Bruce Lenman concludes, their rule 'was an enlightened manipulation of the existing system to facilitate Scottish participation in the advantages of an incorporating union, while still upholding that distinct Scottish identity which nobody denied that the first two Viscount Melvilles always showed.'[5] Both men died, like Pitt, deep in debt.

An island, once again

One reason to focus on George III in 1760 is that his accession marked a curious moment in Britain's involvement with the wider world. The victories of 1759 – Britain's so-called annus mirabilis, when it was successful in arms throughout the world – had made Britain more globally dominant than ever before. One writer in that year gushed that

> such were the events of that prodigious year in which Great Britain displayed her power and influence beyond what she had ever done, in the most shining periods of history. In Europe, in Asia, in Africa, and in America, her greatness had conspicuously shone out.

Imperial success followed imperial success. It was hardly a surprise that sorrow at the death of George II was overshadowed by joy of an accession of a handsome fresh-faced twenty-two-year-old king. Celebrations happened throughout the empire. In Boston, for example, local newspapers hailed the new 'patriot king,' and hoped that his reign heralded a 'new Era for North-America.' Joy over the accession of a new king even compensated for Boston's devastating fire of 20 March 1760 in which four hundred houses were destroyed and which resulted in £100,000 in damages. The Pennsylvania painter Benjamin West left for Italy and then Britain just as news of this tragedy reached Philadelphia. His arrival in the Old World made him think hard about the glories of the British Empire in the Americas, a vision of future glory that informed his 1771 masterpiece, *The Death of General Wolfe*. This vast panorama of the fields of Quebec conveyed visually the sentiments expressed in the proud boasts of the writer noted earlier, celebrating Britain's push to global superiority.

But just as Britain's 'fleets rode triumphant in all seas; her armies conquered wherever they appeared' in the glorious years between 1759 and 1762, the horizons of Britain's rulers narrowed. George III saw himself as a patriotic Briton which, in the context of politics in the 1760s, translated into a Tory navalist and colonial strategy and an abandonment of European entanglements, especially in Germany where George distrusted Frederick the Great, ruler of Prussia. If he distrusted Frederick, he hated his chief minister, William Pitt the Elder, the architect of British victory in the Seven Years' War, thinking him a 'snake in the grass' with 'the blackest of hearts.' He preferred the company of men like himself – men who saw themselves as British patriots and conventional country gentlemen, such as the Earl of Bute and even more so his good friend and the very model of an English conservative, Frederick, Lord North. North's very ordinariness, his self-deprecating humour, easy urbanity and clubbability, and even his unprepossessing appearance – overweight, awkward, with eyes that the waspish Horace Walpole, with typical malice, declared rolled about to no purpose and which gave him the air of a blind trumpeter – were very appealing to George and to members of the House of Commons, where he was a popular and well-trusted leader. George III remained North's most steadfast supporter during his long prime ministership between 1770 and 1782, refusing to let him resign, giving him awards such as a knighthood in Britain's leading order, the Garter, which he gave to no other favourite, and even paying off North's substantial debts.

George III and Lord North were urbane and cosmopolitan men – George's John Bull demeanour did not extend to such things as cuisine, where he had a sophisticated palate – but they were also men with a limited understanding of the new geopolitics of the 1760s. Spain and the Dutch Republic had ceased to be European powers by then, though both countries remained significant players in the colonial sphere. The five great powers in Europe by 1760 were Britain, France, Austria, Prussia and Russia – a configuration that lasted until the First World War. France hated Britain because of its humiliation between 1759 and 1762 and the embarrassment of the Peace of Paris in 1763. Its foreign policy for the next sixty years was predicated on getting revenge for what it had suffered in the early 1760s. The other significant power was Prussia, yet George III went out of his way in the early part of his reign (he became more sensitive to German matters and to Hanover later) to alienate this vital ally. He and the Earl of Bute dropped subsidies to Prussia as soon as they could and unceremoniously dumped Frederick by withdrawing precipitously from Europe in 1762, to Frederick's everlasting fury. Pitt and the Duke of Newcastle resigned as a result, thus depriving George III of the most experienced and skilled operators in the diplomatic minefield of European geopolitics. As Brendan Simms comments, 'once again, Britain was baling out of a European war at the expense of her allies. Britain was, in strategic terms – at least in terms of strategic self-perception – an island once again.'[6]

Hubris had overcome common sense. Britain had deliberately gotten rid of its allies, uniting most of Europe against it. And it now had a massive territorial empire to defend and pay for, which made finding and keeping allies in Europe more imperative than ever. Warning signs that controlling this empire would not be easy to do started to emerge in the early 1760s, In Ireland between 1761 and 1765, a mostly Catholic agrarian protest movement of small farmers and labourers, the Whiteboys, engaged in low-level but highly disruptive and troublesome protest, which was often violent, showing that the Protestant Ascendency's control of the kingdom was constantly precarious. More disturbingly and more violently, Native Americans in the Great Lakes region of the North American interior and in the Pennsylvania backcountry revolted against British rule in a series of serious revolts, the most significant of which was led by Pontiac, an Ottawa chieftain from near present-day Detroit. The British 'fix,' the Proclamation Declaration of 1763 – George III's order to establish new colonies and regulate land grants in territory acquired from the French by declaring a line over which American expansion could not occur – proved highly contentious, not satisfying Native American allies whom it was intending to protect and infuriating the many American colonists who had an expansionist vision of settler expansion in the seemingly empty lands of the American interior (which were lands, of course, that were occupied by Native American sovereignties who had no intention of ceding their land easily).

Benjamin Franklin, along with George Washington, who made major investments in western land, was a firm advocate of this expansionist vision of a single, unified British geopolitical space on the North American continent, reaching from the Atlantic Ocean to the Gulf of Mexico. Franklin argued in 1766 that 'a well-conducted western colony would be of great national advantage with respect to the trade, and particularly useful to the old colonies as a security to their frontiers.' The Proclamation Line, he thought, was a disaster. If American colonists were forced to be cooped up east of this line, Franklin predicted that settlers would be forced to give up agriculture and take up commerce to survive. Meanwhile, he believed, France and Spain would move into the vacuum. Western expansion was thus a preventative measure to secure the interests of the British Empire. Britain's decision to distance itself from European allies and its antagonism to France and Spain aggravated a combustible situation in a region which had already led to a world war and which proved to be an area of constant tension between Americans and Britons during the 1760s and 1770s.

Troubles were also emerging elsewhere. The Caribbean was flourishing as never before but was also a tinderbox, given the disproportion between white masters and black enslaved persons, as the nearly calamitous slave revolt of 1760–61, called Tacky's Revolt, had shown. This revolt had been put down, in part, due to the skilled tactics of one of the few distinguished colonial governors of the period, Henry Moore, who received a baronetcy and the governorship of New York as a reward, but the most economically valuable of all British colonies had nearly been destroyed in what was the biggest and most serious challenge by non-white subjects of empire until the Sepoy Rebellion in India in 1857. In India, the great acquisition resulting from the Seven Years' War, French and local Indian rulers challenged the new order of British rule established after the Battle of Plassey. The position of the East India Company was by no means secure in the early 1760s, as discussed later. And then in 1765 the seemingly most loyal and least problematic part of the empire, the coastal colonies of mainland North America, exploded into what turned out to be a permanent revolt.

By early 1763, the honeymoon between George III and his public was over, exacerbated by local political difficulties, especially by attacks on the hated Lord Bute and his Tory-leaning monarch by George's most-hated English opponent, the radical Whig pamphleteer, John Wilkes. George's antagonism to Wilkes was not just due to Wilkes's politics and lèse-majesté: it also came about, as was also the case in the 1780s with the prolific gambler and rake, Charles James Fox, from distaste for Wilkes's louche behaviour, so different from that of George himself. Wilkes adopted in his notorious pamphlet, issue no. 45 of the *North Briton*, a tone of xenophobic patriotism, attacking Bute as a Sottish interloper and a court favourite who seemed as malign to national interests as had been the Stuart favourite, the Duke of Buckingham, in the 1620s. Wilkes had more serious aims, however, than just being a provocateur (at which he excelled, more than almost anyone in British history). One of his most important aims was to support Pitt the Elder's view that Britain needed to support Prussia and, especially, Frederick the Great. Wilkes was arrested, but his subsequent trial showed that he retained great support in the country.

The aristocracy

The British aristocracy which governed Britain in this period, in combination with a monarch who accepted the constitutional limits of monarchy established in 1688, were not up to the immense task that faced them as a new empire emerged from the triumphs of the Seven Years' War. The plan for a new empire was clear from the Treaty of Paris in 1763 when, as one of the British heroes of the Seven Years' War, Admiral George Brydges Rodney declared, the 'empire of Great Britain [was] at stake.' British negotiators wrestled with a vision of a grand territorial empire populated by millions of subjects occupying millions of acres. But they also wrestled with a smaller vision of British settlement in the west extending into a frontier populated by Native Americans. Under the Earl of Bute, the ministry tried, without stunning success, to square the circle of two visions of empire. The first step was removing France from the Americas, allowing Britain what it had long desired – unbroken sovereignty across the western shores of the North Atlantic. The second step was adding four new Caribbean islands to the British West Indies, thus making the Atlantic empire one of tropical plantations and mainland settlements, integrated into a more tightly regulated Atlantic commercial empire. The final steps were confirming British conquests in Asia and Africa. British aristocrats, such as William Petty, Earl of Shelburne, the twenty-five-year-old leader of the Board of Trade in 1762 and later the prime minister who was brought down from office by a subsequent Peace of Paris in 1783, thought of the empire in narrow terms, as something intended to benefit the interests of the home country, even at the expense of the colonies. The colonies were places that had to serve national interests, just as tenants on country estates were required to show deference to landed grandees such as himself. As Max Edelson notes, Shelburne thought that 'to reform colonization,' it was necessary that 'the state must unleash the power of commercial exchange across space.' Indeed,

> once it became clear that the 'Well-being of the Universality' of the British archipelago depended on its colonies, it became intolerable to consider that Britain should not command what was 'essentially necessary, for its Preservation.' This newly acknowledged dependence sharpened a sense of risks to this artificial domain, distended across thousands of miles of maritime space – especially as colonies grew into more prosperous, autonomous, and developed societies.[7]

Such thoughts came naturally to men like Shelburne and his successor as president of the Board of Trade, Wills Hills, Earl of Hillsborough, Irish Protestants whose instinctive response to opposition and possible sedition and disorder was to respond with coercion. For Hillsborough, as for Shelburne and other leading ministers, the empire existed for only one purpose: to enrich Britain, colonies being there 'to improve and extend the commerce, navigation, and manufactures of this kingdom, upon which its strength and security depends.' North America was valuable for fisheries in the North Atlantic, for raw materials useful for the navy, as a captive market for British manufactures and as a supplier of goods to the West Indies. The West Indies were valuable for the sugar and other tropical commodities it produced, India was important for tea and textiles and the coastal forts of Africa were valuable for their role in supporting the Atlantic slave trade.

George III was determined to reform the aristocracy so that it was less dissolute and more public-spirited and less complacent in the face of all the privileges that aristocrats enjoyed. One of his concerns, however, which proved unfortunate about the aristocracy gaining a proper understanding of Britain's place in the world was to wean the aristocracy from foreign influences and make them more clearly aligned to the ideals of Britishness. Reverend John Brown reflected his future monarch's view in his influential *An Estimate of the Manners and Principles of the Times* (1757) when he lambasted 'the higher ranks' for indulging every 'Foreign Folly . . . or Vice.' The result, Brown argued, was an aristocracy devoted to 'vain, luxurious, and selfish EFFEMINANCY' who lived off their rents and did little of value to the nation and instead did nothing but indulge in 'Dress and Wagers, Cards, and Borough-jobbing, Horses, Women, and Dice.' Of course, one would expect a clergyman to engage in moralising: that is their job. Brown condemned aristocrats going on European Grand Tours as being a means of succumbing to 'foreign degeneracy.' Brown's comments struck a chord with British leaders who were conscious that in a world of politeness and commerce with a rising middling class of respectable urban citizens that aristocratic leaders needed to set an example of uprightness and virtue. The problem was that such concerns about morality at the top end of society coincided with Britain entering the world stage in a much more direct way than previously. What Britain did not need, but got, in the 1760s, was a leadership retreating into isolation when Britain needed more leaders with an international outlook.

Few aristocrats, and certainly not George III, had much foreign experience and even fewer had any experience in the empire (although the origins of the Pitt fortunes came from their ancestor, Thomas 'Diamond' Pitt's, activities in India in the early eighteenth century when he was governor of Madras). Those noblemen that did have international experience, moreover, were sidelined in favour of men whose background was solidly and stolidly British. The effect was to isolate Britain from the world. It was hard in the 1760s to even get peers to serve in prestigious overseas posts. Horace Walpole noted in 1767 that 'Sir James Gray goes to Madrid. The embassy has been sadly hawked about; not a peer would take it.' The rare men of distinction and rank who were experienced in European affairs found this situation lamentable. William Nassau de Zuylestein, Earl of Rochford, wrote in 1772 that 'the situation of Europe at this very instant of time is become . . . critical' because 'we have not a single friendly power or ally to boast of.'

If it was difficult to get men of parts to serve as ambassadors in agreeable European capitals, appointing men with the requisite pedigree that would have given them a place in British politics to become colonial governors was close to impossible. The quality of governors in British America in the 1760s and 1770s was extremely poor with positions being given to local notables such as Thomas Hutchinson in Massachusetts and Cadwallader Colden in New York who were out of their depth in their roles and who did not command enough local respect in a time when rank was vital for securing the respect of the political nation. Americans expected lords to lead them but seldom got them. When peers were made governors, they tended to be men such as John Murray, Earl of Dunmore, who were trying to escape a dubious past, which in Dunmore's case included a background as a supporter of Jacobitism. One sign of how low the regard for Dunmore was in the highest circles of British leadership is that when Dunmore's daughter, Lady Augusta Murray, married George's son, the Duke of Sussex, George III considered the marriage a violation of the Royal Marriages Act of 1772, which required royal princes to have the consent of the monarch for marriage.

To a great extent, the problems Britain's ruling elite had in understanding a more complicated wider world that Britain was entering into from the 1760s arose from the consolidation of that elite into an effective governing class in the eighteenth century and the general prosperity of the elite in the second half of the eighteenth century as agricultural land became increasingly profitable as the effects of agricultural innovations, including more extensive use of enclosure legislation to maximise agricultural income, became apparent. There have been few periods in British history when the British aristocracy has been more powerful, more secure in its position in the nation and wealthier than in the first twenty years of George III's reign. It is a period often described as an 'aristocratic century.' The reduction of party-political conflict between Whigs and Tories made politics a means of personal advancement by the well-born and rich. The agricultural and industrial revolutions made many aristocrats, especially those fortunate enough to be sitting on rich coal deposits, very wealthy. Some sense of the confidence of the mid-eighteenth-century British ruling elite can be discerned in the portraits of them, their families, their houses and their animals commissioned and painted by Joshua Reynolds, Thomas Gainsborough or George Romney, from which we get a sense of grace and elegance that is lacking for earlier periods and which contrasts with the sterility of Victorian portraits, which often seem to focus more on horses and stuffy dress than on humans.

It is important, however, to be careful about what is being claimed here about Britain being especially propitious for aristocrats in the middle of the eighteenth century. Aristocrats probably did not increase their share of British wealth over the course of the eighteenth century. The percentage of land tax paid by the top thirty people in Buckinghamshire in 1784 was about the same as in 1650. Britain has always had highly concentrated landownership and inequitable wealth distribution, not just in the eighteenth century but today. In 2019, 432 private landowners in Scotland own more than half of Scottish land, making that country have the most concentrated pattern of land ownership in the developed world. Moreover, as aristocrats were careful not to push their political dominance so that it roused protest, they tended not to seek to increase their elected influence against the wishes of local political communities. Paul Langford concludes that in this time 'the great families mainly rested upon their laurels and often observed an ostentatious neutrality' in county politics. There were only three county elections in the 1760s and 1770s in which a noble family sought to increase their electoral influence against the wishes of freeholders and in each case their efforts were unsuccessful.[8]

Indeed, Langford contends that the fashion among aristocrats for enclosure acts provoked concern among contemporaries. The novelist John Cleland, for example, 'presented a morbid image of the nobleman's annual journey from London to his country seat as a kind of cortege making its way through a lifeless landscape.' It is not too much, he argues, to see the 1760s as signifying a crisis in the paternalism that sustained aristocrats' conceit of contented peasants under benevolent noble rule. 'It was thought,' he notes, 'that men whose ancestors had been content with the rural round . . . now preferred life in London, Bath, and Brighton.' Criticism coincided with bad harvests, poor winters and terrible storms. The magnificent homes that grandees built with their massive and impressive gardens both seemed to many to be founded out of the misery of people evicted from their homes to allow for great aristocratic parks and allowed landlords to build a distance between themselves and their tenants that aggravated social tensions. Not surprisingly, these social processes that showed that paternalism was in retreat as the rage for improvement replaced it led to comments that nobles needed to pay more attention to their communities than to urban pleasures and even more so the concerns of a wider world.[9]

While peers and their children had preferential access to sinecures and took good positions in the armed forces or in the Anglican Church, those careers were not entirely closed to ambitious members of the middling classes. George III himself was a conscientious promoter of merit rather than just a tool of his courtiers, seeking positions for themselves and their families. Aristocrats always had great advantages in gaining government patronage, but demographic changes in upper-class families meant larger families from 1750 than in the early eighteenth century when mortality rates in aristocratic families were high and marriage rates low, leading to many extinctions of titles. This increase in the aristocratic population made competition for places more intense.

By European standards, however, the British aristocracy was relatively open and not quite a caste to which entry was denied and which was set apart from every other section of society. Aristocrats had few exclusive privileges and tended not to exercise such privileges, such as giving testimony in court under rules of honour rather than under oath. Laurence Shirley, Earl Ferrers, allegedly took advantage of an ancient privilege allowed peers, which was to be hanged by a silk rope, when he was executed at Tyburn on 5 May 1760 for the murder of his servant. The fact that he suffered a public spectacle of death for a crime in which he was judged just as if he was a commoner says something about how even aristocrats were ostensibly equal to other subjects in their treatment before the law. Nevertheless, what is notable about the eighteenth-century peerage, and thus the pool from whom almost all of Britain's statesmen were drawn, is that it remained a very small body of (mostly) men. During the entire eighteenth century, there were only 1,003 persons (43 of whom were women) who were peers. George III was very resistant to suggestions that he make people peers, and thus, the total increase in the size of the peerage was just 4, from 181 in 1750 to 185 in 1783. The contrast with the seventeenth century, when the peerage doubled, and the nineteenth century, when the peerage increased enormously, is striking.

Lord North

What this meant was that the eldest son of an earl, such as Lord North (he only succeeded to his title as Earl of Guildford in 1790, when he was fifty-eight), was an especially privileged person. Such men led extremely sheltered lives, educated at public schools, most particularly Eton, where they had a standardised upbringing that forged through immersion in classical literature and the ordeals of boarding school a common identity which made the members of the peerage and gentry have greater shared values than in the seventeenth century. That sense of identity was reinforced by study (or at least residence) at Cambridge or Oxford. The English universities were in an especially low point in the 1760s and students used them more as means of making social contacts than in indulging in scholarship. It was a terrible period in the history of British higher education. The numbers of students matriculated at English universities halved to just three hundred per annum by mid-century, meaning that university attendance in a period of rapid population growth was something experienced by a vanishingly small percentage of the population.

Oxford and Cambridge suffered from religious exclusiveness, ridiculous academic rules, lethargic teaching, limited research, and an increasingly aristocratic complexion. Nearly 60 per cent of peers born in the mid-eighteenth century were educated at one of the two universities. The only students at Oxford or Cambridge apart from generally indolent aristocrats were men studying for the Anglican Church, where a degree was virtually obligatory to get a post. Edward Gibbon wrote of his two years at Oxford in 1752–53 that they were 'the most idle and unprofitable of [his] whole life.' It was a common experience for students wanting more than a jolly time. One of the remarkable features of the age is how little the major intellectual and scientific developments of an age seemingly devoted to the advancement of human knowledge emerged from English universities (it was quite a different matter for Scottish universities, where Enlightenment thought found an agreeable home and where scholars such as Adam Smith propounded major theoretical insights into the human condition).

North was educated at Eton and Christ Church, Oxford, in a traditional pattern, and was elected unopposed, aged 22 as member of Parliament in 1754 for the seat of Banbury, Oxfordshire, which was in his family's interest. Thus, he became a public figure at the same youthful age as his friend, George III, did a few years later. North quickly showed he had administrative talents, and his genial nature made him much respected within the House of Commons. He soon was given major offices and became a political figure of consequence. His heart, however, was not in Westminster but in the beautiful Oxfordshire village of Wroxton, where the North family spoke for half the acres in the village and exercised a dominant influence over all the remaining land and people. They controlled everything that mattered in this little slice of traditional rural England. Benjamin Disraeli, a nineteenth-century prime ministerial successor of Lord North, described the English system that produced his predecessor as 'a territorial constitution,' based on a ruling elite of large landowners supported by a church whose ministers preached deference to established authority every Sunday to parishioners and who both exhibited noblesse oblige in their communities, expecting and receiving deference to their desires and unchallenged political power in return for their sometimes limited benevolence. The system had many virtues, encouraging men such as North and his royal patron to repay their privileges through showing virtue in public life – their insistence that the rulers of the elite were providing service to the nation was not mere conceit but accorded with deeply held values, one of the most important of which was an assumption that peers and even royalty had to risk their lives through participating as soldiers and sailors in Britain's very frequent wars.

But the system had conspicuous faults. It bred in its beneficiaries such as Lord North a narrowness of vision that made it close to impossible for them to understand, let alone identify with, rebellious colonists in North America or nabobs in India. As Nick Bunker argues,

the system set mental boundaries that they could not transcend, raised as they were in a culture where the landscape and the parish church bore everywhere the signs of privilege . . . The very qualities George III liked best in him [North] – his devotion to his church, to his king, and to the landed gentry – were precisely those that rendered North incapable of governing America.[10]

North defended until his death aged sixty on 2 August 1792 his role in the American War. He insisted that 'it did not originate in a despotic wish to tyrannise America, bit from the desire of maintaining the constitutional authority of Parliament over the colonies.' He even argued that if he needed to 'mount the scaffold in consequence of the part I have performed in its prosecution, I shall continue to maintain that it was founded in right and dictated by necessity.' His failure was one of understanding and imagination, not, as Americans believed, because he wanted to punish America, let alone be a tyrant to its white residents.

George III and America

No more was George III a tyrant. Indeed, if he had been more tyrannical, or at least less respectful in obeying the requirements of limited constitutional monarchy, as Americans begged him to be (following the ancient theme of believing that if only a wise king knew about the activities of his wicked ministers, he would have taken action to restore proper order: Americans also tended to have a view of George's constitutional authority that resembled that of their governors, who could exercise their prerogative more easily than George III could do against Parliament), then the resulting conflict in America may have turned out differently. George III did not instigate the policies that led to the American Revolution. He followed the advice of his ministers, on whom initially he was a restraining influence. It was only after the Boston Tea Party (1773) that he ceased his conciliatory stance and became determined to ensure that Americans respected royal authority. The lack of respect that Bostonians showed for that authority in refusing to allow tea to land in the harbour against the express instructions of their rulers and with a lack of concern for the effects that such actions would have on the East India Company's position made George III furious – a fury he shared with the great majority of the political nation, who were mostly united in opposition to American radical acts. He endorsed strongly the Coercive Acts of 1774, expressly designed to punish Boston for their intransigence, which united the Thirteen Colonies in opposition to British policy and which forced the conflict between America and Britain to war. It was only after the Coercive Acts that Americans began to personally target George III as their opponent. Thomas Jefferson, a young Virginia planter and aspiring politician, led the way, in *A Summary View of the Rights of British America* (1774), where he explicitly asked George III to intercede against Lord North and use the power of his veto against Parliament. Jefferson, far distant from the centre of imperial power, could not appreciate that to do so would not just have seemed to George III a violation of the constitution he had sworn to uphold but a crass abandonment of his close friend and compatriot. If British aristocrats had little understanding of what drove American rebels, Americans were just as clueless about how power worked in Britain and how irrelevant Americans – men without rank or fortune – seemed in the rarefied circles of actual British leadership. The radical writer, Thomas Paine, knew more than did Jefferson about how power worked in Britain but cared less and in *Common Sense* (1776) – in a publication to match John Wilkes's *North Briton* as a means of making the British monarch incandescent with rage – went further than Jefferson, calling George III 'the Royal Brute of Britain,' a charge Jefferson now enthusiastically took up in 1776 in the Declaration of Independence. By 1776, George III was being targeted as a menace to American liberty. It became evident to Americans contemplating revolt that, just as in 1649, the king had to be 'killed,' at least symbolically, through being removed from any new American system of government. The pulling down in that same year of the statue of George III in New York City was not just a symbolic rejection of George III as a monarch: it was a demonstration that Americans no longer respected a monarch whose motivations they both misunderstood and feared.

George III returned the favour. By 1776, he was determined to teach Americans a lesson. He never deviated from that ambition in the following years. His main role in the American Revolution was not in causing it but in continuing it. He refused to entertain ideas of negotiation or surrender until he was eventually forced to concede defeat and accept that his favourite prime minister had to depart, as he did in 1782. The war in America became a deeply personal crusade, in which he became convinced that Britain had to win if 'we are to rank among the Great Powers of Europe, or to be reduced to one of the least considerable.' Even after the British defeat at Yorktown, George III was determined to win the war at all costs. When he was finally forced to accept American independence, George III offered to abdicate, at least in a letter which eventually he did not send, a potentially personally devastating act which must have caused him utmost grief, not just because it signified failure on a grand scale but because it would have meant handing over the Crown to his irresponsible eldest son, whom he greatly disapproved of, in traditional Hanoverian fashion for fathers and heirs.

It was his personal traits, even his more admirable ones, such as devotion to duty, which shaped his conduct as king and which led him into trouble in his empire. Like North, he never deviated from his view that waging war against rebellious Americans was highly justifiable. He thought that British willingness to make peace with America in 1783 was a sign that Britain was 'absorbed by Vice and Dissipation,' thus associating his disappointment with his wayward sons into unhappiness with social relations in the nation. It was a bitter pill to swallow to have to accept as prime minister in 1784 William Pitt the Younger, the son of the politician he most detested and whose warnings in the 1760s about British policy in America, based on a much deeper and richer understanding of global affairs than was ever possible for most English noblemen, had proved remarkably prescient. As Andrew O'Shaughnessy argues, 'George III

Figure 8.1 John Singleton Copley, *The Three Youngest Daughters of George III*

Source: Artepics/Alamy Stock Photo.

appreciated the portent of the American Revolution for the end of the Ancien Régime in Europe' and 'used every means to defend the empire against revolutionaries whose victory he believed would annihilate the national greatness of Britain.' In the end, however, George III probably reflected his country's will more accurately than his aristocratic opponents. Pitt may have been right about America but people in power were not listening to him. They, like George III, thought that Lord North had the right attitude to the colonies. George III's and Lord North's political and social conservatism was simply more appealing to the prejudices of the majority of the members of Parliament than the reforming views of the leading opponents of the war in America.[11]

India

The perspective of history makes scholars focus on the war with America as the defining event in George III's life and the focus of British attention on the wider world in the 1760s and 1770s. It was only after 1774, however, that this conflict came to take centre stage in British public life. In the 1760s, the issue that was most important was British rule in India and the plight of the East India Company as it faced financial ruin in the early 1770s. That Britain would come to have a large territorial empire in India came about almost by accident. The East India Company's intentions in India, where it been involved in trade since the early seventeenth century, was to limit the company's political and military involvements to the minimum that would protect its commercial interests. As Robert James, the secretary of the company told the House of Commons in an enquiry into its affairs commissioned by Pitt the Elder in 1766–67, the company's involvement in Indian affairs arose out of fierce competition with the French which led to military commitments that 'grew insensibly from one trouble to another' and were unwelcome developments as 'we don't want conquest and power. It is commercial interests only we look to.'

Those commercial interests, with tea being an especially important component of the company's trade by the 1750s, supplementing if not supplanting an older trade in Asian textiles, were considerable. Robert Clive, the face of the company in India and the Victor of Plassey told Parliament during another inquiry, in 1772, that 'INDIA yields at present a clear produce to the public and to individuals of between two and three millions sterling.' That was an underestimate. Total government income from all sources, according to the company's books, was £311,317,805 between 1750 and 1781, including customs and excise revenue of £36 million. In 1769–70, this customs revenue was £2,739,257, which was one-third of all revenue for Britain in that year. Clive himself had made a colossal fortune from India, bringing back perhaps £300,000 to Britain on his return from India in 1760. That torrent of riches meant that Britain could not retreat from its accidental rule over the wealthy province of Bengal, even though what the company was doing there was deeply disturbing to Britons worried about the morality of overseas empire. Its activities in Bengal were especially concerning, as the company's extortionate taxes contributed to a famine that killed millions and in which the company, and by extension Britain, acted with disgraceful indifference. The British conquest largely freed the company's servants from Indian government regulatory acts limiting corruption, and they took full advantage. British traders monopolised food supplies to drive up prices and strong-armed Indian merchants to drive down costs. When drought struck, and famine followed in the late 1760s, the company 'violently' sought to maintain its revenue, turning a natural hazard into one of the world's worst-ever tragedies.

Clive became the most famous and richest of a new social type in Britain that emerged mostly in the 1760s, the wealthy nabob, or a European employee of the company who had enriched himself at Indian expense and returned to Britain. Nabobs out-bought even very wealthy aristocrats for desirable proper-ties on which they built ostentatious, if not vulgar, country mansions. Clive outdid by some margin previous imperial plunderers like the seventeenth-century privateer-governor, Sir Henry Morgan of Jamaica, in his rapacity. For Americans such as Virginian Arthur Lee, the lessons of Clive seemed clear: he had started in 'blood and plunder,' and his enterprise would end in 'servility and dependence' as his 'wealth would be insecure under the crimes by which it was acquired without ministerial influence and protection to cover them.' George III, he thought, needed to act if Britain and its new empire was not to fall, 'as Greece and Rome have fallen,' corrupted from within by tolerance of lux-ury and illegal avarice. That individuals were making hand over fist while the Company itself was by the early 1770s nearing bankruptcy only compounded the moral indignation of Britons and Americans. It also led Lord North to pass the Tea Act of 1773, reducing the duty of tea re-exported to the American colonies to make British tea cheaper than smuggled tea and thus providing the East India Company with enhanced revenues. It was perceived to be, and was a none-too-subtle attempt to bring America to provide a modest contribution to imperial funds, which had proved impossible to obtain through the hated Stamp Tax of 1765.

In addition, the company was highly vulnerable in Britain to being consid-ered an illegitimate form of sovereignty, not properly subordinate to the king in Parliament. It was for this reason that Pitt ordered an inquiry into its affairs in 1766 and which led to the Regulating Act of 1772, an act initiated by Lord North which placed the relationship between the company and the British government on a different footing. Sovereignty by the British in India was always a vexed issue. Even in the early stages of the conquest, Clive had admit-ted to Pitt the Elder that he wondered whether 'so large a sovereignty may possibly be an object too extensive for a mercantile Company.' Pitt's inquiry in 1766–67 was an attempt to settle that sovereignty question. Pitt's inten-tion, not realised, was to establish that Bengal was conquered territory and thus belonged properly to the British state. North's Regulation Act was an unprecedented parliamentary intervention into Indian affairs. North spoke of 'such continual excesses, such frauds at home, oppressions abroad, that all the world may cry out, let it go on the crown.' Yet the Regulating Act, for all the reforms it forced on the company, did not reform Bengal as a new America. Parliament's role in regulating the Company was increased but the act did not create a new constitution for Bengal or extend British law to the inhabitants of the newly conquered territories. It maintained a distinction between Britons in India, subject to British law, and 'native inhabitants,' who were to be governed by their own customs. As P.J. Marshall comments, this emphasis on preserving the rights of native inhabitants of Bengal to be governed by their own laws fitted with a broader current of paternalist imperial rhetoric led by English aristocrats and their like-minded monarch to insist that how they imagined relations between benevolent Oxfordshire landlord and grateful tenant should also work in wildly different places such as Bengal, French Canada and the slaveholding plantations of the eastern Caribbean.[12]

But empire in India was the total antithesis of a quiet parish in England's home counties. And it was very far from aligning with the ideal for a British Empire based on fairness and freedom. Instead, what it showed was how easily Britons overseas could fall into 'Asiatic despotism.' William Pitt the elder, despite himself being the grandson of a nabob whose methods of enrichment much resembled Robert Clive or Henry Vansittart, governor of Fort William in Bengal, exclaimed that 'The riches of Asia have poured in upon us, and have brought with them not only Asiatic luxury, but I fear, Asiatic principles.' The most sophisticated thinkers on empire, like the increasingly influential politician and political thinker, Edmund Burke, declared that the British Empire in 1769 was an 'object . . . wholly new to the world,' and needed to be governed on new principles. Britain's duty, he averred, was

> in all soberness, to conform our government to the character and circumstances of the several people who compose this mighty and strangely diversified mass. I never was wild enough to conceive that one method would serve for the whole; I could never conceive that the natives of *Hindostan* and those of *Virginia* could be ordered in the same manner; or that the *Cutchery* [Calcutta] court and the grand jury of *Salem* [New England] could be regulated on a similar plan.

As Marshall explains, 'for Burke, an empire based on ideological propositions about Protestantism, commerce, maritime power and freedom had given way to an empire based on the practical needs of the very diverse peoples who were now the king's subjects.'[13]

Burke put in a blast in this speech that 'I am persuaded that government was a practical thing made for the happiness of mankind, and not to furnish out a spectacle of unity, to gratify the schemes of visionary politicians,' against men like George Grenville, prime minister in the mid-1760s and Lord North, prime minister from 1770 to 1782. His charge was unfair: North tried his best to vary government practice against different perceived needs. The strident advocates of imperial uniformity tended to be North Americans and their British friends. The radical writer Samuel Sayre expostulated that all

Englishmen wherever they were had to live under the same rules that governed people living where George III resided. He insisted that there was a broad vision of an imperial constitution so that 'Englishmen, and their descendants, wherever they go, and wherever, they plant themselves, are Englishmen, with all their rights, privileges, and freedom.' He continued: 'Nor is he less an Englishman who lives in India, Africa, or America, than he who daily basks in the immediate sunshine of royal presence.' By 1775, Americans were starting, along with Jefferson, to think that royal presence might be infected with alien influences, even 'Asiatic despotism.' The American author of a serial publication, *The Crisis*, quoted George III calling the American colonists his hated slaves and while admitting that this quote was false suggested that one might expect George III to say such a thing for 'we have fairly cloathed an eastern spirit, in an eastern garb . . . we have not . . . meanly suffered the sentiments of an insolent mogul to be cramped by the poverty of princely diction.' To drive home the point, Americans widely republished an insulting print (an early example of photo-shopping!) depicting George III as an Asian despot, wearing a turban, Asian jewels and a banyan (Asian headdress). To add massive insult to injury, the heading of the print was 'Ecce homo,' a direct reference to the words of Pontius Pilate ('behold the man') condemning Christ the Saviour to death.

The reality, of course, is that George III, Lord North and most of the 'visionary politicians' of the 1760s had far too limited a grasp of the world to be capable of 'Asiatic despotism.' At bottom, they could not understand, let alone control, the new forces of the 1760s arising from Britain's rapid acquisition of a worldwide empire. And instead of trying to comprehend this new world, they retreated into the safety and familiarity of the world they knew and loved – that of a virtuous monarch, a dutiful people, an obedient church and a hard-working Parliament composed of men of limited horizons and national rather than international ambition. George III 'gloried' in 'the name of Briton.' Sadly for George III, as the American Revolution and the loss of the Thirteen Colonies proved, such attachment to the solidities of his native country was not enough in changed circumstances.

Notes

1 Holger Hoock, *Empires of the Imagination: Politics, War and the Arts in the British World* (London: Profile, 2010), 23.
2 Linda Colley, *Britons: Forging the Nation, 1707–1837* (New Haven: Yale University Press, 1992), 206.
3 Ibid., 210.
4 Marilyn Morris, *Sex, Money, and Personal Character in Eighteenth-Century British Politics* (New Haven: Yale University Press, 2014), 5.
5 Bruce Lenman, 'From the Union of 1707 to the Franchise Reform of 1832,' in R.A. Houston and W.W.J. Knox, eds., *The New Penguin History of Scotland from the Earliest Tomes to the Present Day* (London: Penguin, 2001), 324–5.
6 Brendan Simms, *Three Victories and a Defeat: The Rise and Fall of the First British Empire, 1714–1783* (London: Penguin, 2007), 492.

7 S. Max Edelson, *The New Map of Empire: How Britain Imagined American before Independence* (Cambridge, MA: Harvard University Press, 2017), 43, 45.
8 Paul Langford, *A Polite and Commercial People: England 1727–1783* (Oxford: Oxford University Press, 1989), 592.
9 Ibid., 440–2.
10 Nick Bunker, *An Empire on the Edge: How Britain Came to Fight America* (New York: Vintage, 2014), 368–9.
11 Andrew Jackson O'Shaughnessy, *The Men Who Lost America: British Leadership, the American Revolution, and the Fate of Empire* (New Haven: Yale University Press, 2013), 41, 46.
12 P.J. Marshall, *The Making and Unmaking of Empires: Britain, India, and America c.1750–1783* (Oxford: Oxford University Press, 2005), 182–96.
13 Ibid., 204.

Bibliography

Black, Jeremy, *George III: America's Last King* (New Haven: Yale University Press, 2006).

Bowen, H.V., "British Conceptions of Global Empire, 1756–83," *Journal of Imperial and Commonwealth History* 26 (1998), 1–27.

Brewer, John, *Party Ideology and Popular Politics at the Accession of George III* (Cambridge: Cambridge University Press, 1976).

Bunker, Nick, *An Empire on the Edge: How Britain Came to Fight America* (New York: Vintage, 2014).

Colley, Linda, 'The Apotheosis of George III: Loyalty, Royalty and the British Nation, 1760–1820,' *Past and Present* 102 (1984), 94–129.

Colley, Linda, *Britons: Forging the Nation, 1707–1837* (New Haven: Yale University Press, 1992).

Hoock, Holger, *Empires of the Imagination: Politics, War and the Arts in the British World* (London: Profile, 2010).

Langford, Paul, *A Polite and Commercial People: England 1727–1783* (Oxford: Oxford University Press, 1989).

Marshall, P.J., *The Making and Unmaking of Empires: Britain, India, and America c.1750–1783* (Oxford: Oxford University Press, 2005).

Morris, Marilyn, *Sex, Money, and Personal Character in Eighteenth-Century British Politics* (New Haven: Yale University Press, 2014).

O'Shaughnessy, Andrew Jackson, *The Men Who Lost America: British Leadership, the American Revolution, and the Fate of Empire* (New Haven: Yale University Press, 2013).

Thomas, P.D.G., *George III: King and Politicians 1760–1770* (Manchester: Manchester University Press, 2002).

Thomas, P.D.G., *Lord North* (London: Allen Lane, 1976).

9   Global victory and imperial defeat, 1756–88

Introduction

The eighteenth century, like the twentieth, was dominated for Britain by two global wars; the Seven Years' War, 1756–63 (although it really started unofficially two years earlier, in 1754); and the American Revolution, 1776–83. One war was a glorious victory for the British; the other, a signal defeat. One difference between the historical treatment of these two eighteenth-century wars as compared to their counterparts in the twentieth century was that in the eighteenth century, the first war has been relatively little studied compared to the reams of material produced on the latter war. To take one example, Linda Colley's 1992 exploration of Britishness, *Britons*, mentions the Seven Years' War on five pages compared to twenty-four pages on which the American Revolution is mentioned. And relatively little attention is given to its causes.

It seems an almost accidental war, coming out of contingencies and accidents, and escalating tensions between two warring nations which boiled over after a small conflict begun by the young George Washington, a Virginia officer, in the Ohio Valley in 1754. In 1755, these interior conflicts led to the rout by the French of a large army under Edward Braddock, who himself died in the massacre, in the Battle of the Monongahela. The contest seems, in this reading, to be an almost inevitable consequence of the relentless mid-eighteenth-century growth of the British mainland colonies which occasioned alarm among a less expansionist French America that the British might displace the French as the principal suppliers of goods to Native Americans. A showdown, by this reckoning, had to occur, and it was likely to do so in the backwaters of the empire, given that the war was more about imperial conflict, at least in the beginning, than a tussle for dominance in Europe.

Causes of the Seven Years' War

Admiral Roland-Michel Barrin, Comte de la Galissoniè, reflected this idea of an inevitable conflict in a memorandum he wrote to Louis XV after having served two years as governor of Quebec. His main point was that the expansion of the British mainland colonies was a dire threat to the French West Indies, a region increasingly valuable to France. Moreover, the growth of American trade augmented British maritime power to a degree that threatened France's superior standing in Europe. 'If we do not halt the rapid progress of the English colonies, he urged the French government, or 'if we do not form a counter-weight capable of containing them within their bounds,' then 'it will take them little time to carry large forces either to Saint-Domingue or to the island of Cuba, or to our Windward Islands,' and then 'there will be no hope of keeping them except at enormous expense.' Of course, governments get warnings such as this from departing officials all the time and seldom act on them. This time, France did. These thoughts struck a chord with French officials alarmed at British growth in North America. And they were thinking about more than America. The Seven Years' War reflected new geopolitics.

It operated in every ocean, except the Pacific (and even there was fighting in the Philippines in 1762, with a British expedition to acquire Manila). There were significant theatres in the Atlantic, the Caribbean and the Mediterranean. Fighting in Europe was important, but the war was fought primarily in North America and India, as well as in central Europe, where Britain's ally, Frederick the Great of Prussia, had some amazing victories. In this global context, dominance at sea was essential, and the Royal Navy was important everywhere. The capture of Havana in 1762 was a signal example of the navy's importance. The absence of naval battles is not so much a sign that fighting at sea was unimportant but a recognition that British naval power by the late 1750s was too great for the French to overcome. It was the command of the Western Approaches (the Atlantic seas at the edge of western Europe immediately west of Ireland and parts of Britain) won at the Battle of Lagos in 1759 off the coast of Portugal, and in the same year under Sir Edward Hawke at Quiberon Bay (off the coast of France) that enabled the subsequent expeditions to Cape Breton, Canada, Havana, Manila and elsewhere.

To the extent that historians have examined the long-term causes of the Seven Years' War, they have connected the war to the end of the war of the Austrian Succession in 1748, which left too many points of worldwide contention unsettled not to be resolved except through force. The two areas of contention were in south-east India and even more so in the Ohio Valley of the North American interior. These were areas where there was daily tension between the French and the British. Another point of contention was in Europe and around the difficulties Britain found itself in with another empire, the Holy Roman Empire, where the geopolitical system erected by an earlier generation was in a state of terminal disrepair.

We need to remember that leading British statesmen always had their eyes on Europe much more than on Africa, Asia or America. Britain's international position in the early 1750s was under serious threat from deteriorating relations with their ally, Prussia. Britain's inability to fix German issues in a region where it had a possession that George II cared deeply about was a major headache for British statesmen. Just because the war started in America and had the most serious long-term consequences in America, does not mean that it did not

Figure 9.1 Dominic Serres (1779), *The Battle of Quiberon Bay*, 20 November 1759.

Source: Niday Picture Library/Alamy Stock Photo.

have deep European roots which shaped British policy at the most fundamental level. One sign of how important Europe was in the causes of the Seven Years' War is the British reaction to an unexpected French takeover of Minorca early in the war, in June 1756. The press was in an uproar and demanded a victim, who turned out to be the unfortunate Admiral John Byng. He was court-martialled and shot to death on his own ship.

The loss of Minorca rankled in Britain more than the defeat on the Mononga-hela because it was a major reverse in European waters rather than a lurid skirmish in a place no one had heard about. Britain's reaction was to restore relations with Frederick the Great. He quickly invaded Saxony in August 1756, thus setting off with a vengeance the continental war Britain had been wanting very much to avoid. The accident of invasion, however, led to the winning combination of the Anglo-Prussian alliance, which turned out to be vital to British success.

The main cause of war appears to be mutual fear of each other by France and Britain, which made minor conflicts seem to presage more serious conse-quences. In short, each nation started a pre-emptive war for defensive reasons, the reasons being the need to defend interests around the globe. But what started off as a defensive war became by 1759 a war of conquest. Britain seized French and Spanish possessions in North America, the Caribbean, West Africa, India and even in the Philippines. This global war made Britain more aware of their colonial possessions and their value to Britain while more Britons than ever before were drawn directly into the empire as soldiers and sailors, serving alongside colonial Americans, Indians, Native Americans and Africans.

William Pitt and America

The Seven Years' War fell into two stages: failure and defeat between 1754 and 1757 and outrageous success after 1758. Braddock's defeat in 1755, the fall of Minorca in 1756 and the uninspired leadership of the Duke of Cumberland's protégé, the Earl of Loudoun, as commander-in-chief in America, allowed France under Governor Pierre de Rigaud de Vaudreuil and General Louis-Joseph de Montcalm to capture British forts on Lake Ontario and Lake George in the Pays d'en Haut region of the Great Lakes. These embarrassing defeats brought to power (for the second time) William Pitt the Elder and the Duke of Newcastle. Pitt proved to be the leader Britain needed. A bombastic, egotistical, ambitious hypochondriac, Pitt boasted in Parliament about how in his new ministry he had spent enormous amounts of money in sending large numbers of soldiers to America, India and Europe – 167,000 men in total at an annual expense of £18 million. In addition, large sums were being funnelled to Frederick in Prussia. No empire had ever spent so much money on imperial warfare before.

Pitt's gamble, to throw money at the problem, worked extremely well. In 1758, the Royal Navy, as noted earlier, won control of the Atlantic Ocean, devastating French shipping. The British army captured the great French fortress of Louisburg on the St Lawrence River, captured Quebec in a stirring victory under General James Wolfe in 1759 and got Vaudreuil to surrender all Canada in 1760. Not everything went well. In Jamaica, a major slave revolt broke out in April 1760, nearly destroying white control of Britain's most important colony. British reaction to this non-white challenge to its authority – the most serious before the Sepoy mutiny in India in 1857 – was savage. Captured rebels were tortured to death in excruciating rituals of punishment. But if we exclude this event, British arms succeeded magnificently, not just in America and Europe but in the Lesser Antilles and West Africa.

The colony which contributed most to British victory was the colony that was to cause it most problems in the American Revolution, Massachusetts put ten thousand men in the field in 1758 and overall kept one man in seven under arms during the war. In addition, it provided nearly one-third of all money raised in America for the benefit of British war making. That sum is impressive as Massachusetts was not a rich colony. It idolised Pitt and Wolfe and celebrated wildly in public celebrations when Quebec fell. It raised a statue to Lord Howe, who was killed at Ticonderoga in 1758, which was to prove an ironic act when Howe's brothers became military commanders of the British army and navy during the American Revolution. The residents of Massachusetts felt proud of its contributions and the result of the war left them more than ever attached to the empire, expecting after 1763 a larger role in that empire with further recognition of their rights as English people and entitlement to greater self-government. Their efforts also led them to compare themselves favourably with other colonies. Governor William Shirley detailed to London the failings of colonies to the south of New England, arguing that this meant that 'parliamentary union' should be imposed on North America and that Britain should tax these delinquent colonies more intensely.

During the years of Pitt's leadership, the American view of empire as a partnership was accepted by many Britons and the idea of colonial government as 'negotiated' was understood to work well. Imperial reform schemes were abandoned in favour of the status quo. Nevertheless, Pitt never conceded that Parliament was anything other than sovereign and that America could govern itself without the help of a permanent army in the colonies. Other Britons were less tolerant than Pitt of the idea of a negotiated empire; they preferred command and obedience over discussion and some respect for American contributions to the war effort. These opinions mattered little in the West Indies, where planters accepted imperial dependency in return for security against internal slave revolts and external attacks from empire. As the West Indies were at the forefront of the imperial mind, it was easy to think that the situation in the West Indies world also pertain in North America. That was a calamitous calculation to make.

India

The most astounding result of the Seven Years' War was Britain's triumph in India under the East India Company, where its defeats of the French and the Mughals led to it taking over the rich province of Bengal. For contemporaries, this result was unexpected, but with historical hindsight, it fits into a larger picture of the break-up in Asia of the general agrarian empires of the Qing, Ottoman, Safavid and Mughal empires from the 1720s onwards. In India, the Mughal Empire started to fragment with provinces becoming semi-independent while north India was invaded by Persian and Afghan armies in 1739 and 1759, leading to the sack of Delhi. Thus, European expansion occurred at a time of Indian weakness. The Mughal Empire did not have a good solution to the cost of defending and paying for its multiple imperial possessions in the ways that Britain had worked out in the early eighteenth century. It was caught in a vice of rising military expenditure and stagnant revenues. That Europe decided to embark on war in Asia only accelerated the problems the Mughals faced.

This worldwide set of imperial crises occurred in India when the British shifted from peaceful trade to wars and Indian conquest. The contrast between the two halves of the eighteenth century is remarkable, with peace in the first half matched by violence in the second half. Why violence happened is harder to explain, except as a by-product of global conflict between France and Britain. Britain was happy with what it was doing in India as a sponsor of a state-controlled trading company, buying textiles and tea. One consequence of British victory in Bengal was that the focus of British attention changed, from seeking India's trade goods to lusting after India's territorial revenues, revenues it needed after 1757 and after its outward expansion from Bengal after 1783, to pay for its growing army of Indian Sepoys and British troops. The date conventionally chosen for the outbreak of hostilities is 1744, with fighting at sea between France and Britain and war on land from 1746 in south-eastern India. War only stopped in 1761 with the complete victory of the British in southern India.

The peak period of violence came after 1756, when relations between the East India Company and a new nawab of Bengal, Siraj-ud-Daula, broke down. Robert Clive, later ennobled as Lord Clive of India, led a military force against the nawab, comprehensively defeating him at the Battle of Plassey in 1757, making Bengal a client state and then from 1763 a province under British rule. The victories of the British were rewarded in the 1765 Treaty of Allahabad when the Mughal emperor awarded the East India Company the *Diwani*, or responsibility for running Bengal while gaining its revenue. Suddenly Britain had acquired 20 million new subjects and an annual Indian revenue of £3 million.

This account is the traditional story, but scholars are making some modifications to it. Britain is not seen as being as peaceful in the eighteenth century before 1744 as it was once thought. Ideas that Britain walked without direct intention to engage in conquest into an empire that was tearing itself apart seem unconvincing. The empire was weakening, but it was not paralysed. One current view is that British rule was not built on the collapse of the Mughal Empire but was a consequence of the emergence of a new order, in which there was a complex interplay between the East India Company and Indian rulers. For one thing, northern India, where the Mughals had their power base, was prospering in the first half of the eighteenth century and the Indian economy was probably strong in various other parts of the subcontinent. That the Mughals declined in the mid-eighteenth century is clear. What is contested is that this led to anarchy, which the East India Company was able to exploit. The British won power as participants in Indian political struggles and exercised their power in some ways as other Indian rulers did, including continuing running their possessions under Indian legal structures.

It is likely that the East India Company was skilled at insinuating itself into local elite politics, although the extent to which Indian elites collaborated with Britain is hotly contested within the existing historiography, especially by scholars from South Asia. They see the British less as actors in an Indian play but as alien aggressors, introducing brute force into Indian politics in ways not previously seen. What is clear is that individual Britons, from Robert Clive downwards, and Indians associated with the company acted in their own interests to cloud larger geopolitical objectives. The greatest opportunities after Plassey were in internal trade. The result of internal internecine warfare was something new in India. The East India Company, in fact, was not just another regional Indian power but had made India into a British national possession, making those who ruled it bound to fulfil British national aims. Britain did not leave India to the East India Company; it poured resources into the region on an almost unlimited scale, especially to support its growing and large army. This army soon eclipsed all other Indian armies and began to exert its power over the whole subcontinent.

The conquest of India had multiple results. For Britain, one major result was that India became increasingly important in Britain's domestic economy. After 1760, the company reconfigured its trade, most notably in moving away from its long-standing dependence on the exportation of South American silver to buy Chinese and Indian commodities. Successive drives to increase the flow of tribute to Britain through the *Diwani* led to increased commerce within India and China, including more manufactured British goods going to these countries. The importance of East India goods in Britain's overseas trade balance grew from the mid-eighteenth century, with exports to Asia increasing from 7.9 per cent of total exports in 1752–54 to 14.7 per cent in 1794–96, while imports peaked at 21.8 per cent in 1784–86. This increase in trade, moreover, took place at a time when Atlantic trade was also increasing rapidly, meaning that the totals involved in Asian trade became increasingly substantial.

The conquest of India also altered sovereignty in India and the empire. The East India Company gave large sums to the emperor in return for his favour. The 'bribery,' as it seemed in Britain, left it highly vulnerable to criticism in Britain that the company was systematically corrupt. That led to questions over the governance of a large territory by a private company. Robert Clive admitted to William Pitt the Elder whether 'so large a sovereignty may possibly be an object too extensive for a mercantile Company.' The Crown wanted the new territories to be administered by them rather than by the company. Discussions on this topic eventually led to compromise, with the company agreeing to pay to the government an annual tribute of £400,000 to the Treasury for securing its powers in Bengal. Its rule was a hazy middle ground between Mughal and British sovereignty. Concerns about this uncertain formal status led eventually to Lord North's Regulating Act in 1773, where North argued that the company should be 'farmers for the publick' rather than just a private concern.

A great advance in British power

The result of the Seven Years' War was a transformation in Britain's geopolitical situation. When the war began, France was easily the strongest power in Europe, with an advanced economy and a population three times that of Britain and Ireland. Its navy was not as strong as Britain's, but its army was vastly more powerful and important, especially in Europe. It was for this reason that Prussian support was vital to maintain British interests in Europe. It was no surprise, therefore, that until the end of 1757, France was winning the war against its old foe.

But by 1760, Britain had defeated France everywhere, on land and at sea. It had won Canada, preserved Hanover and taken Guadeloupe, Senegal and Bengal. Soon it would conquer Havana and reduce France to penury. Britain had an inspiration leader in Pitt, a skilled administrator in Pitt's lieutenant, the Earl of Hardwicke, an experienced politician in the Duke of Newcastle and some able military commanders, especially in the navy. It also had support from settlers in America, who provided men and materials to aid the British war effort to a much greater extent than did French settler in French colonies to their nation's war aims. That Britain did not acknowledge this help did not make it any less real. The costs to Britain of the war were substantial. The cost in 1761 of supporting the navy and the army and maintaining Prussian subsidies was a massive £9, 991,598.

But despite gloomy talk by advocates of making peace that this expense would lead to national bankruptcy, the financial reforms noted in a previous chapter that led to the fiscal-military state meant that Britain could support an ongoing war, no matter the demands that William Pitt's subsidy policy of paying colonies to compete in support of imperial goals, which cost Britain £200,000 per annum but which raised twenty thousand troops for imperial warfare. The problem was that George II's new administration, led by the Earl of Bute, with the Duke of Bedford as a chief negotiator in Europe, botched the peace plans, as Pitt angrily declared. Pitt commented on the peace deal as follows:

> France is chiefly, if not solely, to be dreaded by us in the light of a mari-time and commercial power . . . [and] by restoring to her all the valuable West-India islands, and by our concessions in the Newfoundland fishery, we had given to her the means of recovering her prodigious losses and of becoming once more formidable to us at sea.

Pitt was self-interested in his analysis, but it was an analysis that was generally correct. He had changed the direction of the war by concentrating on coop-eration with American settlers, encouragement of Frederick in Germany and Clive in India and by lack of concern about the costs of doing battle, convinced that a peacetime dividend of enhanced British power would soon wipe off any debts. But the administration which replaced him and the Duke of Newcastle focused on the years of failure, from 1754 to 1757, which had preceded Pitt's new system. All the acts reshaping empire in 1764 and 1765 replayed the diffi-culties of 1757 rather than the achievements of 1758–62. If we employ a coun-terfactual to imagine a different settlement after 1763, we can think of what might have happened if Britain had extended the lessons of victory by con-tinuing to do as Pitt had done to win the war rather than to embrace projects stimulated by the fear of defeat. Instead of devising an unpopular Stamp Act to get more taxes out of the colonies, which would, in any event, not have been enough to do more than raise a small proportion of the costs of maintaining a British army in America, it should have constrained Pitt's subsidy policy which may have stimulated at less cost a larger voluntary response from the colonies.

Parliament kept trying to address the problems of 1754–57 between 1764 and 1766, which Pitt had largely solved by his wartime system of spending lots of money on troops and subsidies. Between 1767 and 1770, America suffered under the reforms of Charles Townshend, who was mostly concerned with government policy of even earlier years, between 1748 and 1754, when he worried about the lack of an independent salary for colonial governors. Even more remarkably, John Murrin contends, 'in the final crisis of 1774, Parliament reached back even farther to the early years of the century . . . by resurrect[ing] the Board of Trade's ancient nostrum of depriving charter governments of special privileges by act of parliament.' The Coercive Acts of 1774 were a replay of a policy of 1701 to deal with events three-quarters of a century later. As Murrin concludes, 'the Revolution truly was a paradoxical aftermath of the Great War for the Empire. Britain may actually have lost her colonies because, in the last analysis, the English simply did not know how to think triumphantly.'[1]

Consequences of victory

The American Revolution was an imperial civil war as much or than a nationalist rebellion. Its origins lay in the Seven Years' War and the problems of imperial governance that followed from Britain's overwhelming victory against France and Spain. It was not due, as an older generation of historians focusing very much on America rather than the war as a global event argued, from the resentments that Americans had about their treatment, especially when serving as soldiers, from haughty and intolerant British officers. More important than American dissatisfaction with British treatment was the low opinion British officers had about American contributions to the imperial war effort. The Seven Years' War was the first time in which substantial portions of the British ruling class came to have a direct experience of North America, and they were not impressed by what they saw – braggadocio accompanied by self-interest, poor soldiering and inadequate support from colonial assemblies. They repeated their dissatisfaction to their superiors, family and friends in Britain, thus contributing to an atmosphere in which the colonies were parasitical rather than helpful to the empire. More important, however, the Seven Years' War revealed just how valuable North America was both economically and geopolitically to the British Empire and encouraged imperial officials to indulge in fantasies of imperial reorganisation.

Britons were convinced that Americans were not pulling their weight in defending the empire and that their contribution to British victory had been slight. If you read the British press on the war, it was highly negative about what colonists did, arguing that they got in the way rather than aiding Britain in the quest for victory. With very few exceptions, British commentators saw the war as a British victory, secured despite rather than because of American support. They thought that it should be the colonies who should be grateful to them, given that they had removed the common enemy of the French from their internal borders, allowing for rapid westward expansion. Colonists, of course, thought the opposite. They considered that their contribution to victory had been massive and they resented what they saw as punishment for their support of the British by the imperial reorganisations of the mid-1760s.

But it was practicalities, not emotions that were the most important legacy of the Seven Years' War in causing the American Revolution. Perhaps Britain should have kept Guadeloupe rather than Canada as their reward for victory.

It may have been better for Britain to have had a foe constraining American actions in the mid–1760s rather than having Americans feel that they
could move across the continent freely and complain about imperial actions
without geopolitical consequences (although in this respect this omits the
extremely serious constraints that powerful Native American nations continued to impose on settler expansionist dreams). The real issue was that the
size and nature of British victory brought new problems to an inexperienced
British government under the direction of a brand-new king. These questions
included, How was the American interior to be governed? How were Catholics in Quebec to be incorporated into an Atlantic empire that was firmly
anti-Catholic, to an extent that was more pronounced than in Britain itself?
and How was the empire in the Atlantic to be coordinated with the new and
massive empire Britain had acquired in Asia and with the flourishing trade in
slaves and other goods with Africa and even with a potential new empire in
the Pacific?

Most important, the Seven Years' War had resulted in a large and multi-
ethnic empire developing, quite suddenly, which had many more imperial
subjects in Bengal than in Massachusetts. Most imperial subjects were non-
white and had no personal or emotional allegiance to Britain. The specialness of British colonists in the Americas, with their constant claims that they
were the equal of Britons at home, started to seem less convincing in this
multi-ethnic empire. As Stephen Conway argues, Britain, 'perhaps subcon-
sciously downgraded the colonists. Americans who had enjoyed the special
status of fellow-Britons across the Atlantic were now viewed alongside French
Canadians, Native Americans, and even Bengalese, as just another set of people to be governed.'[2] These tendencies to lump all imperial subjects together
was enhanced by feelings in London that their new empire was vulnerable to
French and Spanish attempts to regain power. Moreover, the totality of British
victory had made Britain proud and insensitive to others. Britain had always
needed support from allies in Europe; in the 1760s, as described in the previous chapter, Britain felt powerful enough to go it alone in the world, breeding
great resentment among European powers already predisposed against it. This
imperial 'hubris' of believing that Britain was inviolable overseas came to haunt
Britain in the 1770s as its war against America was fought largely without any
European assistance, except from German mercenaries willing to fight for pay
in the British army.

After 1763, Britain looked at its huge and diverse global empire and tried to
bring the North American part of that empire into an increasingly rationalised
system, where local differences were eliminated in favour of economic policies
imposed on colonies by metropolitan decrees. As Eliga Gould comments, 'for
all their cocksure certainty, the British saw their actions towards the colonies as
fundamentally pacific.'[3] What they wanted to do was to make the empire more
harmonious and safer through making policies that brought all parts of the
empire into common submission to a beneficent British Parliament.

The vision of empire that Britain had in 1763 was based on some assumptions of what the empire should look like which were very different from those that Benjamin Franklin had advanced in 1760, covered previously in this book. We can see the difference in examining the views of another major theorist of empire in the 1760s, William Knox, a protégé of Lord Halifax at the Board of Trade who had worked in Georgia under Governor Henry Ellis. Ellis was an especially insightful thinker about empire who wrote an important report in 1763 which advised the Board of Trade and hence the government that colonies needed to be bounded and contained by firm lines on the large maps that imperial officials were staring at in Whitehall. Knox continued Ellis's cautious and conservative analysis of colonial boundaries in which the ideal colony was, as Max Edelson notes, 'a clearly delineated territory that was compact, well-governed and connected to Britain through Atlantic trade.'

Knox differed from Franklin, who thought uninhibited westward expansion a boon to empire, by seeing the movement of settlers outside the bounds of settled societies as a potential for imperial disorder. Knox agreed with Franklin's prognosis of a growing colonial population and how early marriage allowed by easy settlement of lands encouraged greater population growth than normal. He disagreed, however, with Franklin that this growing native-born population was a good thing. American breeding habits were vices, not virtues, showing lack of sexual and moral restraint and was part of settlers' headlong pursuit of self-interest over collective goals, all of which collective goals, Knox thought, should be around setting bounds to population increase and to new settlement in areas where Americans would only antagonise Native Americans. Because Britain's 'possessions in North America were so many times more extensive than the Island of Great Britain, if they were equally well inhabited, Great Britain could no longer maintain her dominion over them.' Thus, settlement should be confined 'within proper Limits,' which would be before the Appalachians.

His whole diatribe seethed with opposition to colonists, whose character he denigrated in ways familiar to Britons hearing from British officers about the deficiencies of Americans during the Seven Years' War. They were not obedient 'Children' but rebellious 'Rivals to the Mother Country,' as much like Native American 'savages' as Native Americans themselves in their propagation practices and their chaotic settlement patterns. As subjects, colonists were known for their 'excessive licentiousness,' making them like drunks at a public house, degenerates whose claims for 'privileges' in the 'wilds of America' showed that they had no respect for their monarch or for British officials generally. It was this sort of information that British officials relied upon in their schemes for reorganisation – it was Knox, not Franklin who represented the imperial mind. Order needed to be imposed, and quickly, if British America was not to become ungovernable. In detailing Knox's plans, one can see why imperial plans were bound to lead to disaster. As Edelson concludes,

> Britain succumbed to the predictable hubris of modernising states, so confident in their technologies for order almost inevitably fracture when faced

with unforeseen contingencies, especially when people resist schemes that they believe aim at their subjugation. Its struggle to impose a particular spatial order on America generated its own undoing, which went beyond a contribution to the general discontent that drove colonial power.[4]

Causes of the revolution

The simple causes of the American Revolution are easily told. There were tensions in the colonies immediately following the Peace of Paris in 1763, when there was a flurry of British interventions into America, such as a Royal Proclamation that sought to preserve the interior west of the Appalachians for Native Americans while encouraging Protestant settlement into newly acquired Canada and Florida and a tightening of the Navigation Acts; a Mutiny Act in 1765, providing stricter discipline for colonial soldiers; and the Revenue Act of 1764, which reduced a prohibitive duty on foreign molasses entering North America from the Caribbean, Americans bristled from interventionist and ill thought-out, as they saw it, commands from Britain to change established practices, hinder trade, favour Native Americans over colonists and stymie westward expansion. Already, ham-fisted British policy in the Great Lakes region had set off a rebellion among Native Americans, already alarmed by the result of the Seven Years' War, which meant that they could no longer so easily play one empire off each other. The rebellion rather misleadingly called Pontiac's rebellion, after one of just several Native American chiefs (from the Ottawa people) who joined in what was a multi-tribal rebellion started in spring and summer in 1763. It was a brutal war, which hardened racial animosities, and encouraged a vigilante groups, the Paxton Boys, in Pennsylvania, to emerge, who in December 1763 massacred peaceful Indians of Conestoga and in February 1764 marched on Philadelphia to demand more violent imperial attacks on native Americans in the 'Middle Ground' of the western interior.

The real furore, however, only emerged when Britain tried to make Americans pay more for the cost of empire through imposing taxes through a Stamp Act, passed in 1765. Almost everywhere in the British Atlantic, especially in North America, unrest, sometimes violent, emerged as colonists protested what they considered to be an unjust tax, imposed without consultation with local political assemblies. The Stamp Act was repealed in 1766, but further attempts by the British to find a way to tax Americans in ways that Americans found acceptable failed. More important, a constitutional rift appeared between colonists and Britain, as setters refused to accept that Parliament's insistence that it alone had the authority to make laws in the empire and could not have its authority tested was allowable, except insofar as it deprived them of their 'liberty' through 'tyranny,' reducing them to 'slavery,' a condition Americans knew well and which they feared, seeing how abjectly African American enslaved people lived.

An attempt to solve one problem of empire – the parlous financial position in 1773 of the East India Company – by addressing another – the unwillingness of Americans to accept parliamentary sovereignty – failed dismally, resulting in the Boston Tea Party, when Boston residents, disguised very poorly as Mohawk Indians, threw tea into the harbour rather than allowing a ship laden with East Indian Company product to discharge its goods to customs collectors. Americans' flagrant disobedience against imperial authority provoked a stern response, with Britain imposing four Coercive Acts in 1774 against Massachusetts and its ports, alongside an act, the Quebec Act, which incorporated French Catholics into the empire, outraging strongly anti-Catholic Protestants in the northern colonies.

It is worth pausing at the Boston Tea Party to note how this event shows the ways in which one part of the empire became connected to other parts of the empire in the imperial mind. We have noted aspects of India's connection to America in Chapter 6. Tea was one of the most important imperial commodities – grown in China, bought by the East India Company, transported to Britain and then re-exported throughout the empire, including to Boston. Generally, the Tea Party is described in American-centric terms, as an act of provocation by Britain, a ministerial scheme to trick Americans into accepting taxed tea. But it would have been strange if an event sparked by a debate over the nature of imperial taxation, about a commodity produced and sold from various parts of the world, not just from within the British Empire, and designed to benefit Britain overall, not just America, would be discussed in terms that were confined to British North America. And it was not. What British ministers were interested in was how lowering taxes on tea in America might help the stricken East India Company. That was Britain's priority, over and above how they thought sending tea to Boston might help, rather than inflame, the imperial problems faced in that town.

The East India Company was more powerful in the imperial government than were American colonists. Its shareholders were rich, well connected and determined to defend the privileges of the company through its powerful House of Commons lobby. The government was always extremely careful in dealing with the East India Company, because it feared how its supporters might use any conflict to cause trouble in domestic politics. If the government tried to make the company more accountable, it raised fears in Country Whigs (a faction of the political nation predisposed to see ministerial action as tyrannical) of a growth in the royal prerogative and a belief that the government might exploit the wealth of the company as Crown patronage and as money for ministers to bribe and corrupt Parliament. It was these fears that helped bring down in 1783 the Fox–North administration after it tried to pass an East India Act.

Americans had little understanding of the complicated place of India and the East India Company in British politics in the 1760s. Americans were hugely hostile to the East India Company and to British imperialism in India. John Dickinson, a very influential political pamphleteer, argued that a corrupt British ministry hoped to support a broken East India Company 'by the ruin of American freedom and liberty,' lambasting the company as a vile institution that for years 'have levied war, excited rebellion, dethroned lawful princes and sacrificed millions for the sake of gain' and now 'cast it eyes on America, as a new theatre whereon to exercise their talents of rapine and cruelty.' He thundered that 'we are not Sea Poys, nor Marathas, but British subjects, who are born to liberty, who prize it high.'

The problem which Dickinson did not appreciate was that it was the East India Company, not the American colonies, which was a model of imperial docility which Britain preferred dealing with rather than with troublesome American colonists. The East India Company accepted the right of Parliament to legislate for it; American settlers did not accept this. What the events of the 1760s showed was that Britain's control over North America was fragile and based on voluntary cooperation. The American colonies had evolved within an imperial system, from the 1640s, implosion of metropolitan authority during the Civil Wars in which imperial authority was negotiated rather than imposed in the ways that Britain was finding customary when dealing with the East India Company. American opposition to British authority appeared to Britain as a direct challenge to their major institutions of government that was like, if different in form, to the challenges Stuart monarchs had posed to the liberties of the nation in the seventeenth century. Thus, Americans were defining consent in terms repugnant to the heirs of the Glorious Revolution, British Whigs.

As P. J. Marshall notes, 'Americans asserted that the people did not authorise their betters to govern for them as the considered best by an act of consent in the remote past, as was conventional British doctrine; rather they continued actively to give or withhold their consent, treating those in authority, in John Adams's words, as their 'attorneys' and maintaining 'a popular check upon the whole government.' For the House of Lords, such an attitude was 'a dangerous doctrine, destructive to all government.' Faced with such an existential threat to their authority, Britain doubled down, not just to control America but to set an example to other parts of the empire, notably Ireland, and to the disaffected in Britain. Scotland by 1773 was secure and committed to British rule from London, but politicians with long memories, who were few on the ground in the 1760s, much to the cost of the imperial government, remembered the lost revolt against Parliament, the Jacobite Rebellion in 1745–46. To add to Britain's difficulties, it understood that if it provoked further unrest in the colonies, it would incur interest from France and Spain in interfering in British affairs in the Atlantic.

But, as Marshall writes, 'international rivalry made a coercive response hazardous, it was also an argument against inaction, Britain's standing as a great power in the eyes of the other European states would be fatally compromised were Britain unable to impose its will on its own colonies.' Britain thought, however, that in 1775 it could run the risk of forcing the colonies to back down because France was perceived to be weak and for the moment pacifically inclined, and thus 'believing that its greatest rival would be unable or unwilling to exploit the breach between Britain and its American colonies, the government felt that it could act against its rebelling colonies without serious international consequences. If the revolt had been suppressed quickly, the risk might have been justified.'[5]

The war for American independence

By 1775, thirteen colonies in British North America were at war with Britain, while the West Indies, Bermuda, Canada and Ireland stayed loyal. From July 1776, with the Declaration of Independence, until 1783, Britain and America were involved in a messy, complicated and violent set of civil wars, in which relatively few people were at first committed to either rebellion or else to staying loyal and in which it became clear over time that sides had to be taken and allegiances upheld. Like all civil wars, the American Revolution was a nasty business, with neutrals hounded until they chose which side they were on. Patriots were especially good at exploiting the hesitancy of their fellow country people, so that more and more people felt they had to support rebellion rather than stay within the empire. The war split communities and families apart. American allegiances were often determined more by local issues than by imperial concerns or by ideological conflict. In North Carolina, for example, fierce disputes in the early 1770s, termed the Regulator disputes, led to the losers in this dispute staying neutral and then loyalist in the War for American Independence, not because they supported Britain but because they saw the war as a project of elite men who they opposed and who the felt would damage the local interests they had fought to defend just a few years earlier.

The war itself was long, bloody but was eventually won decisively by the American rebels. American troops under the inspirational leadership of George Washington, a Virginian planter whose actions had started off the Seven Years' War in 1754, managed to hold off British attacks for long enough for the French in 1778 to declare war on the British in support of America, followed a year later by Spain. These declarations of war transformed an imperial civil war into an international conflict. The key battle came at Saratoga in October 1777. It was a rare American victory and showed that their amateur army could defeat a professional field army. 'It was a glorious sight,' one American soldier declared, 'to see the haughty Brittons march out and Surrender their arms to an Army which but a little before, they despis'd and called poltroons.'

The equally decisive battle at Yorktown in Virginia in 1781, was won by Washington in part because the British army had stopped a blockade of the American shoreline in order to chase the French and Spanish fleets planning to capture British West Indian islands. American victory ensured British defeat in the war, and the two sides settled for peace and the eventual creation of the United States of America. Britain, however, was not as upset at the loss in America as might have been expected. A few individuals, notably George III and Lord North, who had committed fully to winning the war, found the loss intensely hard to bear. But for many Britons, it did not even seem as if they had lost the war. The loss at Yorktown was compensated for by a bigger naval victory in April 1782 against the French at the Battle of the Saintes in the Lesser Antilles. That victory persuaded the British that they had not fared that badly in the war, especially as they gained Gibraltar and Minorca at the Peace of Paris, after having kept control of the West Indian islands that contributed a great deal to imperial economic prosperity. Thus, the loss of America was more a matter of national embarrassment than an economic disaster. In the 1780s, Britain enjoyed a period of sustained economic prosperity and geopolitical dominance in Europe. As J. G. A. Pocock quips, 'the Revolution was less of a traumatic shock to the British than a display of their capacity for losing an empire without caring very deeply.'[6]

Why did the British lose? It was not because its army or navy were not very good or that it relied on unsuitable European battlefield tactics when guerrilla warfare was what was necessary in American terrain. These are explanations for military defeat previously put forward, but they are unconvincing. British forces were strong, and their leadership, if occasionally pedestrian, invariably professional, accomplished and the equal of anything on the American side. One problem that Britain had was that the fighting started in New England, where the concentration of British troops in 1775 weakened the army elsewhere in America. The nature of the American war also made it impossible for the British army to operate at peak efficiency. The country was large and close to unmanageable while the absence of a capital city meant that conquering New York and Philadelphia merely moved the fighting elsewhere. The biggest problem, however, was not a military one but a psychological reality, As John Adams argued, the battle was not over land or money but was a contest to 'gain the hearts and subdue the minds of America.' Britain could never do this by force and it never convinced Americans that its argument in favour of parliamentary sovereignty against local autonomy was correct.

The war was lost by the time that France entered the war in 1778, as Britain then had to make sure it or Ireland was not invaded. It had to expand conflict with European armies in the Caribbean, West Africa, Asia and the Mediterranean. As Stephen Conway argues, 'from 1778, then, the war in America should not be seen as a David and Goliath type struggle, in which the Americans triumphed against the odds.'[7] Of course, we should not just concentrate on why Britain lost; America also won. It beat Britain at Saratoga and Yorktown, and its continental army was never properly defeated, despite many severe setbacks. Washington's ability to survive in 1776, as commemorated in a famous painting by Emanuel Leutze in 1851 of him crossing the Delaware River in winter, and his bold attacks on British forces at Trenton and Princeton in that winter, played an important role in securing American victory. In addition, the politicians in the Continental Congress managed to keep the Thirteen Colonies united and mostly in favour of their aims for independence, even given considerable domestic setbacks and hardships. The unity of the Americans in pursuit of their goal proved remarkable and a strong factor in ultimate victory.

Britain and the American Revolution

Britain was not terribly affected by the American War of Independence. Ordinary Britons had to pay more taxes, although Lord North managed before 1778 to limit tax rises to an increase in the land tax, which was paid by the wealthy. The British state had developed a coherent fiscal-military machine, as outlined previously, which allowed it to fight for America relatively cheaply, at least when compared to the debts incurred during the Seven Years' War. Some businesses, like shipbuilders, did well out of the war, while food producers and retailers benefitted from increased demand for their products. Where people suffered most was in transatlantic trades such as the tobacco trade to Glasgow and the Atlantic slave trade. In the latter, supplies slowed to a trickle while demand fell away entirely, as planters struggled to meet costs. Trade with America, in general, became more expensive due to rising insurance rates, the costs of providing naval convoys to ships so they would not be attacked at sea, and rising sailors' wages, as the supply of sailors dropped due to impressment and volunteering in the British navy and more men staying on land rather than venturing to sea.

Britain was divided by the war. Americans had their supporters in parliament, especially before the war started. Once war began, however, and especially after France and Spain entered the war, partiality to Americans greatly reduced, as supporting them seemed close to treachery. Opposition was confined to the press and the world of print. The Dissenter Richard Price, for instance, produced best-selling attacks on the war. He thought the war to be an unmitigated disaster. Irish support of America was more pronounced and more dangerous, given security risks in the island. What the Revolution did not do, unlike the French Revolution, was radicalise the British population. The loss of America brought down a popular government that had the support of the king and led to popular reform movements in both Britain and Ireland. But political changes were short and ephemeral in their effects. The main reason was that the loss of the American colonies had little economic or geopolitical effect. Moreover, Britain was not a big loser after the war was finished. It kept its trade to America largely intact and, indeed, by 1794, when Britain and the United States signed a commercial treaty, Americans were buying far more goods from Britain than the other way around. By the 1790s, Britain was once again America's main market, its chief supplier of imports and a major provider of immigrants to America.

Canada and revolution

Canada occupied a special place in the American Revolution. It was the only place which Patriots tried to enlist into rebellion. That desire to add Canada to the Thirteen Colonies continued throughout the war, even after an invasion from America in 1775–76, conceived of by Americans as liberation rather than invasion but seen very differently by Canadians, had failed dismally. The

Americans hoped that by invading Canada that they would secure their northern boundary and prevent the British from rallying Native Americans to raid interior regions. Their appeals to French Canadians, however, fell on deaf ears, mainly because constant Protestant attacks on Catholics in the previous century had aroused huge suspicion about American intentions from French *habitants*. The American invasion was chaotic and unsuccessful, a catastrophe that cost five thousand American lives, either dead or captured. No other invasion was attempted, despite George Washington contemplating it in 1782. Britain was able to defend this part of the empire with ease, not just in the 1770s but also forty years later when America once more tried to invade it, during the War of 1812.

Canada next came into importance after the end of the War for American Independence. It marked a remarkable transformation in the composition of the population from overwhelmingly French to one with a mixed French and British population. Some six thousand Loyalists came to what was to become Upper Canada after 1750 with a large single integration of people in 1787 when thirty thousand white and free blacks moved from New York to Nova Scotia. These people wanted and did acquire land within French settlements. The governor, Guy Carleton, was committed to constructing new Loyalist societies based on hierarchy and dependence, but new settlers firmly rejected such thinking. They wanted land but did not want to be in places where Old World customs and values had been transplanted. The Loyalists entering Canada were part of a large outmigration of sixty thousand Loyalist refugees and fifteen thousand enslaved people moving everywhere in the British Empire. There were eight thousand Loyalists who went to Britain, thirty-five thousand to Nova Scotia, two thousand to Quebec and six thousand in Lower Canada. The latter migration was the most successful of these migrations, due to a propitious climate for agriculture. In the late 1780s, these settlers were joined by a surge of immigration from New York, making the colony viable and prosperous.

The Loyalist influx made French Canadians nervous because it pointed to a rapid transformation of Canada away from its New French origins. Loyalists were anxious to go to Canada because land was cheap and easily dispersed. In 1791, Loyalists helped draft the Canada Constitutional Act, dividing power between Anglophones and Francophones. It was an act done in the immediate aftermath of the American Revolution and reflected the government of George III's eagerness to allocate Native American land for cultivation by settlers. Loyalists did not always take the comfortable political side, which was reasonable, given their understanding of a post-war society that was more hierarchical, authoritarian and paternalistic than before. Britain was determined in the act to learn lessons from the American Revolution as understood by its subjects, who had rejected the American option of republicanism. Britain wanted 'to avoid, if possible, in the Government of Canada, those defects which hastened the independence of our antient possessions in America,' in which, Britain argued, colonies had become republics 'because no care was taken to preserve a due mixture of the Monarchical and Aristocratical parts of the British Constitutions.'

Britain insisted that the new constitution in Canada would provide for representative assemblies firmly under royal control. The idea was that if Canada had an assembly, properly restricted in its activities, it 'would afford,' in the words of Lord Grenville in 1789, 'a juster and more efficient security against the growth of a republican or independent spirit, than any which could be derived from a Government more arbitrary in its form or principles.' The new government was to be a royal favour, not given as a popular right. Nevertheless, this top-down authoritarian policy was balanced by more lenient practice. The act reiterated a pledge made by Parliament in 1778 to never again tax its white colonial subjects for revenue, as Grenville's father had done in 1765 with the Stamp Act. The costs of government were paid for by the British government, leading to lower taxes in Canada, cheap land and a higher standard of living than in the United States. It led to great migration from the United States into Canada, as well as migration from Britain after 1800. Canada was less democratic than the United States but more content. Lord Thurlow explained that the British 'had given them more civil liberty, without political liberty,' reducing the risk of further rebellion by generous imperial subventions to its subjects.

The West Indies

The effects of the American Revolution in the West Indies were more mixed than in Canada. No West Indian colony joined in rebellion with North America or was asked to do so. It is doubtful that any overture to the West Indies would have worked, given that planters there relied more than in North America on imperial support, not least in sustaining a slave trade providing its plantations with labour and seeing that its largely immigrant white population was instinctively Loyalist in ideological orientation.

The Caribbean suffered considerably during the War for American Independence. It was heavily dependent on food imports from North America and Britain. The war meant that the former source dried up, and the cost of getting goods from the latter soared. Prices for food and other necessaries increased dramatically, resulting in famine for enslaved people in Barbados and Jamaica. Perhaps fifteen thousand enslaved people in Jamaica died as a result of wartime deprivation in the early 1780s. Once the war was finished, however, the plantation economies of the islands quickly recovered, along with the Atlantic slave trade. Indeed, they prospered as never before in the 1790s, when the implosion of the French colony of Saint Domingue removed the principal competitor to the British West Indies, as a provider of sugar and coffee to Europe.

The political and cultural effects, however, of the American Revolution were more long-lasting. Despite its loyalty to Britain, and even though retaining the West Indies was a major victory for the British over the French, the position of white West Indians in the empire declined after the American Revolution.

Figure 9.2 Craskell (1763), illustration to map of Surrey, Jamaica

Source: ART Collection/Alamy Stock Photo.

The British Empire in the 1780s was more authoritarian than before and more dependent on metropolitan direction, exercised tightly among a close group of like-minded military men. Imperial officials in the Caribbean after 1783 were less inclined than before to put up with any opposition from settlers, especially those who upheld the principles of local autonomy that had led settlers in North America into revolt. Britain acted less consultatively and less in the interests of the West Indies than before. In 1784, for example, against West Indian protests, Britain severed the Caribbean from North America by insisting on recognising the United States as a foreign power which, in a mercantilist framework, meant that it had to be banned from providing goods to the West Indies. This disrupted long-standing commercial relationships that had led to a vibrant plantation economy. The favoured position of the West Indies within the empire which had shaped imperial policy between 1688 and 1776 was ended. For the first time, advocates for the West Indies in London were unable to get their own way over West Indian policy matters.

Much more worrying for white planters, however, was how their public reputation plunged during the 1780s as an abolitionist campaign against the slave trade developed and grew in extremely rapid fashion from virtually nothing in 1780 to a major social reform movement by 1787–88. Increasingly, West Indian planters were not seen as fellow countrymen but, like Americans, as foreigners and as hypocrites, wanting liberty for themselves while depriving others of liberty. That those others were black and thus, according to planters, not entitled to British liberty no longer cut much ice by this time. The white West Indian became depicted, like the Indian nabob, as a tyrant, and as someone outside the normal boundaries of polite British society. Planters were caught up in an intense debate in the 1780s and 1790s over the meaning of empire in a time when Britons were migrating to South Africa and Australia, free blacks to Sierra Leone and American Loyalists to a range of places. West Indians were the first in a long line of loyal subjects of Britain to be dropped by Britain as insufficiently British by metropolitan standards. Planters saw themselves as British gentlemen of upright character, working tirelessly in the interests of the empire. That is not how they were seen in Britain by the 1780s. Britons thought that planters and the societies they ruled to be monstrous, so monstrous that they needed reform even if that would harm the economy. In this respect, that abolitionism occurred when the Industrial Revolution was transforming the British economy is significant. Britain could afford the economic hit of abolishing the slave trade because the ending of that trade was not devastating to an economy purring along on all cylinders.

Global impact of the American Revolution

The American Revolution is all too often depicted as a purely American event with American results. It is sometimes seen as an event that had a major impact on Britain and on the restructuring of the British Empire. It also, however, had global consequences. As David Armitage argues, it was 'the first major act of state-creation and decolonization in world history,' an unprecedented 'birth of an entirely new state (or states) within the contemporary international order.'[8] The American Revolution was an Atlantic crisis that encompassed all areas of the British Atlantic world as an imperial civil war that turned into an international conflict among Britain, the independent Thirteen Colonies, and American allies, such as France and Spain. It formed a precursor to other international conflicts, like the Latin American Revolutions of the early nineteenth century. It was a crisis of sovereignty and about American claims to local autonomy that was not singular but part of a general pattern in European empires after 1763, each of which embarked on extensive projects of imperial reform. France, as much as Britain, used its experience during the Seven Years' War to rethink empire. It reconstituted its navy, it overhauled its commercial policy which from 1763 was focused on the immensely valuable colony of Saint-Domingue and it looked for ways to revenge itself on Britain. That vengeance finally occurred in 1778, when it joined the Americans in rebellion.

Spain was left in 1763 with the only possessions in North America, after France had ceded Louisiana. But it was a vulnerable empire, as had become clear in the conquest by Britain of the seemingly impregnable fortress of Havana in Cuba in 1762. Spain also, like Britain, had a new and dynamic young king, Carlos III, who became king in 1759, and embarked on a widespread set of reforms of the empire, with the aim being greater oversight from the centre and more fiscal demands on colonists. Spain succeeded in their objectives, partly due to experience where central control had always been important but also by watching what Britain did in America and not following Britain's confrontational strategies with its colonies. Nevertheless, France and Spain might have been watching even more closely, because the actions of the Americans in creating states out of colonies was replicated later in their empire. Making new states was a radical act of transformation, as the politician and imperial thinker, Edmund Burke, recognised. He saw in British recognition of American independence 'as great a change in all the relations, and balances, and gravitation of power, as the appearance of a new planet would in the system of the solar world.' The American Revolution was revolutionary not because it led to any change in social structures or even in governance but because the United States was a new state, the precursor of all future secessionist movements, anti-colonial and anti-imperial, and well as anti-state, to the present.

What did Britain learn from its defeat? It perhaps learned the lesson Franklin wanted to teach it, that settler self-government had to be respected. Britain never conceded that the sovereignty of Parliament was dissoluble, as Americans argued. It continued to claim its sovereignty was unlimited. Britain, however, did not press its claims too strongly after that, as we have seen in Ireland. It also learned, more ominously, that colonial revolts had to be put down with more force than happened in Boston in 1773. When Irishmen rebelled in 1798, the revolt was met with fierce and unremitting hostility that amounted to brutality. One thing Britain did not change, however, was its commitment to empire. The American Revolution did not mark the end of a British Empire but the beginnings of a larger empire that was not so much different from the pre-1776 British Empire in basic assumptions but was remade from the heritage of the past to meet the challenge of rule in settlers' dominions in Canada and Australia, a vast commercial and landed empire in India and a tentative foray into Africa.

Notes

1 John M. Murrin, *Rethinking America: From Empire to Republic* (New York: Oxford University Press, 2018), 125–6.
2 Stephen Conway, *The American Revolutionary War* (London: I.B. Tauris, 2013), 38–9.
3 Eliga H. Gould, "Fears of War, Fantasies of Peace: British Politics and the Coming of the American Revolution," in Gould and Peter Onuf, eds., *Empire and Nation: The American Revolution in the Atlantic World* (Baltimore: Johns Hopkins University Press, 2005), 20.
4 S. Max Edelson, *The New Map of Empire: How Britain Imagined America before Independence* (Cambridge, MA: Harvard University Press, 2017), 12, 49–53.
5 P.J. Marshall, 'Britain's American Problem: The International Perspective,' in Edward G. Gray and Jane Kamensky, eds., *The Oxford Handbook of the American Revolution* (Oxford: Oxford University Press, 2013), 21–2.
6 J.G.A. Pocock, 'British History: A Plea for a New Subject: A Reply,' *Journal of Modern History* 47 (1975), 627.
7 Stephen Conway, 'The British Army and the War for Independence,' in Gray and Kamensky, eds., *The Oxford Handbook of the American Revolution*, 189.
8 David Armitage, The First Atlantic Crisis: The American Revolution,' in Philip D. Morgan and Molly A. Warsh, eds., *Early North America in Global Perspective* (New York: Routledge, 2014), 310–11.

Bibliography

Baugh, Daniel, *The Global Seven Years War, 1754–1763* (Harlow: Pearson, 2011).

Conway, Stephen, *The American Revolutionary War* (London: I.B. Tauris, 2013).

Edelson, S. Max, *The New Map of Empire: How Britain Imagined America before Independence* (Cambridge, MA: Harvard University Press, 2017).

Gould, Eliga H., *Among the Powers of the Earth: The American Empire and the Making of New World Empire* (Cambridge, MA: Harvard University Press, 2012).

Gray, Edward G. and Jane Kamensky, eds., *The Oxford Handbook of the American Revolution* (Oxford: Oxford University Press, 2013).

Marshall, P.J., *The Making and Unmaking of Empires: Britain, India, and America c. 1750–1783* (Oxford: Oxford University Press, 2005).

Marshall, P.J., *Remaking the British Atlantic: The United States and the British Empire after American Independence* (Oxford: Oxford University Press, 2012).

O'Shaughnessy, A.J., *The Men Who Lost America: British Leadership, the American Revolution, and the Fate of Empire* (New Haven: Yale University Press, 2013).

Simms, Brendan, *Three Victories and a Defeat: The Rise and Fall of the First British Empire, 1714–1783* (London: Penguin, 2007).

Taylor, Alan, *American Revolutions: A Continental History, 1750–1804* (New York: W.W. Norton and Co, 2016).

10 The Industrial Revolution

Introduction

As in so many areas of British historiography, the previously strong claims for Britain being transformed in the second half of the eighteenth century by a series of important innovations in industry that led to an Industrial Revolution have been diminished in recent years. No one doubts that change occurred in the economy of Britain between 1700 and 1900; what has changed have been interpretations of this change that consider it revolutionary rather than evolutionary. Such ideas of an Industrial Revolution occurring suddenly with the invention of the steam engine and the Spinning Jenny cotton mill are now discounted in favour of industrialisation being a process which started in the late seventeenth century and which developed in fits and starts but generally gradually for the next 150 years. In short, we now believe in a 'long,' rather than a 'short,' Industrial Revolution and concentrate as much on what Jan de Vries calls 'an industrious revolution,' on long-distance trade and on the continuing importance of agricultural production in Britain. What still remains central, however, to examinations of economic transformation in Britain during the long eighteenth century is that it made Britain exceptional – the first to profit from a new system of economic organisation which in the next century and a half came to take over the world. Historians tend to ask three questions about this remarkable set of changes over this century: why did the Industrial Revolution happen in Britain, rather than elsewhere; why did industrialisation have the ability to change the fundamentals of global economic dominance, with the West taking over from the East in what is now termed the Great Divergence; and what are the long-term climatic possibilities and challenges that arise from extensive man-made change to the earth through industrialisation?

Why Britain?

Explanations of why the Industrial revolution occurred and what caused it are, unsurprisingly, numerous, given it had such a remarkable effect on global history. The changes in the British economy were shared by other nations in Europe and eventually overseas as well, in the period in which the discipline of economics came into existence and people started to talk about and measure a new concept called 'economic growth.' As Joel Mokyr explains, economic growth is a phenomenon unprecedented in history, lifting most Britons out of subsistence and providing them 'with comfort, security, leisure and material satisfaction that in previous ages had been confined to a few.' It took place first in Britain, with the major effects occurring sometime after 1750, 'a deep and irreversible' event that eventually spread from Britain to Europe, North America, Australasia, and then the world. It was an event with deep roots, reaching back to the Black Death in the fourteenth century, when serfdom was undermined by population falls allowing for labour mobility and a high-wage economy that allowed for more consumption by ordinary people. In the sixteenth century, an expansion in trade, first in wool and then in the seventeenth century in products from the plantation colonies of America, fostered urbanisation, above all in London, whose growth encouraged advances in agriculture, a more refined division of labour, greater efficiency and higher wages than anywhere else in Europe. England also had favourable institutional and cultural factors that encouraged capitalism and a scientific revolution in which people looked to science rather than religion (or superstition) to solve their problems. Markets got better at the allocation of resources, leading to rises in output. Mokyr notes that before 1750

> such developments were normally driven by the engines of commerce and institutional improvement, with technology providing the auxiliary source of power. Around 1750, all this began to change. The best definition of the Industrial Revolution is the set of events that placed technology in the position of the main engine of economic change.

Of course, the 'wave of gadgets' that is popularly associated with the Industrial Revolution need not to have been invented around this time – they could have been invented years earlier. But

> what is beyond question is that the relative importance of science to the productive economy kept growing throughout the late eighteenth and nineteenth centuries, and became indispensable after 1870, with the so-called second Industrial Revolution . . . the essence of the Enlightenment's impact on the economy was the drive to expand the accumulation of useful knowledge and direct it toward practical use.

Thus, the Industrial Revolution was the outgrowth of the social and intellectual foundations laid by the Enlightenment and the Scientific Revolution of the late seventeenth and early eighteenth centuries. And it happened in Britain well before it happened elsewhere.[1]

Because of the global significance of the Industrial Revolution, explanations for why it happened abound. One school, usually Marxist, searches for the causes in the rise of capitalism, which was certainly a necessary, if not sufficient, condition for economic growth. Other historians, writing in the liberal tradition, stress the beneficial institutional effects of the Glorious Revolution, which limited the constraining hand of the monarch and guaranteed property rights, thus encouraging people to innovate for personal gain. And a further group, drawing on the works of Max Weber, seek answers in the cultural characteristics of the British, the initial Weberian notion being that Protestantism inculcated behaviour that encouraged scientific inquiry and capitalist behaviour. Few historians hold to this view now, but many adopt a variant of what Weber called 'the disenchantment of the world.' In this view, once the world was seen in material, rather than spiritual, terms, then people could focus on discovering the world's empirical facts and natural laws, as Isaac Newton famously did in the late seventeenth century. Thus, a new scientific understanding of nature preceded mechanised industry and assisted in its development. The scientific revolution thus created a new person – the entrepreneur. He (it was usually a he) approached the productive process mechanically, seeing it as something to be mastered by machines, which he spent attention to inventing. Machines thus replaced labour and the dictates of science guided everything.

These explanations do not connect that well with each other and require us to make choices about what seems most sensible. At present, the historical consensus is that cultural explanations of the Industrial Revolution as an outgrowth in changes in personal behaviour emanating from the Scientific Revolution make sense. To this explanation must be added three contributory factors: the spread of literacy and numeracy, the emergence of consumerism as a motivation for working hard (one worked harder than one might in order to get additional income to spend on disposable goods and more agreeable food and drink) and late marriages that allowed for the standard of living to be higher in England than elsewhere because people did not marry when they could not afford to do so.

Robert Allen argues that a cultural explanation explains much but not all regarding the causes of industrialisation. Cultural explanations, he argues, explains the supply of inventions but not the demand for them. He argues that Britain's high wages and cheap energy in the form of coal increased the demand for technology by giving British business an exceptional incentive to invent techniques that substituted capital and energy for labour. In short, technical progress had a labour-saving bias that accelerated the growth in output per worker – workers were relatively few but able to produce much because they used machines that were extensions of their bodily exertions. Cheap coal – the major source of driving technological improvements – was essential in this process as it made it possible, in reducing the energy cost of technology, for businesses to pay high wages and remain competitive. What Allen insists on is that to understand how machines came to replace labour, we need to look back to the capitalist transformation of the countryside and rapid urbanisation, as well as successes in international trade, to understand that despite the poverty of many Britons (and the great majority of the Irish, in a country where industrialisation hardly existed in our period), Britain had relatively high wages and relatively low-priced consumer goods, with wages high compared to the price of both capital and energy. It was not, moreover, just Britain that was a high-wage economy with cheap consumer goods. Settlers in British North America, although not enslaved people, were in a similar situation to Britain. In those places without extensive slavery, such as Massachusetts and New York, similar incentives as in Britain existed to try to replace expensive labour with machines.[2]

If high wages are crucial to creating the demand for industrial products, then we should accept that Britain did not have a 'traditional economy' by the early eighteenth century. It had an economy that allowed many people to make enough money to spend on consumables, including luxury products, that, in turn, encouraged technological innovation. A middling class of people, especially in towns, earned enough to live substantially above subsistence levels. More and more people drank tea and chocolate, used sugar, smoked tobacco, owned ceramic plates and dressed in inexpensive but still fancy clothes made from imported fabric. The access that Britons had to goods from overseas was crucial in the so-called consumer revolution of the eighteenth century. Household earnings grew as people worked harder because they desired luxury products. The rise of a middling group in Britain, especially in England, was crucial to the growth of this huge wage economy with excellent standards of living by global standards. The goods they purchased were increasingly produced by skilled artisans (a key constituency in the Industrial Revolution – many inventors came from this group) or imported from within the empire and thus created a demand for a set of skills and a trading infrastructure that were part of a modern economy. In this economy, markets were very important. Markets meant specialisation and gains from trade, a more efficient deployment of resources and the cushioning of adverse events such as bad harvests. Markets included local shops; goods traded nationally, such as flatware from Sheffield in Yorkshire; and international and especially imperial trade. All these factors in Britain facilitated economic growth and thus industrialisation, within an economy in which agriculture continued to be the main occupation of most people.

Agricultural change and continuity

Historians in the past were very fond of describing changes in early modern England as revolutionary. The early modern period was a revolutionary time – the political 'revolution' of the Civil War being accompanied by an agricultural revolution, an industrial revolution, a financial revolution and a scientific revolution. A major theme in the recent historiography of the period and place is to minimise the revolutionary changes that were previously argued to have occurred between 1600 and 1800. There are fewer 'revolutions' in the historiography of early modern Britain now than there was in the heyday of work on seventeenth-century England done in the 1970s, reflecting a tendency to see history as more shaped by contingency and continuity than by dramatic change.

One 'revolution' that has largely disappeared in this re-evaluation of early modern and eighteenth-century English and British history is the Agricultural Revolution. Up until the 1980s, the history of rural England was depicted as being one of revolutionary change in the early modern period. Economic historians argued that profit-oriented farmers and landlords led increases in farm productivity, made possible by large landlords enclosing land for private use which had previously been used as land held in common by a community. Social historians concentrated on the proletarianisation of the rural population, with small farmers being forced to become impoverished wage labourers through the spread of capitalist agriculture and through new forms of capitalist agriculture and new forms of landholding such as enclosure, engrossment and leasehold tenure. This argument is based on an undeniable fact: there is no doubt that between 1350 and 1850 the English countryside was transformed from a society of small farmers to one of large farms worked by wage labourers. The class connotations of this transformation in the countryside were thought unfortunate but it was agreed that the result was growing productivity and the ability of British farmers to feed a growing population while the share of the agricultural workplace dropped sharply and, in this way, eliminating famine. Thus, the overall effect of the 'agricultural revolution,' as described by a previous generation of historians, was mostly to the good, for the nation if not for individuals. The explanation for this change was relatively simple and was connected to the modernisation of agrarian institutions and the introduction of capitalist assumptions into rural settings. The mechanisms for change were the enclosure of open fields, the replacement of peasant cultivators with large-scale capitalist farmers and the production of more food per acre produced with considerably fewer people than under inefficient peasant labour.

The arguments in favour of such an 'agricultural revolution' seem overstated today. Medieval agriculture was surprisingly productive, the proletarianisation of the rural population was preceded by centuries when it was meant to happen and technological changes did not result in remarkably high improvements in productivity. Continuity in agriculture is now seen as more marked than change. England, for example, remained deeply rural in our period. The percentage of people involved in agriculture dropped as late seventeenth- and eighteenth-century urbanisation proceeded so that the 95 per cent of the population working in agriculture in 1520 reduced to 79 per cent in 1750. The drop was significant – apart from the Dutch no European country saw such a decline in agricultural workers – but the total number of workers in agriculture was still very large. Most people were involved in agriculture in 1750 rather than in industry or in services. It was only after 1800 that the numbers of people employed in industry really started to kick off. And the percentages involved in agriculture were higher in Scotland and Ireland than in England/Wales, and higher still in the Americas.

Land, and the ownership of land, was central to the social structure and culture of English and British society and was a sine qua non for entry into the political nation – land was the key indicator of status and power in England.

Viewed from a global perspective, change in the countryside over time seems minimal in the early modern period and into the first half of the eighteenth century. England, from this perspective, had one basic system of agriculture, which was mixed farming and combined growing grain with raising sheep and cattle and which was based on plough cultivation. From a more local level, there were persistent differences based on whether a place fell into the 'champion' or 'wood pasture' landscape. The first agricultural system existed in a broad central band from East Yorkshire to Dorset in the south. It was characterised by large, nucleated villages; by open-field systems that were carefully regulated; and by an absence of hedges, woodland and pasture. 'Champion' land was the land most likely to be enclosed in the eighteenth century. 'Woodland pasture' existed to the east and west of 'champion' land and comprised more scattered villages, hamlets and isolated farms; more trees and pasture; and less open-field agriculture, with the communal regulation of agriculture and village life weaker. As Jane Whittle concludes, 'these regional differences had their origins before the Norman Conquest, were recognised by sixteenth century observes . . .; and are still apparent in the English landscape today.'[3]

If there was an 'agricultural revolution,' it emerged very slowly. As far as we can tell and bearing in mind that data on the aggregate agricultural economy are poor and scarce, land productivity as seen in crop yields rose only slowly from the sixteenth to the nineteenth century. Estimates of the average yield of wheat in the three relatively advanced eastern counties of Lincolnshire, Suffolk and Norfolk suggest an annual growth rate of 0.24 and 0.32 percent. National rates of growth, including less forward-thinking counties, were probably lower. The productivity of meat production between 1660 and 1760 was higher, but annual growth at 0.8 per cent was not exactly remarkable. What made these rates of growth seem more impressive than we might think is that output seems to have increased alongside productivity, while agricultural workers became efficient in their working patterns. The rise in output per agricultural worker increased by 75 per cent over two centuries or annually by 0.3 percent. Moreover, we need to think about rates of growth by early modern rather than by modern standards. Agricultural rates of growth in the early eighteenth century were comparable to those in the industrial and service sectors and contributed more than either to agricultural improvements in the economy after 1700.

In addition, we now are more sceptical that the innovations in agriculture that have been claimed by proponents of an agricultural revolution were adopted with enthusiasm. The spread of new crops, such as clover and turnips, and the practices of selective rotation of crops in order to keep soil productive, as well as the applications of new technology, were comparatively limited. For example, the seed drill, first promoted by Jethro Tull in 1731, failed to become commonplace in agriculture until the mid-nineteenth century.

Agricultural conservatism and enclosure

Julian Hoppit gives four reasons why the enthusiasm for agricultural improvement was less than what was needed for an 'agricultural revolution.' The new

ideas of agricultural change were ad hoc, amateur and sometimes contradictory; the cost of certain developments relative to alternatives was high;
variations in the natural environment made it difficult for national adoption
of agricultural improvements; and farmers were both conservative and risk-
averse. Even if a farmer was willing to adopt new ideas, heard probably at the
tavern or market place rather than read in a book written by an agricultural
propagandist, such as Sir Arthur Young, he was faced with a bewildering set
of options. That meant that whatever option he chose could only be put
into operation by years of trial and error. Given these constraints, what was
achieved in our period in the area of agriculture was impressive – an increase
in food production and the end of subsistence crises and, beginning in the
early eighteenth century, six unusual decades in which there was more food
than people needed and where England became an exporter of grain rather
than, as has been the case from the late eighteenth century until today, an
importer of foodstuffs.[4]

One possibility is that growing efficiency in the agricultural sector may have
been due to changes in English social structure. Robert Brenner is the principal
proponent of such a view. He argued, following Marx, that peasant agriculture is not competitive against high-efficiency farming, such as developed in
England in the early seventeenth century. It was only capitalist modes of farming with high levels of competition and more effective forms of management
which could bring about high labour productivity levels in agriculture.[5] More
recent research has cast doubt on whether peasant agriculture is so easily distin-
guishable from capitalist agriculture, given that peasants could be as attuned to
market opportunities and prices as capitalist-oriented farmers. What Brenner
successfully does, however, is insist on how change in the countryside was contested and was shaped decisively by class conflict. Conflict was especially tense
over the spread of leasehold tenures which Brenner, following R. H. Tawney,
argued were devised by landlords to recoup losses in customary tenancy, where
rents were fixed by custom at 8d per acre, which in the early seventeenth century was one-tenth of the market value of the land. Brenner overestimates the
ease by which landlords could deprive customary tenants of their rights, and it
is hard to see that landlords were able to get rid of such tenants, to be replaced
with wage labour, quite as easily as Brenner thinks. It was precisely in the
period Brenner analyses, from the sixteenth to the mid-seventeenth centuries,
in which yeomen farmers were at their apogee, with output nearly doubling
between the 1520s and the 1730s.

In short, the idea of an 'agricultural revolution' in the eighteenth century has
less force than it once did, mainly because British agriculture was very efficient
well before 1700, at least compared with most of continental Europe. At the
start of the Industrial Revolution, Britain was already a rich and sophisticated
economy by the standards of the time, with gross domestic product (GDP)
well below the United Provinces of the Netherlands but already well ahead of
France. If England is subtracted from Britain, then average GDP rises more.
Daniel Defoe, who knew Britain better than anyone else in the first half of
the eighteenth century, often noted British wealth, especially in its southern

agricultural regions while the Scotsman Adam Smith, writing half a century later, had no doubt that

> the annual produce of the land and labour of England . . . is certainly much greater than it was a little more than a century ago at the Restoration of Charles II . . . and [it] was certainly much greater at the restoration than we can suppose it to have been a hundred years before.

'Improvements' on this system were modest because farming had largely, in an age before significant adoption of technology in agriculture, reached the limits of productivity, according to knowledge of such things at the time. Mechanisation, for example, and the use of steam power was largely absent until the mid-nineteenth century and farmers found it hard to deal with pests who attacked grain crops. What remains true is that the people involved in agriculture were hard-working and skilled, responding capably to favourable market conditions, good at bringing more land into cultivation and able to make farming productive enough to make Britain self-sufficient in food until the last quarter of the eighteenth century. Farmers, however, were losing importance in England, as the population became more urban and less willing to defer to traditional rural leadership. By the end of our period, in 1815, the percentage of the population of England which was urban had increased to a new majority, meaning that England was no longer an agrarian society and that agriculture was just another industry, albeit the largest and most important. This was a fundamental change in the long history of Britain and separated Britain out from other European nations. In Spain and Russia, for example, nearly two-thirds of the population still worked in agriculture as late as 1900. In 1700, while the rural sector in Britain was large, the number of men working directly in agriculture was comparatively small, at 32 percent. Nearly as large a percentage were in commerce and manufacturing as early as this date, an astonishingly high figure for a pre-industrial economy – suggesting, in fact, that Britain, especially England, was more a mixed than a preindustrial economy.

The biggest issue in agriculture was less technological innovation than the vexed issue of enclosure. Landowners, previously condemned by landlord and landless alike in the sixteenth century, as heartless and unproductive, was now thought by landowners as a central means by which agriculture could be improved. They argued that enclosure was inherently good because private ownership was also good, encouraging people to improve land which would not be possible under common ownership. It was something that landowners did with care, however, as opposition to enclosure was fierce, as it deprived ordinary people of something they considered part of their customary rights. Perhaps for this reason, using Parliament to get land enclosed was relatively rarely done, at least compared to the use of Parliament to promote infrastructural developments. By 1740, a little over a quarter of England's surface area was enclosed by act. The remainder of land tended to be enclosed by agreement between landowners and people affected by enclosure. Enclosure by agreement was a tricky process, which often was abandoned by landowners facing hostility. It was only in the second half of the eighteenth century that a push to enclosure really developed, with 1,800 Acts for enclosing between 1760 and 1800 compared to just 50 between 1660 and 1727. For all the attention given to enclosure and the tension it caused in rural communities, it did not have that much effect on agricultural productivity, perhaps at most an 18 per cent improvement. It did lead, however, to a great increase in rent income, boosting rentals by 64 per cent in the second half of the eighteenth century. It was income rather than 'improvement' that encouraged landowners to seek to enclose land through fencing and ditching.

Additional agricultural productivity, moreover, meant not just more output per acre but more output per worker. Enclosed fields tended to increase labour productivity by reducing employment, especially of women and children. Thus, we can say that these changes in agricultural ownership placed the burden of coping with low agricultural prices on those who could least afford it while helping the fortunate who maintained and increased their income as land prices soared. A counterfactual is worth considering: perhaps more intensive cultivation of smaller farms by independent peasant proprietors and their families might have had the same effect on productivity in the countryside with the very adverse social effects of destroying the customary fabric of rural society and making the poor suffer.

Women's work

Gender historians have taught us that traditional topics look different when broken down by gender. For example, scholars studying Britain between 1700 and 1850 tend to see the pre-industrial family income as beneficial to women compared to the capitalist wage economy, when home and work became separated. But we should not see this pre-industrial period as static. Women's work patterns changed in the seventeenth century, with more women becoming weavers and being involved with textiles, after having been excluded from this craft in the sixteenth century.

Jane Whittle and Mark Hailwood have analysed what women worked at in the early modern period. They show that most of all adult women's work was taken up with unpaid household duties and child care rather than work in the wider economy. Men did little of this work. Gender segregation in work was highly pronounced. Men dominated hunting and fishing, crafts, building work and transport. Women dominated dairying, child care, midwifery, cleaning, laundry and collecting food and water. In agricultural field work, women did almost all the weeding and half of the sowing – men dominated otherwise. They also cared for pigs, poultry and bees. In the vibrant textile economy, women dominated the preparatory processes. They cleaned, combed, carded and spun wool. In commerce, women participated equally to men in buying and selling goods, with a dominance in textile selling. Regarding the amount of time spent on an activity, women engaged in agriculture as much as in housework and spent more time in commerce than in care work. It is also apparent that the gender division of labour was flexible, with men and women doing different things in all categories of work. Changes in farming systems altered work patterns considerably. Small farms found female workers, who could be deployed in many tasks, desirable, especially given a price differential making women cheaper to employ. Large farms preferred male servants and used day labourers.[6]

Was pre-capitalist and pre-industrial England a 'golden age' for women's work? Older literature, predicated on Marxism, argued that industrialisation destroyed female autonomy in working practice, to the extent that any such autonomy existed in a strongly patriarchal society. This led to female 'parasitism,' as they became more confined to the home than to household production in which work and home were the same. Writers in this tradition saw industrialisation as a very bad thing, as it increased gender inequality, as male workers were valued more highly than female workers. Recent work has been less strident about female 'parasitism' with historians arguing that if we move away from the countryside to concentrate on urban areas, then we see opportunities from industry for women increasing rather than decreasing overall female work patterns. What changed most dramatically was not women's work but their potential for economic agency through greater access to capital. Women were investors as well as producers, and their increased presence in the economy as creditors suggests that female autonomy did not altogether disappear.

The Industrial Revolution caused great changes in women's work and in the household as an economic unit. Whether these changes were good or not is open to debate. One fact to consider is that in the first half of the eighteenth century, women participated in significant cash-generating activities. With the advent of the Industrial Revolution, as industries increasingly had to compete with mechanised production, the incomes they generated declined and women and children had to join in work to keep cottage industries afloat.

Where there was significant change was the advent of manufacturing and a sharp increase in demand for the skills of urban women in that sector. The rise and fall of cottage industry or household production forced working women to reconsider their finances. In textiles, by far the biggest industry employing women, there was a double blow after 1790 when domestic spinning disappeared and was replaced by mechanised weaving. Many of the women facing this reduction of work turned to domestic weaving, but by 1820, that, too, had been greatly reduced. If there was an end to the relatively good times for female employment, it did not happen in our period but after 1820. That is not to say that women were especially well treated in the manufacturing economy before that date. They were often paid by the piece rather than by time, they were more often fined for errors than were men and their employment was more sensitive than men to business fluctuation. Employers hesitated before getting rid of male breadwinners; they had fewer compunctions when women were involved. In short, the idea of a 'golden age' is overstated and probably wrong, as it focuses very narrowly on just one aspect of women' lives and adopts an attitude on work opportunities that few women would have shared, but inequities in female employment remained constant from the start of our study until the end.

Choice and consumption

The accumulated economic changes of the long eighteenth century led to changes in consumption patterns that had a significance beyond economics and the development of taste. It encouraged people to have a new experience that some historians such as Colin Jones and Timothy Breen, writing about the French Revolution and the American Revolution respectively, have considered to have had revolutionary implications, in politics as well as in economics. *Choosing* goods among a plethora of options was both new and increasingly commonplace in the eighteenth century. As Breen notes,

> what gave the American Revolution distinctive shape was an earlier trans-
> formation of the Anglo-American consumer marketplace. . . . Suddenly,
> buyers voiced concerns about color and texture, about fashion and eti-
> quette, and about making the right choices from among an expanding
> number of possibilities.

When people had 'the invitation to make choices from among many competing brands, colors and textiles – decisions of great significance for the individual – it held within itself the potential for a new kind of collective politics' in which 'the concept of freedom of choice was elevated into a right.'[7]

Jones is even more explicit in the implications of growing consumer ability to choose, for the course of the French Revolution. He argues that consumption patterns made the activity of making choices novel so that 'citizen-voters were presented with a series of political consumer choices and were called on to evaluate the quality and the utility of the political commodities offered,' meaning that 'the post-1789 citizen had [already] been fashioned in the marketplace,' in a 'community of buyers and sellers who contrary to traditional culture, were committed to exchange on a relatively egalitarian footing.'[8]

The product that most initiated such ideological changes was Indian cotton, whose arrival in Britain has been skilfully outlined by Giorgio Riello. Cotton was a crucial ingredient of the Industrial Revolution but was a product that had been cultivated, best of all in India, for centuries before becoming transformed in the late eighteenth century into manufactured cloth going from Britain to the world, including, tragically and ironically, back to India, where industrial cloth undermined Indian cotton manufacture. Where Britain had the advantage was less in the quality or even the price of cotton but in the ability of the people who made cloth to provide fashions that women wanted to buy.[9] Before then, it was India who shaped fashion. Indian cloth, or calicoes, was deeply alluring to ordinary people, with women leading the way, because it was cheap, compared to silk, and endlessly adaptable, unlike wool. Nearly everyone, except the very poor, could suddenly by the early eighteenth century adorn their homes and their bodies in bright colours and exotic patterns, many of them customised by Indian manufacturers specifically for British buyers.

The arrival of calicoes in the early eighteenth-century British market was not uncontroversial. Its arrival and popularity threatened existing commercial networks and led quickly to protectionist legislation and state-mandated bans on the importation, sale, purchase, and even the wearing of India cotton. Protectionists adopted moral arguments against calicoes, usually focused on how wearing such clothes would lead to female infidelity and insubordination, and made economic arguments, familiar today in our new protectionist climate, about foreign goods threatening local livelihoods.

But these arguments were to no avail against incessant demand for calicoes from eager consumers, augmented by an aggressive trading strategy by the East India Company, which was adept at giving consumers the cottons adorned with shapes, checks and flowers that they desired. In the meantime, as Riello also details, domestic British manufacturers of textiles produced cloth with new patterns and new kinds of decorative accessories, at an accelerated rate and with real attentiveness to a local and fickle market of fashion and taste that British manufacturers knew better than Indians how to cater for. We need to be careful, however, as John Styles reminds us, not to argue too strongly for the importance of cotton in the eighteenth-century British economy. Cotton, or imitations of cotton, did not displace in popularity all other kinds of cloth in the middle of the eighteenth century; that development belongs to a much more modern moment associated with industrialisation and nineteenth-century imperialism.[10]

What is true is that cotton and other printed decorative fabrics became central to how fashion operated in Anglo-America in the long eighteenth century. Cotton goods were significant less because they satisfied a new need – clothing is eternal, after all – but because they were valued for their aesthetic or decorative potential like other goods, such as porcelain, which signified affordable luxury in the period of the industrious revolution. Industrious revolution is a term that applies to an expansion of production that is mediated by commercial incentives, relies on exchange and specialisation of production and fosters the sort of growth that Adam Smith wrote about in *The Wealth of Nations*.

These goods, and new goods such as tea and sugar, each with strong imperial connotations, created a market for luxury goods and provided the basis for what Michael Kwass calls 'a buying spree of historic proportions,' which changed psychology regarding opening up possibilities of choice as much as developing social and economic change.[11] The first change was how these new fabrics and other imperial goods were sold. They were sold in cities and provincial towns in a new system of marketing and distribution, based on fixed location shops, clustered together with goods visually available to the new category of shoppers. Instead of having, as in the seventeenth century, to accept what merchants provided 'without,' and not being able to choose many goods for themselves, consumers had a plethora of choices in the eighteenth-century shopping environment between similar but differentiated products that were often bought either on credit or, increasingly, with cash. Paying in cash meant that consumers were not dependent on others to justify their shopping choices. The result was a transformation in trade and city life. The prolific social commentator, Daniel Defoe, described the effects of this change in 1726: 'It is true that a fine show of goods will bring customers . . . but that a fine sow of shelves and glass windows should bring customers, that was never a rule in trade till now.'

As Sophia Rosenfeld reminds us, in a book chapter from which this analysis is largely drawn, choice was not unlimited.[12] Merchants had a pre-selected but not inexhaustible range of goods available. They directed taste, as much as they were responsive to it. We might see the development of a consumer culture as a delicate formation of a set of understandings between mostly male shopkeepers and auctioneers and a mostly female group of potential buyers. One could only buy what a merchant provided; but if you did not like what was on display, there were increasingly multiple places where one could go to get the goods that you wanted. Shopping also became a leisure activity, with great opportunities for sociability as people met each other while shopping or (the word is revealing) 'window-shopping.'

Because shopping was as much fun as a necessity, the purpose of shopping changed. People bought things they did not really need or which they desired for reasons that were not just for practical advancement. As Jan de Vries has argued, the desire for goods made people work harder than they ought to have done in order to buy the consumer goods that they wanted rather than needed. The result was an increase in overall productivity and a rise in living standards as the good effects of an 'industrious revolution' kicked in.[13] Shopping took on important meanings over and above the purchase of goods. It was a way of displaying status and taste, a social activity and an arena for asserting one's knowledge and preferences.

Of course, Breen and Jones's assumptions are that to choose either in shopping or in politics should be seen within the realm of *Homo economicus*, or how a rational actor exercised his or her intention to maximise his or her utility and express his or her freedom through personal preferences in a variety of stable and logical markets. That rationality is not how contemporaries thought of shopping. They saw the activity as frivolous, a mostly feminine activity rooted in irrationality and fleeting desire for shiny objects, as much as the outcome of deliberate choice about purchases, viewed with rational thinking. As Rosenfeld argues, 'the appearance of something like an expanded menu of options and the cultivation of consumer choice, especially in the world of silks, cottons, and other textiles, does not seem to have produced anything like an ideal consumer consciousness.' She is dubious that political choice making is closely connected to the decision to choose between different kinds of calicoes. She suggests that the idea of individual choices in politics occurred only in the 1870s, a hundred years after the start of the age of revolutions. Breen and Jones's equation of consumer choice with political decision making 'inadvertently warn us against any kind of determinism' and that what one bought 'predisposed a person to make a particular choices, or indeed any kind of choices, in the political realm or even to support a politics in which choice was celebrated as an ideal for human flourishing.'[14] However, thinking about the ideological import of the choices people made in buying goods tells us much about changes in the British economy that led to an Industrious and then to the Industrial Revolution.

The Great Divergence

The Industrial Revolution led to what historians call the Great Divergence, a term coined by Kenneth Pomeranz in 2000 and expanded on by Prasannan Parthasarathi in 2012 in an explicit comparison of how Asia fell behind Europe from the end of the eighteenth century in economic activity and economic growth.[15] The Great Divergence is simply expressed but hard to explain as a historical process. The Great Divergence is the understanding that China and India were supplanted around 1800 by Western Europe, especially Britain, in global economic importance, due to the economic advantages that Britain gained from early industrialisation. Pomeranz argued that in the late eighteenth century, Britain, unlike the Yangzi Delta (the most economically advanced region in China), was able to overcome pressures on their land, which provided the food, fuel and fibre needed for survival. Britain was able to overcome its land constraints by substituting wood with coal and by importing foodstuffs and raw cotton from the Americas. In this reading the Americas, in effect, served as 'ghost acres' for Britain, providing an additional amount of land that could be devoted to food which allowed Britain to devote more land to industry. What has made Pomeranz's explanation for what used to called, rather insensitively, 'the rise of the West' is that it avoids having to rely on cultural explanations of European superiority in religions, intelligence or scientific brilliance or Douglass North's assertion that the political and economic institutions established in England after the Glorious Revolution, which get perilously close to arguing that Europeans got rich because they were smart. Pomeranz's argument avoids such cultural explanations in favour of wealth and prosperity coming mainly from ecological windfalls.

Debate over the Great Divergence has been intense and productive. One handicap has been a lack of good data. Because GDP is a concept only invented in the twentieth century to measure national economic well-being, historians have had to resort to proxies for living standards from data not produced for the purposes now intended, while population levels usually must be guessed at. In short, as is the case for most attempts to do statistical work in past societies, a lot of heroic guesswork must be involved. Problems of data make it difficult to answer whether Britain was already by 1700 or only from after 1750 on a path of economic growth that showed a clear break with post-Malthusian patterns, where resources were constrained, meaning that a shortage of resources would eventually put a halt to rapid population increase.

Heroic research by a team led by Stephen Broadberry has shown that all the growth in English and then British GDP per capita between the Middle Ages and the eighteenth century was due to growth in the immediate aftermath of the Black Death (1340s–1400s) and the late seventeenth century (1650s–1700s). For 250 years after the Black Death, when income gains came from severe population decline, economic growth in England was non-existent. Between 1650 and 1700, however, a significant structural transformation in the economy, which can be termed early industrialisation, coincided with small population decline to create a significant surge in income per capita, which was not sustained in the early eighteenth century, when rates of growth per capita were roughly half of what occurred in the late seventeenth century.[16]

The structure of transformation was threefold. There was an increase in textile manufacturing in 'new draperies' that were blends of wool and other fibres. New agricultural techniques imported from the Netherlands spurred increases in agricultural productivity. In addition, religious strife in France brought Protestant refugees into Britain with considerable capital and skills. In the next half-century, however, economic growth slowed, although the picture would look somewhat different if growth in America and the West Indies was added into the calculations. That growth would be offset by stagnant economic growth in Scotland and probably declining per capita wealth in Ireland. What an analysis of pre-modern growth rates seems to show is that substantial economic growth was hard to achieve. Certainly, before 1750 no European country was doing well enough economically to diverge substantially so that it exceeded the wealth of China. The strong empirical evidence that Broadberry and his co-authors bring forward shows that it is incorrect to see any medieval or early modern roots of the Great Divergence. Rising economic growth in Europe, including in Britain, was a relatively late phenomenon, not a centuries-long period of exceptional growth.

The Great Divergence, therefore, dates to the late eighteenth century and the nineteenth century, not to most of our period. It was only the advanced stage of the Industrial Revolution in which British living standards rose significantly and national wealth started to really advance. The gap grew rapidly after 1800, mainly because non-agricultural workers in Britain were generally far more productive in Britain than in China. Pomeranz also argued that advances in science were relatively unimportant in making Britain richer than China, though artisanal inventions were significant. Although our basic understandings of the Great Divergence are clear – that the differences in wealth between East and West that were so apparent in the mid-nineteenth century were of recent, rather than old, standing and were connected almost solely to the economic advantages of industrialisation from 1750 onwards and that what Britain had as key advantages were coal and colonies – there is still much we need to know. We would like to know more about relative levels of economic development in the advanced areas of Europe and Asia, the nature of the industrialisation process, the contribution of institutions and the role of science and knowledge in this process. Future research will illuminate this developing debate.

The wealth of the Americas

The wealth of Britain was enhanced in the eighteenth century by dynamic growth in Britain's Atlantic colonies. Of course, imperialism was not a cost-free activity. The colonies needed defending from attack from European empires and from Native Americans and African Americans, and in wartime, these costs could be extremely high. The Seven Years' War was immensely expensive, leading Britain to try and recompense financial losses after victory after 1763. The mercantilist regime also imposed costs to both producers and consumers that might have been less if Britain operated under policies of free trade. A previous generation of economic historians argued that empire was a cost to Britain rather than a benefit, mainly due to the marginal cost of investing in empire rather than in more productive domestic industries. The idea was that money that could have gone into running cotton factories was wasted in running slave plantations in the Caribbean when these plantations were not as wealthy as before, as Eric Williams had argued in his seminal *Capitalism and Slavery* (1944). This line of argument derives ultimately from Adam Smith. He argued in *The Wealth of Nations* that the American colonies were not as valuable as people at the time thought. He thought slavery inherently inefficient as the 'experience of all ages and nations, demonstrate that the work done by slaves, though it appears to cost their maintenance, is, in the end, the dearest of all.'

Here he was especially critical of colonies in how they took capital from metropolitan Britain that could have been expended in other more economically beneficial and efficient activities. Smith argued that 'the stock which has improved and cultivated the sugar colonies of England has, a great part of it, been sent out from England, and has been by no means altogether the produce of the soil and industry of the colonists.' Without money from Britain, he argued, 'the progress of our North American and West Indian colonies would have been much less rapid, had no capital but what belonged to themselves been employed in exporting their surplus produce.' His main target was the mercantilist system which he believed led to the misallocation of capital investment from Britain. Thus, rather than creating more trade, he argued, colonial ventures distorted it.

The loss of America seems to prove Smith right. Defeat in America was simultaneous to the take-off of industrialisation in northern England but does not seem to have had done much, if anything, to slow it down. The United States remained in Britain's commercial sphere until the 1830s, without Britain having to pay much to defend it. Thus, while trade with the empire, in this telling, might have been important before the Industrial Revolution, it was not that important during the years when industry boomed in Britain. For Joel Mokyr, 'the Industrial Revolution did not require the creation of British India or the control of Canada, nor did it depend on the cheap sugar from the Caribbean.' Britain could have sourced what it needed without any help from the empire. After all, British exports to the Americas were never more than 40 per cent of total exports, even in the 1770s and 1780s, and over half of these exports went to what became the United States. In the 1840s, at the height of the imperial mission, exports to the colonies were just under a quarter of all exports and slightly more than a quarter of all exports. Of course, that would imply Britain moving to free trade and away from mercantilism, which was politically impossible until well into the nineteenth century. He concludes that 'on the path to a more modern economy driven by technological progress, empire was, on balance, a distraction, not a stimulus to progress and the blue water policies were more atavism than path to economic development.'[17]

Other evidence, however, points to Smith being wrong and the colonies being a considerable addition to the wealth of Britain in the eighteenth century. The colonial economies, especially in the West Indies, were efficient and highly profitable, with lots of the profits from the plantations being sent back to Britain. Recent research suggests that by 1800, including the quasi-colonial dependency of the United States, plantations made up about 10 per cent of British GDP, up from about 7 per cent in 1774. What needs stressing, also, is that what Smith and Mokyr did not see the colonies as an extension of Britain, with settlers claiming to be British. Rather, they saw them as international places with no connection to Britain except costs which would not be incurred if these places were independent. But, as has been explained earlier, that was not what the position of the colonies were in the eighteenth century. Settlers saw themselves as British and thus deserving of as much imperial support as was the case in Scotland or Yorkshire. It is curious that no one ever counts the expense of defending and provisioning, say, Yorkshire in the way that is customarily done for Jamaica or New York. The reason for this, of course, is that Yorkshire is seen as properly British and thus cannot have costs separate to that of the state. Settlers wanted to argue that the same was true for the colonies they resided in.

By the 1740s, the colonies in British America were producing considerable profits. Reports by the surveyor general of the southern colonies, Robert Dinwiddie, give an economic snapshot of the economic health of the American colonies between 1743 and 1748. Dinwiddie's analysis reflected the imperial priorities which were as much about the military strength of colonial populations as about their economic capacities. Thus, New England's large reservoirs of manpower made it very valuable, given Britain's need for military manpower in campaigns in the Caribbean which were very destructive of soldier and sailors' lives in a malign disease environment. Dinwiddie suggests that the total value of American trade in the 1740s was £9.5 million, of which the plantations accounted for 22 per cent and 57 per cent of a total annual produce of £3.7 million. Dinwiddie boasted that the trade of America was 'of inestimable value to the Nation of Great Britain' being a 'grand Source of Britain's Opulence.'

Another way of establishing how valuable the colonies were is to look at total worth in the colonies as compared to total wealth in Britain. In 1774, I estimate that British America had a total physical wealth of £162 million, which was 58 per cent of the £278 million that was the wealth of England

and Wales. Plantations were valued at £104.3 million or 24 per cent of the total wealth of England/Wales and Britain combined. If we assess wealth per capita, then America, including very poor enslaved people whom most settlers would have not considered worthy of including in such statistics, had wealth of £57.5 compared to £42.3 in England and Wales. If we include Scotland and Ireland, which were poorer than England, then the differential in favour of America, especially plantation America, would have been even greater. To this, we must add the ghost acres that Pomeranz has detailed. To compensate for the calorific inputs from sugar brought from the New World around 1700, an extra 150,000 acres of wheat (out of 10 million acres of arable land) would have had to be put into production. In addition, the most important plantation product, sugar, had many other multiplier effects that were conducive for British economic growth, such as prolonging the durability of meats, fruits and vegetable and allowing hot drinks to be substituted for beer, thus reducing the need for cereal production.

Britain's involvement in the outside world was a boost for local manufactures. The growth of Atlantic trade, for example, was essential for the late seventeenth-century development of the copper industry, as well as for sustaining industries such as shipbuilding. Early mechanisation in Britain alongside a protective wall for the benefit of British American planters were the means whereby Britain's innovative merchants were able to offer an impressive and growing array of consumer goods to British settlers. These settlers had strong purchasing power due to imperial preferences that gave them privileged access to a highly desirable British market, full of high-wage-earning consumers eager to incorporate plantation products such as sugar into evolving cultural practices like the afternoon tea ceremony. The industrial development of metalworking and the arms industry in Britain was stimulated by the Atlantic economy, with West Africa in the mid-eighteenth century demanding ever more guns in order to embark on slave-raiding and warfare. Britain provided nearly 1 million guns to West Africa between 1750 and 1807 and 1 million pounds of gunpowder. Selling guns to Africa developed a gun-making industry in Birmingham. Guns also went to the East India Company and to America, being used ironically in the American War of Independence against British troops. Colonial demand thus drove the industrialisation of this trade from the early eighteenth-century way of making guns in small workshops. Possibly such innovations would have occurred without empire, but empire was the means whereby such developments were done.

The Industrial Revolution and global economic change

The Industrial Revolution was a quintessentially British, even English, event. Britain, of course, was only the first nation of most nations to experience industrialisation and to scour the world for industrial ingredients. Other nations followed, in Europe and North America in the late eighteenth and early nineteenth centuries, with the rest of the world following in the late nineteenth and twentieth centuries. The Industrial Revolution was also a global event, with profound ecological ramifications. The main issue was the vast and increasing use of fossil fuels. The real impact came after our period, especially since 1850, when the impact of coal mining, oil and gas drilling, energy transport and fossil fuel combination started to be felt worldwide.

The first century of the Industrial Revolution helped to inspire changes in global vegetation. As John McNeill notes, 'charcoal stratigraphical analysis shows that global biomass burning declined for seventeen centuries before 1750. It then spiked until 1870 or so, before again declining for several decades.'[18] The ecological teleconnections, or linkages, involving places far apart, helped to shape the vegetation cover of every continent and originated from the start of the Industrial Revolution in Britain.

The major impact of the Industrial Revolution is thus global and yet to be fully worked out. It is a worldwide historical event so important that scholars now see it as initiating a new geological age, 'the Anthropocene,' the name given to an age which recognises the great power that humans exert over the earth's basic biogeochemical systems and life on earth itself. This age seems to have started with the advent of sustained fossil fuel use and coal-fired industrialisation. Steam engines were crucial as they convert the chemical energy of coal into heat and then kinetic energy. It was amazingly successful as a means of increasing economic activity. British coal consumption doubled in the second half of the eighteenth century and quadrupled in the next half-century. Coal releases carbon dioxide into the atmosphere as a greenhouse gas with carbon dioxide starting to rise around 1800. What we can say is that the Industrial Revolution unleashed forces we have yet to know how to control. The Industrial Revolution saw rates of economic growth in the nineteenth century and beyond grow in ways never experienced. These rates of economic growth made Britain rich and important. But the hundred-fold increase in energy from 1750 that followed this rise in economic growth, extended globally, has also meant that the price of ecological change has exceeded even increases in rates of economic growth. This entirely new global situation means that we cannot yet determine whether the Industrial Revolution in Britain is ultimately a good thing.

Notes

1 Joel Mokyr, *The Enlightened Economy: Britain and the Industrial Revolution 1700–1850* (London: Penguin, 2009), 3–5, 9–10.

2 Robert C. Allen, *The British Industrial Revolution in Global Perspective* (Cambridge: Cambridge University Press, 2009).

3 Jane Whittle, *The Development of Agrarian Capitalism: Land and Labour in Norfolk, 1440–1580* (Oxford: Oxford University Press, 2000), 156.

4 Julian Hoppit, *Land of Liberty?: England 1689–1727* (Oxford: Oxford University Press, 2000), 364.

5 Robert Brenner, 'Agrarian Class Structure and Economic Development in Pre-Industrial Europe,' in T.H. Aston and C.H.E. Philpin, eds., *The Brenner Debate* (Cambridge: Cambridge University Press, 1985), 10–63.

6 Jane Whittle and Mark Hailwood, 'The Gender Division of Labour in Early Modern England,' *Economic History Review* (2018), online, 9 December 2018.
7 Timothy Breen, *The Marketplace of Revolution: How Consumer Politics Shaped American Independence* (Oxford: Oxford University Press, 2004), xv, xvii, 190.
8 Colin Jones, 'The Great Chain of Buying: Medical Advertisement, the Bourgeois Public Sphere, and the Origins of the French Revolution,' *American Historical Review* 101 (1996), 39.
9 Giorgio Riello, *Cotton: The Fabric that Made the Modern World* (Cambridge: Cambridge University Press, 2013).
10 John Styles, *The Dress of the People: Everyday Fashion in Eighteenth-Century England* (New Haven: Yale University Press, 2007).
11 Michael Kwass, *Louis Mandrin and the Making of a Global Underground* (Cambridge, MA: Harvard University Press, 2014), 2.
12 Sophia Rosenfeld, 'Of Revolutions and the Problem of Choice,' in David A. Bell and Yair Mintzker, eds., *Rethinking the Age of Revolutions: France and the Birth of the Modern World* (New York: Oxford University Press, 2018), 236–72.
13 Jan de Vries, *The Industrious Revolution: Consumer Behavior and the Household Economy, 1650-to the Present* (Cambridge: Cambridge University Press, 2008).
14 Rosenfeld, 'Revolutions and Choice,' 262–3.
15 Kenneth Pomeranz, *The Great Divergence: China, Europe and the Making of the Modern World Economy* (Princeton: Princeton University Press, 2000); Prasannan Parthasarathi, *Why Europe Grew Rich and Asia Did Not: Global Economic Divergence, 1600–1850* (Cambridge: Cambridge University Press, 2012).
16 Stephen Broadberry et al., *British Economic Growth, 1270–1870* (Cambridge: Cambridge University Press, 2015), appendix 5.3.
17 Mokyr, *Enlightened Economy*, 160.
18 J.R. McNeill, 'The Global Environment and the World Economy,' in Tirthankar Roy and Giorgio Riello, eds., *Global Economic History* (London: Bloomsbury, 2018), 168.

Bibliography

Allen, Robert C., *The British Industrial Revolution in Global Perspective* (Cambridge: Cambridge University Press, 2009).

de Vries, Jan, *The Industrious Revolution: Consumer Behavior and the Household Economy, 1650-to the Present* (Cambridge: Cambridge University Press, 2008).

Mokyr, Joel, *The Enlightened Economy: Britain and the Industrial Revolution 1700–1850* (London: Penguin, 2009).

Overton, Mark, *Agricultural Revolution in England: The Transformation of the Agrarian Economy, 1500–1800* (Cambridge: Cambridge University Press, 2010).

Pomeranz, Kenneth, *The Great Divergence: China, Europe and the Making of the Modern World Economy* (Princeton: Princeton University Press, 2000).

Riello, Giorgio, *Cotton: The Fabric that Made the Modern World* (Cambridge: Cambridge University Press, 2013).

Wrigley, E.A., *Continuity, Chance and Change: The Character of the Industrial Revolution* (Cambridge: Cambridge University Press, 1988).

11 Gender relations

Introduction

When James VI and I wanted to justify the rule he began in England in 1603 and the manner of that rule, it was natural for him, as it was natural for just about everyone in Britain in this time, to turn to gender relations as a model from which to explain his idea of kingship. The book that he wrote for the guidance of his eldest son, Henry, called *Basikon Doron*, was written with lots of references to ideal gender relations, as men saw them. A perfect king owed duty to God because he has 'made you a little God to sit on his throne.' The king's court was like a patriarchal household and a model of a good order in which men acted responsibly. It should be a household in which the well-ordered 'little commonwealth' of the household meant that subjects 'know no other father' but the king. To be a good king was to be a good man. When he married, the prince's responsibilities were clear: 'Ye are the head, she is your body. It is your office to command, and hers to obey.' Patriarchal political thought was based on the biblical injunction to 'honour thy father and mother,' with the father's authority being most important and the mother to be honoured more for her character than for her rights to be obeyed.

James VI and I extended his understanding of the monarchy as being modelled on the patriarchal family in another work published in the same year, *The Trew Law of Free Monarchies* (1598). '[K]ings,' he argued, 'are called Gods . . . because they sit upon God his throne in the earth' with the king being 'a natural Father to all his lieges at his Coronation.' He was like 'a father of children, and to a head of a body composed of divers members . . . the head cares for the body, so doeth the King for his people.' Because a king was like a father, resisting him would be like disobeying a father, something 'monstrous and unnaturall.'

James VI and I often used the language of gender to emphasise his authority. Thus, in 1604, when attempting to persuade (unsuccessfully) English members of Parliament that union with Scotland was a good idea, he stated, famously, 'I am the husband and the whole isle is my lawful wife; I am the head and it is my body.' The marriage metaphor, Amanda Capern notes,

> framed the entire speech, extinguishing any distinction between the public and the private sphere: God united the kingdoms and he was the head of

this multiple body that he gendered female in order to describe the relationship of duty of obedience upwards from the body to the head and the duty of care downwards from the head to the body. . . . James co-opted notions of the godly householder in a move that de-mystified but simultaneously empowered his role as king.[1]

Western gender relations

For James VI and I, gender was both crucial but also unchanging. The relation between men and women was as much a constant in life as was the relation between king and subject. Of course, as we know, the role of the monarch changed greatly over time, while the office of monarch was key to British political life, even during the Commonwealth, which was defined by the absence of a monarch, as much as by republican ideas. Change and continuity went together in that institution. Did gender undergo a similar trajectory – a central fulcrum of difference in early modern Britain and British America while undergoing significant alteration in function between 1603 and 1815? In my view, change was constant in gender relations but continuity in practice was more significant. But because gender was a pervasive category of identity did not mean it was a stable category. Gender difference was highly fluid, changing depending on age, social status and marital position. The works of William Shakespeare are, once again, a great guide to how varied gender could be thought of in the same years that James VI and I was putting together his dogmatic ideas about gender. Many of his plays directly concern gender relations, none more so than the play he wrote as James VI and I took the throne, *King Lear*, in which he explored how violations of patriarchal norms could lead to disaster, as well as a deeply insightful exploration of the varieties of gender experience in Lear's three daughters. James VI and I himself was not quite the model of manliness his writings would suggest he should have been as king. He was not the virile young Henry VIII or the manly Henry V. He was awkward and ungainly, with mild cerebral palsy, meaning he had to lean on the arms of young men as he walked. He was considered rude, uncivil and, as noted previously, probably had homosexual inclinations. Just because gender roles were prescribed does not mean that people followed them.

The fluidity of gender and sexuality in this supposedly rapidly patriarchal age is a recent topic explored by historians, arising in part out of works in the 1970s, such as Michel Foucault's *History of Sexuality* (1976). Foucault's work ranged much more widely than the early seventeenth century, but his argument that the very concept of sexuality is a construct of Western scientific discourse is one historians of this period have taken to heart, Gender historians, in particular, have challenged essentialist assumptions, such as what James VI and I enunciated, that sex, gender and sexuality were fixed and biologically produced. Instead, gender historians tend to argue that culture as much as biology determines these three categories of difference, meaning that they must be studied in respect of relations of power and are subject to significant variation over time. What is clear, however, is that gender and sex were at the forefront of the mental worlds in the past. Our interest in gender and in changes in gender over time do not just arise from our fascination with gender in the last fifty years with the rise of second-wave feminism; they were concerns of intense interest to people living in the seventeenth through nineteenth centuries.

One thing that we understand now is that household relations in western Europe are historically unusual, not normative, as people in early modern Britain, such as James VI and I (although not William Shakespeare) assumed. To use the language of anthropology, England had a bilateral system of descent, from both the paternal and maternal sides, with brides coming into marriage with a dowry, if from families with assets, that was folded into the conjugal fund and came under the control of the husband. It then devolved on the children of the marriage in the same way as the inheritance of the patrilineage. The paternal side was the favoured side, as it had naming rights (children took the surname of the father) and had control over the family firm that resulted from marriage. Families were strongly shaped by religious doctrine. Christians – Catholics and Protestants – enforced serial monogamy (only one marital partner at a time) and forbade polygyny.

That ban on polygyny may not have ensured that husbands were faithful to wives – adultery was common among the monarchy and aristocracy, if seemingly less common, because more consequential, in less favoured social sectors. It did mean, however, that illegitimacy was uncommon, as the risks for unmarried women of having bastard children were severe, leading to social ostracism and often penury. Of course, this does not mean that premarital sex was uncommon: a large percentage of women were pregnant at the time of marriage, baptism registers reveal. What was important was that legitimate heirs were less in number than in polygynous societies in Africa, Asia and the Americas.

Who controlled marriage varied. The church allowed, as in *Romeo and Juliet*, for children to marry without the consent of fathers, although the tragedy in that play warned contemporaries of the dangers of marrying young and for love rather than with parental consent. Over time, this aspect of the western European household pattern changed, with more people marrying for love and affection and without worrying too much about financial concerns. Nevertheless, opposing affection and finances in determining marital choices is a false dichotomy between romantic love and material concerns. Most couples, then and now, took both matters into consideration. Law was firm in the view that consent of both parties was crucial so that arranged marriages were not theoretically possible. Most marriages, of course, were subject to the multilayered consent of all parties involved, not just couples but also friends and family. As Linda Pollock notes,

> material interest, affection, practical considerations, influence of friends and family, parental love, honour, and personal piety, along with a miscellany of other intangibles, shaped marital choice, Any one individual thus

weighed countless issues, making marriage, even for those with resources, a leap of faith that things would work out.[2]

What was most distinctive about the Western European household system was that people postponed marriage for far longer than is known in any other historical society, with men marrying in their late twenties and women marrying in their mid-twenties, with a relatively high proportion of people, 15 to 20 percent, never marrying at all. The oldest average age for marriage came for women marrying in the last quarter of the seventeenth century, when they married at age twenty-six and when nearly a quarter of women never married. Not surprisingly, population faltered in the first third of the eighteenth century.

What late marriage did was to depress fertility, which helps explain low population growth in the late seventeenth and early eighteenth centuries. It also reduced a couple's dependence on the patrimony, as generally couples had been working and saving money for years before they wed, meaning that married couples set up new households rather than taking up residence with parents, siblings or other relatives. Britain, especially England and Wales, was devoted to the nuclear family, with relatively few people living in families that were multigenerational or larger than a married couple and children. Of course, mortality within marriages was high by modern standards and remarriages frequent, leading to families being blended, with second partners and stepchildren common.

Britons came to understand that their household system was unusual when they encountered different household systems in their empire and in Africa as part of their involvement in the slave trade. In North America, for example, Native Americans followed the practice of matrilineal rather than patrilineal descent, with property coming to children through the mother's kin group, not the father's. They also exhibited matrilocal characteristics, with children being in the house of their mother and their mother's lineage. The husband had to maintain his links with his mother's lineage group, even after marriage, meaning that matrifocality prevailed. Women married in their teens. While the matriarchal system gave women some power, men were still in charge. Matrilineality did not mean matriarchy. Matrilineality also existed in West Africa, but what Europeans noticed most about West African societies was less matriarchy, as, in general, West Africans tended to favour patrilineal kinship with bride-price payments, than polygamy, the practice of men having multiple wives. Only some of these practices crossed the Atlantic and survived into chattel slavery; although certainly polygamy did exist and may have been what men in slave societies wanted if they had some choice over marriage partners.

Britons did not celebrate these different kinds of household patterns. What Africans and Native American family patterns showed, British observers thought, was that British household patterns were best and were derived from God's intentions on earth. They had no sense that diverse family and household patterns and a different attitude to sexual morality, especially sexual relations outside marriage, which was common for unmarried people, were either

Figure 11.1 Quarrels with her Jew protector, plate II: *The Harlot's Progress*, William Hogarth, 1732

Source: D Hale-Sutton/Alamy Stock Photo.

possible or desirable. They were not aware, for example, that this loose set of sexual mores they saw in West Africa only pertained to life before marriage: married women were expected to be as faithful to their husbands as was the case in marriages in Britain. There was a lot of commentary in our period about 'unnatural' gender and sex relations by outsiders, with this commentary justifying seeing Native Americans and Africans as uncivilised. It was how one behaved in a family that was very often determinative of whether a people or race was thought to be savage or not. And they interpreted the fact that field work in the Americas was done by Native American women rather than, as in Britain, mostly by men as a sign of Native American men's laziness, not appreciating just how important hunting and war making was within Native American societies.

Patriarchy

Britain, like every European society, was patriarchal in structure throughout our period. It is important to note that the fundamental features of gender relations remained unchanged for centuries, with substantial change only occurring very recently in the perceived ideal relationship that should exist between men and women. The changes in our period are ones of nuance rather than revolutionary in their intent and consequences. One constant was patriarchy as a governing principle in society. Patriarchy meant the domination of men over women in every aspect of life, with women subordinated, marginalised or excluded, sometimes officially in law, more often unofficially in custom. As we have seen in the statements of Jams VI and I, male domination was so rooted in the culture that men and women found it impossible to imagine a society based on different principles. Consequently, the evolution of gender relations so that some women such as the radical reformer, Mary Wollstonecraft, thought around 1800 that there was a possibility of the sexes having a degree of equality in their interactions was an extraordinary transformation and one that extremely few people accepted.

Patriarchy in 1603 was justified in scripture, especially the Creation story of Adam and Eve, and was played out in all sorts of day-to-day life. Medical science thought that men were physiologically different from women and superior. The theory of the humours had women rendered as irrational, emotional, impulsive, and sexually rapacious. Patriarchy was also the basis of both domestic and political authority. A man ruled his family just as a king ruled his kingdom. For this reason, dissent by wives, children or servants was treated in law as akin to treason. Capital punishment for wives who killed their husbands was different from that given out for husbands killing their wives. Men were hanged; women were burnt to death, the justification for the difference being that the woman's crime was more heinous, as petit treason.

The law recognised male supremacy in every way. A man's word carried more weight than a woman's in court hearings. That made attaining convictions for rape very difficult. If a woman was raped but a man denied it, the court favoured the man, as it presumed that women were untrustworthy, libidinous and swayed by passions such as malice and revenge. More important in everyday life was a husband's legal right to use and dispose of his wife's property, even without her consent. Few people disputed the rightness of such doctrines, as they lived in societies that accepted hierarchy as a universal principle of nature, with gender as an integral part of the natural order.

The effects of these entrenched patriarchal attitudes were manifest everywhere. Women played no formal part in public affairs, although many were influential behind the scenes. It is for this reason that a female monarch – Elizabeth I and Anne, who ruled between 1702 and 1714 – was inherently problematic. Contemporaries saw a female monarch as a contradiction in terms or an exception to a general rule and not something that applied to any other part of life. The church leadership was entirely male, with fewer opportunities under Protestantism than under Catholicism for women to exercise any sort of power, except moral influence. Women could not go to university or become lawyers and were increasingly excluded by guild regulations from trading independently.

All these restrictions seem to modern minds a licence for domestic tyranny and public humiliation for elite and ordinary women alike. That was sometimes true but women, while dependent, were neither slaves or, if married, servants. The power they had may have been largely informal, but it was real nevertheless. Men were meant to treat women properly and respectfully and it was a dereliction of their roles as men if they did not do so. Every description of the proper gender order insisted that men had duties as well as rights and that husbands and wives were as one flesh and were meant to love each other and treat each other decently. The idea was that husbands should be mild and forbearing and should leave the running of the household and the care (though not the control) of children to their wives. Of course, such views were not supported in law. Judith Bennett argues that companionate marriage, as increasingly celebrated as the progressive norm within marriage depended entirely on the husband's goodwill and was at best a 'voluntary egalitarianism shadowed by inequality.'[3]

The social order that shaped gender relations was strongly misogynist, with lots of jokes about hitting women when they misbehaved and ribaldry around women's behaviour in general. William Shakespeare's *The Taming of the Shrew*, a comedy about 'subduing' a woman who was too feisty for her own good, reflects popular opinion among men. If a wife nagged, she deserved chastisement. Of course, women shared some of the assumptions of the age too – they also believed in hierarchy. Most had no problem in accepting that men had not only rights but also duties and that women needed to obey, just as children and servants needed to obey mothers and mistresses, and, if they did not, they deserved to be beaten or punished.

How did women cope in a system that was oriented so firmly against them? Not all women accepted their fate as dependents. Some women writers spoke out, for example, on behalf of their sex. Many more accepted conventional wifely duties as models to fashion their lives around. Most women welcomed being a wife and a mother, and both statuses provided them with respect and with authority. Pious and diligent housewives were widely praised as examples of the goodness of their sex.

But not all women accepted male authority in practice. Men knew this and had only some powers to change their behaviour without permanently alienating their wives and female dependents. Men may have been able to compel women to obey but that did not make for pleasant family relations. The gap between theory and practice disturbed men who wanted, on one hand, to be compassionate and reasonable and, on the other hand, expected compliance with their will. It seems that there was a widespread sense of anxiety among men in the Stuart period that they were being undermined by women who dreamed of subverting masculine privilege and worked hard to do so. Not all 'Shrews,' as Shakespeare would have put it, could be 'tamed.' A common joke was that real power resided in the hands of women rather than men and that men were being 'unmanned' by secret resistance from women. Indeed, David Underdown has argued that the period witnessed a crisis in gender relations, with plays, sermons, ballads, and jokes, and a formidable battery of repressive sanctions directed at single mothers, witches, and 'unruly women' of all kinds. These written expressions of concern about women's behaviour demonstrated men's anxiety that when they gave orders, these orders were not obeyed, leading to men being laughed at by other men for their inability to control their womenfolk.[4]

Bernard Capp suggests that the British Civil Wars reinforced fears that patriarchy was in crisis. 'The traditional association of family and commonwealth,' he notes, 'prompted a natural alarm that overturning the political and social order would trigger a parallel inversion of gender order, an alarm strengthened by the fact that women were playing a more public and visible role than ever before.'[5] There were among them preachers and crypto-Catholic seducers of innocent men. It is hardly surprising that in a time when authority was described so often in gendered terms, that a crisis in authority would be seen as a crisis in gender. If order was breaking down everywhere else, why would it also not break down within the nuclear household and family?

One problem we have, however, in ascertaining whether a gender crisis in mid-seventeenth-century England was real or not is that the subaltern (a term to describe the relations between coloniser and colonised in nineteenth- and twentieth-century India), who, in this place, is the Englishwoman, finds it hard to speak naturally. When women did not like aspects of the patriarchal order, they used what political scientist, James Scott, calls 'the weapons of the weak,' such as grumbling, joking and not respecting authority except when they were forced to do so.[6] Capp has looked at one way in which women could contest patriarchy on their own terms, which is to use 'gossip,' something women were meant in theory to be addicted. Gossiping was one way in which women negotiated patriarchy, creating space and autonomy for themselves in the face of laws that consigned them to positions of subordination. In short, women negotiated patriarchy through evasion, accommodation, negotiation and resistance. Gossip was essential in providing the networks of support women needed to separate themselves out from men. As Capp concludes,

> gossip networks played an essential role in the exchange of small loans, favours, and advice, oiling the wheels of household management and family care. They offered a sense of belonging, and a social identity that balanced a woman's identities as wife and mother. They furnished advice, help, support, diversion, companionship, relief, a safety valve, and *in extremis*, a place of refuge.[7]

Of course, as Capp reminds us, we should not invest women with too much wisdom while we celebrate the ways in which they gained some autonomy for themselves. Women often worked together and provided each other with mutual support, but they were also as quarrelsome and competitive as men, and as keen as men on implanting their own sense of hierarchy on inferiors.[8]

And while they created female networks, these networks often led to friction between competing groups of women. Moreover, for most women, female networks were only parts of their lives. Relations with men – fathers, sons and, most of all, husbands – were always as, or more, important than the parallel worlds of female competition and cooperation. But that female worlds existed separate from those controlled by men shows that there were always spaces within the structure of patriarchy which women could use to their advantage.

Gender frontiers and race

British movement into the Atlantic created 'gender frontiers,' defined by Kathleen Brown as 'the meeting of two of more culturally specific systems of knowledge about gender and nature.'[9] 'Gender frontiers' also existed in British interactions with West Africans and Asians, but the numbers involved were much smaller than in the Americas and so can be passed over quickly, with a comment that one of the advantages that white men thought agreeable in working in West Africa or India was easy access to local women and casual sexual morality.

'Gender frontiers' were of two kinds: mesalliance, to use a word from the time, between mostly Native American women and British men (Pocahontas from early Jamestown, Virginia, is the most famous example of a Native American woman involved in mesalliance) and sexually exploitative relations between white men and their enslaved African women. My study of the sexually explicit diary of the Lincolnshire migrant to Jamaica, Thomas Thistlewood, who listed his 137 different sexual relations over a thirty-seven-year period with enslaved women illustrates the stark realities of what black women had to put up with. A portion of his sexual relationships were consensual, notable with the Creole slave, Phibbah, who was essentially, by Thistlewood's death, his established mistress, being the mother of Thistlewood's only son, who did not survive his father but, if he had, would have fallen into that uncertain category of mixed-race people in the island. Many of Thistlewood's sexual encounters were coerced – women consenting to sex without really having any choice in the matter, as refusal would lead to punishment – or were rapes, sometimes purposefully to punish an enslaved woman for a transgression.

Thistlewood did not give much respect to the integrity of enslaved unions when embarking on his reign of sexual terror. It is hardly surprising, therefore, when such unions, not protected by either law or custom, dissolved – there was little incentive to make these unions work, except the wishes of those in the relationship. Marriage, monogamy, illegitimacy and the whole panoply of the Anglican church's role in weddings and supporting stable relationships was deficient for white people and wholly missing for black people in the eighteenth century Caribbean. It took the pressure of abolitionism in the early nineteenth century for white colonists in the West Indies to reluctantly agree to measures to support slave marriages. They refused, however, to regulate white men's sexual behaviour towards black women, making migrants to these colonies continue to sexually exploit black women and live with them in irregular unions by British standards without any legal or social sanction of disapproval.

Thistlewood's world was that of Jamaica in the middle decades of the eighteenth century (he lived in Jamaica between 1750 and 1786), but this world of highly distorted sex ratios with lots of people neither marrying nor having legitimate challenge was common in many parts and time periods of colonial British American history. Carole Shammas calls these places where the social pattern faced by Thistlewood existed 'marriage-challenged zones' and notes that it was a feature of white society in seventeenth-century Virginia when family formation was difficult, when men vastly outnumbered women, and when mortality at all levels was very high.[10] Virginia and the rest of British North America overcame these demographic constraints by the early eighteenth century and established family patterns that were very similar to the nuclear family of married couple and dependent children that existed in Britain and Ireland.

But in the West Indies and in India, settlers did not achieve this demographic solution and continued to be 'marriage-challenged zones' for both whites and blacks throughout our period. Moreover, even in British North America, where the demography of the enslaved was reasonably good after 1740, many of the features of relationships and family life in 'marriage-challenged zones' continued well into the nineteenth century. In short, there were more people in British America living in families that Britons would have considered irregular than there were people living in standard nuclear families. English settlers were very often unable to replicate metropolitan gender models in the plantation world or in the frontier regions of the interior where people lived together but did not marry, in part, because these were under-institutionalised places without such things as ministers to conduct marriage ceremonies or perform baptisms. In Jamaica, the effects of a dire demography and the racial structure of the island, allowing white men easy access to black women, with whom they sometimes formed temporary unions, and where even among whites marriage was not recognised is reflected in very high rates of illegitimacy, which were about 33 per cent compared to under 2 per cent in Britain. Men refused to form attachments with white women (who in turn were happy to live in informal unions), preferring in many cases to 'riot in the goatish embraces,' as the historian Edward Long disapprovingly observed, of coloured mistresses than marry.

In slave families, irregular unions were almost a function of enslavement. The restrictive sexual climate that happened after women in West Africa married, with legal and social penalties for infidelity, could not be replicated in British America, in part, because slaveholders had no interest in regularising slave marriages, as this would have stopped them from breaking up marriages to sell enslaved people when they wished and would have lessened their ability to fornicate with enslaved women when they wanted. African enslaved men without access to the lineage groups that they relied on in West Africa to maintain their patriarchal privileges could not reproduce in the Americas

African family patterns and male patriarchal privilege. Slave owners tended to favour men over women and accepted male dominance over women within slave communities, but whatever slaves wanted took second place to the work and security concerns on plantations.

The result was a highly dysfunctional family environment for most enslaved people, especially in the West Indies. Enslaved women faced even more severe problems. Not only did they have to worry about near-constant sexual exploitation, but they were also forced to undertake the hardest physical tasks on the plantation just at the time when they should have been bearing children. Working in sugar was exhausting and dreadful for health in general, and especially for reproduction. Matters were especially bad before the start of abolitionist agitation in the 1780s, as during the period of the slave trade planters made a calculated decision that it was better to buy rather than breed. Like the worst kind of modern employer, slaveholders thought workers getting pregnant a bad thing, as it deprived them of a good worker for a few weeks. As infant and child mortality among the enslaved was very high, planters thought that the expense and bother of raising children to adulthood was not worth the bother, when fresh inputs of adult labour could be purchased from slave ships. Planters in North America, where slave demography was better and profits from planting lower than in the West Indies, were more willing to invest in what was needed to ensure enslaved women reproduced safely but their motives were equally suspect. In the Chesapeake, they wanted to keep enslaved children alive so that they could sell them to planters in more southern states, thus making the breeding of the enslaved a profitable activity.

'Gender frontiers' and the mixing of races through sexual contact created issues that went past gender and into birthright. British settlers insisted that as British Protestant blood flowed through their veins, they were the equals of British people in the metropolis. But what happened when Britons mated with Africans and produced people who were of mixed race? In general, these people, if free or freed by their father, were treated as a discrete and marginalised racial class, tainted by illegitimacy and the intermingling of African and European bloodlines. The presence of mixed-race free people proved problematic in societies such as Jamaica, where whiteness was valued as the determinant of 'belonging' within the group who alone could exercise the privileges of British inheritance. As Brooke Newman argues,

> in mid-eighteenth century Jamaica, racial classifications based on hereditary status soon created new challenges, and opened up new possibilities, as a result of two key local developments: pervasive sexual relations between white men and enslaved women of African descent and the manumission of enslaved individuals, mostly women and their mixed offspring, with blood ties to the white community.[11]

The British were always far more rigid than Iberians and, to an extent, the French in refusing to face up to the consequences of what was termed miscegenation. They never recognised interracial marriage, unlike Spanish and Portuguese America, and placed restrictions in places such as Jamaica on what mixed-race people could inherit from their white parent. This systematic discrimination based on an increasingly rigid idea of what constituted whiteness and what did not, made mixed-race people an ambivalent group in society, without all but the most basic rights. Who was white in Jamaica, and in British America generally, varied considerably over time in ways that reflected changes in local circumstances, but what continued to be true was how officials kept on redefining what 'race' was in order to keep it in accord with local concepts of blood, lineage and race that both preserved the inheritance of free-born English people and kept intact a slave regime characterised by bondage and legal disabilities for the enslaved and great privileges for all white people, rich or poor. By holding out, however remotely, the dim possibility that the product of interracial sexual mixing might be classified as white Jamaicans cemented white men's dominance within their society. As Newman argues,

> interracial sex played a constitutive role in Jamaican slave society: as a means of asserting white male dominance over the enslaved through control of black female sexuality, and as a vehicle for the production of illegitimate mixed offspring whose unsanctioned parental blood ties could, in extraordinary cases, receive legal recognition and act as a buttress for the colony's socio-racial order.[12]

Population changes in the eighteenth century

Underlying changes in gender relations in eighteenth-century Britain and British America, as hinted at when looking at the differences between British North American and West Indian demographic patterns, was rapid population growth in the northern colonies of British America (covered earlier in this book in a discussion of Benjamin Franklin's views on empire) and in Britain. In Britain, almost all population growth occurred after the mid-eighteenth century. Between 1701 and 1801, England's population grew by two-thirds; Scotland's, by 46 percent; and Ireland's more than doubled. By comparison, France's population increased by 36 per cent in the century and that of the United Provinces by just 11 percent. In population terms, alone, Britain was becoming more powerful in the world. It also meant that Britain had a more youthful and, from the 1780s, more productive population, with lots of people in the ages between fifteen and forty-nine, which were the ages when the population was most likely to be productive. It also allowed Britain to solve the perennial problem of finding manpower to fight its imperial battles.

Before 1750, population increase was haphazard, with the population declining between 1727 and 1731. The reasons for population growth in the second half of the eighteenth century were rising fertility, a declining age at female first marriage (which allowed for more children in an age without contraception) and more children born illegitimately. The authoritative work of Tony

Wrigley and Roger Schofield, re-creating the population history of England for more than 330 years, consider that people lived a little longer than before but that the reduction in women's first age at marriage from twenty-six to twenty-three over the century was the biggest contributor to rapid population growth, despite net migration of more than five hundred thousand people during the century. Also important was a growing incidence of marriage, with fewer women in society aged forty who had never married. Some doubt has recently placed on parts of this interpretation, with suggestions that improved nutrition and better standards of hygiene, as well as some advances in medicine, such as vaccinations against smallpox, meant that people lived for as much as ten years longer by the end of the century than they did at the start of the century, increasing the numbers of women who completed all their child-bearing years without dying. This figure suggests that life expectancy might be seven years more than Wrigley and Schofield have suggested.

But, still, marriage patterns seem one key to population increase. Why did people marry earlier? One explanation is that a new ethos of love emerged, where people married freely and married for love and affection rather than having marriages supervised by parents and for dynastic economic advantage. Such theories underestimate the extent to which love and affection always underlined marital choices in the seventeenth century and overestimate the extent of change over time. A study of couples in the late eighteenth century who married earlier than normal, often in the late teens, suggests that another factor encouraging early marriage was ideological. Couples marrying early, often without having the resources to support themselves, trusted to the future to make love affordable, doing so in a period of strong economic growth, where people had some confidence that they would be able to do well economically, even if they married young and had large families.

The age of George III was an age in which large families were both common and welcome. Franklin's delight in people marrying early in Pennsylvania and having large families (somewhat ironic for a man with one illegitimate son and only one daughter surviving to adulthood) was echoed in Britain by delight at the fifteen children of the monarch, George III and his devoted wife, Charlotte. Whereas in the late seventeenth and early eighteenth century, 41 per cent of aristocratic families died without heirs, having large families became normal among peers, gentry and the middling sorts. The five children, all daughters, of the Bennetts in Jane Austen's *Pride and Prejudice*, were a large but not unusually large family by the standards of genteel society in the late eighteenth century. Infant and child mortality declined gradually but by modern standards remained very high: even George III and Charlotte suffered the deaths of two infants from their seventeen births and few families managed to have all their children live to adulthood. Between one-fifth and one-quarter of babies died before the age of ten. There is not much evidence, moreover, that the death of children was not a blow to families, in ways that they are tragedies for families today. The texture of family life was shaped always until very recently by the likelihood that not all children would survive their parents. The sadness of those deaths of children tended to remain in the emotions of those people enduring such losses.

What may have changed in this period, however, was attitudes to children and there may have been a decline in child-rearing strategies based on parental sternness and corporal punishment in favour of child-rearing strategies influenced by the sentimental philosophies of the Enlightenment. The second half of the eighteenth century was a more child-centred and permissive age than in the early seventeenth century, with patriarchy a good deal softer, especially in practice, where fathers prided themselves on their empathy and solicitous concern for their children, seeing them as individuals to be loved and cherished, as much as being useful additions to the family economy as workers. The harsh doctrines of patriarchy were modified by the gentler tones of paternalism, a version of patriarchy in which the rule of the father was depicted more in terms of mutual obligations between family members rather than stark commands of dependents to obey patriarchs.

Literate parents based their child-rearing strategies on the influential principles on this topic and on the instruction of the young in John Locke's *Some Thoughts Concerning Education* (1693). Locke argued for a child education policy which was based around recognising a child as an empty vessel that needed to be filled with lessons drawn from sympathetic adult teachers. He argued that play was not a frivolity but essential to the development of a child and stressed that in education a child's personality had to be considered. He stressed the value of giving praise over the usefulness of physical correction, though he did not rule out the latter – that would have been beyond anyone's conception in a period where selective violence was thought of as a useful way of resolving debates and teaching people lessons. Corporal punishment seems to have declined, as did rates of interpersonal violence generally, despite the high profiles of eighteenth-century criminals like underworld mastermind Jonathan Wild and highwayman Dick Turpin.

It was not just ideology but social and economic structures that help explain why people married increasingly younger during the late eighteenth century. In the countryside, men often had to wait until fathers died before becoming a farmer or a master craftsman on inheriting property. As men tended not to marry until they could afford to set up independent households, this waiting for a father to die, as life expectancy was on the increase, meant that men married later, usually to women roughly their own age, and had fewer children than they might have done. After 1750, some of the constraints of the early eighteenth century were reduced. Apprenticeship was shortened, and the expansion of domestic industry, especially proto-industrialisation or cottage production, gave more opportunity for young people to make enough money so that marriage came about when they were in their early as opposed to their late twenties. In the village of Shepshed, Leicestershire, for example, where framework knitting was very important, women by the early nineteenth century married five-and-a-half years younger than their peasant ancestors in the seventeenth century.

Population increase meant both a younger population and one in which large numbers of people were aged in their thirties and forties, doing most of the work that provided wages to support a family. Early marriage was also associated with urbanisation. People in cities married earlier than in the countryside so that early marriage increased as the populations of towns burgeoned. London took an increasing share of the English population, from 7 to 12 per cent between 1650 and 1750, then, although its population kept on increasing, stayed at around 10 per cent throughout the eighteenth century. Urbanisation elsewhere exploded, with industrial towns such as Manchester and Birmingham expanding from virtually nothing in 1700 to being major metropolises by 1801 with seventy-five thousand and sixty-nine thousand people, respectively. Towns encouraged more freedom from parental controls, greater possibilities for making money and, in the case of women, potentially greater economic and sexual freedom. Illegitimacy rates tended also to be higher in urban settings than in the countryside.

Interestingly, while fertility increased after 1750, fecundity, or the ability of women to conceive and the time differences between births, does not seem to have changed over time. Fecundity depended not just on the level of nutrition and the health of women but on their lactation habits. In this respect, an ideological commitment to breastfeeding among all classes after 1750 was important, as breastfeeding delays conception. British mothers after 1750 tended to breastfeed for longer than on the continent, and this contributed to both lower marital fertility, given the age of marriage as a condition of fertility, and lower infant mortality. Women did not just breastfeed to reduce family size. They believed, following Rousseau's teachings, that breastfeeding was a technology for producing an improved human being. Breastfeeding brought women, it was believed, closer to their children and to making sure they developed into strong and smart adults.

Sex and sexuality

Gender is connected to sex and sexuality, but trying to discover much about the latter is difficult. It was rare for people to write about their sex lives in the early modern period, which makes Samuel Pepys's Restoration diaries and Thomas Thistlewood's explicit Jamaican diaries so unusual and valuable, in their frankness about male sexual desire. Otherwise, we must find out about sexual practice either from conduct books, which are not that reliable a guide except to ideal behaviour and which were notoriously didactic, or from court cases, which by their nature tended to dwell on sexually deviant or disruptive activities. In general, we know more about the regulation of sex than about how it was practised.

And in regulating sexual activity, it was the Christian Church that was dominant. Protestant churchmen argued that sexual relations outside marriage and which did not lead to the procreation of children were sinful, denouncing these practices from pulpits and pursuing people in church courts, when they could. Individuals respected some but not all the church's extensive proclamations about what was proper or improper sexual conduct. They accepted, for example, that illegitimacy was not conducive to good social order and participated in rituals of shunning unfortunate single mothers. They were less willing, however, to accept that premarital sex was all that bad, at least when it was clear that such sexual activity would eventually lead to marriage. After all, sexual pleasure was significant as one of the foundations of a happy marriage. Thus, in some places, 'bundling' occurred, which is where future partners shared a bed together ('bundled' to restrict improper access) to see if the partners were sexually compatible.

Respecting sex, the double standard was well and truly alive throughout the period. Men could fornicate as they pleased without much social disapproval – prostitution was a constant presence in urban cities and existed also, if less obviously, in the countryside. Women were less able to experiment sexually. They were meant to be chaste before marriage and faithful within marriage after they had wed and were usually expected to turn a blind eye to male infidelity, although officially such actions by men were subject to social disapproval, Any sexually deviant behaviour from women, however, led women to be labelled as whores or jades and meant they faced social opprobrium or worse. Where men were most castigated was if they were believed to be cuckolds. These men were publicly ridiculed and sometimes subject to charivaris, or public demonstrations of contempt for them. The abuse directed against them reflected less the shame of an unfaithful wife than the embarrassment of a man that he could not govern his dependent. Women who were adulterous were punished very seriously, more so than were men. Husbands enjoyed more sexual license than wives, with less at stake if discovered. It remained very hard for women to leave even abusive husbands, with divorce reserved only for the very rich and very noble, and even then, divorces were hard to obtain and condemned as disgraceful when divorce was achieved within the press and by popular opinion.

The one area where women had an advantage over men was in same-sex relations. Lesbianism was generally ignored. Male homosexuality was not similarly ignored. Sodomy was punished with extreme rigour. Nevertheless, since so much of male life was spent in the company of other men, homosexuality was probably reasonably frequent, if carefully hidden. And the image of the sodomite was such a potent image less because it showed deviant sexual behaviour than because it was a sign of systemic depravity. When Mervyn Touchet, the Earl of Castlehaven was prosecuted and executed for sodomy in 1631, the scandal was more his failure to govern himself and his household in a proper patriarchal way rather than for his penchant for buggery and rape. Over time, homosexuality became less willingly tolerated. By the eighteenth century, Randolph Trumbach describes a shift in social attitudes from a century previously where sexual relations between the sexes and same-sex desire became seen as mutually exclusive in ways not previously so obvious.[13] It was a growing rigidity in how sex was categorised that caused this change and was also reflected in the official denigration, rather than avoidance of mention, of prostitution.

Both homosexuality and prostitution were depicted in similar ways, as unclean. The representation and treatment of prostitutes were as women who were apart from society. They were often described in medical terms by the mid-eighteenth century, as vehicles through which men received syphilis. Hogarth's famous set of prints about the fall of a prostitute, *A Harlot's Progress* (1731), is an example of how sex and disease often went together. Homosexuals were described as 'others,' so, too, were Native American 'beraches,' men who were, in British opinion, transgender and thus effeminate sodomites. British sexuality was normative; sexual degeneracy was part of Asian, Native American or African behaviour. Africans were especially likely to be sexually slandered, with observers thinking them hypersexual and deviant. Nevertheless, it was customary to attribute to anyone who seemed different from British people accusations of sexual deviancy.

Female behaviour

The question of how women should behave evolved over time but within a social structure that never deviated from being patriarchal. As in Stuart England, propriety was the watchword of genteel women in Georgian Britain and propriety meant agreeing to patriarchal norms of female submissiveness. To an extent, women behaved because they had to, as rebelling against seemingly pre-ordained roles handed down, their preachers told them repeatedly, from God, would bring little profit. To argue against the rightness of patriarchy was to argue that the whole basis of society was awry. Resignation and accommodation to patriarchy were sensible. Nevertheless, women did not live a life of quarrelling subordination. They had their own place and rights and when they were wronged, they protested.

What changed between the sixteenth and eighteenth centuries was an idea that marriage should be one of romance and loving domesticity. Marriage was also facilitated at the highest levels of society by the institutionalisation of a national marriage market in the London 'season' and at fashionable resorts, such as Bath. Moreover, the eighteenth century was the age of sentiment and nothing was sentimentalised as much and as often as motherhood. Mothers, of course, have been honoured from biblical times. What differed in the second half of the eighteenth century was the adding of secular practices to religious associations. Breastfeeding, for example, became ultra-fashionable, as we have seen, and added to ideas that women were instructing children through the very giving of their milk and blood to their infant children.

Women also benefitted from the economic changes of the eighteenth century. The rise of shopping made female lives, especially those of the genteel, much more comfortable and gave a role to women as arbiters of taste. They were also arbiters of politeness, a key Enlightenment concept, favouring easy and inclusive elite social intercourse, conducted usually in homes – the normal domain of female influence. In salons, the informal influence of women was immense, as Julie Flavell shows in a forthcoming book on Caroline Howe, the spirited sister of the aristocratic three famous Howe brothers who served with distinction in American wars, and as Stella Tillyard has described in her marvellous evocation of the lives of the mid-eighteenth-century daughters of the Duke of Richmond. These women had considerable, if informal, influence on high politics in which their husbands, including the opposition leader, Charles James Fox, were heavily involved.[14]

Perhaps the biggest change in the eighteenth century for women was an increase in their literacy rates, which increased overall from 5 per cent of women being literate, at least to the extent of being to sign their name, around 1600 to 25 per cent by 1714 and near 40 per cent by 1740. Signing one's name is the barest form of literacy but probably an increasing number of women were literate as we would understand it by the late eighteenth century. At the genteel level, women were highly literate and were devoted readers and writers. The number of women who wrote letters to each other makes the Georgian period after 1750 the golden age of female correspondence, allowing women to develop intense friendships over often long distances. It was also the age in which the romantic novel was in the ascendant. As Amanda Vickery comments, 'the well-turned letter became an unavoidable performance of the long-standing female work of kin, but in addition, it enabled unprecedented numbers of women to participate in worldly exchange and debate. It was in their tireless writing no less than in their ravenous reading that genteel women embraced a world far beyond the boundaries of their parish.'[15]

It was a time, too, in which sociability became essential to genteel women's experience. Gillian Russell has traced the development of sociability within the so-called provincial urban renaissance of the eighteenth century, whereby towns mushroomed in size and importance, connecting sociability to the Georgian craze for the theatre. It was the period in which actresses became nationally famous, such as Sara Siddons, and was the world of the demimonde where aristocrats and actresses mixed, often salaciously, Many actresses served as royal mistresses, such as William IV's long-term mistress, Dorothea Jordan, and George IV's erstwhile mistress, Mary Robinson, or as paramours for peers. These relationships often led to scandals. One of the great scandals in the mid-eighteenth century involved an actress who was a mistress when the Reverend James Hickman shot dead his lover, the mistress of the Earl of Sandwich, when she was leaving Covent Garden.

Russell argues that there was a crisis in the 1760s and 1770s over fashion and luxury concentrated on the allure of the theatre, which was a dangerous but exciting place of scandal and sociability.[16] Sociability took many forms and was ideologically inflected in many ways. It underpinned a model of society which, according to Adam Smith, was a conversational one in which pleasure arose 'from a certain correspondence of sentiments and opinions, from a certain harmony of minds, which like so many musical instruments coincide and keep time with each other.' Sociability allowed for a range of activities, what Elaine Chalus has called 'social politics,' such as balls, theatricals, dinners, card parties and general visiting. In these activities, women found a public role, which,

Chalus suggests, compels us 'to rethink our definition of politics.' She claims that we should not just look at high politics, such as parliament, for understanding where power resided. Women did not have power but could have a presence in public life and as more frequent players in the political process, such as seen on the behaviour of Elizabeth Seymour Percy, Duchess of Northumberland and her incessant attendance at public events. It was evident more dramatically in the life of the famous beauty Georgiana Cavendish, Duchess of Devonshire, who was both the arbiter of fashion in late eighteenth-century Britain, just as her descendant, Diana, Princess of Wales, was to be two hundred years later, and an active attendee at contested elections, bestowing kisses on electors in return for their votes, making her an active player in Whig politics.[17]

The stormy sexual politics of the 1770s have been seen by Paul Langford as showing that 'feministic tendencies glimpsed with such alarm thirty years before seemed to have developed into a full-blown revolution.'[18] Women's voices were increasingly heard, with female poets, playwrights, novelists and even an outstanding female historian, Catherine Macaulay, making themselves prominent. Macaulay was an independent and sometimes fiery spirit, tending towards a republican viewpoint in an age wary of such sentiments and who was addicted, it seems, to cosmetics and who scandalised society by marrying for a second time a man thirty-six years her junior. That such women existed, however, shows how women were getting more of a public voice in the time of the American Revolution. Not everyone welcomed this development. It seemed to anxious men that gender roles were reversing. And men seem to have been especially anxious about changing gender roles in the 1760s and 1770s, mirroring a similar anxiousness that was the case in the first half of the seventeenth century.

Gillian Russell sees these tensions around appropriate gender roles in a time of change playing out most obviously, if distinctively, in the theatre. The theatre was a curious place, an arena to articulate patriotic values based on stalwart manliness, as well as being a place of dangerous effeminacy with more than a hint of illicit sexuality. That royals and leading aristocrats cultivated actresses only added to the excitement of the theatrical space. The theatre was an institution engaged in a dynamic interplay with its world and a place where the Georgian penchant for theatricality – a mode of enthusiastically engaging with the public sphere – opened opportunities for women to participate in fashionable sociability. 'Women were the main beneficiaries,' Russell tells us, 'of the expansion of entertainment that occurred after 1760,' an expansion in which the theatre, as the pre-eminent mode of public entertainment throughout Britain and its empire, played a crucial role in establishing alternative public spaces to the older male-dominated areas of sociability as 'palaces of the fashionable world.' Its moment, however, did not last long. As we will see, women who were overly prominent in the public sphere, no matter how distinguished, were found threatening as the easy days of the 1760s and 1770s in Britain gave way to the more ideologically pressured world of the 1790s and the tumults of the

French Revolution. Indeed, these decades were later explained away as 'the eighteenth-century's bad dream, an interlude of frivolous dress styles, of high heads and high heels, and crimes and misdemeanours in high life.' These dramas were often played out in the space of drama – the Georgian theatre.[19]

Sex and politics

Women's involvement in a new and theatrical public sphere in the 1770s backfired, mainly because elite women were battered by the sexual double standard when they engaged in political activities. From the 1780s onwards, there was a conscious drawing back by elite women from engaging openly in politics in ways that the Duchess of Devonshire and her sister, the Countess of Bessborough had done, most notably in the infamous election of 1784, when they supported the Whig leader, Charles James Fox, against the Tory, William Pitt the Younger. What the Duchess of Devonshire had hoped to do was to show the anomaly of a woman being able to wear a crown but not cast a ballot, although neither the duchess or almost anyone else thought that women having a vote was a reform worth considering: the importance of women in politics was confined to suggesting that as the sex that had a near monopoly on virtue that their involvement in public affairs would make public life more appealing. That the duchess was campaigning for the libertine Fox made that argument a little hard to sustain. She also wanted to advance the more dubious and politically partisan view that contrasted Fox's manliness and appeal to women with Pitt's inability to attract women and his chaste priggishness.

Judith Lewis argues that this tactic failed badly. The Duchess of Devonshire was relying on one model of masculinity as being acceptable, one performed in hard drinking, womanising, and sports, when another model, adopted by George III and by William Pitt, was emerging as part of an evangelical revival in the late eighteenth century. This later model stressed that men should be pious, uxorious, frugal and devoted to the simple pleasures of family life. As Lewis argues, women such as the Duchess of Devonshire and her friends, descending on the populace from the highest reaches of fashionable society, like modern-day celebrities do on occasion today, and showcased for their beauty and aristocratic demeanour, may have been welcomed with enthusiasm by an electorate who enjoyed seeing these glamourous creatures in person, but they were pilloried in the press and in Parliament as doing something unnatural. The duchess and her friends, in this rendering, were exposed to a lower-class male gaze in ways that were inappropriate for women of their rank and gazed at in ways that diminished, rather than promoted, them and their feminine proprieties.

By *giving away* kisses to constituents as part of their strategy to win votes, they contrasted themselves unfavourably to the male candidate *taking* such votes (as assertive upper-class men were meant to do). These female proto-politicians could thus be represented by people hostile to them as akin to prostitutes, giving favours rather than receiving them. In the end, Lewis argues, Foxite libertinism, which included high-status women involving themselves in affairs that were by custom reserved for men, would by the more politically straightened and contentious decade of the 1790s be associated mainly with the political licentiousness of revolutionary France and thus considered a first step on the road to perdition.[20]

The end of the American Revolution was important, too, in changing opinions about how much women should be in the public sphere. It initiated, along with concurrent developments in religions, where evangelicalism was growing and which emphasised female modesty and virtue above all other values except piety, a dramatic change in moral climate, which made the actions of high-placed aristocratic women seem less like celebrity fun than a dangerous precedent to disorder, including sexual excess. For every person who loved seeing a glamourous fashion plate such as the Duchess of Devonshire mixing with plebeians and the genteel alike, there was another person who was scandalised by her loose morals and excessive devotion to luxury and to the enervating frivolity of card-playing. Despite the vast fortune of the Cavendish family, Georgiana was constantly in debt, due to excessive and very bad card-playing.

This was not the type of woman that the earnest evangelical women of the late 1780s and 1790s wanted to emulate. They thought the Methodist countess of Huntington, who was an informal source of financial and moral support for early abolitionists, was a much more fitting model, as was the almost silent but utterly respectable Charlotte, consort of the king. The excesses of hard-living aristocrats and royals such as George III's unruly and sexually licentious sons were highlighted in this period in a number of high-profile scandals in the courts, such as the trying for bigamy in 1776 of the Duchess of Kingston and the notorious Grosvenor case of 1770, outlining an adulterous affair between Lady Henrietta Grosvenor, wife of a very rich nobleman, Lord Grosvenor, and the king's brother, the Duke of Cumberland. These scandals attracted vast attention and great public condemnation, suggesting that women in fashionable society had lost their moral compass. Their derelictions of womanly virtue indicated that Britain was losing its way morally, even as it was flourishing economically and as part of a growing and large and diverse empire.

These scandals and the loss of America fed into a sense that Britain was a sinful nation who through their defeat in America was being taught by God a painful lesson, that lesson being the need to reform their ways. That was bad news for libertines such as Fox and the earlier political hero, John Wilkes. It was also bad for women such as the Duchess of Devonshire, who thought there was a place for women in public life. The lesson from the 1770s and early 1780s that was learned in the late 1780s and 1790s was that women needed to be more discreet than the duchess and her friends if they wanted some place in public life. If they wanted to be part of the public sphere that was involved in politics, then they needed to confine themselves to operating informally in salons and dinner parties and to be careful to confine their public advocacy to carefully contained acts of sympathy for moral reforms such as abolitionism, temperance, the protection of children and the promotion of Christian values of tolerance, modesty and good behaviour.

Figure 11.2 Joshua Reynolds, Lady Worsley, 1776.

Source: Art Heritage/Alamy Stock Photo.

A move to separate spheres?

Two final questions are, Whether women's lives changed much over the seventeenth and eighteenth centuries? and If so, was this change for the good? In my opinion, women's lives were much enriched by the end of the eighteenth century, primarily as they were more visible in a world that was more sympathetic to the roles they were given, notably as shoppers and consumers and the judges of what was fashionable and in good taste. One dominant theme in the historiography is that women enjoyed a 'golden age' in the late medieval and Tudor period which diminished as commerce became culturally important. It is hard to see the seventeenth-century female world as a 'golden age' compared to the richer and more vibrant world of the early nineteenth century, with its softer relationships between men and women and its valorisation of shopping and involvement in the world as consumers and participants in public entertainments as a culturally valuable activity. Even in the world of work, the argument that the arrival of capitalism crucially constricted women's opportunities compared to the past seems unconvincing. Women's work was already low skilled, low status, low paid and narrowly confined to a small part of the economy well before industrial capitalism in the early nineteenth century. The narrative that women had less autonomy, freedom and enjoyment over time is at odds with what seem to be improvements in the female condition, as their voices were heard more often, as the material conditions of their lives improved, as the law discriminated less obviously against them and as they participated in a rich world of female companionship based on visiting, consumption and print make not much sense. The world of women that Jane Austen describes is circumscribed by male privilege but offers women more than the world that Shakespeare portrays his female characters living in.

Historians debate over whether the changes in the period after the so-called 'golden age' did much to improve the position of women. Ideas about the roles that women should occupy in society became increasingly more rigid over the eighteenth century with less chance for women to move outside their customary roles to establish a place for themselves in the public world. The Duchess of Devonshire's experience shows how fraught doing this could be, even to a beautiful wife of a powerful aristocrat. It has been suggested that from the end of the American revolution women retreated from most public life in order to focus on a domestic life, in which they had a special place as makers of home and protectors of the hearth from outsiders.

The name for this strategic retreat from aspects of public life is 'separate spheres, a notion introduced into gender history of the eighteenth century by Leonore Davidoff and Catherine Hall to explain how from the 1780s there was a sharpening of the differences between male and female social roles that meant that men and women were increasingly living in 'separate spheres.' The sphere for women was in private life, with exclusion from the public sphere becoming increasingly common into the first decade of the nineteenth century. Davidoff and Hall argue that the development of an ideology of separate spheres – men were in charge of public matters; while women's particular expertise was in the private realm – was a very significant change in gender relations, which rendered patriarchy less all-encompassing than it had been, given that women were now recognised to have power in the house, although less and less in the world outside the home.[21]

The emergence of separate spheres as an ideological justification for keeping women in the house was accompanied by a ramping up of a view of middle-class women as the moral guardians of Britain, thus encouraging them to take a prominent role in certain kinds of reform movements, such as the abolition of the slave trade and the prevention of cruelty to children, that seemed to demand a moral dimension. Not all historians are convinced that the development of a separate spheres' ideology was either new or all that revolutionary. Amanda Vickery, a quarter of a century ago, cast doubt on whether the changes Davidoff and Hall claimed were all that special, suggesting that a basic separation in gender relations, with men working outside and women inside 'could be applied to almost any century or any culture.'[22]

The jury is still out on whether the separate spheres theory has any historiographical relevance today, but it looks like arguments in favour of women's lives being marked more by continuity than by change are in the ascendant and that women did not suffer as much by being removed from public life as might be thought, given that the only women in public life were high-status women who had fewer restrictions on them and more money to do as they wished than ordinary women. Change did occur: gender differences became more sharply delineated over time and changes in medical practice away from humoral theories had enormous difference in female lived experience. But women in 1800 lived under patriarchy in remarkably similar ways to women in 1600. As in so much recent historiography on seventeenth- and eighteenth-century Britain and its empire, the dramatic changes we used to see in family formation, in seeing patriarchy giving way to egalitarianism in family life, have become muted and negated by findings that suggest continuity shaped gender relations in this period, ever as much as change.

Notes

1 Amanda Capern, *The Historical Study of Women: England 1500–1700* (Basingstoke: Palgrave Macmillan, 2008), 179.
2 Linda Pollock, 'Little Commonwealths I: Communities,' in Keith Wrightson, ed., *A Social History of England 1500–1750* (Cambridge: Cambridge University Press, 2017), 65.
3 Judith Bennett, 'Medieval Women, Modern Women: Across the Great Divide,' in David Aers, ed., *Culture and History 1350–1600: Essays in English Communities, Identities and Writing* (Detroit: Wayne State University Press, 1992), 154.
4 David Underdown, 'The Taming of the Scold: The Enforcement of Patriarchal Authority in Early Modern England,' in Anthony Fletcher and John Stevenson, eds., *Order and Disorder in Early Modern England* (Cambridge: Cambridge University Press, 1985), 116–36.
5 Bernard Capp, *When Gossips Meet: Women, Family, and Neighbourhood in Early Modern England* (Oxford: Oxford University Press, 2003), 22.

6 Scott, J.C., *Weapons of the Weak: Everyday Forms of Peasant Resistance* (New Haven: Yale University Press, 1987).
7 Ibid., 376.
8 Ibid., 381.
9 Kathleen M. Brown, *Good Wives, Nasty Wenches, and Anxious Patriarchs: Gender, Race, and Power in Colonial Virginia* (Chapel Hill: University of North Carolina Press, 1996), 33.
10 Carole Shammas.
11 Brooke Newman, *A Dark Inheritance: Blood, Race, and Sex in Colonial Jamaica* (New Haven: Yale University Press, 2018), 271.
12 Ibid., 21.
13 Randolph Trumbach, 'From age to gender, c. 1500–1750: From the Adolescent Male to the Adult Effeminate Body,' in Sarah Toulalan and Kate Fisher, eds., *The Routledge History of Sex and the Body 1500 to the Present* (London: Routledge, 2013), ch. 4.
14 Stella Tillyard, *Aristocrats: Caroline, Emily, Louisa and Sarah Lennox, 1740–1832* (London: Vintage, 1994).
15 Amanda Vickery, *The Gentleman's Daughter: Women's Lives in Georgian England* (New Haven: Yale University Press, 1998), 287.
16 Gillian Russell, *Women, Sociability and Theatre in Georgian London* (Cambridge: Cambridge University Press, 2007).
17 Elaine Chalus, 'Elite Women, Social Politics, and the Political World of Late Eighteenth Century England,' *Historical Journal* 43 (2000), 669–97.
18 Paul Langford, *A Polite and Commercial People: England 1727–1783* (Oxford: Oxford University Press, 1989), 603.
19 Russell, *Women, Sociability and Theatre*, 4, 12–13.
20 Judith S. Lewis, *Sacred to Female Patriotism: Gender, Class, and Politics in Late Georgian Britain* (New York: Routledge, 2003), 135–42.
21 Leonore Davidoff and Catherine Hall, *Family Fortunes: Men and Women of the English Middle Class, 1780–1850* (London, 1987)
22 Amanda Vickery, 'Golden Age to Separate Spheres? A Review of the Categories and Chronology of English Women's History,' *Historical Journal* 36 (1993), 383–414.

Bibliography

Berry, Helen, ed. *The Family in Early Modern England* (Cambridge: Cambridge University Press, 2007).

Capern, Amanda, *The Historical Study of Women: England, 1500–1700* (Basingstoke: Palgrave Macmillan, 2008).

Capp, Bernard, *When Gossips Meet: Women, Family, and Neighbourhood in Early Modern England* (Oxford: Oxford University Press, 2003).

Chalus, Elaine, *Elite Women in English Political Life ca. 1754–1790* (Oxford: Oxford University Press, 2007).

Gowing, Laura, *Gender Relations in Early Modern England* (Harlow: Pearson, 2012).

Newman, Brooke, *A Dark Inheritance: Blood, Race, and Sex in Colonial Jamaica* (New Haven: Yale University Press, 2018).

Shepherd, Alexandra, *Meanings of Manhood in Early Modern England* (Oxford: Oxford University Press, 2003).

Shoemaker, Robert B., *Gender in English Society, 1650–1850* (London: Longman, 1998).

Vickery, Amanda, *Behind Closed Doors: At Home in Georgian England* (New Haven: Yale University Press, 2009).

12 A new empire?

The loss of America and the resurgence of monarchy

The defeat of Britain in North America and the subsequent creation of the United States, confirmed by the acceptance of a new system of government as made manifest in the constitution approved in the auspicious year of 1788 and in the election as president of the new republic of the foremost enemy of Britain (and, ironically, a committed Anglophile), George Washington, was commonly thought to be a disaster. It was thought a disaster even though it led more or less directly to the concurrent establishment of Canada to become in the nineteenth century, Britain's most important settler colony. It was heralded by the comprehensive defeat of a large British army at Yorktown, Virginia. According to legend, after the defeat, the British army band at Yorktown, played the traditional tune 'The World Turned Upside Down,' later to become the title of a song in the major musical hit, *Hamilton*, in 2015. It seemed to portend the end of the old order, even if it took another two years for peace to be concluded and another eight years before revolution was spread to France.

On 25 November 1781, Lord George Germain, the cabinet minister most in control of Britain's war effort, heard of the British loss and summoned up the courage to go, with Lords Stormont and Thurlow, to see the prime minister, Lord North. 'Courage' was a characteristic notably lacking in Germain, according to unkind gossip at the time, as noted above. He had been court-martialled for disobeying orders at the Battle of Minden in 1759 during the Seven Years' War and was henceforth to be labelled as 'the coward of Minden.' Despite his high rank as a son of a duke, Germain never quite escaped the epithet applied to him. When George III made him a peer in February 1782, mainly so to prevent the opposition leaders in Parliament using Germain's departure from office as a way of discrediting the war in America, several peers were so outraged at 'the greatest criminal his country had known,' in the words of the Earl of Abingdon entering the House of Lords that the marquess of Carmarthen, supported by the Dukes of Devonshire, Rutland and Portland and the Earls of Shelburne, Derby and Craven, moved a motion of disapproval.

Lord North's response to Germain's visit was extreme, 'as he would have taken a ball in the breast.' He paced up and down in an agitated fashion, wildly exclaiming 'O God! It is all over!' George III, on the other hand, responded with stoic resolve, writing back to Germain a letter that showed no sign of either desponding nor despair in handwriting or content, except that George had not dated the letter, unlike almost every other letter he wrote on official business. George III was in denial, refusing to accept that Britain had lost nearly half of its Atlantic colonies and over 3 million people – the great majority of whom as recently as the early 1770s had proclaimed themselves to be devoted monarchists.

As Andrew O'Shaughnessy notes, Britain 'had spent eight years waging what the staunchest supporters regarded as a "holy war" against "dangerous" revolutionary principles, which threatened every system, religious or civil, hitherto respected by mankind.' He continues: 'even moderates believed the retention of America was essential to the survival of Britain as a great power within Europe.'[1] The political economist, Adam Smith, no lover of empire usually, described in 1776 how the 'expectation of a rupture with the colonies . . . has struck the people of Great Britain with more terror than they have ever felt for a Spanish armada or a French invasion.' What calmed fears was a widespread belief that Britain's humming economy and impressive military strength would make victory in America easy. When the implausible happened, and Britain had to face up to the fact that it had lost, it led, as was the case in America after 1975 with the fall of Saigon in a war thought equally unlosable, to a blame game ensuing, with Britons looking for scapegoats among the military and political leaders of the nation.

The loss of America was especially thought to be a disaster because it was the first partition of Britain and its empire since the English loss of much of France in the mid-fifteenth century. It had been imperial growth, not imperial loss, that was the normative experience of eighteenth-century Britain. American independence entailed the departure from Britain of more than 3 million unhappy white Protestants, and their nearly seven hundred thousand enslaved people, whose most firm belief in 1765 had been that they were Englishmen abroad, with all the rights and liberties of English people, and with a fervent attachment to the Crown and to the person of the monarch. Just as France had discovered in 1763, Britain was to find that it had lost most of the most valuable part of the North American continent which it had settled. Subsequent British imperial expansion in the Atlantic World into Canada and the southern Caribbean and the growth of informal empire in Latin America as Spain and Portugal imploded after 1810 did not make up for the loss of Britain's most important eighteenth-century colonial possessions.

The adverse result of the American Revolution seemed to contemporaries to be not just a national humiliation but an international setback of the most serious kind. Britons felt that Europeans were glorying in British discomfort. In July 1782, the new prime minister, the Earl of Shelburne, on taking office, remarked that 'the independence of America would be a dreadful blow to the greatness of this country; and that when it should be established, the sun of England might have been said to have set.' The experienced diplomat, the Earl

of Buckinghamshire, declared that he saw 'this unhappy disgraced country sur-
rounded by every species of embarrassment, and . . . now circumscribed as a
human body in the last stage of decline.'

Who was to blame for this unhappy situation? For the opposition leader,
Charles Fox, the blame lay squarely on the Crown, both in general and in the
person of George III, and by the replacement of 'Whig ministers' and 'Whig
measures' by a 'Tory system' in which 'we have lost our respect abroad and our
unanimity at home; the nations have forsaken us; they see us as distracted and
obstinate, and they leave us to our fate.' Defeat showed the machination of the
Crown, ministerial corruption and a failure to consult parliament, as well as
moral decline. Fox thought that the major culprit was the Crown:

> to the influence of the Crown we must attribute the loss of the thirteen
> provinces of America; for it was the influence of the Crown in the two
> Houses of Parliament, that enabled His Majesty's ministers to persevere
> against the voice of reason, the voice of truth, the voice of the people.

The implications of such celebrated attacks on the body of the king were
clear to students of seventeenth-century British history. Fox was making omi-
nous references to revolution against corrupt authority and was invoking the
parliamentary opposition of the 1640s against Charles I. George III felt some
of the blame warranted. After being so resolute for so long in 'driving' the war
in America onwards, George III felt so bewildered and devastated that when
he was finally forced to acknowledge American independence, he drafted a
letter of abdication to Parliament. If Parliament had accepted any such letter,
George III would have joined Charles I and James VII and II in ending his rule
in disgrace.

Instead, he ended it in madness, spending nearly a decade before his death
aged eighty-one on 29 January 1820 virtually a prisoner at Windsor Castle.
His first bout of madness had occurred in the summer of 1788, that auspicious
year in British and imperial history, from which he recovered, but only after
a series of painful and humiliating medical treatments. Ironically, however, his
popularity as a monarch began from around this date. Between 1781, when
Fox assailed him, and his recovery from illness in the winter of 1789, George
III reached a peak of popularity. He enjoyed, in short, an apotheosis in the
final years of his reign, as did the monarchy itself. Indeed, we can date the
growth in respect for the British monarchy from George III's madness in 1788,
a growth in respect which survived the vicissitudes of George III's unpopular son, George IV; the wilfulness of Victoria after the death of her beloved
husband; and the philandering of Edward VII and Edward VIII. Today, with
Elizabeth II on the throne and the succession secured until at least the twenty-
second century, the monarchy's popularity is at an all-time peak. On the surface, it appears that the survival and strength of the monarchy is a surprising
constant from 1603 to the end of our period and beyond. No other institution
in British life, not even the Church of England or the ancient universities, has

had a longer presence and authority within British public life. The execution of Charles I and the resignation of James VII and II seem to have done little damage to the royal 'brand.'

This popularity, however, needs to be explained with more nuance than just showing Britons' long-term devotion to monarchs and to monarchy. George III only became popular when he lost almost all his power, along with his reason. That loss of power was largely the result of the politics of the 1780s. George III was saved from serious criticism about the loss of America because it was accepted that he was a limited monarch, who accepted the restraints on his behaviour imposed from the 1688 Glorious Revolution settlement. The popularity of the monarchy and of George III after 1788 personally reflected his political impotence – an impotence made abundantly clear by his illness, one that elicited sympathy for him from the nation as a man who was vulnerable rather than powerful – and indicated how the monarchy from this time forward was a symbolic rather than a really powerful institution. The monarchy became more expensive to run, with the country paying millions on renovations to existing royal dwellings and to new buildings such as castles and the future George IV's Orientalist fantasy of the Brighton Pavilion. It did not regain its political importance.

Devotion to the monarchy became increasingly a means whereby Britons could channel their patriotism – 'God Save the King' became the national anthem during the latter part of George III's reign, as noted earlier. As Linda Colley argues, 'defeat in America and, above all, revolution in France fostered in Britain a more splendid monarchy and influenced the nature and direction of that splendour.' Britain increasingly focused patriotic and public display around the monarchy while insisting that this royal ceremonial 'was hallowed by tradition, as distinct from the upstart and synthetic contrivances of the French.' The British were especially contemptuous of the artificial and phoney, as they saw them, celebrations of imperial grandeur orchestrated by Napoleon Bonaparte, with dignified royal ceremonies in Britain contrasted, as the London *Times* put it, with the fake shows of an 'unprincipled and sanguinary usurper' daring 'to imitate, by a splendid mockery, he long recognised, the consecrated and venerable institutions of the unpolluted honour of ancient state.'[2]

The point, however, was that Napoleon, however gauche, was a real ruler while George III, like all subsequent British monarchs, exercised little actual power after the end of the American Revolution. The persistence of monarchy may seem to be one of the big themes of British history between 1603 and 1815, but the reality of persistence masks the enormity of functional change in what a monarch could or could not do. As O'Shaughnessy comments, 'in terms of wielding real executive power, George III's reign was the last hurrah of the British monarchy.' Britain could from the start of the French Revolution be considered a 'republic disguised as a monarchy.' There was no need for a king to be executed, as in France, because power by the 1790s lay elsewhere than in the monarchy.[3]

Britain in the 1780s

The loss of America provoked some soul-searching within Britain but for most Britons the defeat in America was passed over quickly. The population moved onto more pressing concerns, such as benefitting from the booming economy established as industrialisation really took off. Britain's success in retaining its Caribbean possessions following Rodney's victory at the Battle of the Saintes in April 1782 and triumphs over the French and Spanish in the Mediterranean convinced people that victories in 1782 came close to outweighing losses in 1781. Britain had largely come to terms with losing the Thirteen Colonies as early as 1778 when an imperial war became a global conflict. By early 1782, British public opinion was no longer prepared to support a war to reconquer America or to keep Lord North's government in office. This overturn of a government that had the full and enthusiastic support of the monarch was a spectacular political revolution but one which was accomplished with such a minimum of fuss that its implications only later became clear. The Earl of Shelburne negotiated a peace in 1783 with European powers and the new United States of America in ways that were surprisingly successful, given how Britain started from a poor starting position. Shelburne's deft diplomacy was thus a contrast with how badly Britain had negotiated a previous peace in 1763, when it had started from a position of unprecedented strength but made a mess of negotiations.

Peace in 1783 was welcomed not by lamentations but by rejoicing. Bonfires were lit in many British towns and the ringing of bells signified happiness that the ordeal of a second Civil War between British peoples had been ended without the nation falling apart. One reason for complacency was that whatever the criticisms of the Peace of Paris (and there was a torrent of criticism of the peace as a national humiliation, with the main attack being on how Britain had abandoned its loyalist supporters to an uncertain future), Britain could move forward without the burden of financial catastrophe that had been the result of complete victory in the Seven Years' War in the 1760s.

The American war, like other wars, had been very expensive, with Britain's annual expenditure increasing from £10.4 million in 1775 to £29.3 million by 1782, with the national debt nearly doubling from £127 million in 1775 to £232 million in 1783. Taxes increased substantially, meaning that by 1783 Britons were more heavily taxed than any of their enemies. But the reforms to state financing outlined previously to create a dynamic fiscal-military state worked very well by the 1770s. Even in the dark days of 1780–81, the British government was able to raise more money, more easily, than its rivals. Lord North's major achievement during the War for American Independence was to fight an overseas war without creating a financial crisis. By 1787, the economic travails of the early 1780s had largely vanished under the sophisticated economic management of William Pitt the younger. Christopher Wyville of the Yorkshire Association told Pitt admiringly that 'the prospects of the county has been advanced with a rapidity beyond all expectation . . . and government has

Figure 12.1 Death of the Earl of Chatham, by John Singleton Copley, 1779.

Source: Lebrecht Music & Arts/Alamy Stock Photo.

been steadily conducted on the principles of a virtuous oeconomy.' By 1780, just as financial crisis was overwhelming France, Britain was in financial surplus and government bonds had increased in value by 48 per cent from 1784 – a clear vote of confidence by city investors in the financial management of Pitt and his government.

The prosperity of the 1780s meant that Britons could look forward with confidence rather than dwell on the past with dread. They did so in remarkable ways in what Arthur Burns and Joanna Innes call 'a unique decade' in which 'a wide variety of "reform" and "improvement" campaigns about public health, prisons, and the slave trade 'commanded support across a broad front.'[4] It was a decade in which the eighteenth-century passion for 'improvement' came to fruition. It was also a decade when Britain decisively entered a worldwide empire. It settled its relationship with the East India Company in the India Act of 1784, bringing the company under effective state regulation with it becoming a partner in the Asian empire as a subordinate partner of the British state. Pitt declared that the national importance of India had 'increased in proportion to the losses suffered by the dismemberment of other great possessions,' with the country 'in every instance rising in political and commercial consequence to Greta Britain' so that it 'bids fair to be a counterpoise to the western world.'

In the remarkable years of 1787–88, Britain initiated settlement in Sierra Leone in West Africa and in the Malay Peninsula in south-eastern Asia, as well establishing a new beachhead for settler colonialism by sending convicts to Botany Bay in New South Wales in Australia to found a penal colony that eventually became a major destination for both free and coerced British migrants. In Australia, the same patterns of conquest and expropriation of indigenous land as in seventeenth-century eastern North America occurred, although more rapidly and more completely. In those years, also, an abolitionist movement emerged virtually from nothing to become the first and most important national social reform movement in Britain, urging Britain to translate its economic superiority into making the country and its empire morally respectable. If the French Revolution had not interfered, scaring conservative aristocrats and members of Parliament (MPs) so that any concession to liberalism would lead to social disorder, and if the Haitian Revolution of 1791 had not frightened Britons about the racial implications of revolution, then the abolition of the slave trade would probably have occurred in the early 1790s, a few short years after it had been secure within British life as a major source of colonial wealth and mercantile profit.

In 1788, the trial for corruption of Warren Hastings, the ex-governor of Bengal, started. This trial, which lasted until 1795, exonerating Hastings but showing up 'Asiatic despotism' within the East India Company, was prosecuted by the imperial statesman, the Irishman, Edmund Burke. It inspired a profound debate about this new empire of conquest in Asia and what it was doing to the good reputation of Britain in the world. H.V. Bowen comments that

> the forces and influences emanating from the periphery were deemed to be of such peculiar strength that they were held to pose a serious threat to the delicate economic, social and constitutional balances that existed at the very heart of the Empire. It was thought that misrule, corruption, greed, vice, and arbitrary government would not remain confined to India but might serve to act as corrosive agents and weaken traditional liberties, values, and virtues within metropolitan society.[5]

The spirit of 1783

One problem of empire of immediate concern in 1783 was what to do with the sixty thousand loyalists who had fled from the United States. Of these, 8,000 whites and 5,000 free blacks had gone to Britain, 30,000 mostly whites had gone to Canada, 6,000 whites with 15,000 enslaved persons had gone to Jamaica and the Bahamas, 1,200 free blacks had settled in Sierra Leone and even a few loyalists went as convicts to Australia or served in the East India Company. Maya Jasanoff has argued that how these loyalists were treated was part of what she calls 'the spirit of 1783,' a 'spirit' which 'cemented an enduring framework for the principles and practice of British rule, as British power regrouped, expanded and reshaped itself across the world.'[6] The British world that resulted was a liberal, constitutional empire committed to global expansion and, what was new, a commitment to humanitarianism, even if this humanitarianism was tinged with strongly racist and hierarchical principles. In retrospect, Britain established a model of global 'liberty' that was in contradistinction to the famed principles of liberty, equality and fraternity that animated the ideology of the French Revolution, The British 'spirit of 1783' was a more limited but more achievable and long-lasting of liberty under a strong monarchical state and within a social structure shaped by a commitment to tradition and hierarchical stability.

A painting by Benjamin West, Jasanoff argues, exemplifies the virtues of this model of liberty, one in which the loyalists of 1783, now incorporated into a vibrant new empire were prominent. *The Reception of the American Loyalists by Great Britain* (1812) showed a benevolent Britannia extending its help to prominent white loyalists, such as William Franklin, Benjamin's son, with Native Americans in attendance (highlighting the British belief that they treated Native Americans better than did the United States) and African Americans, 'looking up to Britannia in grateful remembrance of their emancipation from slavery' (which was rather premature, given that slave emancipation was two decades into the future). 'Religion' and 'Justice' held up Britannia's mantle, with the crown in the most prominent place in the painting. Here was in visual form an alternative approach to the world than that enunciated by American and French revolutionaries, and one utterly different from the apocalyptic vision of the world that Europeans imagined was in the minds of the black revolutionaries in charge of Haiti in the Caribbean. It was a vision that was of a society that was traditional, stable and based on inherited status and clear hierarchies. It had the king at the centre, supported in his rule by the church and by the law. The empire it celebrated was benevolent and multi-ethnic, where enlightened white men extended paternalistic protection towards people of African descent, Native Americans and indigenes everywhere. The benevolence of the empire was exemplified in the extension of humanitarian relief to the poor and powerless. It might be a tableau which emphasised white nationalism – the notion that the interests of white citizens came first without non-whites being deprived of all rights – but it downplayed ideas of white supremacy – the belief in the biological superiority of the white 'race' and the desirability of creating spaces where non-whites were not present. By the standards of the time, its racial thinking was relatively benign. The vision, Jasanoff suggests, was a proud and happy one, of an empire 'suffused with national pride,' with loyalists, who many people had been thought to have been badly treated in the 1780s, 'poster children for British imperial success.'[7]

It would not have been lost on observers that this painting was composed when Britain was securing its southern boundaries in North America against American aggression in the War of 1812. It was reprinted as the frontispiece to a memoir by John Eardley Wilmot, the Loyalist claims commissioner in 1815, the year in which on 18 June, Britain brought the Napoleonic Wars to an end at the Battle of Waterloo. Britain seemed to have survived the age of revolution almost unscathed. Of course, this self-congratulatory elite response to British ideological superiority over the French and the Americans belied an undercurrent of radicalism in the 1790s that, to frightened conservatives, of whom there were many in Pitt's government, threated rebellion in Britain, as in France and America. No revolution occurred, but it was feared and instilled a period of fierce repression and strict curtailment of British liberties, according to the many critics of government.

The violence that Britain had unleashed overseas for two centuries was now matched by violence at home: against radicals, working-class protestors and supporters of what the mystical poet, William Blake, called the 'red round globe hot burning.' Peter Linebaugh has told the story of one such radical rebel and his fate. Edward Despard was an embittered military ex-governor of Honduras in the 1780s, who was cashiered after trying to implement in this far-flung slave society measures of racial, class and gender democracy. He joined with Irish revolutionaries from the rebellion of 1798 in increasingly wild discussions about radical reform and was tried and convicted for a quixotic and possible imaginary plot to murder George III. His plot was easily discovered – the pubs he drank in had lots of government spies – and he was hanged and then beheaded as a traitor in London in front of twenty thousand people who largely supported his cause. His death came on 21 February 1803. He gave an impassioned speech in which he expressed his belief 'that the principles of freedom, of humanity, and of justice, will finally triumph over falsehood, tyranny and delusion, and every principle inimical to the interests of the human race.' The sheriff in charge wanted him to stop his harangue, lest he got himself into trouble (!) and then he was hanged. It could indeed have been worse, as he did not have to face his actual sentence which was to be drawn and eviscerated before being quartered. He died without religion, in the manner fitting a radical revolutionary, and as a brave Irish revolutionary soldier who was a comrade and friend of Britain's greatest hero Admiral Horatio Nelson, Viscount Nelson. The crowd booed Despard's executioners, and at least one of the crowd, a lad of thirteen named Jeremy Brandreth, ended up with the same fate as Despard, being hanged and then decapitated as a traitor as a leader of the working-class Pentrich Uprising in Derby in 1817. Thus, the prints of Despard's death should be contrasted to West's more pacific painting as a sign that the workers of England did not share the ruling elite's belief in beneficent aristocratic rule and did not celebrate a triumphant liberal and hierarchical empire.[8]

What also would have struck observers at the time was the continuity in the vision of West with that of a fellow American, Benjamin Franklin, in his pamphlet, *Observations on the Increase of Mankind* (1760), published a few years before revolution was even contemplated. Both West and the pre-revolutionary Franklin rejected revolution, celebrated white British identity, and saw the British Empire as a welcoming institution in which the aims of Britons at home and overseas could be realised. British attitudes to the rest of the world had subtly changed between 1760 and 1812. The biggest change was the rise of humanitarianism in both Britain and the north of the United States. Seeking to do good in the world has, of course, an ancient history. What changed from around the mid-eighteenth century was an increased appreciation that the opportunities afforded by the rise of a market economy allowed individuals and societies to imagine that they had the capacity to improve the lots of suffering strangers, be they enslaved people in the West Indies or suffering widows in India. The boundaries of moral responsibility grew over the eighteenth century.

They coincided with a renewed insistence by imperial officials that governance should be based upon coercion and control rather than consent and cooperation. They were confirmed in their opinion that the best colonial government was paternalistic and benevolent authoritarianism by the bad behaviour they saw settlers in the West Indies, Canada and Australia displaying toward non-whites and especially by the actions of an aggressively white nationalist United States. Increasingly, Britons distinguished themselves by contrasting their own willingness to force British liberties on non-white peoples throughout the world with white American tendencies to confine their much-vaunted liberties solely to themselves.

The differences in attitude between republican 'democratic tyranny' and British benevolent and autocratic humanitarianism can be seen in the early settlement of Botany Bay in Australia. Australia was a giant social experiment, an outdoor prison, envisaged also as a place where freedom and liberty would be paramount values, to be imposed by dictate from above rather than relying on uncertain efforts from below. Lord Sydney, home secretary and an old-fashioned Whig who believed in the Country Whig values that motivated the American Revolution. He saw Australia as a place of redemption for convicts who had made a mistake when in Britain but whose experience in Australia was meant to liberate them from their past. Sydney insisted that convicts arriving in Botany Bay arrived with their rights intact and their crimes wiped off by the punishment of transportation. Sydney's views did not prevail, however. The ruler on the ground, Captain Arthur Phillips, a forward-thinking despot such as Edward Despard had been in British Honduras, although Phillips came to a better end, was unprepared to allow convicts any substantial independence until they had served the terms for which they had been condemned for transportation. Phillip's actions soon superseded Sydney's old-fashioned Commonwealth intentions for Australia. He placed the authority of the state as superior to the liberties of the people, arguing that the people of Australia would quickly abuse those liberties, just as the French and American revolutionaries had done. Humane authoritarianism triumphed over ancient notions of commonwealth. One of the first things Phillips did on arrival in 1788 was to decree, without consulting anyone else, that slavery would not exist in Australia, thus making that country the first European society to be founded and to continue without slavery as a lawful economic institution. It is hard to see that the American Revolution had played an appreciable role in these changes. The start of the French Revolution had only hardened British resolve that its fundamental beliefs about empire and involvement in the world outside Britain and indeed Europe remained unchanged.

Perhaps the major difference in Britain's governance by 1815 from earlier times was that the British state had become much stronger – the ultimate beneficiary of all revolutions and wars is the state. Nevertheless, we should not overestimate how strong that state was. Britain's imperial state was more powerful than the American one, which, Jack Greene argues, was 'a weak American state' that had replaced 'a weak British state.'[9] But it remained constrained by local opposition from British and imperial subjects, aware of their rights as British subjects under a limited monarchy. Britain learned from its disaster in America to be henceforth very careful in exerting its power, at least in settler colonies such as Australia, South Africa and Canada and especially against white Protestant subjects who professed loyalty to the British Crown. The iron fist of the British state was only ever unleashed against imperial subjects who were non-white, as in India in 1857, in New Zealand in the New Zealand Wars between 1845 and 1872 and in Jamaica during the Morant Bay rebellion in 1865. No similar demonstrations of British force happened to white settlers in settler colonies. Of course, Ireland, as ever, remained the exception, as can be seen in the fierce repression that followed the subduing of rebels in 1798.

The centrality of Europe

The advent of the French Revolution in 1789, and Britain's entry into a fully fledged European as well as worldwide conflict from 1793 made clear a central reality of Britain's foreign policy that we might emphasise more in this volume than has been done, Europe always came first in the attention of individuals and the state in seventeenth- and eighteenth-century Britain. The question of Britain's position in Europe structured British politics and public political discourse in ways that made it, rather than taxation, popular unrest, religion, elections or global expansion, the central political preoccupation in eighteenth-century Britain. When the Hanoverian kings addressed Parliament at the opening of each parliamentary session, they invariably talked about Britain's European policy. Indeed, in the Oscar-winning film about Anne, *The Favourite*, this insistence on the primacy of Europe became the object of a gag, when Anne pretended to faint rather than having to discuss British war with France. Europe was always a serious, rather than frivolous, matter. Within national politics, what most divided Whigs and Tories was differences over what role Britain should play in the international state system. Many Britons were convinced that British security and prosperity could only be achieved through engagement in Europe with a vocal and increasingly important minority believing that Britain's destiny lay in commercial, imperial and naval expansion.

The French Revolution brought to the fore the part of Europe which had been the focus of attention in the late seventeenth and early eighteenth-century concern over the expansionist policies of Louis XIV. That part of Europe on which British interest was directed was the realm where George III was king – Hanover in the Holy Roman Empire. That obsession with the Holy Roman Empire – always a region of volatility where the major powers of Europe competed for influence – was matched by British worries over the defence of the Low Countries of Flanders and the Dutch Republic. There was a great continuity in English and British foreign policy: the defence of the Low Countries was a vital part of foreign policy in Europe from the mid-fourteenth to the mid-twentieth century. It was just as important an area of British interest in the late eighteenth and early nineteenth century as before or after that date. The Battle of Waterloo in 1815, for example, which secured British dominance in Europe and the world from 1815 through to 1914, was fought in present-day Belgium, fifteen kilometres south of the present capital of the European Union, and the bête noire of modern British anti-Europeans, Brussels.

The Low Countries could not be defended by British forces alone, even with the support of local populations. They needed the help of European allies – Austria and Prussia for the majority of the eighteenth century. This need for allies meant that even if the main threats to British worldwide influence came from southern places, like Spain and especially from France, Britain's European policy was always centred on Germany and in maintaining a balance of power in that region so that France could not dominate there and thus becoming overly powerful in Europe as a whole. The actions of the French revolutionaries in the 1790s and especially their push to war under Napoleon Bonaparte in the 1800s merely underlined this long-standing reality in British foreign policy, in which the Holy Roman Empire was central to foreign policy making.

Daniel Baugh notes regarding the Seven Years' War that 'the ultimate object of statemen in London . . . was to maintain and increase security, power and influence in Europe.'[10] The British Empire that was established by the late 1780s was primarily valued in Britain for how it played in Europe. As P. J. Marshall notes, 'eighteenth-century British opinion considered that the nation's standing rested not, as some later generations were to think, on its possession of a world-wide empire, but on its eminence among the powers in Europe.'[11] Ironically, the result of the American Revolution was to keep Britain's position in Europe higher than it had been since the 1760s. It was France, not Britain, that was isolated in Europe, and even more so after 1789, when the actions of French revolutionaries horrified European monarchies more than any event since the creation of an English republic following the execution of Charles I in 1649.

Indeed, one lesson that Britain learned from the War of American Independence was that in their concentration on building an empire after 1763, they had neglected their traditional priorities in Europe. The Whig leader, Charles Fox, declared in 1787 that 'America had been lost for want of a continental war in Germany' and like other critics of government stressed that henceforth Britain should pursue European alliance more purposefully so that it never found itself in the position it was in around 1778, when it found itself isolated in Europe. From 1783, while Britain pursued the expansion of empire vigorously, it made certain that its colonial policy was one in which colonies existed as a main source of wealth on which Britain's status as a great power rested and which through this status came a capacity to exert influence in Europe. What the American War made clear to Britain was that it was the years between 1763 and 1783 which were exceptional -and undesirable.

Having an overseas empire made having allies and interests in Europe more vital. Britain, it was clear, was a European power and could not abandon its connections to Europe without its connections to the rest of the world being badly affected. So long as Britain's main rivals were other western European maritime powers – as was the case between 1789 and 1815 – the wealth of the empire and from Britain's increasingly global commercial interests as well as its powerful navy was the basis of Britain's formidable European presence. That does not mean that Britain's power in Europe was uncontested. Between 1775 and 1790, for example, the naval warship tonnage of the European powers increased by 46 percent, reaching its largest-ever levels, placing unprecedented demands on British financial and naval strength, meaning that Britain's imperial power was imperilled, even as Britain continued its global expansion. Nevertheless, Britain managed to maintain and slightly increase its strategic gap over its principal rival, France, despite both nations investing ever more heavily in its navy. That meant that if Britain kept making alliances with other European powers (as it did with the Dutch and the Prussians in the Triple Alliance of 1788), it could keep command of its European seas. The culmination of this naval strategy came in the famous battle of Trafalgar in 1805, off the coast of Spain, when the British smashed the Franco-Spanish fleet.

When in 1783 the British tried to understand why they had been defeated in America, they attributed their failure overwhelmingly to errors of policy in Europe. They concentrated on the moment of hubris noted earlier with the young monarch George III in the aftermath of the great victory in 1763, when Britain felt it could go it alone in Europe. The lesson of their defeat was that Britain had turned its back on Europe and then Europe had taken its revenge. British leaders under William Pitt the Younger, who started his long and distinguished career as prime minister from 1784, resolved never to make this error again. Thereafter, even as Britain's worldwide empire expanded far beyond its eighteenth-century limits after 1800 and as the wealth that Britain was getting from the Industrial Revolution made it the richest and most powerful country in the world, replacing the historical superiority of the Chinese in what historians call the Great Divergence, its geopolitical policies were always informed by a European policy under which other global strategies were negotiated.

In the French revolutionary and Napoleonic wars of the 1790s and 1800s, Europe was once again of paramount importance to British thinking and indeed to British welfare, Compared to previous wars, Britain's colonies were downgraded in importance. The significant exception was in Britain's disastrous wars in the West Indies, the most conspicuous event being the ultimately unsuccessful effort to defeat the greatest and only successful war started by enslaved persons against an imperial power in Haiti through the occupation of Saint Domingue (the French colonial name for Haiti) between 1793 and 1798. Neither Britain nor France was able to defeat the forces of ex-slaves led by the charismatic black generals, Toussaint Louverture and Jacques Dessalines.

Of course, the Napoleonic wars were so immense that they extended outside Europe into other parts of the world. In South Asia, Charles, Marquess Cornwallis, who had been the losing general at Yorktown in 1781, led as governor of Bengal, presiding over an expansion of British rule from the late 1780s. That expansion involved wars with not just France but with native Indian leaders, notably Tipu Sultan, the ruler of the southern state of Mysore, with the British war effort run by the two Wellesley brothers, Richard, Marquess Wellesley and Arthur, later Duke of Wellington. Under the Wellesleys and their successors, the East India Company army expanded from 88,249 soldiers in 1793 to 227,183 (of whom 195,572 were native) in 1815. But the main fighting in these wars, and Britain's geopolitical and economic emphasis was in wars in Europe, notably in the Iberian Peninsula and in the customary British fighting zone of the Low Countries.

We can see the results of an enhanced pro-European strategy in the 1790s onwards in how policy was conducted in the Caribbean, which was a major area of conflict in this period and where British expansion continued almost unabated. Britain failed in Saint-Domingue but its other efforts in the southern Caribbean resulted in the acquisition of valuable territories from the Dutch, Spanish and French. In 1797, Britain occupied Dutch Guiana and in the next year took over Trinidad from Spain. In the Peace of Amiens of 1802, Britain had its occupation of Trinidad confirmed and in 1815 transformed its occupation of the three Dutch colonies of Demerara, Essequibo and Berbice into formal colonisation. In the Vienna settlement of that year, it retained not just Guiana and the Cape of Good Hope in South Africa but also the small islands of Tobago and St. Lucia. On one hand, it seemed that even with abolitionists starting to flex their muscles to abolish the Atlantic slave trade (achieved in 1807) and then slavery (achieved in 1834 and 1838), Britain remained committed to an Atlantic empire in the Caribbean, north-east South America and parts of Central America.

But this new Caribbean empire was different from the one that existed prior to the American Revolution. There was no question of recognising settler rights in these new territories – each colony had more direct rule and less self-government than was usual in the Atlantic world before 1783. As Christer Petley notes,

> It was the radicalization of the French and Haitian Revolutions that . . . shattered the self-confidence of white slaveholding colonists in the British Empire . . . and limited the options of any West Indian colonials who dreamed of leaving the British Empire, provided cautionary examples about the inherent security risks of slavery and slave trading, worsened the image of the Caribbean in the metropole, and provided new momentum to the extension of British imperial power over the sugar colonies.[12]

The cost of Caribbean wars was over £20 million, and this cost was not something that could be got back from planters, over whom Britain was determined to keep close control. Planters were clearly dependent on the British government and especially the military support of Britain. That dependence took away any necessity for the imperial government to listen to settlers and to follow what settlers wanted, except when those needs coincided with the interests of the government – something that happened less and less frequently.

Britain broke in the Caribbean with the principles that had shaped the eighteenth-century colonial system. It neither allowed settlers much say in colonial governance nor allowed in the new frontiers of Trinidad and the Guianas to unleash the full force of the logic of the plantation system. Slavery was to be ameliorated, whatever planters wanted, and brought under the close supervision of a much more intrusive state. Britain was determined not to make the mistakes it believed it had made that allowed the Thirteen Colonies to secede and for Europe to turn against it. Its policies in the late eighteenth-century Caribbean suggested that it thought its mistake in America was not that which Benjamin Franklin thought it had made – not respecting settler self-autonomy – but was the exact opposite – letting settlers get too accustomed to governing themselves, a rule which seemed to be as much about oppressing others, such as enslaved people, as in respecting settler 'rights.' And if what settlers in the Americas or Australia or Protestant elites in Scotland or Ireland wanted to do got in the way of larger policies designed to maintain Britain's position in Europe, then the reaction against these self-proclaimed Britons was swift and decisive.

The swing to the south and a new empire?

Was the British Empire different after the loss of America? A former generation of historians, led by Vincent Harlow in the 1930s and Ronald Robinson and Jack Gallagher in the 1950s, argued that the loss of America signalled a new British Empire, one based in South Asia and which was defined by the quest for new markets and raw materials rather than the creation of settler colonies and direct control of territories taken from indigenes. Few historians today would agree with such a sharp break in the character of British imperialism from the middle 1780s. For one thing, the colonies of settlement in North America and the Caribbean remained more important than India until well into the nineteenth century while Parliament's determination to tighten the governance of empire in the Atlantic World before the American Revolution was not an aberration or a passing phase but was a trend that continued and intensified after 1783. Moreover, settler colonies did not disappear after the creation of the United States. The British Empire was always far more expansive than just being concerned with extracting wealth from colonies in Asia and later in Africa. Indeed, the end of the American Revolution initiated the start of what scholars call 'settler colonialism' in the predominantly European-majority populations of Canada and Australia, each of them being colonies that would have not have existed in the form that they did except for the results of the American Revolution.

The lineaments of these settler colonies are studied as a subdiscipline of imperial history called 'the British World,' a trend that proved very popular after the turn of the twenty-first century. Its origins lie in reflections by the historiographer J.G.A. Pocock that there should be a new subject within British history writing, that acknowledged 'a British world, both European and oceanic, in the nineteenth and twentieth centuries,' a development which had its roots in the making of Britain and British expansion into the Atlantic, Asia and Pacific in the seventeenth and eighteenth centuries. The British world thus 'had a history, that, as Jamie Belich argues, was 'a transnational cultural entity based upon a populist form of pan-Britonism.'[13] These settler colonies were 'neo-Britains,' similar in kind to the colonies of eighteenth-century North Americas, where migrants formed societies that they shaped around ideal of Anglicisation. The dream of transforming overseas spaces into replicas of British countryside remained a constant throughout our period. In short, the themes that dominated British imperial expansion before 1788 were not themes that disappeared with the creation of the United States.

Saul Dubow has enunciated these themes and their persistence over time especially vividly in his work on Anglophone South Africa, one of the more ambiguous places of settler colonialism, with similarities to the West Indies, given the disparity in the numerical ratios between whites and non-whites. South Africa was also similar to Canada, in having a large and pre-existing European population, in this case of Dutch descent, who were less keen than British settlers on transforming the African colony into an approximation of southern England. Dubow argues that the concept of a British world for the nineteenth century onwards helps tease out a Britishness which was neither ethnic nor racial but was 'a composite, rather than an exclusive form of identity.' It encompassed being South African as well as being British. His South African British World is an imagined community, distinguished from the British Empire, with 'British' being used in an 'adjectival' rather than a 'possessive' sense. The British World he describes is thus not just a synonym for the British Empire. This definition allows for the United States to be included within a post-1783 British world, as Jamie Belich has done in a pioneering work on settler colonialism in which the United States is seen as continuing to act like a settler colony, especially regarding its expansion westward across the North American continent, well after independence was gained.[14]

P. J. Marshall has been the historian who has most contested Vincent Harlow's belief that a second British Empire developed in Asia and Africa in the second half of the eighteenth century. He notes that the East never replaced the Atlantic in economic and geopolitical terms in the eighteenth century. The West Indies, Canada and the new possession of Australia more than outweighed India in importance to Britain in this period, although there may have been a start to a 'swing to the east' in the late 1790s, as wars engulfed the subcontinent and Napoleon's invasion of Egypt between 1798 and 1801 threatened British control of its Indian territories. If there was a 'swing to the East,' however, in the later eighteenth century, there was no corresponding swing away from the

Atlantic. The West Indies remained central to Britain's economy and geopolitics until the 1820s at least and was at the forefront of attention after the sudden success of the antislavery movement formed in 1787.

Marshall notes that

> changes in the very diverse links that had bound the old thirteen colonies into the British Atlantic world were much less cataclysmic in the immediate aftermath of the war than the constitutional separation and political alienation that put Britain and America apart and kept them apart.

He argues 'that the pre-revolutionary British Atlantic World was able to survive the upheavals of war and American independence' because

> it was a world that functioned through the links that bound together families, ethnic communities, or groups with common interests on both sides of the Atlantic . . . the strengths of the links holding together the British Atlantic world ensured its rapid recovery from the ultimate failure of politics that had led to a fratricidal war.[15]

Humanitarianism and the long-term view

If we are to assess the importance of Britain's involvement with the world from 1603, we need to ask what the long-term benefits and costs were for both Britons and for the people they colonised. The answer to the latter is usually thought to be that British influence on non-British peoples is generally negative. Some conservative historians such as Niall Ferguson consider that British imperialism was overall a good thing, for the world just as much as for Britons. The contrary view, one held, for example, by Shashi Tharoor, an Indian politician, diplomat and writer, who sees Britain's empire as 'inglorious' and British involvement with his home country as being very negative, tends to have more sway in this long-standing historiographical battle about empire's influence on the present. Tharoor argues, more for the nineteenth and twentieth centuries and from a perspective informed by a long tradition of Indian nationalism, that

> the British conquest of India was the invasion and destruction of a high civilisation by a trading company utterly without scruple or principle, careless of art and greedy of gain, over-running with fire and sword in a country temporarily disordered and helpless, bribing and murdering, annexing and stealing.

The data of Angus Maddison on the world economy suggests that India was the world's largest economy around 1700, with around 25 per cent of both the world's population and the world's gross domestic product (GDP). By the time the British had left in 1947, the population share of the subcontinent was still large, at 16 per cent but its share of world wealth was down to less than

4 percent. The reason, Tharoor argues, was that 'India was governed for the benefit of Britain.'

Less polemically, Prasannan Parthasarti has demonstrated through convincing economic data that the European global dominance over Asia that occurred around 1800 – the Great Divergence – was, in the case of India, not because Europe possessed superior markets, rationality, science or institutions but because Britain used its political power over India to cause Indian deindustrialisation and thus replace India as the chief supplier of cotton textiles to the world. In his view, the threat of being outcompeted by Indian textiles on global markets and the increasing scarcity of traditional sources of energy acted as triggers for revolutionary technological breakthroughs in Britain that led to the Industrial Revolution and then to Britain being able to displace a weakened India from its traditional place in cotton manufacturing. Politics thus preceded economics and those politics acted entirely for the benefit of British consumers and not in support of Indians.[16]

The question we need to ask, however, in conclusion, is, If empire was so bad for the world, why do Britons continue to think that it was overall a beneficial institution which Britons should be proud of? Surveys of British opinion continually show a large majority – about 60 percent, or quite higher than the percentage in favour of Brexit in 2016 – who think the British Empire was a force for good rather than evil. The differences between popular acceptance of empire and academic disdain for what imperialism has wrought lies in each constituency seeing empire in very different ways. The academic view of empire is focused on the extractive colonies of Asia and Africa after our period. The nineteenth-century volume of the Oxford history of the British Empire, for example, starts its regional analysis of empire with four chapters on Asia, one on the British West Indies, and another on Ireland before four chapters on settler colonies (and none on the United States), ending with three chapters on Africa. The public thinks, however, when it thinks of the British Empire, more about Australia, New Zealand and Canada than about India or Nigeria, because that is where the greatest contacts are between Britons in the metropolis and their kinspeople migrating away from Britain.[17]

If we think of British imperialism in the nineteenth century as part of the movement of the British people throughout the world, part of which movement led to the establishment of settler colonies from 1607 onwards and to continuing British migration to the United States after 1783, and if we add to this historical understanding an appreciation of the consolidation of British power in the British archipelago in a process that had been occurring since the incorporation of Wales into England between 1535 and 1542 (with conquest by England in Wales and Ireland from the early twelfth century), then formal and informal empire after 1783 looks less exploitative than it might appear to the descendants of Indians, Pacific Islanders and Africans whose history of empire is one of British oppression and cultural arrogance. There may be some debate about whether British expansion increased the sum of liberty throughout the world. It probably did not do much in this regard. But, as Avner Offer has argued powerfully for the British Empire of the late nineteenth century and which is true for the eighteenth century and early nineteenth centuries as well. 'The establishment of overseas English-speaking societies was by far the largest benefit created by Britain and her Empire.'[18]

The benefits of empire went almost entirely to British migrants throughout the long period of British expansion – the damages were born by indigenous peoples and by Africans transported to the Americas in the slave trade. Those damages were large enough to outweigh the benefits. The benefits, however, were very real and meant that the communities of Britons that became established in settler colonies did very well. They became, in eighteenth century, North America and in Australia between the 1820s and the 1890s, the richest and most egalitarian societies in the world. By 1900, overseas neo-Britons added almost 40 per cent to British gross national product, 'dwarfing any other actual contributions of Empire in the British Isles alone.' As Offer concludes, 'their inhabitants may not have been more wealthy than Britons on the average, but manual workers (the majority) were much better off in terms of wages and status, and lived in more equal societies' than if they had stayed in Britain.[19] The expansion of Britain outwards had proved by 1900 to be a boon to the ordinary Briton, overseas and at home. It was for this reason that then and now empire has seemed a good thing to most of the British population, and equally seen as a good thing by large sections of the population in the settler colonies of Australia, New Zealand and Canada. Whether British expansion overseas in global terms is a good thing in reality rather than in the perceptions of those who benefited from it is more debatable. It is undeniable, however, that the move by the peoples of Britain to create a new nation out of a composite monarchy and the creation of a great empire spanning the globe is world-historically important. What this book has attempted to show is how the roots of this extraordinary belief in empire's positive effects by the death of Victoria in 1901 were in the dramatic events that make British and British overseas history in the seventeenth and eighteenth centuries so interesting.

Notes

1 Andrew Jackson O'Shaughnessy, *The Men Who Lost America: British Leadership, the American Revolution, and the Fate of Empire* (New Haven: Yale University Press, 2013), 4.

2 Linda Colley, *Britons: Forging the Nation 1707–1837* (New Haven: Yale University Press, 1992), 215–17.

3 O'Shaughnessy, *Men Who Lost America*, 45–6.

4 Arthur Burns and Joanna Innes, eds., *Rethinking the Age of Reform in Britain 1780–1850* (Cambridge: Cambridge University Press, 2003), 10.

5 H.V. Bowen, 'British India, 1765–1813: The Metropolitan Context,' in P.J. Marshall, ed., *The Oxford History of the British Empire: The Eighteenth Century* (Oxford: Oxford University Press, 1998), 531.

6 Maya Jasanoff, *Liberty's Exiles: The Loss of America and the Remaking of the British Empire* (New York: Harper Press, 2011), 9–12.

7 Ibid., 343–6.

8 Peter Linebaugh, *Red Round Globe Hot Burning: A Tale at the Crossroads of Commons and Closure, of Love and Terror, of Race and Class, and of Kate and Ned Despard* (Oakland: University of California Press, 2019).

9 Jack P. Greene, 'Colonial History and National History: Reflections on a Continuing Problem' *William and Mary Quarterly*, 3rd ser. 64 (2007), 246.

10 Daniel Baugh, *The Global Seven Years War, 1754 to 1763* (London: Longman, 2011), 1.

11 P.J. Marshall, 'Britain's American Problem: The International Perspective,' in Edward Gray and Jane Kamensky, eds., *The Oxford Handbook of the American Revolution* (Oxford: Oxford University Press, 2013), 16.

12 Christer Petley, 'Slaveholders and Revolution: The Jamaican Planter Class, British Imperial Politics, and the Ending of the Slave Trade, 1775–1807,' *Slavery and Abolition* 39 (2018), 53–79.

13 Cited in Rachel K. Bright and Andrew R. Dilley, 'After the British World,' *Historical Journal* 60 (2017), 551.

14 Saul Dubow, 'How British was the British world? The Case of South Africa,' *Journal of Imperial and Commonwealth History* 37 (2009), 1–27; Jamie Belich, *Replenishing the Earth: The Settler Revolution and the Rise of the Anglo-World, 1783–1939* (Oxford: Oxford University Press, 2009).

15 P.J. Marshall, *Remaking the British Atlantic: The Unites States and the British Empire after American Independence* (Oxford: Oxford University Press, 2012) 3, 313, 321.

16 Shashi Tharoor, *Inglorious Empire: What the British Did to India* (London: C. Hurst, 2017); Prasannan Parthasarathi, *Why Europe Grew Rich and Asia Did Not: Global Economic Divergence, 1600–1850* (Cambridge: Cambridge University Press, 2011); Niall Ferguson, *Empire: How Britain Made the Modern World* (London: Allen Lane, 2003).

17 Andrew Porter, ed., *The Oxford History of the British Empire: The Nineteenth Century* (Oxford: Oxford University Press, 1999).

18 Avner Offer, 'Costs and Benefits, Prosperity and Security, 1870–1914,' in Porter, *The Nineteenth Century*, 709.

19 Ibid., 709–10.

Bibliography

Armitage, David and Sanjay Subrahmanyam, eds., *The Age of Revolution in Global Context, c. 1760–1840* (Basingstoke: Palgrave Macmillan, 2010).

Bayly, C.A., *Imperial Meridian: The British Empire and the World* (London, 1989).

Benton, Lauren and Lisa Ford, *Rage for Order: The British Empire and the Origins of International Law, 1800–1850* (Cambridge, MA: Harvard University Press, 2016).

Fullager, Kate and Michael A. McDonnell, eds., *Facing Empire: Indigenous Experiences in a Revolutionary Age* (Baltimore: John Hopkins University Press, 2018).

Jasanoff, Maya, *Liberty's Exiles: The Loss of America and the Remaking of the American Empire* (New York: Harper, 2011).

Kinkel, Sarah, *Disciplining the Empire: Politics, Governance and the Rise of the British Navy* (Cambridge, MA: Harvard University Press, 2018).

Marshall, P.J., *Remaking the British Atlantic: The United States and the British Empire after American Independence* (Oxford: Oxford University Press, 2012).

Moniz, Amanda B., *From Empire to Humanity: The American Revolution & the Origins of Humanitarianism* (New York: Oxford University Press, 2016).

Polasky, Janet, *Revolutions without Borders: The Call to Liberty in the Atlantic World* (New Haven: Yale University Press, 2015).

Sexton, Jay, 'Epilogue: The United States in the British Empire,' in Stephen Foster, ed., *British North America in the Seventeenth and Eighteenth Centuries* (Oxford: Oxford University Press, 2013), 318–48.

Index